Wealth, Cost, and Price in American Higher Education

Wealth, Cost, and Price in American Higher Education

A Brief History

BRUCE A. KIMBALL
WITH SARAH M. ILER

Johns Hopkins University Press
Baltimore

Johns Hopkins University Press
2715 North Charles Street
Baltimore, Maryland 21218
www.press.jhu.edu

Library of Congress Cataloging-in-Publication Data

Names: Kimball, Bruce A., 1951– author. | Iler, Sarah M., author.
Title: Wealth, cost, and price in American higher education : a brief history /
Bruce A. Kimball ; with Sarah M. Iler.
Description: Baltimore : Johns Hopkins University Press, 2023. |
Includes bibliographical references and index.
Identifiers: LCCN 2021062994 | ISBN 9781421445007 (hardcover) |
ISBN 9781421445014 (ebook)
Subjects: LCSH: Education, Higher—United States—Costs—History. |
Education, Higher—Economic aspects—United States. |
Universities and colleges—United States—Finance. | Endowments—United States.
Classification: LCC LB2342 .K488 2022 | DDC 378.73—dc23/eng/20220218
LC record available at https://lccn.loc.gov/2021062994

A catalog record for this book is available from the British Library.

*Special discounts are available for bulk purchases of this book. For more information,
please contact Special Sales at specialsales@jh.edu.*

With deep gratitude and esteem, this book is dedicated
to three wonderful mentors, colleagues, and friends:
David Riesman, Stan Katz, and Dan Coquillette,
whose wise counsel, learned insights, and unfailing help,
spanning nearly five decades *in seriatim*, inform every page

CONTENTS

Appendices

This research into the historical finances of higher education began in the 1990s during my collaboration with Dan Coquillette on our history of Harvard Law School, whose two volumes were published in 2015 and 2020. Meanwhile, after I moved from the University of Rochester to Ohio State University in 2007, Ben Johnson, my superlative research assistant, helped immeasurably in broadening and deepening the historical financial research, and we coauthored several articles. After Ben received his PhD in 2013, Jeremy Luke, another exceptional research assistant, aided me in extending the research until he completed his PhD in 2017, and we coauthored several essays.

Since that time, Sarah Iler, my former PhD advisee and coauthor, has worked closely with me on writing this book over the past five years. She has ruthlessly offered insightful and informed feedback on countless drafts of every paragraph, table, figure, and appendix, as well as finding and analyzing innumerable articles and photographs. The argument and narrative are vastly improved thanks to Sarah's superb work. I am tremendously grateful to Ben, Jeremy, and Sarah for their foundational contributions to this book.

I would also like to thank several scholars and colleagues who contributed immensely over the past 20 years in my study of higher education finances: Michael Olivas of the University of Houston; John Thelin of the University of Kentucky; A. J. Angulo of the University of Massachusetts Lowell; Stan Katz of Princeton University; Ben Soskis, editor of the *HistPhil* blog; Thomas Adam and A. Burcu Bayram of the University of Texas at Arlington; Mark Thomas of Garfield Produce; Dave Griswold of Boston University; Dan Coquillette of Boston College; and Randy Curren and Tyll Van Geel of the University of Rochester.

In addition, I wish to express great appreciation to a number of scholars who generously took the time to read the manuscript and provide valuable feedback that improved the book tremendously: Dave Breneman of the University of

Virginia, Linda Eisenmann of Wheaton College, Richard Freeland of Northeastern University, David Hammack of Case Western Reserve University, Stan Katz of Princeton University, Walter Massy of Stanford University, Jim Mohr of the University of Oregon, John Thelin of the University of Kentucky, and Mike Banerjee of the University of California, Berkeley.

Several foundations declined proposals for major grants to support this research, maintaining that the subject belonged to the province of economists. Nevertheless, I am extremely grateful for financial support that came in several ways. One was a Guggenheim Fellowship in 2012 that supported research on the history of cost escalation in American higher education. Another was a Coca-Cola Critical Difference for Women Grant awarded in 2013 by the Department of Women's, Gender and Sexuality Studies at Ohio State University to examine early fundraising campaigns at women's colleges. In 2014 the American Philosophical Society awarded a small grant to examine the financial challenges of liberal arts colleges. In 2017, Thomas Adam invited me to participate in the Walter Prescott Webb Memorial Lecture Series of the University of Texas at Arlington by preparing an essay on the finances of major professional schools in the first half of the twentieth century. Throughout the period from 2007 to 2019, the School of Educational Policy and Leadership and the Department of Educational Studies at Ohio State University provided significant annual financial support that allowed me to travel to archives and obtain important documentary and electronic sources that informed the research. Finally, in 2020, the Emeritus Faculty Academy of Ohio State awarded a small grant that aided me and Sarah Iler in completing the writing and in paying archival fees to reproduce images.

In addition, I am tremendously grateful to Greg Britton, the editorial director of Johns Hopkins University Press, for his interest, support, and counsel over several years.

Finally, I wish to thank Lynne, Zack, Becca, and Stacey for listening, over the past fifteen years, to fascinating stories about the history of wealth, cost, and price in American higher education!

AAU	Association of American Universities
BEA	Bureau of Economic Analysis
CAGR	compound annual growth rate
CASE	Council for the Advancement and Support of Education
EMI	Endowment Model of Investing
GDP	gross domestic product
GEB	General Education Board
GNP	gross national product
HBCUs	Historically Black Colleges and Universities
HEF	Harvard Endowment Fund
MIT	Massachusetts Institute of Technology
NACUBO	National Association of College and University Business Officers
NCES	National Center for Education Statistics
TCJA	Tax Cuts and Jobs Act
UMIFA	Uniform Management of Institutional Funds Act
UPMIFA	Uniform Prudent Management of Institutional Funds Act
YAF	Yale Alumni Fund
YMCA	Young Men's Christian Association
YWCA	Young Women's Christian Association

Full citations are given for sources at the first citation within each chapter, except for the following abbreviations.

Adam and Bayram, *Economics of Higher Education*
Thomas Adam and A. Burcu Bayram, eds., *The Economics of Higher Education in the United States* (College Station, TX, 2019).
https://muse.jhu.edu/book/66852

Angell, *Annual Report [Year–Year]*
James B. Angell, *Annual Report of the President of the University of Michigan [Year–Year]*.
https://quod.lib.umich.edu/a/angell/

Angulo, *Diploma Mills*
A. J. Angulo, *Diploma Mills: How For-Profit Colleges Stiffed Students, Taxpayers, and the American Dream* (Baltimore, MD, 2016).
https://muse.jhu.edu/book/44879

Arnett, *College and University Finance*
Trevor Arnett, *College and University Finance* (New York, 1922).
https://archive.org/details/collegeuniversitooarneuoft

Baumol, *Cost Disease*
William J. Baumol, *The Cost Disease: Why Computers Get Cheaper and Health Care Doesn't* (New Haven, CT, 2012).

Biennial Survey of Education [Year–Year]
US Bureau of Education, *Biennial Survey of Education Year–Year* (Washington, DC, [Year]).
https://catalog.hathitrust.org/Record/100886319

H. Bowen, *Costs of Higher Education*
Howard R. Bowen, *The Costs of Higher Education: How Much Do Colleges and Universities Spend per Student and How Much Should They Spend?* (New York, 1980).
https://eric.ed.gov/?id=ED207368

W. Bowen, *"Cost Disease"*
William G. Bowen, *The "Cost Disease" in Higher Education: Is Technology the Answer? The Tanner Lectures, Stanford University* (Stanford, CA, 2012).
https://www.ats.edu/uploads/resources/current-initiatives/economic-challenges-facing-future
-ministers/financial-issues-research/the-cost-disease-in-higher-education.pdf
http://sites.tufts.edu/strategicplan/files/2012/10/ITHAKA-TheCostDiseasein
HigherEducation.pdf

W. Bowen, *Economics of the Major Private Research Universities*
William G. Bowen, *The Economics of the Major Private Research Universities* (Berkeley, CA, 1968).
https://eric.ed.gov/?id=ED024318

Breneman, "Essay on College Costs"
David W. Breneman, "An Essay on College Costs," in National Center for Education Statistics, *Study of College Costs and Prices: 1988–89 to 1997–98* (Washington, DC, 2001), 2:13–20.
https://nces.ed.gov/pubs2002/2002158.pdf

Burton Files
Office of the President Marion Le Roy Burton files, Smith College Archives.
https://findingaids.smith.edu/repositories/4/resources/394

Carnegie, *Gospel of Wealth*
Andrew Carnegie, *The Gospel of Wealth and Other Timely Essays* (New York, 1901). https://ia800209.us.archive.org/31/items/cu31924001214539/cu31924001214539.pdf

Cavan, "Student and the Financing of the College"
Jordan T. Cavan, "The Student and the Financing of the College: A Study of Student Fees, Student Aid and Factors Affecting the Proportion of the Cost of Higher Education Borne by the Student" (PhD diss., University of Chicago, 1935). https://www.proquest.com/dissertations-theses/student-financing-college-study-fees-aid-factors/docview/301798904/se-2?accountid=9783

Clotfelter, *Buying the Best*
Charles Clotfelter Jr., *Buying the Best: Cost Escalation in Elite Higher Education* (Princeton, NJ, 1996). https://muse.jhu.edu/book/33780

College Board, *Trends in College Pricing* [*Year*]
College Board, *Trends in College Pricing and Student Aid (Year)* (New York, [Year]). Title varies. https://research.collegeboard.org/trends/trends-higher-education

Curti and Nash, *Philanthropy*
Merle Curti and Roderick Nash, *Philanthropy in the Shaping of American Higher Education* (New Brunswick, NJ, 1965).

Dwight, *Annual Report [Year–Year]*
Timothy Dwight (the younger), *Annual Report of the President of Yale University [Year–Year]*. Title varies.

Ehrenberg, *Tuition Rising*
Ronald G. Ehrenberg, *Tuition Rising: Why College Costs So Much* (Cambridge, MA, 2000). https://eric.ed.gov/?id=ED445622

Eliot, *Annual Report [Year–Year]*
Charles W. Eliot, *Annual Report of the President of Harvard University [Year–Year]* https://guides.library.harvard.edu/c.php?g=638791&p=4471938

Fishman, "What Went Wrong"
James J. Fishman, "What Went Wrong: Prudent Management of Endowment Funds and Imprudent Endowment Investing Policies," *Journal of College and University Law* 40 (2014): 199–246. https://digitalcommons.pace.edu/lawfaculty/958/

Freeland, *Academia's Golden Age*
Richard M. Freeland, *Academia's Golden Age: Universities in Massachusetts 1945–1975* (New York, 1992).

GEB, *Account of Its Activities, 1902–1914*
General Education Board, *The General Education Board: An Account of Its Activities, 1902–1914* (New York, 1915) https://babel.hathitrust.org/cgi/pt?id=uva.x000683736&view=1up&seq=7

GEB, *Annual Report [Year–Year]*
  General Education Board, *Annual Report [Year–Year]* (New York, [Year]).
  https://catalog.hathitrust.org/Record/000057205

Geiger, *History of American Higher Education*
  Roger L. Geiger, *The History of American Higher Education: Learning and Culture from the Founding to World War II* (Princeton, NJ, 2014).
  https://muse.jhu.edu/book/36588

Geiger, *To Advance Knowledge*
  Roger L. Geiger, *To Advance Knowledge: The Growth of American Research Universities, 1900–1940* (New York, 1986).

Getz and Siegfried, "Costs and Productivity"
  Malcolm Getz and John J. Siegfried, "Costs and Productivity in American Colleges and Universities," in *Economic Challenges in Higher Education*, ed. Charles T. Clotfelter et al. (Chicago, 1991), 261–392.
  https://eric.ed.gov/?id=ED377762

Goldin and Katz, *Race between Education and Technology*
  Claudia Goldin and Lawrence F. Katz, *The Race between Education and Technology* (Cambridge, MA, 2008).

Gordon, *Rise and Fall of American Growth*
  Robert J. Gordon, *The Rise and Fall of American Growth: The U.S. Standard of Living since the Civil War* (Princeton, NJ, 2016).
  https://www-degruyter-com.proxy.lib.ohio-state.edu/document/doi/10.1515/9781400873302/html

Graham and Diamond, *Rise of American Research Universities*
  Hugh D. Graham and Nancy Diamond, *The Rise of American Research Universities* (Baltimore, MD, 1997).
  https://eric.ed.gov/?id=ED403860

Hadley, *Annual Report [Year–Year]*
  Arthur T. Hadley, *Annual Report of the President of Yale University [Year–Year]*
  https://archives.yale.edu/repositories/12/resources/2590

Harper, *Trend in Higher Education*
  William R. Harper, *The Trend in Higher Education in America* (Chicago, 1905).
  https://brittlebooks.library.illinois.edu/brittlebooks_open/Books2009-05/harpwi0001trehig/harpwi0001trehig.pdf

HEF Records
  Records of the Harvard Endowment Fund, 1916–39, Harvard University Archives.
  http://id.lib.harvard.edu/alma/99001896985020394I/catalog

Historical Statistics of the United States
  Historical Statistics of the United States, Earliest Times to the Present: Millennial Edition, ed. Susan B. Carter et al. (New York, 2006).
  https://hsus.cambridge.org/

Humphreys, *Educational Endowments*
    Joshua Humphreys, *Educational Endowments and the Financial Crisis: Social Costs and Systemic Risks in the Shadow Banking System* (Boston, 2010).
    https://www.tellus.org/tellus/publication/educational-endowments

Johnstone, "Financing Higher Education"
    D. Bruce Johnstone, "Financing Higher Education: Reconciling Institutional Financial Viability and Student Affordability," in *American Higher Education in the Twenty-First Century*, 4th ed., ed. Michael N. Bastedo et al. (Baltimore, MD, 2016), 310–41.
    https://eric.ed.gov/?id=ED573824

Jones, *American Giver*
    John Price Jones, *The American Giver: A Review of American Generosity* (New York, 1954).
    https://archive.org/details/americangiverrevooooojone

JPJ Records
    John Price Jones Co., Records, 1919–54, Baker Library Special Collections, Harvard Graduate School of Business Administration.
    https://hollisarchives.lib.harvard.edu/repositories/11/resources/10477

Keller, *Regulating a New Economy*
    Morton Keller, *Regulating a New Economy: Public Policy and Economic Change in America, 1900–1933* (Cambridge, MA, 1990).

Kimball and Luke, "Historical Dimensions of the 'Cost Disease' "
    Bruce A. Kimball and Jeremy B. Luke, "Historical Dimensions of the 'Cost Disease' in U.S. Higher Education, 1870s–2010s," *Social Science History* 42 (2018): 29–55.
    https://www.cambridge.org/core/journals/social-science-history/article/abs/historical -dimensions-of-the-cost-disease-in-us-higher-education-1870s2010s/17C851D24DF7EF3A4 CE9D4E78224910D

Kimball and Luke, "Measuring Cost Escalation"
    Bruce A. Kimball and Jeremy B. Luke, "Measuring Cost Escalation in the Formative Era of US Higher Education, 1875–1930," *Historical Methods: A Journal of Quantitative and Interdisciplinary History* 49 (2016): 198–219.
    https://www.tandfonline.com/doi/abs/10.1080/01615440.2016.1181997

Lamont Correspondence
    Thomas W. Lamont Correspondence, Records of the Harvard Endowment Fund, 1916–39, Harvard University Archives.
    http://id.lib.harvard.edu/alma/990018969850203941/catalog

Lowell, *Annual Report [Year–Year]*
    A. Lawrence Lowell, *Annual Report of the President of Harvard University [Year–Year]*
    https://guides.library.harvard.edu/c.php?g=638791&p=4471938

Lowell Records
    Records of President Abbott Lawrence Lowell, 1909–33, Harvard University Archives.
    https://hollis.harvard.edu/primo-explore/fulldisplay?docid=01HVD_ALMA211811103370003941&context=L&vid=HVD2&lang=en_US&search_scope=everything&adaptor =Local%20Search%20Engine&tab=everything&query=lsr01,contains,990016384910203941& mode=basic&offset=0

Massy, *Honoring the Trust*
William F. Massy, *Honoring the Trust: Quality and Cost Containment in Higher Education* (Williston, VT, 2003).
https://eric.ed.gov/?id=ED476132

NACUBO, *Endowment Study* [*Year*]
National Association of College and University Business Officers, *[Year] Endowment Study* (Washington, DC, [Year]). Title varies. Some reports were published in conjunction with the Commonfund or TIAA.
https://www.nacubo.org/research/2020/research%20at%20nacubo

NCES, *Digest of Educational Statistics* [*Year*]
National Center for Education Statistics, *Digest of Educational Statistics* (Washington DC, [Year]).
https://nces.ed.gov/programs/digest/index.asp

NCES, *Study of College Costs and Prices*
National Center for Education Statistics, *Study of College Costs and Prices: 1988–89 to 1997–98* (Washington, DC, 2001), vol. 2.
https://nces.ed.gov

Olson, "Cost Effectiveness"
Jeffrey E. Olson, "The Cost Effectiveness of American Higher Education: The United States Can Afford Its Colleges and Universities," in *Higher Education: Handbook of Theory and Research* (1997), 12:195–242.
https://eric.ed.gov/?id=ED403851

Paulsen and Smart, *Finance of Higher Education*
Michael B. Paulsen and John C. Smart, eds., *The Finance of Higher Education: Theory, Research, Policy, and Practice* (New York, 2001).
https://search.ebscohost.com/login.aspx?direct=true&db=nlebk&AN=66836&site=ehost-live

Ryan, "Trusting U"
Christopher J. Ryan, "Trusting U: Examining University Endowment Management," *Journal of College and University Law* 42 (2016): 159–212.
https://papers.ssrn.com/sol3/papers.cfm?abstract_id=2658334

Swensen, *Pioneering Portfolio Management* (2000)
David F. Swensen, *Pioneering Portfolio Management: An Unconventional Approach to Institutional Investment* (New York, 2000).

Swensen, *Pioneering Portfolio Management* (2009)
David F. Swensen, *Pioneering Portfolio Management: An Unconventional Approach to Institutional Investment*, rev. ed. (New York, 2009).

Twentieth Century Fund, *Funds for the Future*
Twentieth Century Fund, *Funds for the Future: Report of the Twentieth Century Fund Task Force on College and University Endowment Policy* (New York, 1975).
https://eric.ed.gov/?id=ED121220

US CommEd, *Report [Year]*
US Commissioner of Education, *Report [Year]* (Washington, DC, [Year]).
https://catalog.hathitrust.org/Record/009164574

Weisbrod, Ballou, and Asch, *Mission and Money*
Burton A. Weisbrod, Jeffrey P. Ballou, and Evelyn D. Asch, *Mission and Money: Understanding the University* (New York, 2008).

Williamson, "Background Paper"
J. Peter Williamson, "Background Paper," in Twentieth Century Fund, *Funds for the Future: Report of the Twentieth Century Fund Task Force on College and University Endowment Policy* (New York, 1975).
https://eric.ed.gov/?id=ED121220

Williamson, *Funds for the Future*
J. Peter Williamson, *Funds for the Future: College Endowment Management for the 1990s* (New York, 1993).

Yale Secretary Records
Yale University Secretary's Office Records 1899–1953, Series III, Yale University Library Manuscripts and Archives.
https://archives.yale.edu/repositories/12/resources/2873

Zunz, *Philanthropy in America*
Olivier Zunz, *Philanthropy in America: A History* (Princeton, NJ, 2012).
https://www-degruyter-com.proxy.lib.ohio-state.edu/document/doi/10.1515/9781400850242/html

FIGURES

TABLES

"How Much Money Is Spent for Higher Education?"

A century ago, the US Office of Education reported that Americans had begun clamoring for answers to "two questions," namely, "How much money is spent for higher education in the United States? and How is it spent?"[1] This widespread interest prompted a few scholars to begin studying higher education finance in the late 1920s, and a small stream of scholarship on the subject trickled through the next two decades. Then, the cost of higher education began to rise steeply in the 1950s and 1960s, and the stream grew into a torrent, as economists, sociologists, and other scholars concluded that a "crisis in college finance" was emerging in the United States.[2]

The intense scrutiny came from an ever broader audience over the next 50 years. Policy makers, politicians, and the general public increasingly decried the combination of rising tuition and mounting student debt, while the endowments and fundraising goals of the wealthiest colleges and universities soared.

1. *Biennial Survey of Education 1928–30*, 526.
2. Christopher Jencks and David Riesman, *The Academic Revolution* (Chicago, 1968), 111n.

Hundreds of studies of these issues appeared through the 2010s and into the 2020s, as higher education continued to become "way more expensive," according to testimony before the Congressional Committee on Financial Services in 2019.[3] Meanwhile, the long-standing stratification of higher education into tiers of institutional wealth also began to attract scrutiny, partly because it seemed related to the increasing wealth inequality in the American population.

The history of these developments is set forth in this book, starting in the 1870s though adverting to their antecedents. The purpose is to explain succinctly the evolution of *wealth*, *cost*, and *price* in the non-profit sector of American higher education over the past 150 years. To understand this history, these three key terms must be defined clearly because their meanings have often varied in public and academic discussion, creating ambiguity and misunderstanding. At the outset, basic definitions will suffice. The historical narrative explains nuances and refinements of these definitions as they become relevant.

In this book, "wealth" denotes the permanent and productive financial capital, or endowment, of colleges and universities.[4] "Cost" means the expense that schools pay to produce their education, which is often called "production cost" by economists. "Price" denotes the amount charged to or paid by students for their education at colleges and universities.

With that said, it is important, even at the outset, to explain the important distinction between "cost" and "price." In both popular and academic discussion, the terms are often interchanged. But it is critical to distinguish the production cost that schools incur from the price that students pay because these two have never been the same and their relationship has long been complicated and variable for two reasons. On the one hand, although for-profit industries set their prices by adding a markup to their production cost, this familiar approach has never obtained in non-profit higher education. In fact, the production cost of higher education has significantly exceeded the price charged to or paid by students for the past 150 years, because various kinds of gifts, grants, endowment income, and government contributions have heavily subsidized students' education. Failure to understand the role of these subsidies has confounded discussion about price, especially tuition and fees, in higher education. On the other

3. Hasan Minaj, Testimony, US Congress House Committee on Financial Services, *A $1.5 Trillion Crisis . . . Hearing before the Committee on Financial Services*, 116th Cong., 1st sess. (September 10, 2019).

4. "Wealth" therefore does not include nonproductive physical assets, such as campus buildings and campus land, except where data sources dictate their inclusion, chiefly in chap. 6. For further discussion on this point, see app. 2; Kimball and Luke, "Measuring Cost Escalation," 202–4; Kimball and Luke, "Historical Dimensions of the 'Cost Disease,'" 45–48.

hand, the value of the subsidies has fluctuated over time depending on the level and sector of higher education and on the historical context, particularly events in the polity, economy, and individual institutions. Price thus has varied somewhat idiosyncratically, and production cost is the more determinate and fundamental issue that can be studied and explained.

Three Aims

This book thus aims, first, to explain concisely the origin and historical development of specific practices and policies that have influenced wealth, cost, and price in the non-profit sector of American higher education. Many of the most influential practices and policies arose during the formative era of American higher education, extending roughly from 1870 to 1930. Thereafter, new ones emerged, generating controversies as well as theories to understand and resolve them.

Second, this analysis of the historical record intends to show that aggregate wealth and aggregate cost in higher education became mutually reinforcing in the formative era. Indeed, they formed a double helix that continued to spiral upward over the past century, intermittently pulling price higher. Fueled by the expanding American economy, this upward spiral was driven by deliberate policy, by rapidly growing enrollment, and by the Darwinian competition for survival and success in which colleges and universities explicitly engaged. Nevertheless, the per-student production cost of higher education rose slowly and unevenly over the span of 150 years, contrary to the view of prominent scholars. This book therefore reveals the deliberate, helical relationship between aggregate wealth and aggregate cost, the historical factors that nurtured it, and the slower intermittent growth of per-student cost.

Finally, this history aims to reinterpret, and thus clarify or challenge, certain received theories, judgments, and data about the wealth, cost, and price of higher education. In the closing chapters, this reinterpretation leads to an assessment of the relationship between these financial issues and the public responsibility and social benefits of higher education in our democratic republic.

During the century between the 1870s and 1970s, the upward-spiraling wealth-cost double helix produced enormous benefits for the United States, and higher education earned widespread public esteem. Indeed, by the 1970s American higher education was widely recognized as the best in the world, led by the elite, wealthiest colleges and universities. However, while the competition among colleges and universities continued to drive the wealth-cost double helix upward in the 1980s and 1990s, esteem for higher education began to ebb. An undercurrent of criticism welled up in the press, the public, and political circles, as the economy stalled, subsidies declined, middle-class incomes lagged, and wealth inequality increased in the United States.

At the end of the twentieth century, the double helix and the public criticism began to undulate together. Both rose in the 1980s and 1990s until the stock market crashed in the dot.com bust of 2001–2, when they declined sharply. They ascended together again during the economic recovery of the 2000s until the Great Recession of 2009, when they fell once more. Both then rose during the economic recovery of the 2010s and culminated in 2017, when Congress enacted what had been unthinkable for 150 years: a retributive excise tax on the crown jewels of American higher education, the wealthiest, elite colleges and universities. Although a recent populist movement precipitated this legislation, the seeds of the political reaction had been planted decades earlier.

During the financial crisis prompted by the pandemic starting in 2019, the double helix and criticism seemed poised to decline together once more. But the initial recovery in 2020 and 2021 pushed the spiral upward, and public ire resurged, so far had public esteem for higher education declined since the 1970s. In particular, the wealthiest, elite colleges and universities were pilloried and, from a historical perspective, appeared to have forgotten their foundational purposes. Instead, they were perseverating in financial practices and policies that had brought them such success through the 1970s, as discussed in the closing chapters.

Dimensions of the Study

This history focuses on specific practices, policies, and events that fostered the helical relationship between wealth and cost in American higher education. These include annual alumni appeals, fundraising campaigns, efforts to establish and grow endowments, and increasingly aggressive investing strategies. Shaping those developments were two cultural forces that also deserve attention.

One was the rise of industrial capitalism with its "survival of the fittest" ethos. Echoed by many college and university leaders, this phrase was famously employed in 1869 by the English scientist Charles Darwin, who borrowed it from the account of his theory of evolution written by English philosopher Herbert Spencer.[5] Though the phrase originally referred to biology, leaders of American colleges and universities, along with "captains of industry," followed Spencer in

5. Herbert Spencer, *Principles of Biology* (London, 1864), 444; Charles Darwin, *On the Origin of Species by Means of Natural Selection or the Preservation of Favored Races in the Struggle for Life*, 5th ed. (London, 1869), 91–92.

extending Darwin's ideas of evolution to social affairs and frequently applied the term to their own intensifying competition during the formative period.[6]

The other cultural force involved the genesis of the American research university in the late nineteenth century, when the dominant culture of American higher education began to shift away from antebellum collegiate mores devoted to the transmission of received knowledge and inculcation of civic virtue. Over the next century, this collegiate view gave way to university mores enshrining ceaseless academic inquiry and the scientific pursuit of knowledge. According to the new university vision, the pursuit of aggregate wealth in higher education should never end because the pursuit of knowledge must always continue.[7]

This volume divides the historical arc of 150 years into two parts. The first, examining the decades from 1870 to 1930, is defined by the formative institutional development of American higher education, by the invention of new modes of fundraising that supplanted the occasional lotteries and subscription drives run by antebellum colleges, and by the absence of large, reliable, quantitative data sets on higher education finances. In addition, higher education became about three times cheaper to produce for each student, relative to the national per capita income, during this formative period between 1870 and 1930.

The second part, addressing the period from 1930 to 2020, is defined by the compilation and availability of reliable quantitative data sets, by the advent of aggressive investment strategies for endowment portfolios, by the formulation of economic theories pertaining to higher education finances, and, especially, by the increasing concern and complaint about the growing production cost, then the rising price and debt of students, and finally the widening wealth stratification in higher education.

Many different kinds of schools across the nation are discussed, including public colleges, land-grant universities, sectarian institutions, community colleges, women's colleges, tuition-dependent schools, research universities belonging to the Association of American Universities (AAU), and Historically Black Colleges and Universities (HBCUs). Yet much of the analysis focuses on the older, wealthy, private colleges and universities, including Yale, Columbia, Princeton, Dartmouth, Johns Hopkins, Cornell, Chicago, Stanford, Smith, Wellesley, and Harvard. Although this focus might appear narrow, several reasons warrant it.

6. See Thorstein Veblen, *The Higher Learning in America: A Memorandum on the Conduct of Universities by Business Men* (New York, 1918), 89; Ron Chernow, *Titan: The Life of John D. Rockefeller, Sr.* (New York, 1998).

7. Our thanks to Michael Arjun Banerjee, who contributed this insight.

First, this history explains how specific financial practices and policies originated and developed, and most of these innovations occurred at the older, wealthy institutions. Second, those schools often have the most complete and informative historical data, especially prior to 1950. Harvard, for example, is both the oldest college and the oldest corporation in the United States. In fact, Harvard has the longest and most robust record of institutional finances in higher education, as well as the longest continuing investment record of any financial entity in the country. Inevitably, a history of this subject must give Harvard considerable attention, not because it is elite or exemplary but because it has the fullest longitudinal data.

Finally, over the course of the twentieth century, nearly all colleges and universities adopted the financial practices and policies of the older, wealthy institutions. In financial terms, the rest were "following in your wake," the president of Princeton wrote to the president of Harvard already in 1919.[8] True, some colleges and universities initially resisted, and the non-profit, degree-granting schools—about 3,300 in 2020—are enormously diverse. Nevertheless, by the beginning of the twenty-first century nearly every college and university came to regard revenue growth, cost growth, and acquisition of financial capital as standard operational aims and major benchmarks of their academic reputation and quality.[9] This conventional view and the associated practices and policies originated at the older, wealthy schools and proliferated from there throughout higher education, and that is the third reason for focusing on them in the following pages.

In sum, this enchiridion attempts to explain succinctly when, where, and how today's financial "common sense" originated and infused higher education. Often appearing natural or inevitable today, the financial practices, policies, and theories arose for particular reasons in specific historical situations. Understanding the original circumstances prompts us to reconsider what now may seem commonsensical and necessary. If successful, this brief history will thus inform the latest round of discussions that began in the 1920s about wealth, cost, and price, amid the historically slow economic growth, lagging middle-class incomes, and increasing wealth inequality in the United States during the early twenty-first century.[10]

8. John G. Hibben to A. Lawrence Lowell, September 24, 1919, Lowell Records.
9. This book does not address for-profit schools because, historically, they have intermittently entered and abandoned higher education, depending largely on the availability of government subsidies. See Angulo, *Diploma Mills*. Some recent economic studies have viewed nonprofit and for-profit schools as fundamentally similar in their competition for revenue. See Weisbrod, Ballou, and Asch, *Mission and Money*.
10. Documentation in this book is kept to a minimum. Further references can be found in the sources cited. Dollar amounts are stated in nominal dollars, not adjusted for inflation, unless specified as constant dollars, which are adjusted for inflation by the indicated base year.

PART I

THE FORMATIVE ERA, 1870–1930

CHAPTER I

"Endowment" Emerges, 1870–1930

In the twenty-first century, the term "endowment" in higher education denotes funds held "in perpetuity" and "invested to create a source of income."[1] It is also agreed that these permanent productive funds are enormously important, because endowments foster—and serve to measure—academic excellence and prestige. "Everyone knows" that "endowment size, perhaps more than any other single factor, determines the success and the perceived quality of . . . colleges and universities," their leaders maintain.[2]

Since 1970, when the *Chronicle of Higher Education* first published a list of the values of endowments of "leading colleges and universities," their values have soared. In 1974, the National Association of College and University Business Officers (NACUBO) launched its annual survey of the endowments of a growing number of institutions. In subsequent decades, more and more journals,

---

1. Quotations are from American Council on Education, *Understanding College and University Endowments* (Washington, DC, 2014), 2; Dwight Burlingame, ed., *Philanthropy in America: A Comprehensive Historical Encyclopedia* (Santa Barbara, CA, 2004), 2:536.
2. Victor E. Ferrall Jr., *Liberal Arts at the Brink* (Cambridge, MA, 2011), 23.

magazines, and newspapers published lists of endowment values drawn from the NACUBO survey, which became a prominent benchmark in the competition among colleges and universities. "Short of beating an archrival in football, posting the highest one-year investment result [of endowment] ranks near the top . . . of institutional aspirations," observed David Swensen, the renowned chief investment officer of Yale University, in 2009.[3]

Due to this growing prominence over the past half century, it is often assumed that "endowment" always carried this meaning and weight in higher education. After all, European universities have owned permanent invested funds since their inception in the thirteenth century, when wealthy burghers and merchants began creating charitable trusts to support some colleges and schools. Following this precedent, benefactors donated permanent invested funds to Harvard, the first corporation and the first college established in the American colonies, soon after its founding in 1636.

Known at the time as "foundations," "legacies," and "trusts," Harvard's funds are the oldest perpetual investments in the United States. Because Harvard now owns the largest endowment of any university in the world, it is also assumed that the significance of permanent funds and the focus on building them began in 1636, and that Harvard's head start on all other colleges inevitably made it the wealthiest. Indeed, colleges and universities having "the longest time to build an endowment—are the richest," it is said.[4]

Yet the fundamental importance of endowment, the emphasis on increasing it, and even its current meaning are relatively recent in historical terms. These characteristics originated during the formative era of American higher education between 1870 and 1930. During this period, the now familiar institutional types took shape, and colleges and universities began competing for "survival of the fittest," in the words of University of Chicago president William R. Harper (1891–1906).[5] The new appreciation and meaning of "endowment" thus developed amid what leaders conceived as a Darwinian struggle, and private and public institutions started to compete intensively to build their financial capital. In 1920, Harvard emerged out of this scrum with the lead in financial capi-

3. Swensen, *Pioneering Portfolio Management* (2009), 320. See "College Endowment Funds: Their Performance in 1969," *Chronicle of Higher Education*, May 4, 1970; NACUBO, "1974 NACUBO Investment Questionnaire Endowment Market Value . . . of 145 Responding Institutions" (typescript; Washington, DC, 1974); Kenneth Redd to Sarah M. Iler, February 26, 2021, email on file.

4. Ferrall, *Liberal Arts at the Brink*, 24. See editor's note in Paul C. Cabot and Leonard C. Larrabee, "Investing Harvard Money," *Harvard Alumni Bulletin*, May 12, 1951, 628n; Seymour E. Harris, *Economics of Harvard* (New York, 1970), 378.

5. Harper, *Trend in Higher Education*, 375.

tal that it would not subsequently relinquish. Over the following decade, a consensus formed around the new understanding and significance of "endowment," which still prevails today.[6]

Prior to the 1870s, the meaning of "endowment" in America, as in England during earlier centuries, comprehended all the resources or assets belonging to individuals or institutions, including personal qualities, entitlements, immunities, franchises, property, buildings, equipment, money, legacies, trusts, and foundations. The consensus that "endowment" in higher education specifically denotes permanent, productive funds first appeared in the 1920s. This novel, narrow meaning was then called the "correct sense" because it conveyed the new appreciation for the importance of permanent, productive funds that had developed over the prior 50 years.[7]

"The Rock of Gibraltar of American Higher Education"

Endowment confers significant benefits to a college or university because permanent productive funds enhance institutional autonomy, stability, and flexibility over the long term. Autonomy is strengthened because other sources of revenue—tuition, grants, gifts, and state appropriations—depend directly on external agents and their preferences. But the income from invested endowment is controlled by the university and thus fortifies its capacity for self-determination. Autonomy is strengthened even by restricted endowment funds, which are usually fungible, as discussed in the following chapters.

Permanent funds also provide stability because a well-endowed institution is normally assured of meeting its operating costs and does not need to adjust expenses dramatically in response to shifts in other sources of revenue. Even in abnormal times, a significant endowment ensures the institution's stable existence. Finally, endowment allows an institution the flexibility to pursue opportunities and discretionary goals. For example, after the economic downturn in the 1970s and early 1980s, well-endowed colleges and universities were positioned to "buy the best" faculty, students, and institutional support, which less endowed institutions could not afford.[8]

---

6. For additional discussion and documentation on points in this chapter, see Bruce A. Kimball and Benjamin A. Johnson, "The Inception of the Meaning and Significance of Endowment in American Higher Education, 1890–1930," *Teachers College Record* 114 (2012): 1–32.

7. Quotation is from Trevor Arnett, *College and University Finance* (New York, 1922), 24–25.

8. Clotfelter, *Buying the Best*. See Twentieth Century Fund, *Funds for the Future*, 6, 26–27; Swensen, *Pioneering Portfolio Management* (2009), 9–15; American Council on Education, *Understanding College and University Endowments*, 2–3.

Due to these benefits of autonomy, stability, and flexibility, a large endowment imparts a considerable advantage to colleges and universities competing to excel in higher education. As an institution's financial capital grows, this advantage is compounded, because the larger base yields larger returns. In addition, larger endowments have generally enjoyed a higher rate of return historically, as scholars began to observe in the late 1920s.

The amount of permanent funds therefore corresponds closely with academic standing and stratifies colleges and universities within higher education. For example, in 2020 there were about 3,300 non-profit, degree-granting colleges and universities in the United States. The endowments of all 63 members of the Association of American Universities, the most prestigious and exclusive academic association, ranked among the largest 100 endowments of colleges and universities in the United States and Canada.

In addition, the permanent capital is concentrated in the highest tier of endowments. In 2020, the NACUBO survey found that the richest 100 schools owned nearly 80 percent of the permanent invested funds of those 3,300 colleges and universities. And 99 percent of the reported funds belonged to about 700 schools, including about 20 community colleges, most women's colleges, and several HBCUs. For example, Hillsborough Community College in Florida and Elgin Community College in Illinois each reported about $8 million in endowment and ranked 714 and 715 nationally in endowment size in 2020, respectively.[9]

It is true that many schools—likely hundreds—with small endowments do not report their data to NACUBO, which conducts the most authoritative and comprehensive survey of endowments in the United States and Canada. In 2020, for example, nonreporters included Tougaloo College, an HBCU founded in 1871 in Mississippi with an endowment of about $10 million; Greenfield Community College in Massachusetts, with an endowment of about $7 million; and Westfield State University, which established a new endowment fund within its affiliated foundation. Indeed, the vast majority of colleges and universities probably have some kind of affiliated foundation or endowment, and the rest "aspire to have one."[10]

Nevertheless, even if, say, 2,000 schools that did not report to NACUBO each had an endowment of a few million dollars (which is likely true), that would

9. NACUBO, *Endowment Study 2020*; Association of American Universities, "Three Leading Research Universities Join the Association of American Universities," press release, November 6, 2019. The annual NACUBO lists include a few private foundations.

10. Lucie Lapovsky, "Critical Endowment Policy Issues," *New Directions for Higher Education* 140 (Winter 2007): 99.

not change the proportional concentration of permanent invested funds in American higher education. An additional $6 billion owned by 2,000 more schools would amount to less than 1 percent of the $647 billion in endowment reported by NACUBO in 2020.

All these characteristics of endowment today—its very meaning, its importance, the drive to increase it, and its concentration—originated in the formative period of American higher education between 1870 and 1930. During this period, encompassing the so-called Gilded Age (1870–95) and Progressive Era (1890–1920), the accumulation of financial capital became the measure of success, superiority, and even fitness to survive generally in American culture, as an unprecedented, enormous wealth gap widened between the rich and the working classes in the United States.

Concurrently, American universities began to expand their curricula far beyond the traditional liberal arts and to encourage research and scientific and applied studies for the first time. Some of these universities, such as Harvard, Columbia, Chicago, and Michigan, evolved from relatively small, antebellum colleges. Others were newly founded—Cornell and California in 1868, Johns Hopkins in 1876, Stanford in 1891.[11] By the 1920s, the wealthiest universities composed an upper tier in higher education, whose elite status continued into the twenty-first century.

Meanwhile, the number and kinds of institutions, students, degrees, and aims of higher education expanded during the formative period. And the newcomers—including land-grant universities, women's colleges, junior colleges, and HBCUs—sought to emulate the older, wealthier, and more prestigious institutions and to acquire the benefits of endowment. By 1919, advertisements in popular magazines across the nation were touting the "two million-dollar endowment" of Lindenwood College in Missouri and the "large endowment" of Wayland Academy in Wisconsin. In 1926, articles profiling women's colleges in *Ladies Home Journal* routinely included information on their endowments. By 1951, endowment was proclaimed "the Rock of Gibraltar of American Higher Education."[12] In this fashion, the growing appreciation of

11. The classic account is Laurence R. Veysey, *The Emergence of the American University* (Chicago, 1965).

12. Quotation is from R. Keith Kane and Dana Doten, "The Case for Endowment," *Harvard Alumni Bulletin* 12 (November 24, 1951): 212. See "Educational Guide," *Red Book Magazine* 33 (June 1919): 6–10; Charles A. Selden, "Mount Holyoke College Today," *Ladies' Home Journal* 43 (August 1926): 126–28; Charles A. Selden, "Goucher Finds Itself," *Ladies' Home Journal* 43 (October 1926): 210.

endowment profoundly shaped the organization, stratification, and public perception of higher education in subsequent decades.

Tremendous Growth of Permanent Funds

The emergence of endowment during the formative period occurred in several stages amid the new Darwinian competition in higher education. First, the size of permanent funds grew enormously, particularly those belonging to the wealthiest universities. Second, understanding and appreciation of the benefits of such funds increased. That appreciation ignited, third, a deliberate effort to amass these funds. Finally, a novel, specialized meaning of "endowment" gained widespread currency, largely due to the influence of the GEB and the millions it received from John D. Rockefeller. That new meaning became conventional by 1930, culminating the four-stage evolution of endowment in higher education during the formative period.

The first stage—the tremendous growth of permanent funds in American higher education—had no precedent. Prior to 1865, the economy of the United States did not produce enough surplus personal wealth to support huge benefactions, and most gifts to higher education went for current operations or buildings. Consequently, few treatises devoted to endowments appeared in the United States before the Civil War, and those circulating soon afterward were written by British authors. Then, between 1870 and 1930, the economy of the United States grew at a breathtaking pace that was "unique in human history," according to economist Robert Gordon. The gross national product (GNP) rose seven-fold, largely due to immense productivity gains in transportation, communication, and manufacturing stemming from technological developments, as well as organizational and legal innovations. Some industrial corporations and financial trusts grew immense, enriching certain "captains of industry" or "robber barons"—Andrew Carnegie, J. Pierpont Morgan, John D. Rockefeller, among others—with previously unimaginable wealth.[13]

As expressed quintessentially by Carnegie in his famous 1889 essay "The Gospel of Wealth," these multimillionaires believed that they merited their vast wealth by virtue of "the law of competition." Without acknowledging their often illegal or unethical methods, Carnegie maintained that he and his peers possessed "rare" and "peculiar talent," as well as "ability and energy," which

13. Quotation is from Gordon, *Rise and Fall of American Growth*, 1:285–87. See Isaac L. Kandel, "Endowments, Educational . . . United States," in *A Cyclopedia of Education*, ed. Paul Monroe (New York, 1918), 2:458–59; Curti and Nash, *Philanthropy*, 41, 56.

justified the disparity "between the palace of the millionaire and the cottage of the laborer." In fact, this wealth disparity "is not to be deplored, but welcomed as highly beneficial," he wrote, because the economic boom driven by "the law of competition" raises everyone's standard of living. Granted, "the law of competition . . . may be somewhat hard for the individual" because "rigid castes are formed" and "often there is friction . . . between rich and poor." Neverthe-less, "it is best for the race, because it ensures the survival of the fittest in every department."[14]

Yet Carnegie also considered the "unequal distribution of wealth" to be "tem-porary." Before they die, multimillionaires must consider what will happen to their fortunes. Bequeathing all the riches to family is "injudicious" and often works "more for the injury than for the good" of the heirs. Leaving wealth to be taxed "for public purposes" often does not accomplish "much posthumous good," he maintained. Instead, the most efficacious "mode of using wealth" is for the rich to treat their assets "as trust funds" to invest and spend as they deem "best calculated to produce the most beneficial results for the community."[15]

Similarly coupling versions of social Darwinism with the beneficent dispo-sition of wealth, many retiring multimillionaires contributed to an enormous flood of philanthropy across the nation. After selling his steel companies to J. Pierpont Morgan for $331 million in 1901, Andrew Carnegie founded the Car-negie Institution of Washington in 1902, the Carnegie Foundation for the Ad-vancement of Teaching in 1905, and the Carnegie Corporation of New York in 1911. Oil baron John D. Rockefeller, "the most famous American of his day," gave much of his fortune to build and endow the Rockefeller Institute of Med-ical Research and the GEB in the 1900s, the Rockefeller Foundation and the Laura Spelman Rockefeller Memorial in the 1910s, and the University of Chi-cago starting in the 1890s, as depicted in figure 1.1.[16]

These unprecedented gifts were welcomed with few reservations. In England during prior centuries, charitable gifts and trusts had created many "inconve-niences" imposed by the "dead hand" of donors, who endowed charities with highly restrictive purposes. After a great deal of controversy, legal and policy re-forms eased these restrictions in England in the middle of the nineteenth

14. Carnegie, *Gospel of Wealth*, 1–6.
15. Carnegie, *Gospel of Wealth*, 8–13.
16. Quotation is from Ron Chernow, *Titan: The Life of John D. Rockefeller, Sr.* (New York, 1998), xiii. See Curti and Nash, *Philanthropy*, 91–211; Zunz, *Philanthropy in America*, 1–2. These amounts and those below are in nominal dollars.

DELAYED HOLIDAY GIFTS FOR PRESIDENT HARPER OF THE UNIVERSITY OF CHICAGO.

Figure 1.1. University of Chicago President William R. Harper Holding Rockefeller Money, 1898. Courtesy of Special Collections Research Center, University of Chicago Library.

century. In particular, the courts introduced the *cy près* (near by) legal doctrine in order to broaden outmoded or unduly narrow restrictions while preserving charitable trusts.[17]

17. John Stuart Mill, "Educational Endowments" (1866) and "Endowments" (1869), in *The Collected Works*, ed. John M. Robson (Toronto, 1967, 1984), 5:614–29, 21:209–17; Arthur Hob-

Such dead-hand restrictions never became a significant factor in the United States because the number and value of benefactions were relatively small until the 1860s. By that point, the lessons of the English "inconveniences" had "taken effect upon the public mind" in America, as the president of Harvard observed.[18] Nor did complaints from prominent clergymen and social reformers that unethical or illegal dealings "tainted" the benefactions of industrial capitalists dampen enthusiasm for the wave of new philanthropy. "The only trouble with tainted money is t'aint enough of it," the saying went.[19]

Most of the new philanthropy flooded into higher education. "Money madness is the besetting sin in the United States, according to the rest of the world. . . . But the grand passion of the people of the United States is for education, not money," declared newspapers in Washington, New Orleans, Omaha, and other cities.[20] Notable gifts to found new institutions during the 1860s and 1870s included $500,000 to establish Cornell University and $800,000 to found Vassar College in 1868, and $7 million—the largest benefaction to that point in American history—bequeathed in 1873 by merchant Johns Hopkins to establish a university and an associated hospital in Baltimore. During the early 1890s, the $20 million reportedly given by railroad mogul Leland Stanford to found a university in California and the $10 million donated by Rockefeller to rebuild the University of Chicago attracted widespread publicity, as did many smaller but still significant gifts to other universities.[21]

In the view of contemporary observers, this wave of benefactions was "one of the most striking phases of American educational history."[22] Between 1870 and 1900 the aggregate endowment of higher education grew ten-fold to some $195 million. At that point, the "capital invested" in American colleges and universities was "greater by many millions than is invested for a similar purpose in any other country," commented news stories in Dallas, Omaha, Richmond, and other cities. The aggregate endowment then quadrupled between 1900 and 1926.[23]

---

house, *The Dead Hand: Addresses on the Subject of Endowments and Settlements of Property* (London, 1880).

18. Eliot, *Annual Report 1882–83*, 41.

19. See Washington Gladden, "Tainted Money," *Outlook* 52 (1895): 886; Sol Gittleman, "Letter to the Editor," *Boston Globe*, September 13, 2019.

20. Dexter Marshall, "Vast Army of Students in the United States," *Washington Post*, September 17, 1905; Dexter Marshall, "Uncle Sam's Vast Army of Students and Teachers," *The [New Orleans] Daily Picayune*, September 17, 1905; Dexter Marshall, "Uncle Sam's Army of Students," *Omaha Sunday World-Herald*, September 17, 1905.

21. See "Wealth's New Position," in *Pandex of the Press*, ed. Arthur I. Street (San Francisco, 1905), 1:285.

22. Kandel, "Endowments, Educational . . . United States," 458–59.

23. Dexter Marshall, "American University Beginnings," *Dallas Morning News*, September 16, 1906; Dexter Marshall, "The Romantic Beginning of America's Universities," *Richmond Times-Dispatch*, September 16, 1906; Dexter Marshall, "Millions Go for Higher Education in Amer-

TABLE I.I
Values of First-Tier Endowments of Colleges and Universities, 1875–1930
(in millions of nominal dollars)

Institution	1875	1880	1890	1900	1910	1920	1930
Chicago	—	—	—	5.7	14.9	28.4	59.6
Columbia	4.6	4.8	8.1	13.3	25.8	39.6	73.4
Cornell	1.3	1.3	4.9	6.8	8.7	16.0	24.7
Harvard	1.6	4.0	7.0	12.6	22.0	44.6	108.1
Johns Hopkins and hospital	6.0	6.0	3.0	3.3	4.6	9.1	26.8
MIT	0.3	0.3	—	3.1	1.9	15.0	32.2
Princeton*	0.9	1.1	—	2.3	—	10.3	26.0
Stanford	—	—	—	18.0	24.0	33.3	27.8
Yale	0.3	1.3	3.1	4.9	12.5	24.0	82.9

Source: Adapted from Bruce A. Kimball and Benjamin A. Johnson, "The Inception of the Meaning and Significance of Endowment in American Higher Education, 1890–1930," *Teachers College Record* 114 (2012): table 1.
Note: The largest endowment in a given year is shaded.
*Princeton's early financial records are incomplete.

"The great bulk" of the "permanent endowments" established by philanthropists thus went to colleges and universities, reported the president of the Carnegie Foundation for the Advancement of Teaching. In 1913, for example, 15 percent of the total income of the colleges and universities in the country came from grants made just by the GEB and the Carnegie Corporation.[24] By 1926, the GEB estimated that colleges and universities had obtained "approximately three quarters" of their endowments since 1900. Among these institutions, the permanent funds of the wealthiest universities grew the fastest.[25] The staggering increases of the nine wealthiest are listed in table 1.1.

By 1920, a second tier of wealthy colleges and universities had formed, comprising 22 institutions. In any given year, the top three or four institutions in the second tier rivaled the endowment of those at the bottom of the first tier. But those top three or four were not consistent because the rank of endowment value of the second tier changed considerably over time, as listed in table 1.2.

ica," *Omaha Sunday World Herald*, September 16, 1906. See Ernest V. Hollis, *Philanthropic Foundations and Higher Education* (New York, 1938), 200.

24. Quotation is from Henry S. Pritchett, "The Use and Abuse of Endowments," *Atlantic Monthly* 144 (October 1929): 520. See Jones, *American Giver*, 7.

25. Quotation is from GEB, *Annual Report 1924–25*, 4. See William A. Orton, "Endowments and Foundations," *Encyclopedia of the Social Sciences* (New York, 1931), 5:532; Arthur R. Seass, *Endowment Income and Investments, 1926–35* (Washington, DC, 1937), 3–5.

Values of Second-Tier Endowments of Colleges and Universities,
1920 and 1930 (in millions of nominal dollars)

	1920s endowments			1930s endowments	
Rank	Institutions	Millions	Rank	Institutions	Millions
1	Carnegie Institute of Technology	9.6	1	University of Rochester	26.2
2	Washington University, St. Louis	9.1	2	Northwestern University	25.3
3	University of Pennsylvania	9.0	3	*University of Texas*	24.0
4	*University of California*	7.3	4	Duke University	22.6
5	*University of Washington*	6.3	5	Vanderbilt University	19.0
6	Northwestern University	5.5	6	Washington University, St. Louis	17.9
7	University of Rochester	5.2	7	Oberlin College	17.8
8	Amherst College	4.4	8	University of Pennsylvania	17.4
9	Dartmouth College	4.3	9	Carnegie Institute of Technology	16.1
10	Clark University	4.2	10	*University of California*	15.2
11	Bryn Mawr College	4.2	11	Dartmouth College	15.0
12	Western Reserve University	4.1	12	California Institute of Technology	10.8
13	Tulane University	4.0	13	Western Reserve University	10.6
14	Vanderbilt University	3.9	14	Rice Institute	10.5
15	*University of Minnesota*	3.9	15	College of Mount St. Joseph	10.2
16	*University of Oklahoma*	3.7	16	Brown University	10.0
17	Tufts College	3.5	17	Tulane University	10.0
18	Barnard College	3.5	18	*University of Virginia*	10.0
19	Brown University	3.2	19	Wellesley College	9.5
20	Wellesley College	3.2	20	Berea College	9.2
21	Williams College	3.2	21	*University of Minnesota*	8.8
22	Smith College	3.2	22	Amherst College	8.0

Sources: Biennial Survey of Education 1920–22, 2:384–425; Biennial Survey of Education 1928–1930, 2:480–500.
Note: Public institutions are italicized.

Tables 1.1 and 1.2 demonstrate the remarkable persistence of the stratification of wealth in higher education that began during the formative period. These two tables list the 39 schools with the largest endowments in the 1920s, constituting about 4 percent of the some 965 degree-granting colleges and universities at that time. Notwithstanding the tremendous expansion in the number of higher education institutions over the subsequent century, nearly all of those 39 remained in that top 4 percent in 2020.[26]

GEB Promotes Endowment

The second and third stages in the emergence of endowment—the growing appreciation for the benefits of permanent funds and the deliberate effort to enlarge them—were closely related. Both were encouraged by the reasoning in Carnegie's "The Gospel of Wealth," which also explained why the bulk of philanthropy came to the institutions with the most financial capital. The wealthiest institutions deserved more, the poorer ones less. Yet, even among the wealthiest universities, the growth of Harvard's endowment was exceptional.

Looking back, it might appear natural that Harvard topped the list of endowments, as it has since the *Chronicle of Higher Education* published its first list in 1970. But Harvard's top rank was not customary during the formative period, as seen in table 1.1. In the 1870s, Johns Hopkins and its hospital had the most permanent funds, as did Stanford in the 1890s and early 1900s. Yale's endowment rose dramatically in the 1920s. Most often, the biggest endowment belonged to Columbia, whose real estate holdings in New York City made it "rich beyond the dreams of avarice," according to some.[27] Only in 1920 did Harvard attain the lead among universities' endowments that has continued through today, a century later.

Harvard's leading position resulted not from banking huge gifts but from pursuing a novel strategy conceived by President Charles W. Eliot during his administration from 1869 to 1909. Eliot became the first university president to emphasize the importance of increasing permanent funds and to develop policies to achieve this, as discussed in chapter 2. While few universities adopted his new strategy before he retired in 1909, Harvard alumni embraced Eliot's financial teachings, and the university's endowment surged ahead by 1920 as a result.

Meanwhile, John D. Rockefeller focused much of his philanthropy on higher education. In 1903, he founded the GEB with a gift of $1 million and made

---

26. *Historical Statistics of the United States*, table Bc510–22; NACUBO, *Endowment Study 2020.*
27. Thomas W. Lamont to Robert J. Beeckman, October 15, 1919, Lamont Correspondence.

additional gifts of $10 million in 1905, $32 million in 1907, and $10 million in 1909. From that point, the GEB directed its efforts toward increasing the number and size of endowments in higher education. The board hoped to achieve a "concentration of gifts in the form of endowment" throughout higher education and exhorted colleges and universities to build their endowments and to ask donors to make gifts to their permanent funds.[28] This policy ran counter to the traditional habits of college and universities to raise money for erecting buildings, covering deficits, or spending on operations.

Moreover, the GEB aimed extremely high. In its view, endowment income should cover about half of the expenses of "an efficient college," the norm at Harvard and the "better-endowed colleges" in the 1910s. This goal therefore implied that every private institution should be as well-endowed as Harvard! Similarly, the board endorsed Eliot's priority and policies on building financial capital when it published the leading guidebook on finances of colleges and universities in 1922.[29]

The extraordinary GEB goal also implied that the permanent funds of American higher education should be doubled, given that endowment income provided about a quarter of the revenue of all colleges and universities in 1900. In order to achieve this breathtaking goal, the board decided to rely on the "almost indispensable leverage" of "conditioning" its gifts to endowment on the donations of others, so as to multiply the increase of permanent funds. Under the typical condition, the GEB provided about one-third of the amount sought. In 1919 Rockefeller gave the board an additional $50 million to increase the endowments of private institutions. By 1925 the board calculated that it had committed some $60 million to the endowments of colleges and universities nationwide, ultimately yielding about $200 million in combination with the conditioned gifts.[30]

The GEB succeeded in drawing widespread attention to the importance of endowment. In 1913, Edwin E. Slosson, author of the landmark *Great American Universities*, wrote that "the leading institutions from the point of view of graduate study are all of the endowed class." Over the next decade more and more institutions pursued the GEB aim because "the preservation and increase of endowment is so important to the well-being of an endowed college or university," observed GEB secretary Trevor Arnett. By 1929, "few colleges in the

28. Quotations and material here and below are from GEB, *Account of Its Activities, 1902–1914*, 3–17, 142–43.

29. Arnett, *College and University Finance*, 11. See Samuel P. Capen, *Resources and Standards of Colleges of Arts and Sciences* (Washington, DC, 1918), 44.

30. See US CommEd, *Report [June 30, 1900]*, 2:1876; Raymond B. Fosdick, *Adventure in Giving* (New York, 1962), 140–49; GEB, *Annual Report 1924–25*, 4–5.

land . . . are not striving for 'adequate endowment,'" stated philanthropist Julius Rosenwald.[31]

Despite these efforts, the GEB did not come close to its goal that colleges and universities should draw half of their income from endowment earnings. In fact, the fraction declined because higher education expanded enormously between 1910 and 1930. Over those two decades, the number of colleges, universities, and professional schools grew from 602 to 1,409 and the number of conferred degrees rose more than three-fold from 40,000 to over 130,000. To be sure, the board had expected a long campaign, stating in 1914 that "many years must elapse" before its goal would be reached. Nevertheless, the board could not keep pace with the expansion, even though it largely restricted its giving to private schools, which still constituted nearly two-thirds of colleges and universities as of 1930. But the public institutions were growing much faster in size and enrollment.[32]

Merely to sustain the norm of 1900 that endowment income provided a quarter of higher education revenue would have required tripling the permanent funds by 1930. Attaining the GEB goal of doubling the fraction meant a six-fold increase. It was impossible. As fast as the board raced to direct permanent funds to higher education between 1900 and 1930, the finish line receded. Indeed, the fraction of total annual revenue provided by endowment income for all institutions fell dramatically over those three decades. Notwithstanding the millions poured into permanent funds, the percentage of institutional income drawn from endowment earnings decreased from 40 percent to 25 percent for private institutions, from 6 percent to 2 percent for public institutions, and from 25 percent to 14 percent for all institutions.[33]

In the mid-1920s the GEB therefore abandoned its goal "because the amounts . . . were so large and the resources of the General Education Board were relatively so limited." But in the same breath the board declared victory, stating that "its objective in stimulating gifts of endowment for general purposes had been attained . . . because the habit of giving endowment to colleges seemed well established."[34] Though equivocal, the statement was accurate.

31. Edwin E. Slosson, "Universities, American Endowed," in *A Cyclopedia of Education*, ed. Paul Monroe (New York, 1911–13), 5:668; Arnett, *College and University Finance*, 1–2; Julius Rosenwald, "Principles of Public Giving," *Atlantic Monthly* 143 (1929): 599. See Edwin E. Slosson, *Great American Universities* (New York, 1910).

32. Quotation is from GEB, *Account of Its Activities, 1902–1914*, 145. See US CommEd, *Report [June 30, 1910]*, 2:843; *Biennial Survey of Education 1928–30*, 2:2, 339.

33. These figures are approximations based on the available data. See US CommEd, *Report [1900]*, 2:1876; *[1910]*, 2:868; *Biennial Survey of Education 1920–22*, 2:282; *1934–36*, 2:20; Arnett, *College and University Finance*, 1.

34. Trevor Arnett, *Observations on the Financial Condition of Colleges and Universities in the United States* (New York, 1937), 4–5.

On the one hand, the GEB conceded that the goal was unattainable, and the Great Depression further eroded the possibility of enlarging endowments after 1930. On the other hand, colleges and universities now appreciated the benefits of endowment. Looking back, the GEB stoutly declared, "The first two decades of the twentieth century will stand out as the relatively brief period during which endowed higher institutions of learning have suddenly expanded in numbers and have endeavored to obtain the financial resources rendered necessary by their expansion in size and scope."[35] This judgment was validated by the growing body of research and commentary on the topic after 1920.[36]

The "Correct Sense" of "Endowment"

Also confirming the GEB judgment was the fourth stage in the emergence of endowment: the evolution of its meaning. As in England during earlier centuries, the term in the United States during the nineteenth century comprehended all the assets, capacities, immunities, entitlements, and beneficial attributes belonging to persons or institutions. After 1870, this comprehensive meaning of "endowment" narrowed within higher education, and the term began to denote predominantly the tangible assets of colleges and universities, including academic buildings, campus land, other properties, and so forth. Over the next four decades, this denotation of tangible assets came to be considered overbroad, and the cardinal importance of permanent, productive investments became apparent in the 1920s, as illustrated in figure 1.2.

The background to this semantic evolution lay in the notoriously weak accounting practices in higher education. In the 1910s, the GEB found that many colleges and universities "had no organized bookkeeping staff," that their treasurer's reports were "frequently . . . incomplete and confused," and that no uniformity existed in presenting financial data.[37] For example, in 1913, one of the Smith College trustees, who was a financier on Wall Street, agreed to advise the college on investing its endowment. But the college treasurer took "several weeks" to account for Smith's current investments, whereas "an intelligent book-keeper" should have been able to provide the information "within half an hour," the financier complained to the Smith president.[38]

35. GEB, *Annual Report 1924–25*, 4, 6.

36. See, e.g., Jesse B. Sears, *Philanthropy in the History of American Higher Education* (Washington, DC, 1922); Lemuel H. Murlin, "Problems in the Use of College Endowments," *School and Society* 16 (1922): 246–50; James C. Young, "The Dead Hand in Philanthropy," *Current History* 23 (1926): 837–42.

37. GEB, *Account of Its Activities, 1902–1914*, 148–49. See "Business Management in Institutions of Higher Education," *Review of Education Research* 2 (March 1, 1932): 116.

38. Thomas W. Lamont to Marion L. Burton, November 5, 1913, Burton Files.

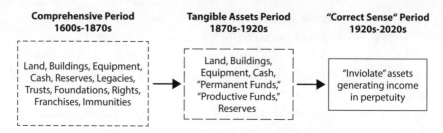

Comprehensive Period 1600s-1870s	Tangible Assets Period 1870s-1920s	"Correct Sense" Period 1920s-2020s
Land, Buildings, Equipment, Cash, Reserves, Legacies, Trusts, Foundations, Rights, Franchises, Immunities	Land, Buildings, Equipment, Cash, "Permanent Funds," "Productive Funds," Reserves	"Inviolate" assets generating income in perpetuity

Figure 1.2. Evolution of the Meaning of "Endowment," 1600s–2020s.

Among the inadequacies of bookkeeping, the GEB identified a particular problem that jeopardized its campaign to emphasize and increase permanent funds in higher education. The board discovered that "all sorts of property were being reported as 'endowment,' the word being so freely and loosely used by colleges in reporting that published statistics were valueless."[39] Finally, apart from incompetence and imprecision, the GEB also concluded that, at many colleges and universities, the "financial reports are made to conceal the situation rather than disclose it."[40]

As part of its campaign to increase permanent funds, the GEB therefore decided to clean the Augean stables of college and university financial reporting and enlisted Trevor Arnett as its Hercules. A graduate of the University of Chicago, Arnett served as that university's chief accountant between 1896 and 1922, when Rockefeller donated millions to the university to the delight of President Harper. From 1920 to 1924, Arnett served as secretary of the GEB and then president from 1928 to 1936. In these roles, he became the national authority on finances in higher education and set forth "the principles underlying college accounting" for endowed institutions in *College and University Finance* (1922). Over the next two years the GEB distributed 5,626 copies of this standard handbook—about six copies for every college and university in the country.[41]

Commensurate with these accounting reforms, the GEB recognized "that, before accurate statements . . . could be made, words must be defined." Hence, the board attempted "to secure the use of terms in their exact meaning" and to address the central question: "what is endowment?"[42] In order to achieve its goal

---

39. GEB, *Account of Its Activities, 1902–1914*, 150.
40. Arnett, *College and University Finance*, 105.
41. Quotation is from Arnett, *College and University Finance*, v. See Carter Alexander, *Bibliography on Educational Finance* (New York, 1924), 79; Richard J. Storr, *Harper's University: The Beginnings; a History of the University of Chicago* (Chicago, 1966), 259; Trevor Arnett, *Suggestions as to the Methods of Handling Endowment and Other Funds* (Chicago, 1927), 1.
42. GEB, *Account of Its Activities, 1902–1914*, 150–51.

of elevating and increasing permanent invested funds in higher education, Arnett and the GEB wished to employ language that reinforced proper financial policy. "It is amazing to find how rarely the term 'endowment' is used in its correct sense," observed Arnett. "This would be a trivial matter if it were simply a matter of definition. But, as the reader will soon perceive, unless the term 'endowment' is properly understood by the trustees and officers, the financial policy of an endowed college may go seriously astray."[43]

Determining that proper understanding entailed winnowing down the comprehensive and varied meanings of "endowment" that had originated centuries earlier. The roots of the English term lie in the late 1400s when the verb "endow" signified "to give a dowry," "to enrich with property," or "to furnish with . . . any gift, quality, or power of mind or body." The noun "endowment" therefore denoted "the property or fund" or "power, capacity, or other advantage" that belongs to either a person or an institution.[44] These broad and varied senses were adopted in American English and continued through the Civil War. The noun had a range of meanings—personal property, rights, capabilities, or other advantages, as well as institutional property, funds, entitlements, immunities, or other assets—and this interchanging of personal and institutional senses long persisted.[45]

In the 1860s, this comprehensive and variable denotation began to narrow in higher education, as "endowment" was distinguished from intangible assets. For example, in 1858 the new Minnesota state constitution provided that "the rights, immunities, franchises, and endowments" previously granted to the University of Minnesota "are hereby perpetuated." In 1890, the new Idaho state constitution employed nearly identical language concerning the University of Idaho.[46] Yale presidents Noah Porter (1870–86) and Timothy Dwight (1886–99) and Harvard president Eliot used "endowment" in a variety of ways but primarily applied the term to all tangible assets, including buildings, real property, "invested funds," and "permanent funds." The reports of the US commissioner of education did likewise.[47]

---

43. Arnett, *College and University Finance*, 24–25; see also 7–8.

44. *Oxford English Dictionary* (Oxford, 1989), s.v. endow, endowment.

45. Noah Webster, Chauncey A. Goodrich, and Noah Porter, *An American Dictionary of the English Language* (Springfield, MA, 1848), s.v. endowment; *Webster's Collegiate Dictionary: A Dictionary of the English Language* (Springfield, MA, 1898), s.v. endowment.

46. *State of Minnesota Constitution* (1858), art. 8, sec. 4; *State of Idaho Constitution* (1890), art. 9, sec. 10.

47. See Eliot, *Annual Report 1881–82, 1892–93, 1900–1901, 1907–8*; Noah Porter, *Annual Report of the President of Yale College 1879–80*; Dwight, *Annual Report 1887–88*; US CommEd,

Some clarifying distinctions among tangible assets were then attempted. In 1900, the monograph on "professional education" prepared for the US Educational Exhibit at the Paris Exposition distinguished "endowment" from "property," the latter referring to "land and buildings."[48] In 1905, Yale treasurer Lee McClung proposed to distinguish sharply between monies reserved for "Land, Buildings and Permanent Equipment" and "Endowment Funds," to prevent "any confusion with respect to the nature and character of these assets." But the president and alumni continued to interchange "endowment" with "working capital," "corporate wealth," "productive funds," and "invested funds."[49]

This varying language reflected different conceptions of institutional assets, which contributed to the accounting problems of colleges and universities. For example, real estate had historically been considered part of an institution's "endowment." But land served a variety of purposes. Institutions owned real estate "for educational purposes," such as classroom buildings; "productive real estate," such as rented parcels and buildings; and "unproductive real estate," such as buffer land that a university had acquired around the campus.[50] Naming all real estate holdings as "endowment" thus created confusion about its meaning and function as an asset. By 1920, the GEB considered the meaning of tangible assets "wrong" and demanded that "endowment" be employed in its "correct sense."[51] But what exactly was that?

"Productive" and "Permanent" Funds

Amid the variation and ambiguity, two cardinal characteristics had surfaced in all the discussion about institutional "endowment": the function and the duration of the assets. Each was expressed by one of the two most commonly circulating terms through the early 1900s. "Productive funds" signified the function; "permanent funds," the duration.

As the GEB began to emphasize in the 1910s, the function of endowment is solely to produce income, so "the word 'endowment' . . . would not . . . mean college buildings." Likewise, Arnett stressed in 1922 that endowment must yield

Report [June 30, 1875], 738–47; *[June 30, 1885]*, 609–21; *[June 30, 1895]*, pt. 2, 2132–47; *[June 30, 1905]*, 1:616–35.

48. James R. Parsons Jr., *Professional Education, Monographs on Education in the United States* (New York, [1900]), 17–18.

49. Quotation is from Lee McClung, *Annual Report of the Treasurer of Yale University 1905*, 4. See "Treasurer Day's First Report," *Yale Alumni Weekly*, September 30, 1910, 31–32; Frederick M. Leonard, "Yale Endowment," *Yale Alumni Weekly*, March 17, 1910, 636.

50. Quotations are from Eliot, *Annual Report 1888–89*, 5; "The President's Report for 1910," *Yale Alumni Weekly*, July 8, 1910, 1026. See US CommEd, *Report [June 30, 1880]*, 601n.

51. Arnett, *College and University Finance*, 24–25.

"income," such as "interest on bonds, mortgages, and loans, dividends on stocks, and rentals from real estate." Consequently, "endowment funds" had to be productive. However, the phrase "productive funds" could signify any invested cash or surplus, leaving unresolved a second fundamental issue: the duration of the income-producing assets. Arnett and the GEB insisted that endowment should be "permanent" and "inviolate" and "last forever."[52] In the late 1800s, this imperative prompted the widespread usage of the term "permanent funds" in institutional and government documents.[53]

Yet, in the early 1900s, even schools with substantial financial capital violated these precepts. Many, such as Smith College, routinely suggested that "a sufficient amount can be taken from the endowment" for building dormitories. Other institutions were "borrowing from endowment on the assumption that the loan would later be repaid," which often never happened. Another kind of violation was "hypothecation"—"the pledging of endowment investments as security for loans for the current expenditures of the college." Finally, trustees sometimes committed an unrestricted gift to endowment and then later decided that they needed the money and revoked the commitment.[54]

Against these practices, Arnett preached that endowment "is sacred and should not be touched or encroached upon for any object whatsoever; its income alone is available." Furthermore, "a college has no right, moral or legal, to 'borrow' from its endowment, to hypothecate endowment securities, to 'invest' endowment in college buildings and equipment, or, in fact, to do anything with endowment except to invest it so that it will produce a certain and steady income." Arnett thus did not endorse the concept of "quasi-endowment" or aggressive investment, which emerged after World War II. He and the GEB insisted that its gifts "shall be invested and preserved inviolably for the endowment" and that endowment should be treated as "permanent funds," which should not be "depleted" or "borrowed" by the institution.

By 1910, the language referring to institutional investments emphasized the characteristics of productivity and permanence. The next step was to associate these cardinal characteristics with a particular term in order that "accurate statements . . . could be made" about financial assets. Without that accuracy,

---

52. GEB, *Account of Its Activities, 1902–1914*, 151–52; Arnett, *College and University Finance*, 14, 25.

53. Henry Kiddle and Alexander J. Schwem, eds., *The Cyclopedia of Education*, 3rd ed. (New York, 1883), s.v. endowment.

54. Quotations are from L. Clark Seelye, *Annual Report of the President of Smith College 1900–1901*, 21; Sears, *Philanthropy*, 95; Arnett, *College and University Finance*, 25–26, 46; GEB, *Account of Its Activities, 1902–1914*, 151.

"the financial policy of an endowed college may go seriously astray."[55] One possible term was "permanent productive funds," which began to circulate in preceding decades and effectively denoted the two cardinal characteristics.[56] But that was an awkward neologism, and the venerable word "endowment" gained more traction, though the new usage required achieving consensus on a refined definition.

Prior to the Civil War, the word "endowment" was rarely employed to denote a colleges' financial investments, contrary to the impression in the late twentieth century. For example, the term did not appear in the 1830 "landmark" legal decision later said to have defined the investing guidelines of "endowment."[57] By the same token, the Harvard treasurer before the Civil War spoke of perpetual "foundations," "funds," and "trusts," not "endowment."[58] Yet the last term had a long lineage in English, and in the early twentieth century those emphasizing permanence and productivity in financial assets began to favor the word "endowment," while narrowing its meaning to the two cardinal characteristics of permanent and productive funds. In the 1910s, for example, the annual reports of the US commissioner of education began to favor this usage, as did the influential *Cyclopedia of Education.*[59]

In 1922, the semantic development was explicitly recognized by Arnett and the GEB when they endorsed "the definition of endowment here given—namely: *a fund which shall be maintained inviolate, the income of which shall alone be used.*" And they had the Rockefeller millions to persuade institutional leaders to adopt their definition, which was subsequently repeated by scholars and commentators.[60] The widespread new usage was evident in the widely read annual report of the Harvard treasurer, who redefined and renamed the university's long-standing category of "funds" as "endowment funds" for the first time in 1929. Equally significant, the treasurer gave no explanation for the shift in terminology.[61] At the end of the 1920s, the university with the most permanent funds in the United States officially adopted the new meaning of "endowment" as a matter of course.

55. Quotations here and above are from GEB, *Account of Its Activities, 1902–1914*, 150–52; Arnett, *College and University Finance*, 24–25; see also 7–8.

56. US CommEd, *Report [1890]*, pt. 2, 1600–1609.

57. Quotations are from William L. Cary and Craig R. Bright, *The Law and the Lore of Endowment Funds* (New York, 1969), 9; Williamson, "Background Paper," 111. See Harvard College v. Amory, 26 Mass. 446 (1830).

58. [Nathaniel Silsbee,] *Annual Report of the Treasurer of Harvard College 1846–47*, 1–6.

59. US CommEd, *Report [June 30, 1910]*, 2:868–942; *[June 30, 1916]*, 2:253–319; Kandel, "Endowments, Educational . . . United States," 458–59.

60. Arnett, *College and University Finance*, 24–25 (emphasis in the original). See Frederic A. Ogg, "Foundations and Endowments in Relation to Research," in *Research in the Humanistic and Social Sciences* (New York, 1928), 323–61; Pritchett, "Use and Abuse of Endowments," 520–24.

61. Charles F. Adams, *Annual Report of the Treasurer of Harvard University 1927–28*, 7.

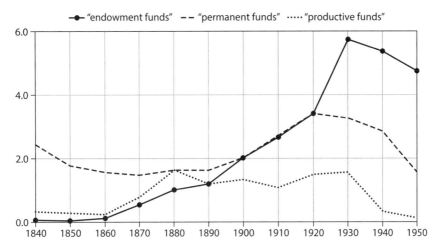

Figure 1.3. Historical Usage of the Term "Endowment Funds," 1840–1950. This graph presents the frequency of the phrases among the total words in English-language books published in the United States in a given year and digitized by Google as of 2019. Each line is defined by the frequencies calculated for 10-year moving averages in decennial years. Values on the *y*-axis are hundred-thousandths of a percent. *Source:* Google Ngram website (https://books.google.com/ngrams). Graph created by Sarah M. Iler.

The shifting semantic consensus is illustrated in figure 1.3. Before 1860, the terms "productive funds" and, especially, "permanent funds" were used much more commonly in the United States than the relatively rare "endowment funds." After 1860, usage of "endowment funds" increased steadily, while wealth and philanthropy also expanded in the United States. In the early 1900s, usage of "endowment funds" caught up to the other two terms. In the late 1910s "endowment funds" began to displace "productive funds" and "permanent funds," while combining their meanings.

In the early 1920s, usage of "productive funds" and "permanent funds" started to decline, and "endowment funds" continued to ascend. Some publications vacillated in their terminology, as did the reports of the US commissioner of education and analyses relying on them.[62] Nevertheless, by 1930, most leaders in higher education employed "endowment" in its new "correct sense," and scholars shifted their attention from defining and appreciating endowment to gathering and studying data about it. In particular, researchers, for the first time, began to track and compare the values of universities' endowments, demonstrating

62. *Biennial Survey of Education 1930–32*, 2:320–68; *1938–40 and 1940–42*, 2:31–33; Orton, "Endowments and Foundations," 5:532–33.

that endowment size had become an important measure of success and fitness to survive in higher education, even apart from its benefits conferred.[63] Culminating in the late 1920s, all these developments emanated from the flood of philanthropy, the guidance of the GEB and Trevor Arnett, and a new financial strategy formulated and propagated by the president of Harvard.

63. See Albert N. Ward, "Making Provision for the College of Liberal Arts," *Liberal Arts College Bulletin* 1 (November 1930): 4; Walter C. Eells, "Endowments in American Colleges and Universities," *School and Society* 41 (February 23, 1935): 263–72; Trevor Arnett, *Trends in Current Receipts and Expenditures . . . of Endowed Universities and Colleges* (New York, 1939), 84.

CHAPTER 2

Free-Money Strategy, 1869–1909

A new emphasis on increasing endowment emerged during the formative period of higher education from 1870 to 1930, driven by enormous philanthropic gifts and by the General Education Board (GEB) initiatives in the 1910s and 1920s. These developments led colleges and universities to appreciate the institutional benefits conferred by endowment, and the tournament to survive and succeed by accumulating financial capital therefore commenced in higher education.

Among the nine universities that emerged as the wealthiest between the Civil War and World War I—Chicago, Columbia, Cornell, Harvard, Johns Hopkins, Massachusetts Institute of Technology (MIT), Princeton, Stanford, Yale—the only one that did not receive a huge single donation was Harvard. Through 1910, at least five American universities received donations to their endowments that exceeded Harvard's largest gift of $1.1 million.[1] The pattern continued through 1930. The $35 million given by John D. Rockefeller to the University of Chicago between 1890 and 1910, the $24 million donated to MIT by George Eastman

---

1. Eliot, *Annual Report 1895–96*, 43; *1901–2*, 35–36; *1905–6*, 27.

during the 1910s, the bequest of $15 million from lawyer John W. Sterling to Yale in 1918, and the legacy of $15 million from industrialist Henry C. Frick to Princeton in 1919 far surpassed Harvard's largest gift of merely $5 million, received only in 1924.[2] Meanwhile, Columbia's legacy of productive real estate in downtown New York City made its endowment the largest in the nation through the 1910s.[3]

Without receiving megagifts, Harvard's endowment attained a lead by 1920 that it has never relinquished.[4] How was that possible? Rather than banking enormous gifts, Harvard built its wealth by adhering to a coherent strategy of financial management that eventually became the common sense—the prevailing ideology—of how to build and maintain the wealth of colleges and universities. President Charles W. Eliot (1869–1909) formulated this strategy over the course of his administration.

In his view, the ultimate aim of "the most far-seeing universities" was "to serve their communities best and deserve best of the republic." Achieving that end required pursuing the intermediate goals of academic excellence and prestige. Affirmed by virtually all presidents of major universities, this pursuit was conceived as a contest governed by the "law of competition" described by Andrew Carnegie. To win that competition, Eliot formulated a singular financial strategy that he summarized quintessentially in 1906:

> In the competition between American universities, and between American and foreign universities, those universities will inevitably win which have the largest amounts of free money [unrestricted endowment]. . . . How is more free money to be obtained? . . . The only way to increase the amount of such funds is to emphasize the urgent need of them, and then to treat them with such steady consideration that they will have . . . an assured permanence as funds.[5]

Eliot's "free-money" strategy included six tenets, which he publicized in his 39 annual reports until he retired in 1909. Harvard alumni then disseminated his view across the nation between 1915 and 1925, when they conducted the first modern fundraising campaign in American higher education and adopted Eliot's statement above as their motto.[6]

---

2. Anson P. Stokes Jr., *Annual Report of the Secretary of Yale College 1918–19*, 42–47; Elizabeth Brayer, *George Eastman: A Biography* (Rochester, NY, 2006), 341–44. Harvard was due to receive $5 million from the Frick bequest, but that share had shrunk to $2 million by 1921. "Bequests of Frick Shrink $30,000,000," *New York Times*, February 23, 1921.

3. Columbia University, *An Official Guide to Columbia University* (New York, 1912), 6; Horace Coon, *Columbia: Colossus on the Hudson* (New York, 1947), 29.

4. See table 1.1.

5. Quotations here and above are from Eliot, *Annual Report 1905–6*, 54–55, 57–58.

6. For further discussion and documentation concerning this chapter, see Bruce A. Kimball and Benjamin A. Johnson, "The Beginning of 'Free Money' Ideology in American Uni-

"Skillful Manager of a Cotton Factory"

Eliot was born in Boston in 1834, and his family fostered an interest in financial strategy and institutional governance. In the early 1800s, his grandfather became one of Boston's wealthiest merchants, and Eliot's father served as treasurer of Harvard, from which Charles graduated in 1853. Four years later, his father lost the family fortune in the Panic of 1857, and the personal experience of suddenly losing his large, anticipated inheritance surely contributed to Eliot's singular concern with financial strategy when serving as president of Harvard. He impressed that concern on both his son, who became the first chief executive of the American Unitarian Association in 1900, and his grandson and namesake, who became a leading landscape architect, depicted in figure 2.1.[7]

In light of this background, Upton Sinclair's portrayal of Eliot in 1923 was certainly paradoxical. Rather than associate Eliot with the "interlocking directorate" and "vested interests of . . . enormous financial power" that governed Harvard, Sinclair cast the president as "a scholar" and an exception.[8] To be sure, Eliot championed major academic reforms in higher education, such as allowing students to elect their own courses. But most writers on higher education during the formative period (and subsequently) charged him with overweening devotion to the business practices of industrial corporations, and considered him the prototype of what Thorstein Veblen labeled the "captain of erudition," playing on the term "captain of industry."[9]

The latter view, in fact, was expressed by the two predominant types of university and college presidents who held office during Eliot's tenure: the clergymen and the academicians. During the first half of his tenure in the 1870s and 1880s, the majority of college and university presidents had served as clergymen prior to entering their office. Embracing the traditional pastoral role of a college president, many in this group chided Eliot, privately if not publicly, because he "never teaches the students and has not the least formative control over their minds or characters. He is really a sort of general manager with duties analogous to those of a superintendent or president of a railroad," in the words of

---

versities: Charles W. Eliot at Harvard, 1869–1909," *History of Education Quarterly* 52 (2012): 222–50.

7. Hugh Hawkins, *Between Harvard and America: The Educational Leadership of Charles W. Eliot* (Cambridge, MA, 1972), 18–19.

8. Upton Sinclair, *The Goose-Step: A Study of American Education*, rev. ed. (Girard, KS, 1923), 1:68.

9. Thorstein Veblen, *The Higher Learning in America: A Memorandum on the Conduct of Universities by Business Men* (New York, 1918), 89.

Figure 2.1. Harvard University President Charles W. Eliot with Grandson, Charles W. Eliot II, ca. 1906. Courtesy of Harvard University Archives.

Martin B. Anderson, a Baptist minister and president of the University of Rochester from 1853 to 1882.[10]

After 1890, the number of clergymen among university presidents rapidly began to decline. Professors ascended from the faculty to take their place, and by 1900 these academicians constituted a majority of the presidents. Most in this

10. Quoted in Arthur J. May, *A History of the University of Rochester, 1850–1962*, ed. Lawrence E. Klein (Rochester, NY, 1977), 101. See also George P. Schmidt, *The Old-Time College President* (New York, 1930), 63–69, 77–107, 184.

group considered financial matters a regrettable distraction from their fundamental duty of elevating the academic standards and enhancing the scholarship at their institution. Like Andrew D. White, president of Cornell University from 1866 to 1885, these visionaries often huffed that Eliot presided more as "a skillful manager of a cotton factory" than as an academic leader.[11] Hence, both the traditional ministerial presidents and the academic reformers likened the Harvard president to a corporate executive.

Viewing Eliot as inordinately preoccupied with the business aspects of university governance, contemporaneous presidents therefore did not understand, or even recognize, his free-money strategy, which he publicly explained in detail. Of course, the presidents of American colleges had long known the importance of money, extending back to the beginning of the colonial era. They responded to financial exigencies by soliciting donations for their institutions, often traveling to England to do so or petitioning "a small group of families" close to the college. After the Civil War, the presidents of the wealthiest universities continued living hand-to-mouth by personally and privately soliciting funds from a coterie of wealthy donors.[12]

Eliot's Singularity

During his tenure from 1869 to 1909, Eliot was unique in developing a long-term financial strategy and in placing a priority on building his university's financial capital. Certainly, no other president developed a coherent strategy, encouraged efforts across the institution, and publicly advocated the approach. Instead, presidents generally depended on a few wealthy patrons to supply most of the university's external funding. Through the early 1900s, whether solving financial crises during the economic panics and downturns or, more often, building academic programs and capacity, other university presidents viewed their financial responsibility primarily as persuading wealthy benefactors to cover budget shortfalls at the end of the year.

At Cornell University in western New York, President White and the founder, telegraph mogul Ezra Cornell, worked harmoniously by keeping within separate domains. Cornell handled the finances; White built academic programs and

11. Quoted in Glenn C. Altschuler, *Andrew D. White: Educator, Historian, Diplomat* (Ithaca, NY, 1979), 147.

12. Quotation is from Ronald Story, *The Forging of an Aristocracy: Harvard and the Boston Upper Class, 1800–1870* (Middletown, CT, 1980), 29. See Story, *Forging of an Aristocracy*, 54, 97; Jesse B. Sears, *Philanthropy in the History of American Higher Education* (Washington, DC, 1922), 31–33; Curti and Nash, *Philanthropy*, 3–59, 143, 164; Geiger, *To Advance Knowledge*, 44–45, 123.

facilities, while trying to extract as much money as possible from the founder.[13] Similarly, at the University of Chicago, President William R. Harper (1891–1906) saw his primary responsibility as determining how to develop the academic programs and resources of the university by spending money as fast as or faster than its major benefactor, John D. Rockefeller, provided it. In pursuing opportunities to enlarge the faculty and the holdings of the university's library or museums, Harper often ran up deficits that Rockefeller had to cover, usually after contentious discussions addressing the budgetary limits that Rockefeller had previously established.[14]

At Stanford, President David S. Jordan (1891–1913) discussed finances extensively with the university's founding patrons, railroad baron Leland Stanford and his wife Jane. But the founders never actually relinquished ownership of the endowment to the university, and after Leland died in 1893, Jane became parsimonious and extremely controlling. Jordan was forced to devote much of his effort to extracting revenue from her until she died in 1905.[15]

In Baltimore, Johns Hopkins University president Daniel C. Gilman (1875–1901) viewed himself primarily as an academic leader who did not need to worry about money because of the founder's extraordinary bequest of stock in the Baltimore & Ohio Railroad. Only after the value of that stock plummeted in the mid-1880s and the university trustees, who also sat on the railroad's board, refused to jettison the stock did Gilman consider raising money for the university. Assuming this responsibility only after the crisis, Gilman unsuccessfully pursued the typical tactic of soliciting a few large donors to cover the deficits, and he witnessed the decline of Johns Hopkins's academic reputation commensurate with its financial resources.[16]

Nor did the presidents of the other three oldest and wealthiest universities— Yale, Princeton, and Columbia—view finances as central to their responsibility. Until 1910, Princeton chose as presidents stiff-necked Presbyterians, who preferred to leave money matters to the treasurer or trustees and recoiled from

13. Carl L. Becker, *Cornell University: Founders and the Founding* (Ithaca, NY, 1943), 87, 118, 173–80; Altschuler, *Andrew D. White*, 67–150.

14. Richard J. Storr, *Harper's University: The Beginnings; a History of the University of Chicago* (Chicago, 1966), 65–78, 245–98, 335–55; Thomas W. Goodspeed, *A History of the University of Chicago* (Chicago, 1916), 275–88.

15. George E. Crothers, *Founding of the Leland Stanford University* (San Francisco, 1932), 24–35; Orrin L. Elliott, *Stanford University: The First Twenty-Five Years* (Stanford, CA 1937), 36–51, 104, 252–99, 326–78, 462–66.

16. Kathleen W. Sander, *Mary Elizabeth Garrett: Society and Philanthropy in the Gilded Age* (Baltimore, 2008), 95–96, 141–70; Edwin E. Slosson, *Great American Universities* (New York, 1910), ix; Hugh Hawkins, *Pioneer: A History of the Johns Hopkins University, 1874–1889* (Ithaca, NY, 1960), 316–24.

publicly asking for money. Princeton therefore fell behind other private universities in financial resources, as evident in table 1.1.[17]

At Yale, the clerical presidents Noah Porter (1871–86) and Timothy Dwight (1886–99) made earnest requests for gifts in their annual reports but delegated financial policy to the university secretary and treasurer. It was the alumni who finally organized a new fundraising tactic to bolster Yale's income, largely unaided by the president. In 1899, political economist Arthur T. Hadley (1899–1921) became the first Yale president not drawn from the clergy, but he continued his predecessors' policy of delegating financial planning and management to the university treasurer and secretary.[18]

Columbia University had the largest endowment of any university in the first decade of the twentieth century, but that wealth lay primarily in real estate holdings in New York City. In 1910, Columbia drew 39 percent of all its revenues from rents of its real estate in downtown Manhattan. Although Columbia presidents Frederick A. P. Barnard (1864–89), Seth Low (1890–1901), and especially Nicholas M. Butler (1902–45) were more entrepreneurial than their peers, they directed most of their efforts to expanding the university campus, buildings, and collections, which required more revenue for support and maintenance.[19]

Alone among his contemporaries, Eliot focused on increasing the productive financial capital of his university and developed a strategy with a coherent set of policies. These he explicated in 39 annual reports, which newspapers frequently quoted and Eliot sent to other college and university presidents, intending to educate them on university management.[20] Fulfilling a long-held plan to synthesize this material into a study of university administration, Eliot published the first book on the subject in 1908.[21] This volume and his annual reports and related

17. "Princeton Cramped by Yearly Deficit," *New York Times*, January 12, 1914; Thomas J. Wertenbaker, *Princeton 1746–1896* (Princeton, NJ, 1946), 389–90; James Axtell, *The Making of Princeton University: From Woodrow Wilson to the Present* (Princeton, NJ, 2006), 24–25, 51.

18. Noah Porter, *Annual Report of the President of Yale University 1879–80*, 9–25; Dwight, *Annual Report 1890–91*, 11–57; George W. Pierson, *Yale College, An Educational History, 1871–1921* (New Haven, CT, 1952), 505–38; Brooks M. Kelley, *Yale: A History* (New Haven, CT, 1974), 333–56.

19. Frederick A. Goetze, *Annual Report of the Treasurer of Columbia University 1909–10*, 9–10; Munroe Smith, "The Development of the University," in *A History of Columbia University, 1754–1904* (New York, 1904), 265; Robert A. McCaughey, *Stand, Columbia: A History of Columbia University in the City of New York, 1754–2004* (New York, 2003), 208–30, 301–30, 416–18.

20. See "The College Education," in *Pandex of the Press*, ed. Arthur I. Street (San Francisco, 1905), 1:488–89; Charles W. Eliot to Charles F. Thwing, February 28, 1896, and February 17, 1898, Charles F. Thwing Papers, Case Western Reserve University Library Special Collections.

21. Charles W. Eliot, *University Administration* (Boston, 1908). Prompted by Eliot's suggestion, President Charles F. Thwing of Western Reserve University had previously published *College Administration* (New York, 1900).

correspondence comprise some 3,000 pages that elaborate his strategy and rationale for accumulating "free money."

Competition to Raise Endowment

Like Eliot, other presidents believed that their universities were engaged in a Darwinian struggle because "the laws of institutional life are very similar to those of individual life, and in the development of institutions we may confidently believe in 'the survival of the fittest,'" as President Harper at the University of Chicago observed.[22] One prominent group of presidents, drawn largely from the clergy, maintained through the early twentieth century that the key to survival lay in upholding collegiate traditions. Another group, coming from the new generation of scholarly faculty, believed that success lay in developing academic programs in new fields of knowledge, as discussed above.

Meanwhile, all college and university presidents recognized that the outcome of the competition depended on adequate financial resources, particularly "external sources of patronage."[23] Like Porter at Yale, they entreated "the friends of the college," which "invites their liberal contributions and requires their generous aid." Similarly, University of Michigan president James B. Angell (1871–1909) called for gifts to endow fellowships for "graduate students" in order to compete with "Harvard, Cornell, and Chicago," which "by the aid of such fellowships . . . are constantly drawing some of our most promising graduates to their halls."[24]

But it was Eliot who recognized that the tournament for academic distinction was fundamentally a contest among universities to accumulate financial capital. This was the first tenet of his free-money strategy. Soliciting and spending gifts from external patrons would not secure victory because a university would remain dependent on those donors. Rather, survival and success depended on increasing the university's own wealth. "If the primacy of Harvard University among American institutions of education is to be maintained, it must not be surpassed by any other in material resources," he declared.[25] The leading university needs the most money in order to succeed, and acquiring that money also validates its fitness "under the law of competition," as announced in Carnegie's "The Gospel of Wealth" and elsewhere.

---

22. Harper, *Trend in Higher Education*, 375. See also Laurence R. Veysey, *The Emergence of the American University* (Chicago, 1965), 317–58; Geiger, *To Advance Knowledge*, 12.

23. Geiger, *To Advance Knowledge*, vii; see also 1–2, 213–14.

24. Porter, *Annual Report 1879–80*, 25; Angell, *Annual Report 1893–94*, 14.

25. Eliot, *Annual Report 1895–96*, 43.

The direct link between academic competition and financial competition reverberates throughout Eliot's writings. For example, he observed in 1897 that "the Harvard Veterinary Department is in competition with those of Cornell and the University of Pennsylvania, both of which are largely endowed," and that the Harvard Semitic Museum needs a new building "like the University of Chicago and the University of Pennsylvania." By the first decade of the twentieth century, private universities also faced "formidable competition with a large number of strong state universities in which tuition is free," Eliot warned. The university was besieged from all sides, in his view. Hence, "we need money," he firmly declared.[26]

Likewise, within Harvard, Eliot linked academic and financial competition and applied the university's historical policy of "each tub on its own bottom" to effect survival of the fittest. This long-standing policy of decentralized financial governance meant that each school and unit of the university balanced its own budget, paid its own expenses, and retained its own debt or surplus.[27] Similar to Eliot's elective system in which students chose their own courses and determined the shape of Harvard's curriculum, the president treated the university as a marketplace in which departments and other units jousted for funding by appealing to their constituents, whose interests they served.

His annual reports repeatedly identify the social benefits, achievements, needs, problems, and efficient solutions for a given Harvard department and then conclude, "It is for the . . . profession and the community to say whether or not the School shall be supported." The verdict of prospective donors determined a department's future in Eliot's strategy. For example, though affirming the value of the veterinary department and the personal sacrifices and commitment of its staff, he nonetheless closed the department in 1902 because it did not obtain sufficient external funding.[28] The department was not fit to survive.

But what kind of money should a university accumulate? According to the second tenet of free-money strategy, a university's wealth is measured by its permanent productive funds. Although Eliot, like his contemporaries, used the term "endowment" in a variety of ways, he relentlessly emphasized the primacy of permanent invested funds. Indeed, "further endowment is the only thoroughly

26. Quotations are from Eliot, *Annual Report 1896–97*, 29, 38; *1906–7*, 16; "Bishop Lawrence Pleads for Funds from the Alumni," *Boston Journal*, June 30, 1904.

27. James B. Conant, *Annual Report of the President of Harvard University 1947–48*, 10–11; *1950–51*, 20–21; *1951–52*, 12; Seymour E. Harris, *Economics of Harvard* (New York, 1970), 226–27.

28. Quotations are from Eliot, *Annual Report 1877–78*, 41; *1899–1900*, 25; see also *1900–1901*, 26–27.

satisfactory and permanent remedy" for any problems that the university may face in the future.[29]

Tuition, Buildings, and "Inexpedient Gifts"

The primacy of permanent productive funds entails three corollaries, according to Eliot. First, a university must avoid relying on "precarious" revenue governed by "the law of supply and demand." Consequently, a leading college or university must avoid the "extremely undesirable" reliance on tuition, "because it threatens the stability and just independence" of the university. In addition, gifts "for immediate use . . . , though very welcome, constitute but a precarious resource" for a college or university.[30] Eliot thus identified the institutional benefits of autonomy, stability, and flexibility that higher education leaders conventionally credited to endowment a century later.

The primacy of permanent productive funds also entails the second corollary of refraining from spending university funds on buildings. After all, "experience has shown that new buildings will be provided by gift nearly as fast as they are needed." Donors like to give and name buildings, and virtually all of Eliot's annual reports describe needs for buildings, often including detailed plans and cost estimates. Yet, before accepting a gift for a building, a university should try to persuade the donor to direct the gift to endowment instead. "It may be doubted," he wrote, "whether a building is . . . so durable and desirable a memorial as a fund . . . devoted to an object of permanent interest." Indeed, "buildings get out of fashion and decay, or are remodeled and converted to new uses . . . but the permanent funds which have come down from those centuries are still doing the very work which the givers meant them to do."[31] Only if the prospective donor refuses to give to endowment should the university accept a donation of a building.

In sharp contrast, President Dwight at Yale made more requests for buildings than any other kind of gift in his annual reports in the 1880s and 1890s. While Eliot extolled the advantage of invested financial capital, Rev. Dwight offered a psalm for bricks and mortar. "New buildings" enhance "the manly and gentlemanly life of the community. The silent power of architectural taste and beauty . . . upon manners and even morals cannot be easily estimated," stated

29. Eliot, *Annual Report 1904–5*, 23. See Charles W. Eliot, "National University," in *The Addresses and Journal of Proceedings of the National Education Association . . . 1873* (Peoria, IL, 1873), 119.
30. Quotations are from Charles W. Eliot, "Inaugural Address . . . October 19, 1869," in *Educational Reform: Essays and Addresses* (New York, 1901), 26. See Eliot, *Annual Report 1893–94*, 28; *1897–98*, 42; *1903–4*, 51.
31. Quotations are from Eliot, *Annual Report 1881–82*, 52; *1882–83*, 42.

Dwight. "The benefactor who gives to the University a building" provides "not only a temporary dwelling place or place of instruction for the students, but also an educating force . . . upon their subsequent life."[32]

Meanwhile, Eliot held that buildings are not "productive" investments unless they yield rents. In fact, buildings drain resources from the university, and this observation implied the third corollary to the primacy of endowment. A university must refuse "inexpedient" gifts, such as donations "bringing new charges on the university itself." Early in his administration, Eliot realized that "as fast as new resources are placed in their hands, . . . the Corporation incur new permanent charges." Gifts, in fact, are expensive, especially buildings, because "enlargements, improvements, and repairs fall upon the Corporation."[33] Some gifts should be refused.

This insight led to a breakthrough in 1898 when Harvard received a gift of $100,000 for a building, along with another $100,000 to endow a maintenance fund for its upkeep. For "the first time in the history" of American higher education, "a new building has been provided with an adequate endowment at the start," Eliot observed. Newspapers also applauded this provision, and in 1903 the Harvard Corporation voted not to accept a gift for a building unless supplemented with an endowed maintenance fund. In contrast, Dwight at Yale rarely mentioned the maintenance costs of the buildings that he solicited.[34]

Eliot's commitment to the primacy of endowment and these corollaries was distinctive among university presidents, who generally focused on developing programs and facilities while relying on the founder or wealthy patrons to cover deficits at the end of the year. For example, in the 1920s President Butler of Columbia, depicted in figure 2.2, was still calling for "unrestricted gifts" for "meeting the cost of current maintenance of the University's work."[35] Such donations to cover operating costs may help the current administration but do not strengthen the university in the long run, held Eliot.

"Free" Money

Beyond striving to increase permanent productive funds, Eliot asserted the third tenet that a university should seek endowment that is "free" in two respects. First, the university should be permitted to invest a gift as it deemed best. In the

32. Dwight, *Annual Report 1886–87*, 18.
33. Eliot, *University Administration*, 27–28; Eliot, *Annual Report 1882–83*, 42.
34. Eliot, *Annual Report 1902–3*, 25; "The College Education," in *Pandex of the Press*, ed. Arthur I. Street (San Francisco, 1905), 1:488–89; Dwight, *Annual Report 1886–87*, 24–25; *1890–91*, 22.
35. Nicholas M. Butler, *Annual Report of the President of Columbia University 1924–25*, 54.

Figure 2.2. Columbia University President Nicholas M. Butler, ca. 1917. Courtesy of the Library of Congress.

seventeenth, eighteenth, and nineteenth centuries, donors sometimes required their gifts to be invested in a certain asset—such as specific bonds or real estate— fearing that their gift would be handled unwisely or improperly. In some cases, donors had a personal interest in the asset, as in the stock of the Baltimore & Ohio Railroad that dominated the endowment of Johns Hopkins University, whose trustees owned the railroad's stock. Whatever the motive, Eliot discouraged gifts from any donor who wished "to dictate the investments in which his money shall be placed."[36]

One reason was to protect the university's autonomy. Another reason was that unrestricted permanent funds could be pooled into a single, large investment fund, increasing its yield and decreasing its risk by diversifying its assets. Finally, pooling the funds enhanced fairness in distributing income back to the schools and departments, all of which received the same rate of return. Unpooled investments led to problems if the permanent funds of one department outperformed the funds of another department. Through the end of his administration, Eliot continued to preach the virtue of gift funds free of restrictions in type of asset.[37]

The second, even more important sense of "free" is that gifts of permanent funds should not be restricted in purpose by the "dead hand" of donors. In 1879, Eliot proclaimed "the imperative need" for endowment "which can be used at the discretion of the Corporation, now for this purpose, now for that, in any department of the University." As munificent gifts came to other universities, he emphasized even more that "the value of unrestricted gifts . . . is always mounting and becoming more generally recognized." Departments must have "free money to devote to new objects." To "serve their communities best and deserve best of the republic, . . . the University needs free money."[38]

The autonomy and flexibility provide "great additional value" to unrestricted gifts, and Eliot publicly praised donors of such gifts as knowledgeable about the best way to donate. Conversely, he explicitly described "highly inexpedient" gifts with narrow purposes that Harvard had to reject. He also identified broad restrictions that were acceptable, while noting his willingness to meet with prospective donors and negotiate satisfactory terms. In fact, he appended model wills and gift letters to his annual reports in order to inform prospective donors of the best way to structure benefactions. Such bequests and gifts set "a high example of intelligent, sympathetic, and far-seeing beneficence" and, therefore, "are always valuable quite out of proportion to their amount."[39] Surely potential donors would wish to earn this public commendation while also making their gift more valuable!

Notwithstanding his emphasis on the value of free endowment, unrestricted in purpose, Eliot also encouraged restricted gifts that are fungible—those

---

36. Eliot, *Annual Report 1878–79*, 36.
37. Eliot, *Annual Report 1904–5*, 40–41; *1907–8*, 51–52; Eliot, *University Administration*, 10–11.
38. Eliot, *Annual Report 1878–79*, 36; *1905–6*, 54–55.
39. Eliot, *Annual Report 1879–80*, 41; *1885–86*, 4; *1887–88*, 28–29; *1892–93*, 46–47; Eliot, *University Administration*, 27–28.

devoted to expenses that the university had to cover in any event. This encouragement might seem paradoxical and was not appreciated by other university presidents and later scholars, who tended to distinguish sharply between restricted and unrestricted endowment and to lament the high proportion of restrictions.[40] But Eliot shrewdly equated unrestricted endowment with restricted endowment that is "devoted to such comprehensive purposes as salaries, retiring allowances, scholarships, administration, and service in the Gymnasium, Chapel, Library, or Dining Hall, and the maintenance of the several scientific laboratories." Endowment income restricted to fixed expenses otherwise paid by general revenue was essentially fungible and, therefore, just as beneficial as unrestricted endowment, he maintained.[41]

Furthermore, fungible gifts offer donors the attraction of specifying a purpose that is important to them. Eliot therefore trumpeted this win-win arrangement and frequently solicited fungible restricted gifts to endow the salaries of the president and treasurer, the administration of the library, and maintenance funds for buildings. Above all, "there is no more desirable gift to a university than a fund to endow a professorship," which "sets free resources now used to meet those charges" for salary.[42] In his view, fungibility was mutually beneficial and therefore twice as attractive to the donor.

Business Practices

Adopting the financial practices of business firms and industrial corporations was the fourth tenet of free-money strategy. At Harvard, this process commenced before the Civil War when businessmen, financiers, and early industrialists began to dominate the membership of the Corporation by the 1830s. These new members demanded "tighter control of finances, better accounting procedures, more aggressive investment policies." In 1829, the Corporation appointed lawyer Josiah Quincy (1829–45) as Harvard's first nonclerical president, and he began to adopt these policies.[43]

But it took another 40 years until Harvard inaugurated a president who wholeheartedly affirmed that "the principle of divided and subordinate responsibilities, which rules in government bureaus, in manufactories, and all great companies, which makes a modern army a possibility, must be applied in the

---

40. Lowell, *Annual Report 1911–12*, 24; Trevor Arnett, *College and University Finance* (New York, 1922), 16; Henry A. Yeomans, *Abbott Lawrence Lowell 1856–1943* (Cambridge, MA, 1948), 248–49; Harris, *Economics of Harvard*, 350–51.
41. Quotation is from Eliot, *Annual Report 1881–82*, 51; see also *1883–84*, 44; *1905–6*, 52–58.
42. Eliot, *Annual Report 1875–76*, 41–42; *1883–84*, 46; *1897–98*, 8–9; *1906–7*, 38–39.
43. Quotations are from Story, *Forging of an Aristocracy*, 42; see also 27–41, 161.

University," as did Eliot in his inaugural address. In the same vein, he urged Harvard's governing board (the Corporation) to increase the return on the university's endowment. "On its invested funds the Corporation should be always seeking how safely to make a quarter of a per cent more," he stated.[44] The inaugural orations of his contemporaries—whether clergymen seeking to preserve tradition or academic visionaries imbued with the university ideal—never offered such admonitions concerning investment policy.[45]

Only much later did other wealthy universities follow this path. For example, at Princeton, Yale, and the University of Pennsylvania, the trustees did not come predominantly from secular and commercial backgrounds until a half century after the conversion of Harvard's Corporation. Then, those governing boards waited another 30 years to embrace business practices and appoint a business-minded president, as Harvard had done in 1869. Only in 1902 did the Yale treasurer replace the university's traditional "cumbersome" bookkeeping with that "of large business corporations."[46]

In particular, Eliot advocated two business practices as part of his free-money strategy, consistent with his personal and familial background. First, he emphasized employing the university's resources effectively and efficiently. This guideline not only saved money but also encouraged new gifts, because a university's acquisition of new free money "depends on widespread confidence in the wisdom and success with which the trustees have used their existing endowments." Only when "it is obvious that all the resources" of a given department "were intelligently and economically employed, and that its influence, usefulness, and reputation are increasing from year to year," could that department expect "further contributions to the permanent endowment." Only at that point would the president endorse and proclaim the need in his annual reports because "the giver would run no risk about the productiveness of his gift."[47]

The second business practice emphasized by Eliot was to present and publicize the finances of the university fully and transparently because this promotes "public confidence in the financial administration of the University," which "is a main root of its prosperity." A university president therefore "should secure

44. Eliot, "Inaugural Address," 33–34.

45. Noah Porter, "Inaugural Address," *Addresses at the Inauguration of Professor Noah Porter, D.D. LL.D. as President of Yale College* (New York, 1871), 26–65; Daniel C. Gilman, "Inaugural Address" (1876), Daniel Coit Gilman Papers, Johns Hopkins University Library Special Collections.

46. Morris F. Tyler, *Annual Report of the Treasurer of Yale University 1902*, 1–2. See Story, *Forging of an Aristocracy*, 54; Edward P. Cheyney, *History of the University of Pennsylvania, 1740–1940* (Philadelphia, 1940), 180–256.

47. Eliot, *University Administration*, 17; Eliot, *Annual Report 1882–83*, 38–39; *1900–1901*, 38.

complete publicity in regard to the financial situation of his university." To this end, the Harvard treasurer made clarifying improvements in his long, complicated annual report throughout Eliot's administration, and this effort was noted in the newspapers.[48] In addition, Eliot frequently commented on aspects of the treasurer's report, explaining how the university financed certain projects, solved financial problems, or utilized significant gifts. Above all, the Harvard treasurer began publishing in 1870 a full annual accounting of each of its endowed funds because "the winning of new endowments depends on widespread confidence in the wisdom and success with which the trustees have used their existing endowments."[49]

Eliot's insistence on complete transparent disclosure was unusual. The only wealthy university to follow Harvard's lead and undertake a full accounting was Yale, although its reports were somewhat obscure. In 1905 a new treasurer at Yale radically revised its financial statements to achieve the "intelligibility and clearness" lacking in the prior reports.[50] Other wealthy universities deliberately avoided publicizing their financial operations, perhaps due to their reliance on a few wealthy patrons. More than a decade after Johns Hopkins opened, Eliot was still trying to convince his friend, President Gilman, of the wisdom of transparency: "Do you not think that you would be more likely to get new endowments, if you now took up the practice of publishing a detailed treasurer's statement?"[51] The president of Johns Hopkins, depicted in figure 2.3, never agreed.

Similarly, a historian of the University of Chicago observed in 1916 that the university did not issue a treasurer's statement because the university "has never dared to disclose to the public the facts [of its finances]. The public confidence is maintained only because the public is not informed as to the true situation." In California, Stanford University made no public accounting because Jane Stanford kept close control over the amounts, records, and purposes of spending until 1902, when the university began to assume legal title to the gifts and endowments that the Stanfords had supposedly conveyed years before.[52]

48. Quotations are from Eliot, *Annual Report 1876–77*, 39; *1904–5*, 59; Eliot, *University Administration*, 234. See *Annual Report of the Treasurer of Harvard College 1886–87*, 166; *1901–2*, 11–15, 33–37, 60; "Deficit, $30,743," *Boston Globe*, January 15, 1906.

49. Quotation is from Eliot, *University Administration*, 17–18. This practice also anticipated fund accounting, which became the standard accounting regimen in higher education until 1995.

50. Lee McClung, *Annual Report of the Treasurer of Yale University 1905*, 3. See Henry C. Kingsley, *Annual Report of the Treasurer of Yale College 1880–81*, 8; William W. Farnham, *Annual Report of the Treasurer of Yale University 1889–90*, 14; Tyler, *Annual Report 1904*, 7–8.

51. Charles W. Eliot to Daniel C. Gilman, October 29, 1887, Gilman Papers.

52. Goodspeed, *History of the University of Chicago*, 286–87. See Storr, *Harper's University*, 269; Crothers, *Founding of the Leland Stanford University*, 1–36.

Figure 2.3. Johns Hopkins University President Daniel C. Gilman, ca. 1890. Courtesy of the Library of Congress.

Columbia was not only secretive but also deceptive in its financial reporting. When Columbia first publicly itemized its endowed funds in 1904, the university did not list investment returns, preventing donors from tracking the performance and impact of their gifts, as they could easily do each year through Harvard's reports. By 1910, Columbia's treasurer was issuing extensive annual reports, but they obfuscated fundamental distinctions, such as between permanent invested funds and building funds or between income-producing real property and nonproductive real property. Nor could a reader discern the flow of revenue from various sources to the expenses of Columbia's various units. One could not tell how much any unit received from endowment income or gifts or tuition. In fact, Columbia's obscure format turns out to be intentional. President Butler and the treasurer wished to make the finances opaque in order to maintain control over them, frustrating his deans and even the trustees.[53]

These maneuvers to withhold or obscure financial information were not unusual. In fact, they fit the widespread pattern observed by the GEB in the 1910s: "financial reports [in higher education] are made to conceal the situation rather than disclose it." The approach to financial reporting differed entirely at Harvard under Eliot, who believed that people with means will give again and give more if they can see exactly the outcome of their gift.[54]

Deliberate Deficits

Eliot's tenet of adopting business practices had an important exception, however. From his inaugural address in 1869 to his treatise *University Administration* in 1908, he affirmed that "a university should not be carried on, like a business corporation, with any policy of laying up undivided profits, or of setting aside unused income for emergencies or future needs. On the contrary, it should endeavor to expend all its available income." In fact, "it is not possible to avoid occasional deficits," asserted Eliot. Doing so "would mean to aim deliberately at an annual surplus, and to keep sufficient reserves to guarantee that annual surplus." As late as 1905, near the end of his tenure, he reported that Harvard had run up serious deficits in eight of the prior 10 years, all of which were described fully in his annual reports and reported in the public press.[55]

This tactic of spending all income and encouraging deficits seems paradoxical in several respects. Though promoting the tactic, Eliot maintained that the university "should never live beyond its means." In addition, he reported that the Corporation sought "anxiously" to avoid deficits and employed "cautious and frugal methods" of spending.[56]

Furthermore, he ran a deficit despite receiving a steady stream of gifts each year. In 1905–6, total gifts amounted to about $1.9 million for endowment and

53. Coon, *Columbia*, 31–32. See John B. Pine, comp., *Columbia University . . . Gifts and Endowments . . . 1754–1904* (New York, 1904); Goetze, *Annual Report 1909–10*, 8–65.
54. Quotation is from Arnett, *College and University Finance*, 105. See Eliot, *Annual Report 1900–1901*, 49–50.
55. Quotations are from Eliot, *University Administration*, 29–30; Eliot, *Annual Report 1902–3*, 53; *1904–5*, 14. See Eliot, "Inaugural Address," 27; "Deficit, $30,743."
56. Eliot, *Annual Report 1880–81*, 40–41; *1889–90*, 36; *1900–1901*, 50; Eliot, *University Administration*, 29–30.

about $360,000 for current operations. Yet the university still ran a deficit of nearly $60,000, "the largest ever experienced." Indeed, Eliot admitted, "it seems strange that, with such a remarkable inflowing of gifts for several years past, it should be necessary to discuss the means of overcoming a large annual deficit."[57] His statements therefore seem contradictory, if not hypocritical. He endorsed and incurred deficits but claimed that Harvard avoided them, operated frugally, and received "remarkable" gifts. And all this he announced in his annual reports.

Eliot's apparent contradiction seemed nonsensical to his contemporaries. College and university presidents normally shunned deficits and sought to build up surpluses in order to prevent deficits. A few wealthy private universities customarily ran deficits because their presidents could quietly cover them at the end of the year by discreetly appealing to a few wealthy donors over lunch. Princeton president Woodrow Wilson (1902–10) relied on a "Committee of Fifty" wealthy alumni to pay off deficits at the end of the year. In New York City, President Butler regularly entreated 25 wealthy acquaintances to cover Columbia's frequent deficits.[58]

Presidents of universities with one primary benefactor who continued to monitor events, such as Jordan at Stanford, had to beseech that donor at the end of each year to pay for expenses that had already been made, sometimes disaffecting the benefactor. President Harper did this at Chicago, infuriating his patron, Rockefeller, who eventually refused to meet with Harper.[59] Eliot is, apparently, the only president who saw virtue in deficits, and certainly the only one to advocate them publicly. His rationale lay in this paradoxical principle: in order to build more endowment, a university had to spend all its money. Wealth growth and cost growth were opposite sides of the same coin.

"Mortgaging . . . Your Whole Income"

Understanding Eliot's view of deficits begins with the fact that he always had reserves to pay for them. At the beginning of his presidency in 1869, he set aside two named funds of unrestricted investments, totaling about $425,000. Over the course of his presidency, he discharged Harvard's repeated deficits against these funds and reported the practice in his annual reports and in the press. The two funds were exhausted by 1905, at which point he admitted that it was "extremely undesirable to use up unrestricted funds bearing a benefactor's name by charging

57. Eliot, *Annual Report 1905–6*, 55–56.
58. "Princeton Cramped by Yearly Deficit," *New York Times*, January 12, 1914; Axtell, *Making of Princeton University*, 24; McCaughey, *Stand, Columbia*, 301.
59. Storr, *Harper's University*, 67, 78, 245–98, 335–54.

annual deficits to them."[60] Indeed, this maneuver appears iconoclastic, contradictory, and imprudent. Along with many others, economist Seymour Harris later excoriated Eliot's practice in the leading history of Harvard's finances.[61]

But Eliot's approach had great advantages. He never had to ask any wealthy donors to pay for a shortfall at the end of the year, as happened routinely at other eminent universities. Doing so, Eliot believed, made the university directly dependent on wealthy benefactors and alienated those who concluded that the university could not manage its affairs. In addition, asking donors to cover annual deficits wasted the opportunity to ask for larger gifts that could contribute to the university's development. Therefore, Eliot broadcast the deficits, so everyone would know that Harvard needed money. Then, he covered them from the two unrestricted reserve funds, so no benefactor had to rescue the university. Finally, he shrewdly employed the deficits to calculate even greater needs, in the following way.

The annual deficit at Harvard usually totaled between $25,000 and $50,000, including a few thousand dollars each from various schools and departments.[62] Deans or directors of those units might request gifts to pay their deficits, but Eliot rarely echoed such requests in his annual reports. Instead, his discussion of a unit's deficit began by touting its excellent work, justifying its expenses in detail, and concluding that its deficit was structural because Harvard must not cut back on the quality or quantity of its work. Furthermore, other kinds of income could not eliminate the structural deficit. Raising Harvard's tuition would exclude students with limited means. Nor could annual gifts or university subventions reliably cover such a deficit every year in the future. Only more endowment could provide a "thoroughly satisfactory and permanent remedy" for a structural deficit. To eliminate a department's recurring deficit of, say, $2,000 required an endowment of $50,000, based on a standard net investment return of 4 percent.[63]

In this way, Eliot's practice of announcing regrettable deficits and paying for them out of unrestricted reserves allowed him to frame and justify his requests

60. Quotation is from Eliot, *Annual Report 1905–6*, 57. See Eliot, *Annual Report 1904–5*, 11–24; "Deficit, $30,743."

61. Harris, *Economics of Harvard*, 213–24; William H. Allen, *Modern Philanthropy: A Study of Efficient Appealing and Giving* (New York, 1912), 185; Arnett, *College and University Finance*, 48, 67; Paul C. Cabot and Leonard C. Larrabee, "Investing Harvard Money," *Harvard Alumni Bulletin*, May 1951, 634.

62. Harvard's annual expenses meanwhile grew from $616,000 in 1880–81 to $1,033,000 in 1889–90 and to $1,412,000 in 1899–1900. *Annual Reports of the Treasurer of Harvard College*.

63. Quotations are from Eliot, *Annual Report 1904–5*, 23–24; see also *1893–94*, 27.

as needs for more endowment to capitalize the deficits. Rather than taking a wealthy benefactor to lunch and requesting $2,000 to cover a program's shortfall for a particular year, as other presidents did, Eliot would request $50,000 to endow the program and promise the donor that the shortfall would be solved in perpetuity. A wealthy donor would find the latter, prospective solution much more attractive than covering a small deficit already incurred, particularly if the donor could name the permanent fund, Eliot believed.

Far from disguising this approach, Eliot explained and justified it in publications. In 1904, he presented data showing that Harvard had carried a surplus in 11 of the 15 years between 1832 and 1857, which "was not a period of rapid development" for the university. Instead, the years when "deficits have been largest and most frequent is the period when the increase of the invested funds . . . has been most rapid." Running deficits leads to "general University prosperity"— if the university has the reserves to cover them.[64] More need attracts more money.

The figures cited above for the year 1905–6 demonstrate the point. The $1.9 million gifts of new endowments, at 4 percent return, would reliably yield about $76,000 to support current programs. Meanwhile, the deficit of $60,000, in Eliot's plan, was essentially an opportunity to demonstrate the existing need for $1.5 million more in permanent funds in the following year. The $360,000 of gifts for current operations would support new initiatives producing future deficits that would need to be capitalized by additional endowment.[65]

While lamenting deficits in order to demonstrate his concern for prudent management, Eliot thus maintained that running deficits is sound policy for a university if it can cover the shortfalls without badgering donors, who may be enticed to give more for an endowment that honors them and permanently solves a problem. Eliot had complete confidence in his novel strategy. As he wrote to President Gilman, "so long as the community sees that the [Johns Hopkins] Trustees can and do build out of income, . . . new endowments will be somewhat improbable." Consequently, "is it not time to mortgage—so to speak—your whole income, as we do at Harvard? A man who can build a good home without touching his principal is sure to be counted rich."[66] Spending money, creating need, and accumulating endowment were complementary.

64. Eliot, *Annual Report 1902–3*, 53–54.
65. Eliot, *Annual Report 1905–6*, 55.
66. Eliot to Gilman, October 29, 1887.

Insatiable Needs and the President's Duty

Perpetually running deficits implied the fifth tenet of the free-money strategy: the university's needs are insatiable. New gifts support new initiatives that necessarily produce deficits that need to be capitalized by new gifts. Thus, Eliot habitually coupled grateful acknowledgments of gifts with new demands: "It may seem strange to urge the need of further endowments immediately after the receipt of the large . . . Endowment Fund," but "the income of that fund is not applicable to charges already incurred, or to any expansions of the work of the College."[67]

Even while accepting "the largest single addition to the resources of the University . . . since it received its charter in 1650," Eliot was utterly shameless in noting another "urgent need" that meant "additional endowment will be indispensable." The scale of Harvard's urgency was sometimes staggering. In 1895, when Harvard's permanent funds amounted to about $8.4 million, he announced that "the Corporation could use the income of additional endowments to the amount of $10 million" for "well-known and urgent wants."[68]

The final tenet of Eliot's free-money strategy held that presidents of colleges and universities have a responsibility to raise money. He therefore exhorted members of Harvard's academic units and their alumni and Visiting Committees to undertake the "hard work" of soliciting gifts, while he also maintained that presidents should make "direct appeals" and adverted to his negotiations with benefactors.[69]

To be sure, such efforts alone were not new. Presidents across the country had long appealed to donors and noted pressing needs here and there in their annual reports.[70] Eliot's innovation lay in directing as many donations as possible into endowment because, he believed, the fundamental duty of college and university presidents is to build the financial capital of their schools.

A president's central duty is not to erect buildings, like Butler at Columbia or Dwight at Yale, or to develop academic programs, like Gilman at Johns Hopkins or Harper at Chicago, or to cultivate scholarship, like White at Cornell or Wilson at Princeton. Eliot did all these things and considered them valuable—so long as they were endowed. The ultimate aim of his new strategy was to acquire more free money for his university. Therefore, his annual reports ceaselessly identify,

67. Eliot, *Annual Report 1904–5*, 24.
68. Eliot, *Annual Report 1895–96*, 43; *1902–3*, 22; *1905–6*, 28.
69. Quotations are from "Way to Get Money Is to Go Out and Get It," *Boston Globe*, September 9, 1923; Charles W. Eliot, "The University President in the American Commonwealth," in *Charles W. Eliot, The Man and His Beliefs*, ed. William A. Neilson (New York, 1926), 1:219.
70. See Angell, *Annual Report 1893–94*, 13, 20, 24.

justify, and publicize Harvard's financial needs and encourage gifts of free money to capitalize them.[71]

Even modest gifts of financial capital should be encouraged. To endow a scholarship "does not require a large sum of money." To endow a book fund requires even less and "is certainly a pleasant benefaction to make; for the readers are agreeably reminded of their benefactor by the book-plate. . . . Establishing a book-fund in a University Library is, therefore, a . . . perpetual service to learning."[72] A need for endowment to suit the interest and pocketbook of every donor should be the president's creed.

Free-Money Strategy

Eliot's foundational precept held that, in the competition among universities for academic accomplishment and reputation, the standing of a university is determined primarily by its wealth. Second, he equated a university's wealth with its permanent productive funds, which came to mean its "endowment" by the end of the formative period. Given this narrow definition, a university must refrain from depending on tuition revenue, spending its own resources on buildings, or accepting any "inexpedient" gifts. Third, a university must strive to keep its endowed funds "free"—unrestricted both in asset type and in purpose—although restricted endowment gifts that are fungible should be strongly encouraged.

Fourth, the university must be managed like a business, operating efficiently and disclosing its finances fully and transparently so that the public appreciates its prudent management. Yet, in striking contrast to a business, a university, fifth, should never carry a surplus but regularly run a deficit because this demonstrates the need that justifies asking for more free money. By implication, therefore, a university's needs are insatiable because spending, paradoxically, increases wealth and revenue. Lastly, the president must assume responsibility for developing the financial capital of the university, including identifying, justifying, and presenting its needs for more free money.

Although Harvard received no huge gifts before Eliot stepped down in 1909, he provided the conceptual framework for establishing and continuing Harvard's financial preeminence.[73] His free-money strategy persisted and proliferated because

71. Eliot, *Annual Report 1871–72*, 33; *1874–75*, 14–15; *1889–90*, 28–29; *1900–1901*, 33–37; *1905–6*, 52; *1907–8*, 30.

72. Eliot, *Annual Report 1897–98*, 41; *1906–7*, 116.

73. In 1903, Gordon McKay, who did not attend Harvard, named the university in a life estate. The bequest slowly started to yield income in 1909 and was scarcely mentioned by Harvard presidents until 1949, when it began to pay fully and became the largest gift received by Harvard in the twentieth century. Conant, *Annual Report 1948–49*, 24; Harry R. Lewis, "Gordon McKay:

Harvard alumni embraced the financial teachings of Eliot, "whose slightest word they regard as law," wrote a Harvard fundraising chairman in 1917.[74] The alumni then advanced his strategy across higher education by way of the first, national, fundraising campaign for endowment, which ran from 1915 to 1925.

Also extending this influence, the GEB in 1922 adopted many of Eliot's tenets as policies.[75] By that point, Harvard's endowment had attained the lead over all other universities that it would not relinquish through today. And these tenets eventually became the common sense of how to build and manage the financial capital necessary to succeed and survive in the competition for academic excellence and reputation, with the ultimate aim "to serve their communities best and deserve best of the republic."[76] Based on this rationale, the double helix of aggregate wealth and aggregate cost spiraled ever upward in higher education.

Brief Life of an Inventor with a Lasting Harvard Legacy: 1821–1903," *Harvard Magazine*, September–October 2007, 48–49.

74. Thomas W. Lamont to Robert F. Duncan, February 5, 1917, Lamont Correspondence. See Richard N. Smith, *The Harvard Century: The Making of a University to a Nation* (Cambridge, MA, 1986), 57–61.

75. Arnett, *College and University Finance*, 6–7, 16, 63–64.

76. Eliot, *Annual Report 1905–6*, 54–55.

CHAPTER 3

Birth of the Annual Alumni Fund, 1890–1925

Throughout the formative era from 1870 to 1930, American higher education needed ever more revenue to support its rising cost. Enrollment and institutions grew rapidly in number and kind, as did academic disciplines, expanding "the requirements for books and periodicals." New scientific research also increased "expenditures required for laboratories and for equipment," wrote University of Chicago president William Harper. "Without money, these demands cannot be met."[1]

Competition to succeed intensified, and colleges and universities came to appreciate that a certain kind of money—permanent and productive funds—was most valuable because it strengthened institutions' autonomy, flexibility, and stability in planning and confronting challenges. In the 1920s, a consensus emerged on narrowly defining "endowment" as this most valuable kind of money. Meanwhile, during the first half of the formative period, Harvard president Charles W. Eliot (1869–1909) formulated a singular strategy by which

---

1. Harper, *Trend in Higher Education*, 375.

every college or university could increase its unrestricted endowment or fungible restricted endowment. Institutions with such "free money" would "inevitably win" the Darwinian "competition between American universities, and between American and foreign universities," Eliot maintained.[2]

While consensus developed around the meaning and importance of "endowment" and the novel strategy, two new modes of fundraising in higher education were introduced, supplanting the occasional lotteries and subscription drives run by antebellum colleges. Widely adopted during the formative period, these new modes occur today at every college and university as regularly as commencement. The first, described in this chapter, was the annual appeal to all alumni for donations. The second, recounted in the next chapter, was the national, multiyear fundraising campaign run by paid staff. Now conventional, these two modes of fundraising arose between 1890 and 1920, concurrent with the competition in higher education and emphasis on accumulating financial capital.

The annual comprehensive appeal to alumni for gifts began at Yale College in 1890, and the innovation immediately faced the problem that it resembled the new national phenomenon known as "mass giving" or "people's philanthropy." How could Yale, an elite and wealthy college, distinguish its innovation from the plebian practice of appealing to the masses for donations? In addition, the new appeal appeared to be "begging" for money. How could the college dignify its innovation and differentiate it from asking for charity?

Yale solved both problems by labeling the invention "democratic," which conferred legitimacy and dignity amid the burgeoning enthusiasm for "democracy" in America in the late nineteenth century. By describing their appeal as "democratic giving," Yale alumni distinguished it from "begging" the "mass" of alumni for charity. Meanwhile, Harvard University inaugurated a second fundraising mode in the 1910s that also resembled "mass giving" and "people's philanthropy" and even borrowed its tactics. Likewise seeking to dignify and distinguish its innovation, Harvard applied the honorific "democratic" to this second mode. Seeking to reclaim the mantle, Yale then pronounced its invention "most democratic," and Harvard soon responded.

This ironic tug-of-war between the two elite universities, each claiming for its own innovation the singular honor of being "democratic," continued until the United States entered World War I. Then, during the 1920s, these two fundraising modes proliferated throughout higher education, even as the "democratic" rhetoric waned in American society. By 1930, the terminology did not matter

2. Eliot, *Annual Report 1905–6*, 55.

because the need to dignify the two new modes had receded. The increased revenue alone justified them. Over the next century, these two modes—along with the traditional discreet appeal to wealthy donors—formed the standard fundraising triad employed by colleges and universities competing for wealth and prestige.[3]

"Mass Giving" and "People's Philanthropy"

The huge wave of philanthropy during the formative era of higher education conformed to the traditional norm that giving was primarily "a prerogative and a responsibility of the wealthy and of the businessman." Meanwhile, between 1890 and 1920 a new phenomenon known as "mass giving" or "people's philanthropy" emerged in the United States. One reason was that the growth of the economy raised the standard of living and increased the average person's disposable income. In addition, the secularization of American society broadened the rationales for giving beyond religious aims, and those in the middle and laboring classes enjoyed exercising a prerogative traditionally reserved for the wealthy elite.[4]

Responding to those developments, various associations dedicated to social welfare and health care became more organized and effective, while developing tactics for appealing to the public for donations. Building on a few scattered efforts in the 1890s, the Young Men's Christian Association (YMCA) and the Young Women's Christian Association (YWCA) organized broad, systematic, public fundraising drives in the 1900s. In November 1913, a campaign broke all records by raising over $4 million in two weeks for the YMCA and the YWCA in greater New York. Meanwhile, in 1907 the Red Cross initiated the sale of Christmas seals, which supported the fight against tuberculosis and prompted widespread acceptance of mass giving. Then, during World War I, the national drives to support disaster relief and to sell US Liberty Loan bonds established mass fundraising campaigns as a fixture in American life.

The yields from mass giving were stupendous, overshadowing the grants from the prominent new foundations established by wealthy industrialists, such as Andrew Carnegie and John D. Rockefeller. In campaigns during 1917 and 1918, the Red Cross raised over $273 million, the YMCA and YWCA nearly $158 million, the Knights of Columbus over $40 million, and United War Work

---

3. For further documentation and discussion on points in this chapter, see Bruce A. Kimball, "'Democratizing' Giving at Yale and Harvard: The Discursive Legitimation of Mass Fundraising . . . 1890–1920," *History of Education Quarterly* 55 (2015): 164–89.
4. Quotations are from Scott M. Cutlip, *Fund Raising in the United States: Its Role in America's Philanthropy* (New Brunswick, NJ, 1965), 110, 203–4. See Zunz, *Philanthropy in America*.

almost $190 million in a single appeal. Even these amounts were dwarfed by the Liberty Loan, bonds issued by the US government in support of the war effort. Over 54 million subscribers purchased nearly $17 billion in bonds in four mass campaigns between 1917 and 1922.[5]

"With each successive drive," a professional fundraiser later recalled, "participating in mass philanthropy became more firmly established as an American value and even as a part of the American standard of living in the sense that a great number of families would routinely budget small contributions." By 1920 a scholarly literature was emerging to estimate how much an average family should give annually to the mass campaigns. In 1921, the American Economic Association held a contest for studies of the amount that an average citizen could afford to contribute to charitable appeals, and 40 scholars submitted academic essays.[6]

Despite this success and notoriety, "people's philanthropy" advanced slowly in higher education. One might expect that the innovation would arise at the colleges and universities that proudly called themselves the "people's institutions"— the new, public, land-grant universities founded under the Morrill Act of 1862.[7] Instead, it was two of the old, private, elite institutions that often relied on discreet appeals to wealthy donors—Yale and Harvard—that pioneered mass giving in higher education. No less surprising in hindsight, their presidents did not lead the way. Independent groups of alumni initiated the two new fundraising modes while departing from the customary approach at their alma maters, and the tradition-minded presidents straggled behind. It was a "democratic" revolution within hidebound colleges and universities.

Passion for "Democracy" and "Democratic Education"

In England, prior to the nineteenth century, "democracy" was "a strongly unfavorable term," according to British sociologist Raymond Williams. Most English politicians and parties endorsed it only in the late nineteenth century.[8] Americans embraced "democracy" much earlier, as Alexis de Tocqueville testified in his two

5. Zunz, *Philanthropy in America*, 44–75.

6. Quotation is from Zunz, *Philanthropy in America*, 72. See Frank A. Fetter, "The E. A. Karlsen Prizes," *American Economic Review* 11 (December 1921): ix; Carl Joslyn, "What Can a Man Afford?," *American Economic Review* 11 (December 1921): 99.

7. Quotations are from Cutlip, *Fund Raising*, 53, 110; George W. Rightmire, *Annual Report of the President of Ohio State University 1927–28*, 26–28. See Earle D. Ross, *Democracy's College: The Land-Grant Movement in the Formative Stage* (Ames, IA, 1942); Allan Nevins, *The State Universities and Democracy* (Urbana, IL, 1962). Compare Robert Lee and Tristan Ahtone, "Land-Grab Universities: Expropriated Indigenous Land Is the Foundation of the Land-Grant University System," *High Country News*, March 30, 2020.

8. Raymond Williams, *Keywords: A Vocabulary of Culture and Society*, rev. ed. (New York, 1985), 83.

volumes of *Democracy in America*, published in 1835 and 1840. However, even in America "democracy" did not become one of the "small number of words" that "legitimized public life" until late in the nineteenth century.[9]

Usage of the words "democracy" and "democratic" grew steadily between 1880 and 1910, rapidly between 1910 and 1915, and even more sharply from 1915 to the early 1920s, after which it quickly declined. Language in major American newspapers illustrates the trend. In the five decades between 1880 and 1930, the number of items published in the *Boston Globe, Washington Post*, and *Los Angeles Times* that included the term "democracy" rose from about 6,700 in the 1880s to 14,600 in the 1910s, before dropping to 9,900 in the 1920s.[10]

Contemporary observers noted the growth of discussion and enthusiasm about "democracy." For many people, "modern Democracy" was becoming "a religion, a passion, an end of inestimable worth," stated philosopher John S. MacKenzie. In 1905, Milton S. Hershey opened a factory in Pennsylvania with a new process that would "democratize" milk chocolate, formerly a delicacy of the rich. In 1908, Henry Ford began manufacturing the Model T in Michigan in order to "democratize the automobile." Such developments prompted satirist H. L. Mencken to remark that "democratic man" has gathered "more followers . . . than any other sophist since the age of the Apostles."[11]

The meanings of "democracy" multiplied with its increased and varied usage. The word "means many things . . . not all . . . consistent with one another," declared a prominent college textbook on government in 1913. In *The Meaning of Democracy*, political theorist Ivor Brown wrote, "The word has come to mean anything; or rather it means so much that it means nothing at all."[12] In particular, the usage and meanings of "democracy" multiplied rapidly in the field of education between 1890 and 1930.

In the 1890s alone, the absolute number of published books employing the terms "democratic" and "education" rose more than six-fold, and the trend continued through the 1910s, when John Dewey published his landmark work *Democracy and Education*. A similar trend appeared in major newspapers. In the five decades between 1880 and 1930, the number of items in the *Boston Globe*,

9. Quotations are from Daniel T. Rodgers, *Contested Truths: Keywords in American Politics since Independence* (New York, 1987), 6. See Alexis de Tocqueville, *Democracy in America*, 2 vols., trans. and ed. Harvey C. Mansfield and Delba Winthrop (Chicago, 2000).

10. Kimball, "'Democratizing' Giving," 169–70.

11. John S. Mackenzie, "The Dangers of Democracy," *International Journal of Ethics* 16 (January 1906): 130; H. L. Mencken, *Notes on Democracy* (New York, 1926), 6–7. See Thomas David, "Democracy as a Religion," *International Journal of Ethics* 10 (October 1899): 29.

12. Quotations are from A. Lawrence Lowell, *Public Opinion and Popular Government* (New York, 1913), 57; Ivor J. C. Brown, *The Meaning of Democracy*, 2nd ed. (Oxford, 1926), vii.

Washington Post, and *Los Angeles Times* including both "education" and either "democracy" or "democratic" rose steadily from about 1,200 in the 1880s to 3,400 in the 1920s. "Democracy" and "education" were strongly associated because "a democracy needs . . . to be both intensively and extensively educated," wrote Abraham Flexner in 1911. In November 1922 President Warren G. Harding proclaimed the very first American Education Week because "the ideals of democratic government and democratic education were planted simultaneously in our country."[13]

This close association made "democratic education" a popular phrase early in the twentieth century. By the 1910s, the phrase echoed in addresses, lectures, sermons, essays, and political debate across the nation, while its meaning varied commensurately.[14] Leaders in higher education inevitably joined the chorus. To Columbia University president Nicholas Butler (1902–45), "democratic education" meant "an education of opportunity," offering students the chance to succeed "according to their capacities and needs." For Stanford University president David Jordan (1891–1913) and New York University chancellor Elmer E. Brown (1911–33) the term signified instruction about the nature of democratic government and citizenship.[15]

Higher education leaders even competed to claim the term. Midwestern, public, land-grant universities considered themselves to be "the culmination of democracy's effort to advance itself by education," in the words of University of Minnesota president Lotus D. Coffman (1920–38). In fact, they competed to be "that most democratic of State universities."[16] Leaders of private institutions responded that "the small colleges in Ohio and Missouri, in Iowa and South Carolina, and in every state of our magnificent Union, are the expression of the democratic spirit." In addition, new institutions founded to serve commuting members of the working class, such as Temple University in Philadelphia and City College of New York, considered themselves the champions of "democratic

13. Quotations are from Abraham Flexner, "Aristocratic and Democratic Education," *Atlantic Monthly* 108 (September 1911): 391; "President Designates Dec. 3–9 Education Week," *Boston Globe*, November 20, 1922. See John Dewey, *Democracy and Education: An Introduction to the Philosophy of Education* (New York, 1916).

14. "Wisconsin Theory Is Found Ideal," *Chicago Tribune*, December 14, 1913; "Gompers Declares Labor's Platform," *New York Times*, March 22, 1920. See "Editorial. Democratic Education," *New York Times*, October 4, 1897; "The Democratic Education," *New York Times*, May 28, 1910.

15. Quotations are from "Half-Million Dollar High School Dedicated," *New York Times*, June 11, 1904; David Starr Jordan, "Education for Free Men," *Los Angeles Times*, July 13, 1925; "Democracy Redefined," *New York Times*, October 22, 1928.

16. Quotations are from "America Stands for Equality in Educational Opportunities," *Boston Globe*, March 2, 1928; "Art of Teaching in Recent Books," *New York Times*, January 15, 1910. See Frederick Jackson Turner, "Pioneer Ideals and the State University," in *The Frontier in American History* (New York, 1920), 269–89.

higher education."[17] Educators at every level wanted their institution to be "democratic."

"Democracy" at Yale and Harvard

After scarcely mentioning "democracy" or "democratic" in their annual reports during the 1870s and 1880s, leaders at Yale and Harvard increasingly employed the terms after 1890. Yet they rarely adopted the popular usages referring to the nation's polity or to preparing students for citizenship or for public service. Occasionally, they mentioned the university's governance, suggesting that faculty, students, or alumni should participate in the university's "democratic system of government."[18] But most often, they used "democracy" in two respects: the socioeconomic composition and the social mores of the student body.

On the one hand, they claimed that Harvard and Yale students "come from families in every walk of life and make a fair cross-section of society at large." Such statements were deeply ironic, given the high barriers, even total exclusion, faced by women, Jews, Latinos, Asians, African Americans, and other groups. At Yale and Harvard, the so-called "democratic" student body was composed almost entirely of white Christian men. Nevertheless, administrators and students at the two universities maintained that enrolling "a fair cross section" of social classes evidenced "the extremely democratic character of our student body."[19] In 1910, one working student wrote in the *Yale Alumni Weekly*, "Yale does not discriminate against the poor," demonstrating "the democratic spirit of the University in regard to the men who work their way."[20] Yale presidents of the time agreed, shown walking together in figure 3.1.

By the same token, raising tuition would mean "interfering with the University's democracy," wrote Yale University secretary Anson P. Stokes in 1911. In Cambridge, President Eliot also opposed raising tuition because that would "impair [Harvard's] democratic quality."[21] Little conception yet existed of tuition discounting—the "high-tuition, high-aid model" that became prominent at the

---

17. Quotations are from Harper, *Trend in Higher Education*, 362–63; "Connecticut Bans Three Law Schools Here," *New York Times*, June 5, 1929.

18. Anson P. Stokes Jr., *Annual Report of the Secretary of Yale University 1910–11*, 80–81.

19. Quotations are from Henry A. Yeomans, *Annual Report of the Dean of Harvard College 1920–21*, 45–46; Eliot, *Annual Report 1895–96*, 42; Stokes, *Annual Report 1910–11*, 52–53, 80. See Jerome Karabel, *The Chosen: The Hidden History of Admission and Exclusion at Harvard, Yale, and Princeton* (Boston, 2005).

20. An Undergraduate, "Working One's Way through Yale," *Yale Alumni Weekly*, December 9, 1910.

21. Anson P. Stokes Jr., "Yale's Financial Future," *Yale Alumni Weekly*, January 20, 1911, 430; Eliot, *Annual Report 1904–5*, 23–24.

Figure 3.1. (*From left*) Yale University President Timothy Dwight (1886–99), US President William H. Taft (1909–13), and Yale University President Arthur T. Hadley (1899–1921) in 1911. Courtesy of Manuscripts and Archives, Yale University Library.

end of the twentieth century.[22] Instead, capping tuition permitted students from outside the wealthy social elite to enroll and diversify the socioeconomic composition of the student body.

On the other hand, Yale and Harvard nurtured the "democratic" mores of the student body in two ways: mitigating social-class privilege and fostering solidarity. Social-class privilege was woven through the fabric of student life at the two universities, evident in their exclusive societies and clubs, which, by their nature, "cannot be thoroughly democratic," wrote Harvard's dean of students. Nevertheless, in the interest of diluting that privilege and fostering "democratic

22. Quotation is from Johnstone, "Financing Higher Education," 332–35.

character," the Harvard administration in 1900 built the Union, a social club that admitted all students for a small fee, in order "to promote the best kind of democracy." In addition, to support the "democratic way," Harvard founded its Dining Association to provide "wholesome board . . . at low rates."[23]

Similarly, in 1902 Yale established the Appointments Bureau, an early work-study and career placement office that served "self-supporting students" and became "one of the bulwarks of the Yale spirit of democracy." Regarding housing, a Yale dean recommended in 1906 "that, in order to maintain the proper democratic spirit . . . , there should not be too great contrast between the rooms of the wealthier students and those of more limited means." This contrast encourages "a distinct class consciousness" that undermines democratic education, said the Yale provost.[24]

Fostering solidarity was no less democratic. As part of the "democratic way" of the Harvard Dining Association, students were forbidden to form exclusive dining tables. Yale's housing policy discouraged off-campus living and urged students to live together in dormitories in order to make "academical life . . . more unified and democratic." In 1906 Yale president Arthur T. Hadley (1899–1921) commended football for "uniting [students] in a democratic fraternity" by "producing an esprit de corps which the miscellaneous scholarly activities of the University would be utterly powerless to evoke."[25] Thus, between 1890 and 1920, Harvard and Yale administrators increasingly encouraged students "to promote solidarity among themselves, to prevent the student body from being divided into exclusive groups, to make the College, in the common use of the term, more democratic."[26]

These efforts to diversify the socioeconomic composition and promote solidarity within the student body prompted officials at both universities to proclaim that "no truer democracy, in the best sense of the word, can be found anywhere than is to be found here."[27] In their view, both Yale and Harvard embraced the passion for "democratic education" that suffused American higher education between 1890 and 1930. The irony only confirms the legitimating power of the word "democracy" during this era.

23. Quotations are from Stokes, *Annual Report, 1910–11*, 80; LeBaron R. Briggs, *Annual Report of the Dean of Harvard College 1900–1901*, 106; Eliot, *Annual Report 1907–8*, 45.

24. Quotations are from Stokes, *Annual Report 1920–21*, 130; Russell H. Chittenden, *Annual Report of the Director of the Sheffield Scientific School at Yale University, 1905–6*, 96; William A. Brown, *Annual Report of the Provost of Yale University 1919–20*, 67.

25. Quotations are from Henry P. Wright, *Annual Report of the Dean of Yale [College] 1906–07*, 20; Hadley, *Annual Report 1905–6*, 19.

26. Lowell, *Annual Report 1910–11*, 13.

27. Dwight, *Annual Report 1891–92*, 42.

Mass Giving Begins at Yale

While democratic rhetoric began to reverberate at Yale and Harvard in the 1890s, mass giving emerged in American society. To that point, gifts to these two universities "depended largely on a comparatively few generous friends to supply needed funds," noted the *Boston Globe* in 1917. At least 95 percent of the gifts came from wealthy individuals.[28] Entirely comfortable with this traditional arrangement, Yale and Harvard leaders gave no thought to making a broad, public appeal to alumni, beyond the pleas in their annual reports.

As at other universities, this long-standing reliance on a coterie of munificent benefactors was sustained by the social norms of privilege: large gifts implied dependence on the donor and deference from the recipient. Giving was "the 'burden' or the 'privilege,' as you may prefer to name it," declared social reformer Lilian Brandt in 1921.[29] For this reason, appealing to wealthy donors was often called "begging," a term normally used in self-deprecating jest that expressed the price of dependence and deference paid for the gifts. As Secretary Stokes at Yale warned, "constant personal begging on the part of a university is apt to be undignified" and to cost the university its "reputation for fearless educational independence."[30] Conversely, university presidents, while showing deference to their patrons, also elevated themselves through their privileged access to the patron. University of Chicago president Harper thus felt humiliated in the early 1900s when John D. Rockefeller refused to meet with him anymore due to Harper's profligate spending.

This entailed privilege meant, for example, that a Yale alumnus who could afford to send only a small check to help his alma mater would feel presumptuous and embarrassed to do so. The gift would suggest that he was an imposter, trying to act like a member of the wealthy elite. Conversely, Yale presidents requesting or receiving such small gifts would feel embarrassed—as though Yale actually depended on and deferred to penurious alumni. Consequently, "no Yale graduate ever thought of giving five or ten dollars or any inconsiderable sum to the college, all appeals for money having been made for contributions of considerable amounts, usually from rich men."[31]

---

28. "Call for Harvard: After Fund of $10,000,000," *Boston Globe*, January 11, 1917. See George C. Holt, "The Origin of the Yale Alumni Fund," *Yale Alumni Weekly*, February 2, 1917, 529.
29. Lilian Brandt, *How Much Shall I Give?* (New York, 1921), 55. See Zunz, *Philanthropy in America*, 17–18.
30. Stokes, *Annual Report 1912–13*, 45. See William H. Allen, *Modern Philanthropy: A Study of Efficient Appealing and Giving* (New York, 1912), 151–52.
31. Holt, "Origin of the Yale Alumni Fund," 529.

Yet Yale did need money to compete with its counterparts. In 1880, President Noah Porter announced that Yale was poor compared to "our sister institutions," including not only Harvard and Princeton but also newly founded universities such as Cornell and Johns Hopkins. Yale's financial straits continued into the 1900s, rendering "competition with our rivals exceedingly difficult. Harvard and Columbia each ha[ve] more than double the endowment of Yale," reported the *Yale Alumni Weekly* in 1910.[32]

Yale's announced need therefore prompted a revolution in March 1890 as mass giving and democratic enthusiasm welled up in American society. A few members of the New York chapter of the Yale Alumni Association proposed that "numbers of men who could afford to give but little" would be "glad to make a small annual contribution if a proper fund of that kind were properly organized and established." Beyond calling for support for their alma mater, these graduates recognized the crucial need to institute a new, legitimate method for regular giving by small donors. In order to ensure that no offense would be taken, the alumni leaders consulted Yale president Timothy Dwight (1886–99) and the Yale Corporation. With their approval, the alumni leaders in 1890 incorporated the Yale Alumni Fund (YAF), whose nine directors were appointed by the Yale president.[33]

At first, YAF passively relied on announcements to attract contributions, but soon the alumni association began annual comprehensive solicitations through a network of agents from the classes of graduates. This approach regularized and systematized the subscription campaigns held in the past when colleges faced crises or special needs. Mindful of the traditional relationship of privilege and deference, YAF declared as its central rationale "that no graduate need feel excluded from giving to the University because he could not afford to give largely."[34] This was a natural extension of the "democratic" ideology cultivated in the Yale student body.

In financial terms, the fund provided critical unrestricted funds to Yale, most of which went to operating expenses, although donors could designate their gifts for endowment. Initially, the monies raised were not large. In the first decade, total gifts amounted to about $86,000, and the principal of its endowment fund totaled less than $8,000. YAF then began to grow rapidly. In 1910, the gifts

32. Quotations are from Noah Porter, *Annual Report of the President of Yale University 1879–80*, 10, 12, 25; "The President's Report for 1910," *Yale Alumni Weekly*, July 8, 1910, 1026.

33. Holt, "Origin of the Yale Alumni Fund," 529. See "The Alumni Fund," *Yale Alumni Weekly*, March 17, 1911, 633; Archibald J. Allen, *Anything Is Possible; The First 75 Years of the Yale Alumni Fund* (Hartford, CT, 1965), 2–11.

34. Yale Alumni University Fund, *25th Annual Report of the Board of Directors* ([New Haven, CT], 1915), 3.

exceeded $131,000 and the endowment principal reached $454,000, about 4 percent of Yale's total endowment at the time.[35]

As Yale's alumni fund increased and attracted attention, alumni of colleges and universities across the nation began to form their own organizations, which joined together to form national associations. In 1913, the Association of Alumni Secretaries was founded; in 1915, the Alumni Magazines Association; in 1925, the Association of Alumni Organizations. By the mid-1920s, at least 20 colleges and universities had established alumni funds like Yale's.[36] State and land-grant institutions also began to replicate YAF. In 1927 the president of the Ohio State University Alumni Association wrote to the university president,

> The Alumni Fund . . . is a comparatively new development . . . , though it has been in effect at Yale with conspicuous success for a good many years. Its whole theory is based upon the fact that it is easier for the average alumnus to give a small amount of money to this university each year for unrestricted use, than it is to pry out of him the capital that would produce annually an interest dividend equal to the smaller amount that he can more easily give each year. I enclose . . . a study of this kind of alumni giving of the Michigan Alumni Association.[37]

Over the next decade, more than 100 colleges and universities followed Yale's lead in establishing annual alumni funds or regular alumni giving programs, including the public universities of Buffalo, California, Illinois, Kansas, Kansas State, Michigan State, Michigan, North Carolina, Pennsylvania State, Rutgers, and Vermont.[38]

The new mode of fundraising thus spread throughout higher education, extending, for example, to a land-grant HBCU, Virginia State University. Founded in 1882 as the Virginia Normal and Collegiate Institute, this was the nation's first fully state-supported four-year institution of higher education for African Americans. By 1920, its alumni association was sponsoring an Alumni Building Fund that became an annual alumni appeal over the subsequent decade. In 1930, the Institute became Virginia State Teachers College, and President John M. Gandy (1914–47) called for creating an alumni office with paid staff, as illustrated in figure 3.2. By

35. Clarence Deming, "Yale's Larger Gifts," *Yale Alumni Weekly*, March 17, 1911, 634–35; "Nineteenth Alumni Fund Report," *Yale Alumni Weekly*, January 14, 1910, 415.

36. Trevor Arnett, *College and University Finance* (New York, 1922), 17; "Universities Ask over $200,000,000," *New York Times*, February 8, 1920; Curti and Nash, *Philanthropy*, 202.

37. James L. Morrill to George W. Rightmire, October 5, 1927, President George W. Rightmire Papers, The Ohio State University Archives.

38. Benjamin A. Johnson, "Fundraising and Endowment Building at a Land Grant University during the Critical Period, 1910–1940" (PhD diss., The Ohio State University, 2013), 337–40.

Figure 3.2. Virginia State University President John M. Gandy (1914–47) and Logo of the Alumni Association, Adopted in 1936. Gandy portrait courtesy of Virginia State University Special Collections and Archives. Alumni logo courtesy of Virginia State University Alumni Association.

1937, the staff had joined the American Alumni Council, consisting of representatives from "the state-supported universities now operating alumni funds or formal alumni giving programs."[39]

Meanwhile, Yale College broke more new ground in alumni giving in 1899, when an appeal to graduates in honor of its 1901 bicentennial raised nearly $2 million to fund new buildings and other projects. Responding to that initiative, Harvard College in 1904 appealed to alumni through an informal, loosely organized campaign that netted nearly $2.5 million in "free money" for the university, guided by President Eliot's recommendation. Then, in 1905 the Harvard College class of 1880 introduced twenty-fifth-reunion giving by donating $100,000 in unrestricted endowment, nearly matching the endowment built by YAF over the previous 15 years.[40]

39. "To the Alumni Building Fund, an Awakening Consciousness," May 1920, Papers of John M. Gandy 1914–47, ser. 2, Virginia State University Library Archives; John M. Gandy, *Annual Report of the President of Virginia State College 1930*, 23; Johnson, "Fundraising and Endowment Building," 339–40.

40. Hadley, *Annual Report 1900–1901*, 26; Yale Alumni University Fund, *25th Annual Report*, 3; Eliot, *Annual Report 1905–6*, 53–54; William Lawrence, *Memories of a Happy Life* (Boston, 1926), 211–20.

Despite raising those large amounts, Harvard alumni considered YAF's annual alumni appeal more effective than "these spasmodic attempts to raise large sums, like . . . the twenty-fifth anniversary." The latter were "hard on men with modest incomes," who could not handle a large donation but whose small annual contributions "would probably amount to considerably more than they give on their twenty-fifth."[41] Taking their cue from the highly successful mass campaigns, Harvard alumni organized the second mode of mass giving that proliferated throughout higher education in the 1920s. This innovation was the Harvard Endowment Fund (HEF), the first national, multiyear, public fundraising campaign, which ran from 1915 to 1925.

Although YAF and HEF eventually succeeded in raising considerable amounts for their respective alma maters, the alumni organizers at both universities initially faced resistance. The presidents, other top administrators, and some wealthy donors were not enthusiastic about the new ventures, which smacked of publicly "begging" for money. How could the Yale and Harvard alumni legitimize their plebian approach, given the traditional custom of discreetly appealing to wealthy donors?

"Democratize This Whole Plan of Giving"

Although several of the YAF and HEF organizers had worked on campaigns for the YMCA, YWCA, Red Cross, and Liberty Loans and adopted some of their tactics, the alumni leaders avoided the campaigns' plebian terms "people's philanthropy" and "mass giving." Instead, YAF and HEF sought legitimacy by invoking one of the "keywords" in American discourse that was gaining great favor and enthusiasm in the 1910s.[42] They labeled their innovations "democratic" and even competed for the rank of "most democratic" in order to dignify mass giving and ease its acceptance at the nation's oldest elite universities.

Unprecedented in fundraising, this "democratic" language echoed other commentary on education at the turn of the century. In fact, educators often distinguished invidiously between the terms "democratic" and "mass," especially when arguing for compulsory schooling. Stories in major newspapers reported that "the masses are 'dull because they have never been cultivated'" by "democratic education." Thus, "democratic education" prepares the "masses" for "democratic society."[43]

41. Malcolm Storer to Thomas W. Lamont, January 12, 1917, Lamont Correspondence.
42. See Williams, *Keywords*, 15–17; Roderick P. Hart et al., *Political Keywords: Using Language That Uses Us* (New York, 2005).
43. "Dr. Leipziger Honored," *New York Times*, May 3, 1903; "Wisdom for the Masses: Birmingham's Work in the Cause of Democratic Education," *Chicago Daily Tribune*, February 5, 1893.

Yale and Harvard administrators and alumni likewise distinguished "democracy" and "democratic" from the "masses" and the "people." The presidents dismissed "a false notion of democracy in education" that involves "lowering educational standards to the level of . . . the mediocre student," as did Harvard president A. Lawrence Lowell (1909–33).[44] Instead, when claiming to cultivate "democratic character," the two elite universities envisioned a "democracy of scholarship"—an "aristocracy" that was also "democratic" in admitting students from any social class.[45] The graduates then adopted this language and conception of democracy to legitimize the novel practices in mass fundraising that they organized for their alma mater.

Discussion about "democracy" at Harvard and Yale rarely touched on the universities' finances during the 1890s. Then, in 1901, during Yale's bicentennial, President Hadley found the term useful to justify receiving modest gifts from a broader range of alumni: "A college that is democratic in its aims and principles cannot expect its income to be furnished by larger endowments exclusively," wrote Hadley. "It must look to the loyalty of its former members for support."[46]

In 1910 Yale secretary Stokes proposed a "democratic" justification for charging different rates of tuition based on students' financial resources. He dismissed the view that "the only democratic arrangement . . . is . . . a flat rate for all students," and he maintained that higher tuition for wealthy students "certainly seems more democratic than a large and uniform increase of tuition charges."[47] Though idiosyncratic at the time, Stokes's proposal anticipated the discounting of tuition that arose late in the twentieth century.

Stokes then invoked "democracy" on behalf of giving to YAF in 1911. "We should aim to double the number of its subscribers during the next quarter century," he wrote in a letter to the alumni. "Such an income coming regularly and being distributed among the rank and file of the graduates would be a continual guarantee of the reliability and democratic character of the University's constituency."[48] Soon thereafter, YAF leaders formally adopted this language, distinguishing between, "on the one hand, the large gifts from wealthy individuals"

44. Lowell, *Annual Report 1922–23*, 69. See Hadley, *Annual Report 1914–15*, 27; Angell, *Annual Report 1922–23*, 1–2; *1926–27*, 5, 7.

45. Quotations are from Joseph H. Beale Jr., "Langdell, Gray, Thayer, and Ames: Their Contribution to the Study and Teaching of Law," *New York University Law Quarterly Review* 8 (1931): 389; Kim Townsend, *Manhood at Harvard: William James and Others* (Cambridge, MA, 1996), 17, 22, 89–97, 120–32.

46. Hadley, *Annual Report 1900–1901*, 21.

47. Stokes, *Annual Report 1910–11*, 52–53.

48. Stokes, "Yale's Financial Future," 430; Stokes, *Annual Report 1910–11*, 80.

and, "on the other hand, the . . . 'Democratic' contribution, represented by [YAF], gathering in annually the smaller gifts, though collectively large."[49]

YAF leaders repeated that argument in 1915 when their twenty-fifth annual report observed that "the fundamental object . . . is to induce universal annual giving, and encourage gifts of any size, however small, for general University use." A copy of this YAF report found its way to Thomas W. Lamont, a Harvard alumnus and chairman of the unofficial group of alumni planning HEF in 1915. Preparing to begin their drive during 1916, these Harvard volunteers began tracking YAF because "this plan works well at Yale, and we ought not to be too proud to copy her example and do it better."[50]

By November 1916, the HEF executive committee, headed by Lamont, began making "democracy" a prominent theme of the Harvard campaign. The secretary reported "that the great virtue of the [HEF] would lie in the widespread appeal and . . . the collection of small contributions from a large number of graduates." The executive committee thus voted to make their Harvard drive "as democratic as it possibly could be and . . . in no sense . . . a 'rich man's' fund."[51] Leading up to the campaign kickoff in January 1917, Lamont announced in his speeches and letters to collaborators, "We are going to democratize this whole plan of giving."[52] Those at Yale did not have to look hard to find the HEF theme because Harvard publicized it prominently. "The decision to carry a wide-spread, democratic appeal to all its graduates and friends" was announced in major newspapers in January 1917.[53]

YAF leaders felt that HEF had stolen their "democratic" thunder and, perhaps, threatened their appeal in the financial centers of Boston and New York. Within a few weeks they responded, asserting their stronger claim to "democratic" fundraising. In a full-page announcement in the *Yale Alumni Weekly*, YAF boldly proclaimed itself "THE MOST DEMOCRATIC ENDOWMENT OF ANY UNIVERSITY."[54]

Continuing to follow the progress of YAF, HEF leaders in March 1917 tried to reclaim the "democratic" mantle. They reaffirmed in *Harvard Graduates Magazine* that HEF will announce "Harvard's needs to every living Harvard man

49. Deming, "Yale's Larger Gifts," 635.

50. Quotations are from Yale Alumni University Fund, *25th Annual Report*, 6–7; Storer to Lamont, January 12, 1917.

51. Robert F. Duncan, HEF Secretary's Notebook, November 24, 1916, HEF Records.

52. Thomas W. Lamont to E. B. Dane, January 8, 1917, Lamont Correspondence.

53. "Call for Harvard: After Fund of $10,000,000," *Boston Globe*, January 11, 1917; "Average Harvard Pay $1,840 . . . Endowment Committee Says," *New York Times*, January 26, 1917.

54. "Alumni Make It Possible to Secure Great Teachers for Yale," *Yale Alumni Weekly*, February 2, 1917, 535.

and . . . will, therefore, be a widespread democratic appeal."[55] Lamont emphasized in speeches and correspondence, "Our idea is to democratize this fund, . . .
every one of the forty thousand . . . living men who have been connected with
Harvard . . . ought to contribute according to his means, be the amount large or
small." In the late spring, YAF responded with "a greater effort at Yale publicity,"
and Lamont obtained a copy of this announcement as well.[56]

At that point, the ironical jousting between YAF and HEF to be recognized
as "most democratic" subsided. The duel likely appeared trivial after April 6,
1917, when the United States entered World War I to make the world "safe for
democracy," in the words of President Woodrow Wilson. In fact, Harvard
alumni called for halting the HEF drive in deference to the wartime campaigns
for disaster relief and Liberty Loans. In May 1917, HEF leaders reluctantly postponed the campaign, and some staff left to help manage the Red Cross in
Washington, DC. Nevertheless, YAF and HEF continued to keep track of each
other's efforts to be the most successful "democratic campaign" through 1918,
and President Eliot, then retired, contributed to the correspondence as well.[57]

Influences of "Democratic" Giving

The effort "to democratize this whole plan of giving" influenced higher education finance in several important respects. First, the terminology helped to legitimize mass fundraising not only at the elite schools Yale and Harvard but also
at hundreds of colleges and universities that had relied predominantly on discreet appeals to wealthy donors. The language of YAF and HEF justified the
broad alumni canvass by dignifying it as "democratic."

In addition, the effort led YAF and HEF to adopt the two "democratic" mores of the student bodies at Yale and Harvard: fostering solidarity and mitigating
socioeconomic privilege. Yale's "democratic" fundraising appealed to solidarity
by "gathering in annually the smaller gifts, though collectively large," from "the
rank and file of the graduates." The Harvard fund tried to reach "every man ca-
pable of giving even the smallest sum, and . . . showing him that his investment
in Harvard College will yield a large return."[58] In the 1900s and 1910s, YAF and

55. Richard. M. Saltonstall, "Harvard's New Endowment," *Harvard Graduates Magazine*,
March 1917, 313.
56. Quotations are from Thomas W. Lamont to Theodore N. Vail, March 12, 1917, Lamont
Correspondence; Yale Alumni University Fund, *27th Annual Report* (New Haven, CT, 1917), 3.
57. Woodrow Wilson, Address of the President, 65th Cong., 1st sess. (April 2, 1917). See letters
to and from Thomas W. Lamont, May and June 1917, April 1918, Lamont Correspondence.
58. Quotations are from Deming, "Yale's Larger Gifts," 635; Stokes, "Yale's Financial Future,"
430; Saltonstall, "Harvard's New Endowment," 313.

HEF emphasized, for the first time at these two universities, that everyone's contribution was important and that all alumni had to pull together in solidarity "to help the University by uniting their gifts, and making one large sum out of many small donations."[59]

"Democratic" fundraising also diluted socioeconomic privilege among alumni by encouraging and honoring all donations, even modest ones. Traditional benefaction by the wealthy elite entailed dependence on the donor and deference from the recipient. "Democratizing giving" meant extending that relationship widely. At Harvard, Eliot identified needs that suited the interest and pocketbook of every donor. At Yale, Dwight wrote that, although "men of large wealth" have "indeed a great privilege" to "give strength and larger life" to their alma mater, "every giver and every worker has, in his measure, the same privilege." The fundamental innovation of both YAF and HEF was to provide a mechanism "to give everyone an opportunity to take part," stated Lamont.[60]

Furthermore, the effort "to democratize this whole plan of giving" prompted appeals to broaden the governance of the elite universities. Only in 1871 had Yale permitted alumni to choose a few members of the Corporation, and in 1912 a Yale alumni class chairman predicted that the number would soon grow, "thus proving that in the affairs of Yale the people rule."[61] Listing reasons to support HEF in 1916, Lamont maintained that the fund provides "the graduates . . . an equal voice with the University." By the same token, the president of the Associated Harvard Clubs argued that alumni should have some say in spending the HEF receipts because "that is a frank and democratic recognition of the fact that the graduates . . . furnish the money" and should "therefore . . . be given some responsibility in its disposition."[62]

Finally, and ironically, the push to make giving "democratic" may have had the opposite effect on admissions. While elite colleges and universities had historically placed priority on admitting children of alumni, the move to "democratize . . . giving" led to emphasizing alumni donations and elevating that priority even higher. As a result, encouraging all alumni to give may have, paradoxically, rein-

59. George P. Day, *Annual Report of the Treasurer of Yale University 1909–10*, 15.

60. Quotations are from Dwight, *Annual Report 1888–89*, 59; Thomas W. Lamont, "Ten Million Dollars for Harvard," *Harvard Alumni Bulletin*, January 11, 1917, 281. See Yale Alumni University Fund, *25th Annual Report*, 3.

61. James R. Sheffield, Speech, Twenty-Fifth Reunion Activities of Yale College Class of 1887, June 1912, Yale Secretary Records. See Brooks M. Kelley, *Yale: A History* (New Haven, CT, 1974), 235–36.

62. Quotations are from Thomas W. Lamont, "Arguments for the Fund," ca. May 1916, Lamont Correspondence; Frederick W. Burlingham to Robert F. Duncan, February 12, 1918, HEF Records.

forced the traditional composition of the student body. Even so, the new modes of fundraising at Harvard and Yale sparked efforts outside of higher education "to democratize social welfare efforts." These implied the duty that everyone should participate in philanthropy, rather than relying on donations from the wealthiest "three to five per cent of the population."[63]

Democracy Discredited

Beginning with a steep recession between 1920 and 1922, the decade following World War I constituted a period of enormous discontent in the United States. It was a decade, some have said, when Americans lost their faith in both democracy and religion. Recovering slowly from the war, Europeans likewise voiced much "discontent with democratic institutions."[64] In 1921, Viscount James Bryce famously observed that "democracy, though assumed to be the only rightful kind of government, has, in its representative form, failed to fulfill the hopes of sixty years ago."[65]

Representative democracy thus came under attack from both ends of the political spectrum—fascism on the right and socialism and communism on the left. In addition, representative democracy was challenged by proponents of "direct democracy," who advocated the ballot initiative, the referendum, and the recall by popular vote. By the late 1920s, many believed that "democracy faces a perilous situation."[66] Indeed, "democracy may still be called a popular idea in the sense that everybody talks about it, but . . . it is very largely discredited," scholars observed.[67]

Nor did everybody talk about it as much. Discussion about "democracy" subsided in the mid-1920s.[68] By that point, the YAF and HEF leaders had abandoned the rhetoric of democracy, while hundreds of campuses launched annual alumni funds and national, multiyear fundraising campaigns. Discursive legitimation was unnecessary because the additional revenue alone justified the two new modes that fueled the accelerating competition for revenue and wealth.

63. Quotations are from John Melpolder, "Democratizing Social Welfare Efforts," *Survey* 37 (December 1916): 303; Brandt, *How Much Shall I Give?*, 55.
64. Moritz J. Bonn, *The Crisis of European Democracy* (New Haven, CT, 1925), 1–2.
65. James Bryce, *Modern Democracies* (New York, 1921), 1:5.
66. Edward M. Sait, *Democracy* (New York, 1929), v.
67. Brown, *Meaning of Democracy*, vii.
68. Kimball, " 'Democratizing' Giving," 170, 188–89.

CHAPTER 4

Fundraising Drives Begin, 1915–25

In the 1910s and 1920s, the General Education Board (GEB) strongly encouraged colleges and universities to build their endowment "in its correct sense," meaning permanent, productive funds. Ambitious schools meanwhile began increasing their revenue by employing two new modes of fundraising: the annual comprehensive appeal to alumni and the national, multiyear, "businesslike" fundraising campaign run by paid staff. Over the next century, both modes became as predictable as commencement, and public and private schools across the United States took pride in describing their multiyear campaigns as "the largest fundraising endeavor in the university's history" or, competitively, "the largest ever in higher education."[1] This phenomenon originated between 1915 and 1925, when Harvard alumni conducted the first such drive, named the Harvard Endowment Fund (HEF). As at Yale, HEF leaders elevated their effort by

---

1. Quotations are from *Ohio State Launches $2.5 Billion Dollar Fundraising Effort* (Columbus, OH, October 2012); Alvin Powell, "Harvard Kicks Off Fundraising Effort," *Harvard Gazette*, September 21, 2013.

calling it "democratic," while they adopted many tactics from "mass giving" campaigns.

Publicized nationwide, HEF exercised enormous influence by propagating not only its own template but also the GEB's "correct" definition of endowment and the precepts of the free-money strategy of Harvard president Charles Eliot (1869–1909). By the same token, HEF disseminated appreciation of endowment's capacity to increase the autonomy, stability, and flexibility of a school and thereby its potential to spend and succeed in the Darwinian competition for "the survival of the fittest."[2] After all, the midpoint of the HEF drive, in 1920, marked the first time when Harvard attained the lead among higher education endowments that it would not subsequently surrender.

Early in the 1920s, even before HEF concluded, scores of prominent colleges and universities began to replicate the fundraising drive, along with the annual alumni appeal. These two new modes—together with the traditional circumspect solicitation of wealthy donors—formed a fundraising triad that virtually all colleges and universities in the United States eventually adopted, accelerating their competition to increase revenue and build endowment over the course of the twentieth century. This chapter focuses on the novel HEF, and the following chapter addresses the contested proliferation of these modes in higher education.

"The Biggest, Longest, and Most Important Campaign"

From the outset, the informal group of Harvard alumni who began planning HEF in 1915 envisioned a pathbreaking venture. It would be "the biggest, longest, and most important campaign of its kind ever undertaken in this country," the chairman Thomas W. Lamont told President A. Lawrence Lowell (1909–33).[3] Indeed transformative, HEF vastly expanded the dimensions and tactics of higher education fundraising. The campaign was unprecedented in the amount to be raised, the years involved in planning and canvassing, and the widespread network of 3,000 volunteers soliciting 36,000 alumni divided into 70 districts around the world. To manage that scope, HEF drew novel tactics from "people's philanthropy," including the preliminary analysis of prospects, the quiet "running start," the orchestrated publicity, the convening and training of the volunteer leaders, the "whirlwind" final push, and the plaint of poverty.

---

2. Harper, *Trend in Higher Education*, 375.
3. Thomas W. Lamont to John J. Jones, ca. December 1916, Lamont Correspondence; Thomas W. Lamont to A. Lawrence Lowell, March 21, 1917, Lowell Records. In this chapter, all letters to and from Lamont are in Lamont Correspondence, unless otherwise noted.

Formerly viewed as an embarrassment, the cry of penury could soon be heard from all elite colleges and universities.

HEF also inaugurated two highly important changes in institutional governance in higher education. For the first time, the university harnessed the fundraising efforts of its various schools, departments, and units, which were accustomed to seeking gifts whenever and however they wished. In addition, the university established comprehensive control over alumni affairs by consolidating and centralizing the disparate alumni organizations and redirected alumni activities toward raising revenue. Taken together, these two changes resulted in employing a legion of alumni and development staff who henceforth would lead the university's efforts in increasing revenue and competing for wealth. A century later, the host of such staff across the nation had grown to 85,000 members, averaging at least 20 at every degree-granting, non-profit college and university.[4]

HEF also introduced into higher education fundraising other innovations that proved paradoxical in several respects. First, due to the unprecedented scope of the campaign, HEF leaders adopted a novel "businesslike" strategy, building an administrative hierarchy, hiring a full-time staff, renting offices, keeping formal accounts, issuing regular reports, and so forth. Unprecedented in higher education, this business strategy included justifying the HEF financial goal through an overall analysis of Harvard's costs, rather than appealing to donors' sentiments as did the mass campaigns. That hardheaded cost justification came to focus on the central purpose of raising faculty salaries, whose value had severely depreciated over the prior decade.

In the end, however, the amount "needed" was not really determined either by the cost justification or by faculty raises. Paradoxically, HEF leaders set the campaign goal by figuring out how much they thought they could get. They privately committed to this "primary" goal to raise as much as they could because everything would go to Harvard's unrestricted endowment, following the dictates of revered, retired president Eliot.

Second, the unprecedented outcome of the campaign was also paradoxical. Beginning with high hopes in 1915, HEF trailed off in 1925, falling short of its goal. Although the dismayed organizers admitted defeat, Harvard publicly declared victory, and the failed drive was remembered as an exemplar of success and a source of admiration in higher education, vastly increasing the fundraising ambitions of colleges and universities across the nation.

---

4. Council for Advancement and Support of Education, *Reimagining CASE 2017–2021* (Washington DC, 2016), 5.

In addition, HEF purportedly gave birth to the new profession of consulting for higher education fundraising. However, unpaid alumni actually planned and directed the campaign. The first consulting firm was formed by a few junior HEF staff who jumped ship just as the drive ran aground when only two-thirds of the goal had been reached. Those who abandoned the campaign and later took credit for its supposed success established the new profession of fundraising consulting for higher education.

Finally, owing to its trumpeted success, HEF was imitated throughout American higher education. But some prominent college and university presidents, including Lowell, considered its approach to be ineffective, inefficient, and even counterproductive. Like many of his peers, Lowell preferred the traditional, patrician approach of quietly soliciting wealthy donors. Furthermore, big givers continued to generate at least 90 percent of the total donations to colleges and universities, even as mass fundraising campaigns multiplied throughout American higher education.[5] HEF, paradoxically, was imitated despite presidents' resistance and the "democratic" campaign's limited impact on the amount of gifts.

Smith and Wellesley Inform the Harvard Drive

Neither contemporaneous observers nor subsequent historians recognized that the famous fundraising drive of all-male Harvard was directly informed by earlier, traditional fundraising drives held by two leading women's colleges. In June 1911, Thomas Lamont, the husband of Smith alumna Florence Haskell Corliss, was elected to the Smith board of trustees and then to its executive committee. A vice president of J. P. Morgan and Co., the leading banking house in the country, Lamont worked at the headquarters on Wall Street in New York City.

Early that summer, Smith College began planning a drive to raise $1 million in endowment, and Lamont and President Marion L. Burton (1910–17) personally led the campaign, appealing discreetly to wealthy donors in keeping with the traditional mode of fundraising. Smith's innovation lay in its stated purpose that the income would be used "*solely for providing larger salaries and increasing the number of the teaching staff.*" In 1913, the Smith drive concluded successfully, and Lamont and Burton continued corresponding regularly until 1917, when HEF was launched and Burton left Smith to become president of the University of Minnesota and, later, the University of Michigan.[6]

---

5. Further documentation and discussion concerning this chapter can be found in Bruce A. Kimball, "The First Campaign and the Paradoxical Transformation of Fundraising in American Higher Education, 1915–1925," *Teachers College Record* 116 (2014): 1–44.

6. Quotation is from Marion L. Burton, "To the Members of the Board of Trustees of Smith College," June 25, 1911, and Marion L. Burton to Thomas W. Lamont, June 22, 1911, Burton Files

As the Smith drive concluded, Wellesley College president Ellen F. Pendleton (1911–35) and board of trustees chairman William Lawrence, an Episcopal bishop and cousin of Harvard president Lowell, began their own drive in 1913. The outline was similar: the goal to raise $1 million in endowment, the traditional mode of appealing discreetly to the wealthy, and the declared aim to raise faculty salaries. The Wellesley drive hummed along, raising $430,000 by March 1914, when disaster struck. Wellesley's main building burned to the ground. Soon after the tragedy, the campaign resumed with a new goal of $2 million on the advice of John D. Rockefeller, who promised to contribute $750,000 conditional upon Wellesley raising the balance by the end of 1914.[7]

The work proved extremely difficult. Wealthy businessmen outside of Boston and New York did not know Wellesley College, and President Pendleton and Bishop Lawrence discovered that the alumnae around the country were not prepared or organized to be canvassed. The Wellesley drive thus provided "severe training" in how to run a national campaign in higher education, Lawrence reported. Nevertheless, the college met Rockefeller's conditional deadline just in time, and Pendleton laid the cornerstone of a new building the following year, as depicted in figure 4.1.[8]

In the subsequent summer of 1915, Lamont and Lawrence imparted the lessons of the Smith and Wellesley appeals to the informal group of Harvard alumni who were starting to plan a fundraising drive. In particular, Lamont and Lawrence had learned both the advantage of framing an appeal for endowment in terms of raising faculty salaries and the necessity of extensive preparation and organization in order to run "a far-reaching, systematic campaign" on "a much larger and more businesslike scale."[9]

Throughout 1915 and 1916, the small group of Harvard financiers and lawyers, led by Lamont, organized HEF "just as any big business project must be handled."[10] In addition to the lessons from Smith and Wellesley and to President Eliot's exhortation to build endowment, the impetus for this approach came from a contemporaneous shift in the prevailing ideology—the meaning and justification—of financial benefaction in American culture and in higher educa-

(emphasis in the original). See letters between Marion L. Burton and Thomas W. Lamont, Burton Files.

7. "Wellesley Needs $625,000 by January, a Letter from the President," *Ladies Home Journal* 31 (October 1931): 109.

8. William Lawrence, *Memories of a Happy Life* (Boston, 1926), 370; see also 341–45.

9. Quotations are from Thomas W. Lamont, "Ten Million Dollars for Harvard," *Harvard Alumni Bulletin*, January 11, 1917, 285; Thomas W. Lamont to Edgar H. Wells, March 22, 1917.

10. Quotations are from Thomas W. Lamont to A. Lawrence Lowell, March 21, 1917, and December 24, 1918.

Figure 4.1. Wellesley College President Ellen F. Pendleton (1911–35) Setting Cornerstone, 1915. Courtesy of Wellesley College Archives, Library & Technology Services.

tion. During the late 1800s and early 1900s, that ideology shifted between two distinct and successive conceptions that historians have termed "charity" and "philanthropy."[11]

From "Charity" to "Philanthropy"

Historians have traced the concept of charity in American culture to the Protestant missionary impulse in Puritan New England, while attributing its motives to altruistic compassion, to an almost subconscious desire to "save" their own souls by saving others, and to the imposition of Puritan morals and norms on others. Whatever the motive, charity means giving directly to specific individuals in order to alleviate the immediate effects of poverty, sickness, misfortune, or other distress. Hence, charitable benefactions are generally personal,

11. The seminal article is Barry D. Karl and Stanley N. Katz, "The American Private Philanthropic Foundation and the Public Sphere, 1890–1930," *Minerva* 19 (1981): 236–71. See Stanley Katz, "Introduction: The Economics of Higher Education and the History of Philanthropy Research," in Adam and Bayram, *Economics of Higher Education*, 1–20.

small, empathetic, and palliative, temporarily satisfying the needs of particular individuals known to the benefactor.[12]

Charity also implies that the recipients are dependent on their benefactor and should respond with deference and humility. We cannot "be charitable to our equals," wrote Progressive reformer Josephine Shaw Lowell in 1879. Critics, such as English politician Arthur Hobhouse, therefore argued that gifts of charity result in "pauperising or degrading all those who come into contact with them."[13] In the United States, Yale professor William G. Sumner, a firm proponent of social Darwinism, wrote in 1883 that for "a free man in a free democracy . . . the next most pernicious thing to vice is charity."[14] The unfit should be left to perish in order to avoid weakening everyone else. Due to the associations with dependence and deference, appeals for charity often prompted references to financial "embarrassment" or "begging" for money.

Such charitable discourse had a long history in higher education. In the late Middle Ages, English universities issued a "license-to-beg" to penurious students so they could pay their bills. Although the American colonial colleges did not issue such licenses, their leaders, when facing a crisis or dire need, often termed appeals for donations as "begging," in line with the deferential relations of charity. Through the twentieth century, leaders in higher education continued to speak in such terms, usually in self-deprecating jest. Bishop Lawrence, one of Harvard's most successful fundraisers in the early 1900s, sometimes called himself "the prince of beggars."[15]

But the implied dependence and deference rankled some college and university leaders. To the very end of his term, Yale president Timothy Dwight (1886–99) distinguished his funding requests from charity and the implication of being unfit. "The call of our University upon its friends is not that of a weak institution, struggling for life and hoping to become something," but from "an institution of strong and vigorous growth, nearly two centuries old," Dwight wrote. By the same token, he maintained that scholarship funds, far from charity, do not "pauperize" a student.[16]

---

12. Further documentation and discussion can be found in Bruce A. Kimball, "Charity, Philanthropy, and Law School Fundraising: The Emergence and the Failure, 1880–1930," *Journal of Legal Education* 63 (2013): 248–52.

13. Josephine Shaw Lowell, *Public Relief and Private Charity* (New York, 1884), 89; Arthur Hobhouse, *The Dead Hand: Addresses on the Subject of Endowments and Settlements of Property* (London, 1880), 9, 194–215.

14. Lowell, *Public Relief and Private Charity*, 89; William G. Sumner, *What Social Classes Owe Each Other* (New York, 1883), 39, 157.

15. Lawrence, *Memories of a Happy Life*, 218, 345, 365. See Alan B. Cobban, *English University Life in the Middle Ages* (Columbus, OH, 1999), 28; Benjamin Soskis, "The Problem of Charity in Industrial America, 1873–1915" (PhD diss., Columba University, 2010).

16. Dwight, *Annual Report 1888–89*, 9; *1889–90*, 35.

Through the 1910s, donations to higher education sometimes still carried the "stigma" of "charity," as the *New York Times* observed. In 1909, the Yale treasurer happily reported that the university did not need to beg or borrow "any money to tide it over a temporary embarrassment." A few years later, the secretary of Yale warned that "constant personal begging on the part of a university is apt to be undignified."[17]

Meanwhile, during the Progressive Era (1890–1920), the rising authority of natural science, the increasing influence of "businesslike" thinking, and the drive for systematic, administrative organization contributed to establishing an alternate conception of benefaction that historians have named "philanthropy."[18] Rather than addressing the symptoms of social dysfunction, as did charity, philanthropy aimed to address their causes. Accordingly, the philanthropic understanding of financial donations eschewed the personal, emotional impulse of charity and sought a "scientific" assessment of need, relying on biological, sociological, psychological, and economic research. Philanthropists thus consulted professional expertise and established intermediary institutions, such as endowed foundations that followed rational policy.[19]

"The much-heralded shift from charity to philanthropy" commenced early in the 1800s and culminated in the early twentieth century.[20] The transition is evident in the widely influential decision of *Jackson v. Phillips* (1867), regarding trusts created by charitable bequests, in which the Massachusetts Supreme Judicial Court incorporated both concepts into the definition of "charity." The court wrote that "charity" benefitted "persons either by bringing their minds or hearts under the influence of education or religion, by relieving their bodies from disease, suffering or constraint, . . . or by erecting or maintaining public buildings or works or otherwise lessening the burden of government." The latter, inchoate concept of philanthropy implied establishing institutions to help those in need on a larger, systematic, impersonal scale.[21]

17. George Gordon, "A Free University," *New York Times,* July 26, 1912; George P. Day, *Annual Report of the Treasurer of Yale University 1908–9,* 11; Anson Phelps Stokes Jr., *Annual Report of the Secretary of Yale University 1912–13,* 45.

18. Robert A. Gross, "Giving in America: From Charity to Philanthropy," in *Charity, Philanthropy, and Civility in American History,* ed. Lawrence J. Friedman and Mark D. McGarvie (Cambridge, 2003), 29–48.

19. Judith Sealander, "Curing Evils at Their Source: The Arrival of Scientific Giving," in *Charity, Philanthropy, and Civility in American History,* ed. Lawrence J. Friedman and Mark D. McGarvie (Cambridge, 2003), 218.

20. Quotation is from Zunz, *Philanthropy in America,* 10.

21. Jackson v. Phillips, 96 Mass. 539, 556 (1867).

Over the next four decades, the distinction between the two concepts and terms became explicit, and by 1910 observers noted the transition in the prevailing ideology of benefaction in the United States. By that point, retiring wealthy industrialists were establishing endowed foundations that adopted the philanthropic approach to social betterment. Usage of the stigmatizing term "charity" therefore declined in public discussion.[22]

Commensurate with the influence of business mores and the Progressive drive for order, system, and organization, the new philanthropic rationale also emphasized effectiveness, efficiency, and economy. Financial benefactions were considered investments that had to realize a tangible return at the lowest cost, as in business. In John D. Rockefeller's famous phrase, philanthropy was "the business of benevolence."[23]

This philanthropic conception strongly influenced the organization and operation of HEF, as did the lessons of the earlier Smith and Wellesley campaigns. Adopting a "businesslike scale," the leaders created "a permanent salaried organization." In October 1916, Lamont hired as HEF secretary Robert F. Duncan, a young Harvard alumnus and newspaper reporter. Over the next six months, Duncan opened offices in Cambridge and New York City, while the paid staff grew to 20 and HEF bookkeepers set up accounts.[24] Likewise, the Yale Alumni Fund (YAF) opened an office, hired a salaried secretary, and publicized its work throughout the year. "The results have been most satisfactory," stated the YAF annual report, after the number of contributors jumped from nearly 4,500 in 1916 to about 6,300 in 1917.[25]

Harnessing "Miscellaneous Begging," Alumni Affairs, and Mass Campaigns

Implied also by philanthropic thinking, HEF effected two critical changes in Harvard's administration that virtually all other schools in the United States eventually adopted. First, the university took control of the fundraising efforts of its departments and divisions. Second, HEF revolutionized the governance of alumni affairs by assimilating, centralizing, and asserting authority over the independent associations, publications, and fundraising projects of alumni.

22. Carl Joslyn, "What Can a Man Afford?," *American Economic Review* 11 (December 1921): 118; Homer Folks, "Philanthropy, Educational Aspects of Modern," in *A Cyclopedia of Education*, ed. Paul Monroe (New York, 1913), 4:671–74.
23. John D. Rockefeller, *Random Reminiscences of Men and Events* (New York, 1909), 184.
24. Quotations are from Lamont, "Ten Million Dollars for Harvard," 285; Lamont to Lowell, March 21, 1917.
25. Yale Alumni University Fund, *27th Annual Report* (New Haven, 1917), 4.

In the late nineteenth century, President Eliot had encouraged the university's departments and divisions to seek funds for themselves and initiate fundraising appeals on their own. But, early in the twentieth century, he realized that the uncoordinated, competitive solicitations were "creating a conflict of benevolences." In the 1910s, university officials concluded that this "miscellaneous begging" was getting worse.[26]

Although the Corporation tried "to coordinate the begging for different University objects," the lack of effective oversight persisted through 1916, and HEF organizers soon recognized that the uncoordinated, competitive appeals would undermine their drive. After repeated pleas, Lamont was assured by President Lowell that he would prevent any fundraising by other university units during the campaign, and the Corporation then formally adopted this "keep off the grass" policy.[27] The HEF idea of soliciting all alumni in a single, comprehensive campaign for the benefit of the entire university thus prompted Harvard's administration to establish control over fundraising by schools and departments, and the Corporation never relinquished that authority subsequently.

Harnessing the five primary alumni entities—two alumni publications and three different alumni groups—proved more difficult. Today, colleges and universities have usually domesticated such entities, which are required to collaborate for the overall benefit of the institution. But in the 1910s, at Harvard and elsewhere, these entities operated independently, closely guarding their autonomy and pursuing their self-interest. HEF leaders needed their help in order to communicate with the university's 36,000 alumni and enlist some 3,000 volunteers to canvass them.

Like alumni associations emerging at other universities across the country, the Harvard Alumni Association was organized by the graduation classes and controlled the university's most direct pipeline to the purses of alumni. But more active and influential was the Associated Harvard Clubs, which were organized geographically by the locale in which alumni lived, as well as the Association of Class Secretaries, which kept the critical lists of alumni who had donated previously to the university. These three organizations assumed that they would handle the HEF gifts and receive a cut, as had been customary in past solicitations that employed their networks. They cited the example of the Princeton Alumni Association, which maintained "that the graduates . . . furnish the money" and

---

26. Quotations are from Eliot, *Annual Report 1906–7*, 52; Roger Pierce to Frederick W. Burlingham, April 16, 1918, HEF Records.

27. Quotations are from A. Lawrence Lowell to Ezra R. Thayer, November 16, 1914, Lowell Records; Thomas N. Perkins to Eliot Wadsworth, May 10 and 18, 1920, HEF Records.

deserve "some responsibility in its disposition."[28] When told that the HEF receipts would go directly to the Corporation, these three groups not only refused to cooperate but also threatened to run their own competing endowment campaigns.

Equally resistant were the two independent alumni publications, the *Harvard Graduates' Magazine* and *Harvard Alumni Bulletin*, which had the only mailing lists of all the alumni. Torturous negotiations with all five entities dragged on, and Lamont became totally exasperated with their self-interest and with the failure of President Lowell and the Corporation to intercede, even though they stood to benefit and claimed to support HEF. Finally, after two frustrating years, agreements to cooperate were reached in spring 1918.

This highly significant outcome effected a new governance model of Harvard's alumni entities that proliferated subsequently throughout higher education. In Lamont's words, the alumni associations "will all be closely linked together and work harmoniously along intelligent lines" within the university and under its authority. By the same token, "a complete rearrangement of our permanent scheme of publicity" at the university resulted. When the university officially established an annual alumni fund in the early 1920s, no such negotiations were necessary. The Harvard alumni had forever ceded to the administration control over funds that they raised for the university's benefit.[29] Indeed, the fundamental purpose of alumni entities had shifted toward raising money for the university.

Meanwhile, in 1916, the HEF Committee officially elected Lamont to serve as chairman, and he balanced the dominance of "cold, fishy, bloodless Boston" by adding members from New York, Philadelphia, Chicago, and St. Louis to a new executive committee.[30] Over the next three years, these individuals participated in "people's philanthropy" associated with the war effort and selectively harnessed tactics from those mass campaigns.

In order to get a "running start," for example, they systematically compiled lists of prospects, evaluated them for giving potential and interest, and quietly obtained a number of large pledges in advance. The tactic backfired on Lamont, however, when he approached his boss, J. Pierpoint Morgan Jr. Hoping to secure a big donation, Lamont cagily asked Morgan to pledge "twice as much

28. Quotation is from Frederick W. Burlingham to Robert F. Duncan, February 12, 1918, HEF Records. See letters to and from Thomas W. Lamont, May 1915–April 1918.

29. Quotations are from Thomas W. Lamont to Edgar H. Wells, January 20, 1919; E. M. Grossman to John Price Jones, July 26, 1919, HEF Records. See Harvard Alumni Association Board of Directors, "Resolution," October 20, 1924, Lowell Records.

30. Quotation is from Edgar H. Wells to Eliot Wadsworth, June 7, 1919, HEF Records. See Robert F. Duncan, Secretary's Notebook, May 6 and November 24, 1916, HEF Records.

as . . . I myself might give." Morgan "replied, with a twinkle in his eye, that he would promise to do this if I would promise to give half whatever he might give," recalled Lamont. Morgan "named $100,000 as his gift, and I was in for $50,000," which was "considerably more" than Lamont had intended to give.[31]

In January 1917, the HEF Committee officially kicked off the campaign with a goal of $10 million—about a third of Harvard's total endowment at the time. But war loomed ominously in spring 1917, and HEF reluctantly agreed to postpone its drive in deference to public fundraising campaigns for Liberty Loans, the Red Cross, and disaster relief related to the war, as illustrated in figure 4.2. Duncan closed the office and went to assist HEF leader Eliot Wadsworth, who was directing the American Red Cross in Washington, DC, and eventually became assistant secretary of the US Treasury.[32]

When the war ended on November 11, 1918, Lamont immediately wrote to the HEF Committee to revive the drive. He projected that it could be completed within two months, since the mass fundraising campaigns by relief agencies had educated Americans "during the war to giving on a large scale." In January 1919, however, Lamont was called to Europe to work on the American Commission to Negotiate Peace, so Wadsworth left the Red Cross to become HEF chairman.[33] Joining Wadsworth on the executive committee were Duncan and Edgar H. Wells from the Red Cross staff, as well as Guy Emerson, who had worked on the mammoth Liberty Loan campaign, and his assistant, John Price Jones, a forty-year-old Harvard alumnus.[34]

These men drew extensively from their experience in the largest fundraising campaigns, disaster relief efforts, and European reconstruction projects, as the press observed. Wadsworth organized a corporate management structure for the campaign and wrote an eighty-page campaign guidebook for the volunteers.[35] "Every Harvard Man Is Expected to Give," marveled the *New York Times*, and so was every woman, including widows, wives, mothers, and Radcliffe alumnae. Extending its reach to the ends of the earth, HEF divided the entire world into 70 zones, each with a management team, and held "Old Grads Summer School" training session for the 70 divisional chairmen.[36] The scope of the organization

31. Thomas W. Lamont to Daniel Kelleher, January 31, 1917.
32. "Call for Harvard. After Fund of $10,000,000," *Boston Globe*, January 11, 1917; "New Harvard Fund Reaches $1,187,160," *New York Times*, July 8, 1917.
33. Thomas W. Lamont to Harvard Endowment Fund Committee, November 15 and December 30, 1918.
34. Duncan, Secretary's Notebook, September 30, 1919.
35. Eliot Wadsworth, "Campaign Book of the Harvard Endowment Fund Committee" (typescript), June 1919, HEF Records.
36. "Every Harvard Man Is Expected to Give," *New York Times*, August 11, 1919; "Society and Entertainment: Woman's Committee of Harvard Fund to Meet," *Chicago Daily*

Figure 4.2. Poster for Red Cross Appeal, 1918. Courtesy of National WWI Museum and Memorial.

was unprecedented in higher education and magnified the risk of embarrassing Harvard if HEF failed.

Borrowing publicity techniques from the mass campaigns, HEF in 1919 opened its Publicity Department, comprising the Press Bureau, the Advertising Bureau, and the Speakers Bureau. John Price Jones, who equated fundraising with publicity, secured widespread coverage in newspapers and magazines throughout the country. In September 1919, newspapers ran over 4,000 columns of news on HEF, and an interview with President Lowell appeared in 55 newspapers nationwide. Lamont was "delighted and amazed."[37]

How Much to Raise?

HEF also innovated the financial terms of giving, in line with its "businesslike" approach. In order to encourage large gifts, HEF allowed pledges to be paid in installments over five years, and HEF leaders made separate contributions to cover the campaign expenses in order to assure prospective donors that their gift would go entirely to the university.[38] In addition, HEF leaders responded to the new taxing of individuals' incomes and estates that Congress enacted following the ratification of the Sixteenth Amendment to the Constitution in 1913.

HEF officials worried that the new taxes would discourage giving in the short run and deplete the sources of philanthropic gifts in the long run by preventing the accumulation of large fortunes. To address that concern, Senator Henry F. Hollis of New Hampshire, who had graduated from Harvard in 1892, introduced a bill in 1917 that gave a tax deduction for charitable contributions. HEF sent a letter, signed by Lamont, Eliot, Lowell, Bishop Lawrence, and the Harvard treasurer, to more than a thousand Harvard alumni supporting the legislation. After the bill was passed, one of the first Harvard graduates and HEF contributors to take advantage of the deduction was Robert T. Lincoln, son of deceased president Abraham Lincoln.[39]

In 1920, Hollis added an amendment to the federal revenue act seeking to increase the value of the deduction, and HEF leaders, joined by representatives of the Princeton and Cornell campaigns, lobbied congressional leaders and government

---

Tribune, October 4, 1919, 21; "Harvard Old Grads Go Back to School," *New York Times*, July 27, 1919.

37. Quotation is from Frank Hoffman to John Price Jones, August 4, 1919, Lamont Correspondence.

38. *Ten Millions for Harvard . . . Reprinted from the Harvard Alumni Bulletin, June 26, 1919* (Cambridge, MA, 1919).

39. Robert T. Lincoln to John W. Prentiss, December 7, 1917, Lamont Correspondence; Henry A. Yeomans, *Abbott Lawrence Lowell 1856–1943* (Cambridge, MA, 1948), 243; Seymour E. Harris, *Economics of Harvard* (New York, 1970), 348.

officials to support the bill. After it passed, HEF published a series of pamphlets explaining the deductions to Harvard alumni.[40] In the end, Harvard officials believed that the impacts of the new taxes and the charitable deduction canceled each other out and did not change contributions to HEF.[41] Impetus for the charitable deduction thus came from higher education, and the deduction certainly contributed to the growth of revenue and wealth of higher education over the next century.

The new "businesslike" model also required a careful analysis of Harvard's finances to justify the breathtaking goal of $10 million and to rebut the popular view "that Harvard is a rich institution which has only to ask for money in order to obtain it in limitless amounts," as President Lowell wrote. In 1916, HEF leaders therefore started proclaiming "the dire need of the University" and declared that HEF would merely "free Harvard from the financial anxiety."[42] Leading universities had previously considered such a cry of poverty as a shameful stigma. But Eliot had taught that need was good and dire need was better.

In order to explain the financial crisis, HEF leaders planned to present a cost analysis "to show clearly to the most practical business man that Harvard needs these additional funds," in Lamont's words. The analysis would demonstrate that Harvard was spending for "reasonable needs," incurred annual deficits due to its inadequate income, and then covered the deficits by expending capital funds and annual gifts.[43] The only solution was to increase revenue. Because tuition had already been raised by one-third in 1913, the students had done their part. Consequently, "the whole sum so greatly needed by the University" had to be raised through a public campaign.[44]

However, this novel commitment to provide a transparent cost analysis did not square with the announced purpose of building Harvard's "unrestricted endowment," which is "the primary need of Harvard" that is "always infinite."[45] To justify this separate aim, HEF leaders invoked President Eliot, prominently

40. Thomas N. Perkins to Eliot Wadsworth, May 3, 1920, HEF Records; Thomas W. Lamont to Joseph W. Fordnay and Boies Penrose, February 17, 1920, Lamont Correspondence; *H.E.F. Bulletin No. 9*, March 1919, and *H.E.F. Bulletin No. 18*, March 1920, HEF Records.

41. R. Keith Kane and Dana Doten, "The Case for Endowment," *Harvard Alumni Bulletin* 12 (November 24, 1951): 214–15.

42. Quotations are from Lowell, *Annual Report 1909–10*, 22–23; Robert F. Duncan to Thomas W. Lamont, November 29, 1916; Thomas W. Lamont to A. Lawrence Lowell, June 7, 1917, Lowell Records.

43. Quotations are from Lamont to Lowell, December 24, 1918; Thomas W. Lamont, "Harvard's New Endowment" (typescript), ca. February 1917, HEF Records, 2–3.

44. Thomas N. Perkins to [form letter to alumni], December 11, 1920, HEF Records. See "Why Harvard Needs Money," *Harvard Alumni Bulletin*, January 18, 1917, 306.

45. [Eliot Wadsworth,] *Harvard and the Future* (Cambridge, MA, 1919), 7, 23; Frank W. Hunnewell to Edgar H. Wells, April 10, 1919, HEF Records.

quoting his words that "the University needs free money." President Lowell, who had earned two Harvard degrees under Eliot, concurred. Hence, HEF leaders never tired of reiterating, "What Harvard as a whole needs most is an unrestricted endowment, and that is the main object."[46]

This innovative plea for free money was all the more remarkable because unrestricted endowment had usually come from wealthy donors, often as bequests. Yet, at the outset in summer 1915, HEF leaders intended "to provide the University with a permanent, unrestricted income, based on . . . gifts, no matter how small, from every Harvard man." Consequently, this call for mass giving of free money extended even further the privilege and status of major donors that "democratic" YAF had previously conferred on alumni giving small, annual amounts.[47]

Nevertheless, business-minded donors would balk at a campaign for an "infinite" goal, so HEF still required a cost analysis to demonstrate the necessity of the campaign's goal. HEF therefore focused on the need to increase faculty salaries, which had not been raised since 1905 and had lost about 44 percent of their purchasing power by 1917 owing to inflation. Here was a justification that the campaigns of Smith College and Wellesley College had shown to be compelling, as Lamont and Bishop Lawrence knew well. Indeed, the university treasurer in 1917 stated to HEF leaders that the university's costs "would not make as strong a case . . . as hammering on the salary argument alone."[48]

Inflation continued to rise during the war, further strengthening the argument. By mid-1919, HEF leaders concluded that "the need of raising [faculty] salaries is the one thing of overshadowing importance," and this need "requires very little investigation or argument."[49] HEF literature and the public press therefore began to proclaim "raising teachers' salaries" as the primary purpose of the campaign even before it was suspended in June 1917. The drumbeat resumed in 1919, and the labor movement gave its "whole-souled endorsement" to the HEF drive for faculty raises, reported the *New York Times*. Harvard's financial "crisis" thus became low faculty salaries—"an invisible moral deficit of $600,000 dollars, met by the self-sacrifice of a loyal, underpaid teaching staff," wrote Wadsworth.[50]

46. Quotations are from Charles W. Eliot, *To All Harvard Men . . . (August 23, 1919)* (printed broadside), HEF Records; Thomas W. Lamont to Carroll Dunham, March 26, 1917.

47. Quotation is from Lamont to Lowell, June 7, 1917. See George P. Day to Alfred P. Ripley, January 24, 1919, Yale Secretary Records.

48. Robert F. Duncan to Thomas W. Lamont, December 16, 1916.

49. Jerome D. Greene to A. Lawrence Lowell and Eliot Wadsworth, August 22, 1919, HEF Records.

50. Quotations are from "Would Pay Teachers More," *New York Times*, September 8, 1919; [Wadsworth,] *Harvard and the Future*, 4. See *Harvard Salaries and the Cost of Living* (March 1917), HEF Records; "The Harvard Endowment Fund," *Outlook*, October 29, 1919, 232–33.

But the amount of $600,000 was contrived. Rather than determining the desired salary scale and computing the amount needed to fund that, HEF leaders in 1919 did some reverse calculating. After estimating that they could raise $12 million in endowment, they assumed a 5 percent return on that principal and declared $600,000 to be the shortfall in faculty salaries. Not only contrived, this reverse calculation combined two inconsistent aims: the endowment raised was to be unrestricted but also designated for faculty salaries. To resolve the inconsistency, HEF leaders equivocated. "Although the income from the Endowment Fund is to be put at the unrestricted disposal of the Corporation, they are . . . bound to use a large part of it to increase teachers' salaries," stated Lamont and others.[51]

Still another problem was that some units of Harvard challenged the priority placed on free money for the whole university. Despite Lowell's promised embargo on "miscellaneous begging," a number of Harvard departments refused to relinquish what they considered their right to solicit anyone at any time for their own restricted purposes. With Lowell unwilling to intervene, HEF had to acquiesce to independent appeals made by several departments and schools. To console themselves, the HEF Committee decided to allow certain restricted gifts to count toward the campaign total. Though fearing that such restricted purposes would draw away unrestricted gifts, they worried more that any potential donations would be lost altogether. "Let no guilty man escape!" they repeated, quoting Bishop Lawrence.[52] By summer 1919, HEF reluctantly agreed to accommodate restricted gifts to various departments of the university.

Meanwhile, the campaign goal increased as the enthusiasm, wish list, and wartime inflation grew. Before World War I, HEF publicized a target of $10 million. Right afterward, the campaign announced a new goal of $11 million, then $12 million, and a month later, $12.5 million in "urgent needs" and $5 million in "other important needs," as departments competed for inclusion and priority in the campaign. By fall 1919, the grand total had risen astronomically to $45 million, more than Harvard's entire endowment at the time. Prudently, HEF settled on a goal of $15.25 million.[53]

In fact, the goal was really determined by how much HEF leaders thought they could raise. Even while calling for a cost justification and for raising faculty salaries, Lamont identified the original goal of $10 million based on a hunch that

51. Thomas W. Lamont to William C. Sanger, April 12, 1917.
52. Quotation is from Thomas W. Lamont to Richard M. Saltonstall, January 30, 1917.
53. Quotations are from Wadsworth, "Campaign Book," 2–5; [Wadsworth,] *Harvard and the Future*, 9–24. See "Harvard Fund $15,250,000. Committee Announces Increase in Amount Sought in Drive," *New York Times*, September 18, 1919.

the amount was an ambitious, likely feasible, and attractively round number. When later asked to identify the needs that justified the campaign goal, President Lowell observed privately "that the needs for the University for additional funds are always infinite, and the sum was really fixed by the amount which Mr. Lamont thought he could raise." For his part, Lowell "could adjust the needs" of the university to justify that amount.[54]

The Whirlwind and a New Profession, 1919

While adopting certain tactics of "popular" philanthropy, HEF leaders resisted what they considered "undignified" techniques, such as citing time pressure, manipulating information, or appealing to impulse or sympathy. The Harvard campaign must be "different from that of a Liberty Loan, Red Cross, or any other 'popular' drive," wrote Wadsworth in the campaign guidebook. "We must aim to develop enthusiasm without rough-and-tumble methods and through refined means."[55] Nevertheless, some HEF leaders began to argue that "we must be eminently practical, and, even distasteful as it may be, turn sentiment to practical uses."[56] This pragmatism intensified soon after the war ended in November 1918.

In the early months of 1919, HEF staff who had been involved in mass fundraising called for ending the drive in a "whirlwind" week. This "unrefined" approach entailed a brief time frame, extensive publicity, dire warnings, and high pressure with progress measured by a graphic clock or thermometer. After some debate, the executive committee authorized a whirlwind week beginning on October 1, 1919.[57] HEF staff feverishly prepared during the two months following the Old Grads Summer School in July 1919. Harvard representatives ventured westward through Kansas, the Dakotas, Wyoming, Utah, and Oregon to promote HEF.[58] During the whirlwind week, the *Washington Post*, *Chicago Tribune*, and *New York Times*, among other major papers, reported the progress.[59] The nation was fascinated by the "democratic" drive of aristocratic Harvard.

54. Hunnewell to Wells, April 10, 1919.
55. Wadsworth, "Campaign Book," 15.
56. Robert F. Duncan to Thomas W. Lamont, January 14, 1919; Lamont to Lowell, December 24, 1918.
57. Edgar H. Wells to Thomas W. Lamont, June 21, 1919.
58. "Harvard Endowment Fund Committee," *Oregonian*, August 18, 1919; "Pocatello Men to Aid Harvard's Fund," *Salt Lake Telegram*, August 22, 1919; "Two Idaho Men Work for Endowment Fund," *Idaho Daily Statesman*, August 23, 1919; "A Greater Chance Than Ever Before in History," *Wyoming State Tribune*, September 8, 1919; "For Endowment Fund," *Grand Forks Herald*, September 14, 1919; "Economic Expert Speaks Here," *Kansas City Times*, September 20, 1919.
59. "Harvard Drives for 15 million," *Washington Post*, October 1, 1919; "Harvard Endowment Fund Reaches $1,904,545," *Chicago Tribune*, October 3, 1919; "$1,745,000 for Harvard," *New York Times*, October 2, 1919.

At the end of the whirlwind week, however, the total pledged reached merely 40 percent of the goal, and the deadline passed without comment. In mid-October the drive still had far to go, and the normally irrepressible Lamont lamented, "I am pretty nearly down with nervous prostration," while Wadsworth conceded to President Lowell, "The campaign is going very slowly."[60] At the end of October, the *Chicago Tribune* reported that the drive had attained but half its goal, and the pace was slowing. In mid-November 1919, the total inched up to 65 percent of the goal. Solicitation in the 70 zones officially ended, and the GEB declined to give more than its conditional grant of $500,000 for Harvard's new school of education, which did not count toward the HEF total. "The Harvard Endowment Fund is dragging seriously," admitted HEF leaders.[61]

Just at that point, Jones, Duncan, and four other staffers left to incorporate a consulting firm devoted to fundraising in higher education. Their move originated in September 1919 when graduates of other colleges contacted HEF asking for help to start a campaign for their alma maters. HEF secretary Duncan reported this correspondence to Jones, who started crafting plans to establish a consulting business.[62]

Having worked at HEF for merely seven months, Jones began writing to alumni groups of other private colleges and universities stoking interest in conducting similar fundraising campaigns. One of his letters went to the head of a Brown University alumni group, who also happened to have graduated from Harvard. He wrote back to Jones, asking why "a Harvard man soliciting a subscription to Harvard's endowment should send such a request to an organization of alumni of another college."[63]

Notwithstanding the questionable ethics, Lamont and Emerson, confident in late September 1919 that HEF would soon end successfully, gave their blessing to Jones and Duncan to leave and form their own consulting firm. But when the time came for them to depart in mid-November 1919, HEF was clearly strug-

60. Thomas W. Lamont to Hugh M. Langdon, October 11, 1919; Eliot Wadsworth to A. Lawrence Lowell, October 20, 1919, Lowell Records.

61. Thomas N. Perkins to Frank P. Sears, November 26, 1919, HEF Records. See "Harvard Endowment Fund Passes Half-Way Mark," *Chicago Tribune*, October 27, 1919; "Harvard Endowment Fund $9,601,560," *New York Times*, November 14, 1919.

62. [Robert F. Duncan,] "A New Force in American Society, Fifty Years of Dynamic Philanthropy, 1919–1969" (typescript), October 9, 1969, JPJ Records, 1–25; Scott M. Cutlip, *Fund Raising in the United States: Its Role in America's Philanthropy* (New Brunswick, NJ, 1965), 175.

63. D. W. Abercrombie to John Price Jones, September 24, 1919, HEF Records.

gling. Nevertheless, the two entrepreneurs recruited four other HEF staff members and left to start the John Price Jones Co. in New York City.[64]

The stated mission of the new consulting company was "planning and organizing and conducting publicity campaigns," because Jones believed that publicity was the core of fundraising. The firm was subsequently considered the most prominent and successful consulting agency on higher education fundraising through 1955, when Jones retired. By that point, all his younger HEF associates had left the firm because Jones never accorded them due recognition or compensation for their efforts over a quarter of a century.[65]

Paradoxes of Success, 1920–25

The HEF campaign limped into December 1919 without acknowledging prior deadlines or identifying new ones. HEF leaders began asking those who had already pledged to increase their subscription. But that orchard yielded no more fruit, and the HEF Committee tried other approaches as the campaign passed $10 million in mid-December. Lamont wrote to the Carnegie Corporation requesting a gift and was immediately rebuffed.[66] Responding to Wadsworth's request to motivate "the slackers," the Harvard Corporation raised faculty salaries by 20 percent on January 1, 1920, and then another 20 percent two months later, moves that were carefully publicized.[67]

On March 1, 1920, HEF reached 79 percent of its goal, as Wells began soliciting graduate and undergraduate students at Harvard College. In the following months, he reviewed the list of noncontributing alumni and began writing to them. No one would escape. At commencement in 1920 Wadsworth spoke to the gathered alumni and observed that over $12 million had been pledged by 17,608 subscribers, including 16,337 alumni. "It is a splendid record but . . . leaves much to be desired," he exhorted, while also pointedly reminding his Harvard audience of "the magnificent bequests of Mr. Frick [to Princeton], Mr. Sterling [to Yale], and Mr. DeLamar [to Columbia and Johns Hopkins]."[68]

64. John Price Jones to and from Thomas W. Lamont, September 20 and 22 and October 6, 1919.

65. [Duncan,] "New Force in American Society," 1–5. See Cutlip, *Fund Raising*, 176.

66. Duncan, Secretary's Notebook, December 17, 1919; Thomas W. Lamont to and from Henry S. Pritchett, December 22 and 23, 1919.

67. Quotation is from Eliot Wadsworth to Thomas N. Perkins, December 4, 1919, HEF Records. See "Harvard Salaries Increased 20 Per Cent," *New York Times*, January 29, 1920; "Harvard Profs Get a 40 to 50% Salary Increase," *Chicago Tribune*, March 17, 1920.

68. "Mr. Wadsworth's Report on Commencement Day, June 24, 1920," HEF Records. In 1918, Joseph R. DeLamar, a wealthy miner who did not attend college, bequeathed about $10.6

In fall 1920, the original HEF Committee planned a final push to raise the remaining $3 million and reach the announced goal of $15.25 million. Lamont even invoked the prospect of Harvard going "bankrupt." Now the driving rationale was to avoid humiliation: "the prestige of the University and its alumni will undoubtedly suffer if we fail to reach the total." Worse still, HEF leaders feared "that we were going to see Harvard College take a licking in something that we have undertaken."[69] Harvard must not fail.

The final push would be "an intensive campaign" lasting four weeks in November 1920 and focused on those who had already donated. HEF leaders calculated that they needed 33 percent more from those who had already given, and their only chance was to convince enough previous donors to double their pledges. Wadsworth, Emerson, Wells, and a number of others threw themselves into the last-ditch effort, doubling their own pledges and soliciting others.[70]

In December 1920, it became clear that HEF would fall short because many major donors refused to double, including Lamont and Morgan. On December 30, the total reached $13 million. HEF closed its offices in New York and Boston, moved the headquarters to the Harvard campus, and hired a new secretary to oversee daily operations. Prompted by repeated suggestions over the previous four years, this relocation gave President Lowell the opportunity to put "all alumni activities together into one place . . . on some systematic basis," as Emerson observed.[71] Beyond harnessing alumni affairs, this step also redirected their purpose toward raising money.

Although the campaign had officially ended, no one wanted to admit defeat, and HEF leaders told former President Eliot that, rather than "announce that we have been beaten," they would let the campaign "drift along for times which are better than they are now." While steering clear of other Harvard efforts to raise money, the drive therefore continued to receive pledges and contributions and to nurse the belief "that by 1925 the total will equal $15 million." In January 1924, subscriptions reached 92 percent of the goal, almost $14 million. In

---

million to be split equally among Harvard, Columbia, and Johns Hopkins universities to support medical research.

69. Quotations are from Thomas W. Lamont to Peter G. Gerry, December 22, 1920; John W. Prentiss to Thomas W. Lamont, October 7, 1920; Thomas N. Perkins to Robert L. Gerry, December 8, 1920, HEF Records.

70. See "Records of Intensive Class Campaign," November 1920, HEF Records.

71. Guy Emerson to John B. Richardson, December 13, 1920, HEF Records. See Eliot Wadsworth to A. Lawrence Lowell, October 7, 1920, Lowell Records.

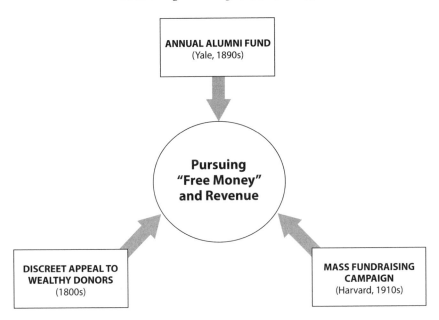

Figure 4.3. Fundraising Triad of Higher Education, 1870–1930.

June the Cambridge office closed, and the drive finally expired in 1925, 10 years after its conception.[72]

Nevertheless, Lowell had already declared the campaign a success, because it "saved the University from bankruptcy," and the president was repeatedly quoted to that effect. Subsequent scholars likewise maintained that the campaign met its goal, relying on the assessment of John Price Jones, who largely took credit for the campaign's achievement.[73] And the campaign did succeed in completing the fundraising triad that persisted in American higher education over the next century and is presented in figure 4.3.

Newspapers reported the shortfall, however, and HEF leaders felt keenly disappointed. Even the 92 percent in pledges must be discounted because 14 percent was either never collected or restricted to purposes apart from HEF aims. Fur-

72. Quotations are from Thomas N. Perkins to Charles W. Eliot, November 20, 1920, and John Price Jones to David M. Little, March 6, 1922, HEF Records. See "Lists, Reports, Statistics, etc., 1919–1925" (typescript), ca. June 1925, HEF Records.

73. Quotation is from Lamont to Gerry, December 22, 1920. See Eliot Wadsworth to [form letter], December 23, 1920, HEF Records; Lowell, *Annual Report 1919–20*, 5–6; Jones, *American Giver*, 14.

thermore, during the "intensive" campaign that raised the final million, HEF allowed subscribers to double the payment period to 10 years. This doubling therefore included amounts that would have come to Harvard anyway as future contributions, a fact that HEF leaders recognized and regretted. Extending the payment period demonstrated their desperation to make the goal. "It does not look as if we should succeed," stated Perkins at the end of the doubling campaign, "and of course I am sorry."[74]

Why did HEF—the fundraising prototype in higher education—fall short? The wartime interruption certainly detracted from the effort, as did the competition from other major drives, such as the Red Cross and Liberty Loan campaigns that raised nearly $18 billion between 1917 and 1922. The departure of Jones, Duncan, and other key staff just as HEF was foundering in November 1919 also took a toll. In 1920 and 1921, a sharp recession dampened giving, particularly during the final intensive campaign. A few alumni "slackers" objected to some of Lowell's policies, but none of these complaints significantly hampered the campaign.[75] The key reason for the shortfall was surely the president's dissembling and lack of cooperation, as explained in the following chapter.

74. Thomas N. Perkins to Alvah Crocker, December 9, 1920, HEF Records.
75. Thomas W. Lamont to and from A. Lawrence Lowell, January 20 and 21, 1920.

CHAPTER 5

Campaigns Proliferate though Presidents Resist, 1920s

Fundraising drives forged ahead at hundreds of colleges and universities during the 1920s, often prompted and led by alumni. It was "the philanthropic decade" and "a golden age" when "everyone thought philanthropy had reached its zenith," wrote John Price Jones, the leading fundraising consultant in higher education. And for Jones, "philanthropy" meant the mass campaigns that consultants began treating as standard practice in higher education.[1]

Nevertheless, many college and university presidents resisted such campaigns in the early twentieth century, and their resistance often slowed the financial development of their school, as fundraising drives multiplied across the nation. Yet such presidents did have one thing in common with John Price Jones: they failed to recognize in the 1920s the new fundraising triad that comprised the annual alumni fund, the mass campaign, and the traditional, discreet appeal to the wealthy. By 1930, these three complementary modes constituted the paradigm

1. Jones, *American Giver*, 15–16.

that hundreds of colleges and universities replicated thereafter in competing for revenue and wealth in order to support their growing expenses.

Presidents Resist "Begging"

Until the late 1910s, when the Yale Alumni Fund (YAF) and the Harvard Endowment Fund (HEF) transformed the fundraising norms in American higher education, many college and university presidents avoided fundraising altogether, regarding it as "begging" that indicated undignified concern for mundane matters or a shameful lack of self-reliance. Former Protestant clergymen often held this view, ranging from President William O. Thompson (1899–1925) at Ohio State University to President George B. Stewart (1899–1926) at Auburn Theological Seminary in New York.[2]

In particular, the stiff-necked Presbyterian presidents of Princeton prior to 1902 clung to their pastoral role and left money matters to the treasurer or trustees. Princeton president Woodrow Wilson (1902–10), a layman but staunch Presbyterian and academic visionary, likewise considered soliciting gifts to be demeaning.[3] Princeton therefore fell behind other wealthy universities in financial resources until entrepreneurial John G. Hibben (1912–32) became president, though he, too, was a Presbyterian clergyman.

At Yale, the Congregationalist clerical presidents in the late nineteenth century were more flexible and forthright in expressing financial needs publicly and privately. But they, too, refrained from personally soliciting gifts and relegated finances to the university secretary and treasurer. In 1899, political economist Arthur Hadley (1899–1921) became the first Yale president not drawn from the clergy, but he did not embrace the free-money strategy of his contemporary Harvard president Charles Eliot (1869–1909). Under Hadley, most gifts went to buildings and current operations, and Yale's endowment grew more slowly than its peers.[4]

Indeed, Yale alumni seemed to have a better grasp of the financial competition than President Hadley and began sounding the alarm in the *Yale Alumni Weekly*, while echoing Eliot's tenets and words. In 1910, one alumnus asserted

2. George B. Stewart to John Price Jones, August 3, 1920, JPJ Records; Benjamin A. Johnson, "Fundraising and Endowment Building at a Land Grant University during the Critical Period . . . 1910–1940" (PhD diss., The Ohio State University, 2013), 69–74.

3. Thomas J. Wertenbaker, *Princeton 1746–1896* (Princeton, NJ, 1946), 389–90; James Axtell, *The Making of Princeton University: From Woodrow Wilson to the Present* (Princeton, NJ, 2006), 24–25, 51.

4. George W. Pierson, *Yale College, An Educational History, 1871–1921* (New Haven, CT, 1952), 505–38; Brooks M. Kelley, *Yale: A History* (New Haven, CT, 1974), 333–56.

that Yale's financial constraints had "rendered competition with our rivals exceedingly difficult. Harvard and Columbia each ha[ve] more than double the endowment of Yale." Another alumnus wrote, "Yale needs money. . . . The solution lies in endowment. The University must face the problem."[5]

In 1919, resuming their effort after the war, HEF leaders tried to enlist both Hadley and Hibben to sign a joint, public letter with Harvard president A. Lawrence Lowell (1909–33) endorsing their fundraising initiative to raise faculty salaries by increasing the universities' endowment. From Princeton, which was already planning its own campaign, Hibben replied to Lowell, "I shall be very glad indeed to sign." But Hadley dismissed the idea and wrote haughtily to Lowell that the HEF draft was not "a letter which you or I would have written or anybody would think we had written." HEF leaders then dropped Hadley from their publicity plans, while retaining Hibben.[6]

The following year, the traditionalist Hadley expressed his disdain for publicly "begging" for money when he announced that Yale was seeking $5 million in endowment to raise faculty salaries. He pointedly sniffed that $3 million had already come anonymously from one donor and that Yale "ought to be able to obtain" the remaining $2 million "quietly, without the necessity of anything like a public 'drive.'" Hadley's sniping at the HEF campaign appeared in his annual report, leading one Yale alumnus to write to the university's treasurer, rather than the president, to ask how to help with Yale's appeal.[7]

After Hadley stepped down in 1921, President James R. Angell (1922–37) started planning a drive and contacted Harvard requesting information about HEF. Over the next three years, Yale planned and conducted its own "round-the-world" campaign to raise $20 million for endowment to boost faculty salaries. While employing the HEF model, Yale hired a newly established fundraising consulting firm, and the university successfully attracted pledges of over $21 million.[8]

Yale's good fortune was bolstered by a gift from John Sterling, which grew in value to $39 million during the 1920s, and also by a gift of $16 million from Edward S. Harkness in 1929. Altogether, Yale received the remarkable total of

---

5. Quotations are from "The President's Report for 1910," *Yale Alumni Weekly*, July 8, 1910, 1026; Frederick M. Leonard, "Yale Endowment," *Yale Alumni Weekly*, March 17, 1910, 636.

6. Quotations are from Arthur T. Hadley to A. Lawrence Lowell, September 24, 1919, and John G. Hibben to A. Lawrence Lowell, September 24, 1919, Lowell Records.

7. Hadley, *Annual Report 1919–20*, 18–19. See George P. Day to William A. Brown, February 26, 1919, Yale Secretary Records.

8. Frank W. Hunnewell to David M. Little, January 22, 1925, HEF Records; George W. Pierson, *Yale, the University College, 1921–1937* (New Haven, CT, 1955), 601.

$91 million in benefactions during the 1920s, an amount exceeding the total of $83 million that came to Harvard and, likely, the total that any other university received in that decade. But Yale spent a great deal of its windfall on beautiful buildings, and its endowment growth ($59 million) trailed Harvard's ($64 million) over the decade. Although presidential resistance to public fundraising finally subsided at Yale in the 1920s, its financial policy did not match Harvard's focus on building its "free money." Consequently, Yale's endowment fell further behind Harvard's even though it received almost 10 percent more gifts between 1920 and 1930.[9]

Meanwhile, neither Johns Hopkins nor Stanford embraced Eliot's strategy or pursued notable fundraising, and their endowments did not increase as fast as their peers through 1930. Johns Hopkins fell behind partly because it relied on endowment income for 70 percent of its revenue until at least 1920. Similarly, Stanford did not charge tuition and relied on endowment income for most of its revenue, so its financial capital plateaued even after 1905, when the university finally secured ownership of its endowment upon the death of Jane Stanford.[10]

President Lowell Dissembles

While President Lowell at Harvard did not explicitly resist the pioneering HEF, his failure to provide support and his disingenuous assertions that he would do so harmed the campaign significantly. Born in Boston in 1856, Lowell belonged to a Brahmin family, whose members included distinguished judges, congressmen, and literary figures, as well as founders of the textile industries who gave their names to the mill towns of Lowell and Lawrence in Massachusetts. After graduating from Harvard College in 1877 and Harvard Law School in 1880, Lowell, depicted in figure 5.1, practiced law in Massachusetts until 1897, when he joined the Harvard College faculty.[11]

During Lowell's presidency, immigrant textile workers in Lawrence famously protested in 1912 against the brutal and unhealthy conditions in the mills, which had been built by Lowell's ancestors, particularly his grandfather Abbott Lawrence, for whom he was named. The mill owners and Lawrence mayor called in mounted police and National Guardsmen with fixed bayonets to suppress the workers' protest. At Harvard, students who volunteered to join the ranks of the

9. See table 1.1; Jones, *American Giver*, 72–73.
10. Orrin L. Elliott, *Stanford University: The First Twenty-Five Years* (Stanford, CA, 1937), 36, 50–51, 104, 252–99, 326–78, 462–66; Edwin E. Slosson, "Universities, American Endowed," in *A Cyclopedia of Education*, ed. Paul Monroe (New York, 1911–13), 5:673; Geiger, *To Advance Knowledge*, 41–47.
11. Henry A. Yeomans, *Abbott Lawrence Lowell 1856–1943* (Cambridge, MA, 1948).

Figure 5.1. Harvard University President A. Lawrence Lowell, ca. 1909. Courtesy of Harvard University Archives.

police were excused from their midyear exams. "Carefully attuned to his times and his class, Lowell was bigoted, racist, and priggish," adjudged historian James Hershberg.[12]

President Lowell therefore faced a dilemma when HEF leaders began to make plans in 1915. On the one hand, he wanted the money, preferred unrestricted en-

---

12. James G. Hershberg, *James B. Conant: Harvard to Hiroshima and the Making of the Nuclear Age* (Stanford, CA, 1995), 57, 70.

dowment, and wished to encourage helpful alumni, particularly well-connected lawyers and financiers. Hence, he repeatedly told them, "I will do anything you desire to help promote the campaign for the Harvard Endowment Fund."[13] On the other hand, Lowell did not favor the "democratic" HEF campaign. He did not mention the drive in his annual reports prior to 1920. Nor did he refer to HEF in public speeches that he gave across the country explaining the need of higher education for "additional endowment," as in Kansas City in 1919.[14]

To negotiate his dilemma, Lowell voiced enthusiasm but gave help slowly or incompletely, and his enthusiasm soon seemed insincere. Initially, it did not occur to HEF leaders that the president could have any reservations about their drive, so they kept him closely informed and sought his advice and approval on every aspect of their plans.[15] But, to their growing dismay and frustration, HEF leaders gradually found that they could not rely on Lowell. Often he approved a request, but conditioned his approval on the agreement of other parties affected, and then left it to HEF to secure that agreement. He did not exercise any authority in support of HEF.

Lowell's equivocation on "miscellaneous begging" clearly demonstrated this behavior. Though assuring HEF chairman Thomas Lamont that he would restrain all fundraising by other departments of the university, the president soon backpedaled, acquiescing to "a certain amount of continuous begging, . . . in the usual way." Lamont had no choice but to accede regretfully.[16] By 1918, the HEF staff became disgusted at all the "schemes for raising money launched . . . by various departments of the University," even though "President Lowell told us that we were to have a clear field."[17]

Meanwhile, rather than telling departments to cease fundraising, Lowell began referring them to Lamont. But the HEF chairman knew that he had "no authority" to stop them and could merely request their cooperation. If departments refused, Lamont was forced to subsume the departmental appeals for restricted purposes into HEF. In one case, Lamont personally paid the economics department $5,000 to postpone its appeal for an endowment of $100,000, until

13. A. Lawrence Lowell to Edgar H. Wells, May 16, 1918, Lowell Records.
14. "Opening the Door to College. . . . A Plain Talk by A. Lawrence Lowell of Harvard," *Kansas City Times*, September 14, 1919.
15. John Price Jones to A. Lawrence Lowell, February 3, 1919, Lowell Records.
16. Quotations are from A. Lawrence Lowell to Thomas W. Lamont, September 26 and December 12, 1916, Lowell Records.
17. Robert F. Duncan to Thomas W. Lamont, March 27, 1917, and Frederick W. Burlingham to Robert F. Duncan, February 16, 1918, HEF Records.

HEF ended. Lowell considered this outcome thoroughly "satisfactory," while HEF leaders, especially Lamont, felt betrayed.[18] By the beginning of 1920 many departments were clamoring to raise money, and Lowell disingenuously asked the HEF executive committee whether his prohibition on other departments' fundraising could be lifted. They responded acidly that many "indiscriminate" appeals were already underway, detracting from the HEF effort.[19]

Even more frustrating was Lowell's reticence to provide personal statements or data supporting the campaign. When asked by the HEF Publicity Department to supply a few expressions of gratitude or affection for Harvard that had come to him from alumni, Lowell replied that he could not think of any. More significantly, the campaign asked Lowell to itemize the university's financial needs in order to develop the cost analysis to justify the campaign goal. Lowell agreed to do so but kept equivocating for nine months.[20]

Finally, in June 1919, Lamont, then in Europe, decided that he had had enough of Lowell's dissembling and conceived a risky plan to circumvent the president by appealing directly to the Corporation. But J. P. Morgan Jr. advised Lamont that his plan amounted to requesting "a vote of lack of confidence" in the president, who would "be antagonized by it."[21] Though Lamont shelved the plan, his disaffection may have reached Lowell, who finally produced an equivocal letter that HEF printed in the *Alumni Bulletin* and in a pamphlet sent to 36,000 alumni. Lowell thereafter became more cooperative, visiting Harvard Clubs in Cleveland, Detroit, Chicago, and New York City and personally soliciting a few individuals.[22]

Nevertheless, the president had undermined the campaign to enlarge the university's endowment. Largely due to Lowell, the financial rationale for the campaign was muddled; restricted purposes blurred the focus on unrestricted endowment, and miscellaneous begging distracted potential givers. Above all, Lowell had alienated Lamont, the driving force of HEF from the start, who never resumed an active leading role in the campaign after returning from Europe in

18. Quotations are from Thomas W. Lamont to H. S. Hunnewell, January 17, 1917, A. Lawrence Lowell to Robert F. Duncan, February 27, 1917, and Frederick W. Burlingham to Robert F. Duncan, February 20, 1918, HEF Records.

19. Edgar H. Wells to A. Lawrence Lowell, May 20, 1919, and March 29, 1920, Lowell Records.

20. Eliot Wadsworth to A. Lawrence Lowell, July 19, 1919, HEF Records.

21. Edgar H. Wells to Thomas W. Lamont, June 5, 1919, Lamont Correspondence.

22. A. Lawrence Lowell, "Urgent Needs of the University," June 20, 1919, and A. Lawrence Lowell, "To All Harvard Men" (electrotyped letter), September 15, 1919, HEF Records; Eliot Wadsworth to and from A. Lawrence Lowell, September 5 and 11, 1919, and John Price Jones to A. Lawrence Lowell, October 9, 1919, HEF Records.

June 1919. By October 1919, entering what would become the most challenging period of the campaign, HEF leaders no longer looked to Lowell for approval, guidance, or support as they had in 1917. Rather, he had become a drain on their time, energy, and goodwill.

"Putting the Institution in a Wrong Light"

Presidents resisted fundraising drives at other private and public colleges and universities, whose permanent funds then failed to keep pace with their peers. In some cases, the presidents' academic inclinations made them resist or disdain raising money. At Amherst College, for example, three successive academicians agreed to serve as president between 1912 and 1931 on the condition that they would not have to solicit gifts. In particular, President Alexander Meiklejohn (1912–23), a Progressive educator who feuded with educational conservatives at Amherst, refused to have anything to do with finances, including the college's centennial campaign in 1920. When alumni leaders asked him to write a supportive message to the alumni, Meiklejohn's draft letter seemed "insulting" to the campaign leaders, who discarded it, wrote their own "message from the president," and then printed and circulated it.[23] Nevertheless, the leadership vacuum cost the college, as the work fell entirely to alumni and trustees.

Amherst's weak fundraising during the 1920s held the college back in the competition for financial capital. Table 5.1 reveals that Amherst's endowment growth ranked near the bottom among the 13 institutions that stood in the second tier of endowments in both 1920 and 1930. Though relatively wealthy, Amherst lost ground among its peers during "the philanthropic decade."

Presidents of public universities had other reasons for refusing to support fundraising drives. Some felt it was unnecessary because they could rely on public subsidies for their needs. Responding to an overture from John Price Jones in 1920, University of Akron president Parke R. Kolbe (1913–25) wrote, "We, as a municipally supported institution, have neither need nor intention of entering upon any campaign for funds."[24]

Other presidents of midwestern and southern universities had previously served as superintendents of large school districts, and they likened funding the state university to financing a public school system. Hence, they feared that fundraising drives might weaken the legislature's willingness to subsidize their institutions. For example, George W. Rightmire became president of Ohio State

23. Stanley King, *A History of the Endowment of Amherst College* (Amherst, MA, 1950), 129, 137–41.
24. Parke R. Kolbe to John Price Jones, July 26, 1920, JPJ Records.

TABLE 5.1
Increases in Second-Tier Endowments of Colleges and Universities
between 1920 and 1930 (in percentages)

Rank of increase	Second-tier endowments in both 1920 and 1930	Increase from 1920 to 1930
1	University of Rochester	404%
2	Vanderbilt University	387%
3	Northwestern University	360%
4	Dartmouth College	249%
5	Brown University	213%
6	Wellesley College	197%
7	Western Reserve University	159%
8	*University of Minnesota**	*126%*
9	*University of California*	*108%*
10	Washington University, St. Louis	97%
11	University of Pennsylvania	93%
12	Amherst College*	81%
13	Carnegie Institute of Technology	68%

Source: Computed from data in table 1.2.
Note: Public institutions are italicized.
*Amherst College and the University of Minnesota are discussed in the text.

University (1925–38) after serving as superintendent of Columbus City Schools, and he believed that a fundraising campaign would depress support among voters for increasing the tax levy that subsidized the university.[25]

Still other university presidents had an aversion to public fundraising because they enjoyed socializing privately with the wealthy elite. By serving as the university's exclusive intermediary with the upper class, these presidents felt they could strengthen their executive authority and social status. This happened at Columbia University, where President Nicholas Butler (1902–45) repeatedly demeaned public drives like HEF, even though he wanted more money. In 1915, he announced that Columbia needed an astonishing $30 million; in 1926, an even more incredible $60 million.[26]

In 1919 and 1920, Butler reported that Columbia was increasing tuition rather than "begging the public to provide new funds," a direct jab at the contemporaneous HEF. Three years later, as scores of colleges and universities were starting

25. Johnson, "Fundraising and Endowment Building," 144–250.
26. Nicholas M. Butler, *Annual Report of the President of Columbia University 1915–16*, 1–2, 10; *1919–20*, 2; *1925–26*, 41–44; "New Harvard Fund Reaches $1,187,160," *New York Times*, July 8, 1917.

fundraising drives, Butler wrote that appealing to "the mercy and pity of the public in the hope of obtaining relief [from expenses] . . . may be called the sentimental method of university administration" and "puts the institution in a wrong light before both itself and the public."[27] Instead, Butler preferred to solicit donations from wealthy New Yorkers at private luncheons, reinforcing his standing and authority at Columbia.

Subsequently, Butler continued to resist the HEF fundraising mode. In 1927, Columbia finally commissioned a study of how to organize a drive to raise funds for endowment, but Butler and the trustees then voted that such a campaign was "not expedient." Butler thus persisted in rebuffing public fundraising even longer than the presidents at Princeton or Yale, and Columbia's major gifts continued to come primarily from wealthy New Yorkers not associated with the university. Finally, in 1928, Butler recognized that Columbia needed to build its endowment and solicit funds more broadly.[28] By that point, however, the large foundations were no longer giving money for university endowments. The stock market crash in 1929 then ended the "Lush Twenties" of higher education fundraising, leaving Columbia still sitting on the sidelines.[29]

As the United States entered the Great Depression, Columbia was drawing 30 percent of its total revenue from the rent of one eleven-acre parcel in Manhattan. This arrangement proved imprudent, particularly after the university's income from its productive real estate declined during the 1930s and 1940s due to unfavorable leases. Butler's resistance to the HEF model and to Eliot's free-money strategy therefore contributed to the failure of Columbia's endowment to keep pace with those of its peers through 1945. The university avoided a crisis during the Depression and World War II but never led the pack again. Only in the 1950s, after Butler retired, did the Columbia trustees approve fundraising campaigns that deans of the university's professional schools had long requested.[30]

Southeastern colleges and universities also missed the fundraising wave of the 1920s. The Civil War had destroyed many of their buildings, drained their relatively small endowments, and scattered their faculty and students. After 1870, both public and private institutions in the southeast resumed their antebellum focus on undergraduate "Christian liberal arts" and lagged far behind the re-

27. Butler, *Annual Report 1919–20*, 4; *1922–23*, 20.
28. Quotation is from Robert A. McCaughey, *Stand, Columbia: A History of Columbia University in the City of New York, 1754–2004* (New York, 2003), 309. See Horace Coon, *Columbia: Colossus on the Hudson* (New York, 1947), 29, 108–9, 280–84.
29. Jones, *American Giver*, 15.
30. Bruce A. Kimball, Jeremy B. Luke, and Jamie M. Brown, "The Formative Financial Era of 'the Major Professional Schools,'" in Adam and Bayram, *Economics of Higher Education*, 133–36.

search, secularization, and technical studies emerging elsewhere in higher education, all of which attracted philanthropy. In 1904, the prestigious Association of American Universities admitted only one southern university, Virginia, and that largely as a courtesy. Few southern students ventured farther north than Johns Hopkins to study for a PhD, and only the most ambitious southern sons went as far north as Princeton for an elite BA.[31] And neither of those two institutions imparted progressive fundraising norms to their alumni. Most of the relatively few southeastern schools in tables 1.1 and 1.2 acquired their endowment through a major benefactor, including Tulane, Vanderbilt, Duke, and Rice.

"The Minimum of Feathers with the Maximum of Squawking"

President Lowell had misgivings about Harvard's public fundraising drives, as discussed above. When Cornell University president Jacob G. Schurman (1892–1920) wrote to him in 1917 inquiring about HEF, Lowell responded curtly and coldly. When a trustee of Mills College requested information in 1919, Lowell did not reply and had his secretary refer the trustee to HEF leaders. When Hadley wrote to Lowell criticizing HEF, Lowell responded sympathetically in a patrician tone, "You are quite right, but when your alumni are working very hard to raise an endowment for the college you hate to decline the requests they make."[32]

Lowell's opinion was not rooted in religious or academic disdain or a desire to hobnob with the rich. Rather, he simply preferred to follow and reinforce the norms and mystique of his Brahmin class by appearing effortless in securing gifts from wealthy donors discreetly and often anonymously. As his authorized biographer wrote, Lowell "rarely solicited a gift; he stated needs and gave all he could himself. Fortunately, anything more from him was rarely required." More precisely, as HEF core leaders observed, Lowell "does not think it is the duty of the president to visit Harvard Clubs, or at any rate, he does not like to do it and does not think he is successful in this particular function."[33]

Lowell's resistance derived not only from his patrician mores but also from a sense of expediency. He believed that quietly approaching wealthy individuals was both more effective and more efficient in acquiring needed funds. Harvard administrators "often heard him say that . . . large sums . . . were best

---

31. Joseph M. Stetar, "In Search of a Direction: Southern Higher Education after the War," *History of Education Quarterly* 25 (1985): 341–67.

32. A. Lawrence Lowell to Arthur T. Hadley, September 26, 1919, Lowell Records. See Jacob G. Schurman to and from A. Lawrence Lowell, January 30, 31, 1917, Lowell Records; Frank W. Hunnewell to W. I. Brobeck, December 5, 1919, HEF Records.

33. Quotations are from Yeomans, *Abbott Lawrence Lowell*, 230; Edgar H. Wells to Charles F. Adams, April 28, 1919, HEF Records.

obtained from a few people rather than from many."[34] Indeed, frequent, loud requests might do damage, Lowell believed, because "a recurring appeal to every alumnus for a small gift might interfere with more substantial donations."[35] As HEF was expiring, Lowell set out to make the point.

Even while declaring HEF a great success, President Lowell, like the alumni leaders, knew that it had fallen significantly short of its goal. The acknowledged problem was that, for all its innovations, HEF did not attract enough major gifts. The "democratic" drive was too democratic! By November 1920, in campaigns lasting only a few months with far less planning and publicity, Brown University had received five gifts over $200,000, and Princeton nine gifts over $250,000. In contrast, the four largest gifts to HEF included three for about $150,000 and merely one for $200,000. As of November 1920, Brown's biggest five gifts totaled $1.1 million and Harvard's $743,000. Princeton's largest nine gifts totaled $2.4 million; Harvard's, $1.1 million.[36] And HEF had been soliciting a lot longer and louder than either Brown or Princeton.

This result seemed to confirm what Lowell often told Harvard deans: a widespread appeal to alumni "brings the minimum of feathers with the maximum of squawking."[37] As HEF wound down in 1923, Lowell and the Corporation therefore initiated their own drive. Aiming for $10 million to support the fledgling Business School and the Departments of Chemistry and Fine Arts, this campaign followed the traditional mode of quietly approaching wealthy benefactors. The organizing committee numbered only nine, including the university treasurer, President Lowell, and his cousin, Episcopal bishop William Lawrence. Publicity was minimal, and no alumni networks were involved.[38]

Led by a gift of $5 million for the Business School from banker George F. Baker, the entire goal of $10 million was virtually achieved by June 1924. Along with another $3 million promised to Harvard's Institute of Biology, Lowell's nine-person committee had nearly matched in 15 months what the HEF legions had raised in 10 years. In his annual reports, Lowell gave at least as much attention to his "ten-million-dollar campaign" as he had to HEF. This was the way to raise money, he seemed to say. After all, Baker, one of the wealthiest men in

34. Ezra R. Thayer to Cornelius W. Wickersham, April 7, 1914, Lowell Records.

35. Yeomans, *Abbott Lawrence Lowell*, 252.

36. Edgar H. Wells to Thomas W. Lamont (July 21, 1920), Lamont Correspondence; Thomas N. Perkins to John W. Geary, November 6, 1920, and "Subscribers Who Have Pledges $25,000.00 and Over, Sep. 10, 1920. Corrected to Nov. 1920," HEF Records.

37. Quotation is from Thayer to Wickersham, April 7, 1914. Lowell was paraphrasing a famous saying by Jean-Baptiste Colbert, the finance minister of King Louis XIV of France.

38. William Lawrence, *Memories of a Happy Life* (Boston, 1926), 417–20; Yeomans, *Abbott Lawrence Lowell*, 230–31.

America, had donated merely $100,000 to HEF. Mass fundraising left a great deal of money in the pockets of the wealthiest donors.[39]

Was the transformation wrought by HEF therefore chimerical? That campaign enshrined mass fundraising in higher education, but the outcome, coupled with Lowell's low-profile drive, put in doubt whether "democratic" appeals actually extended higher education philanthropy outside the province of the wealthy elite. John Price Jones and historian Scott M. Cutlip—advocates of professional fundraising—maintained that HEF transformed higher education fundraising. But neither Jones nor Cutlip considered Lowell's quiet drive to be actual "fund-raising," which they effectively defined as a mass campaign designed and executed by professional consultants.[40]

Lowell thought this was nonsense, as did Hadley at Yale and Butler at Columbia. In the 1920s, Lowell doubted that HEF had changed much about higher education fundraising. When a college wrote to Harvard in 1925 asking about the work of Jones's consulting firm, Lowell had his secretary reply dismissively that the president "knows nothing about the John Price Jones Corporation."[41]

And Lowell was right that mass fundraising would not dramatically alter the proportions of the amount received. Before HEF and during the century afterward to the present day, about 90 percent of the proceeds of higher education campaigns have come from 10 percent of the donors, as a general rule. Lowell's quiet campaign followed this rule by acquiring 95 percent of the proceeds from a few large donors.[42] In the HEF campaign, the top 10 percent of donors contributed only 36 percent of the pledges.[43] The democratic drive was heroic but relatively unrewarding.

"Following in Your Wake"

Although HEF did not change the ratios between givers' wealth and amounts given, the drive was "of prime importance . . . to the whole cause of American education," stated HEF leaders.[44] The significance lay in establishing a new template

---

39. Lowell, *Annual Report 1926–27*, 32; see also *1923–24*, 27–29; *1924–25*, 7–8; *1927–28*, 19.

40. Jones, *American Giver*, 12–13, 24–25; Scott M. Cutlip, *Fund Raising in the United States: Its Role in America's Philanthropy* (New Brunswick, NJ, 1965), 265–68.

41. Frank W. Hunnewell to David M. Little, June 9, 1925, HEF Records.

42. Michael J. Worth, ed., *New Strategies for Educational Fund Raising* (Westport, CT, 2002), 33, 89–104; Heather Joslyn, "Campaign Fever: Fundraising Drives Are Getting Bigger and More Numerous," *Chronicle of Philanthropy*, April 2, 2019.

43. Edgar H. Wells, "Report of the Harvard Endowment Fund," *Harvard Alumni Bulletin*, November 17, 1921, 168–70.

44. "News and Views," *Harvard Alumni Bulletin*, January 11, 1917, 281. See "Lamont Pleads for American Colleges," *New York Times*, September 27, 1919.

for pursuing institutional wealth, the fundraising triad illustrated in figure 4.3. Before Lamont and his associates started their planning in 1915, other colleges and universities had made attempts at public drives, animated by the growing donations from multimillionaires and their new philanthropic foundations.

In the early 1910s, Smith College's successful campaign chiefly employed the traditional model of soliciting wealthy donors, as did that of Wellesley College, while also attempting a broader canvass of alumnae. In 1913, organizers at the University of Pittsburgh employed the YMCA model in a short-term, community-based, whirlwind campaign that reportedly raised $2 million for a new building. In 1917, those same organizers tried this approach on behalf of Elmira College, a women's college in upstate New York, but did not succeed because the geographical, vocational, and demographic range of the alumnae required more planning and organization than they expected.[45]

By the time HEF raised its first million in July 1917, some 50 colleges and universities had announced appeals for money employing various tactics. Nearly all these drives shuttered during World War I, then reopened in 1919, and followed different paths. In Wisconsin, nine denominational colleges—Beloit, Campion, Carroll, Lawrence, Marquette, Milton, Milwaukee-Downer, Northland, and Ripon—banded together in 1919 with the collective goal of raising $5 million. But this federated effort fell well short.[46]

A number of midwestern universities, such as the University of Minnesota, imprudently sought money to build football stadiums, as announced in figure 5.2. The campaign for a stadium rather than endowment may explain Minnesota's below-average performance among second-tier endowments, evident in table 5.1. At least, President Eliot may have drawn this conclusion. Over his opposition, Harvard alumni had raised money in the 1890s to build a stadium. When the structure was completed in 1903, Eliot wrote in his published annual report that the university had "not . . . contributed a dollar to the cost of the structure," and that "the game which has been conducted at [Harvard] with the least intelligence and success is football, except from a pecuniary point of view."[47]

Meanwhile, MIT made the greatest percentage increase between 1915 and 1930 among the nine largest endowments recorded in table 1.1. This jump resulted from the large donations of industrialist George Eastman, several be-

45. Cutlip, *Fund Raising*, 86–88.
46. "New Harvard Fund Reaches $1,187,160," *New York Times*, July 8, 1917; "Colleges Combine to Raise Funds," *New York Times*, December 26, 1919, 11.
47. Eliot, *Annual Report 1902–3*, 41, 43; see Herman Weicking, "Engineers Back Stadium Drive," *Minnesota Technology* 3 (November 1922): 8.

The University of Minnesota
Invites Participation
In a Great Program

FOR fifty-four years the University of Minnesota has received substantially all of her support from the State through the legislature.

A situation now confronts the University in which the legislature is unable to assist.

Necessity demands two outstanding new structures.   The need for them, long recognized, has now become imperative. Their realization will mean much for the University's future success in rendering public service.

To Perpetuation of Those Manly Qualities Which Our Soldiers Exemplified, Minnesota Proposes this Mighty Memorial Stadium

Figure 5.2. University of Minnesota Fundraising Drive for Football Stadium, 1923. Courtesy of University of Minnesota Archives and Special Collections.

quests, and the proceeds of a "Technology Plan" that called for industrial corporations to donate to MIT in exchange for help "in dealing with technical problems." This Technology Plan, however, led some philanthropic foundations to reject MIT's requests for funding on the ground that its technical research was too utilitarian. In any event, HEF leaders examined the plan and concluded that Harvard could not adopt it.[48]

48. Quotations are from Massachusetts Institute of Technology, *The Technology Plan* (Cambridge, MA, 1919), 2. See Merton L. Emerson to A. Lawrence Lowell, December 12, 1919, HEF Records; Geiger, *To Advance Knowledge*, 178–80.

Among these diverse ventures, the HEF model soon became standard owing to its widespread publicity, supposed success, and Harvard pedigree. In fall 1919, requests for information began pouring into the HEF offices from presidents, trustees, education journals, and entrepreneurs across the United States, Canada, and Britain. The inquiries kept flooding in over the next six years, and HEF staff heroically tried to answer each inquiry. Finally, the secretary created a form-letter response itemizing key aspects of the HEF template, concluding with the soon conventional admonition, "Above all, raise as much as possible no matter the goal."[49]

One inquiry, in November 1919, came from the editor of the *Spectator* in London. HEF staff replied that they would be glad to share their experiences "if your ancient universities . . . undertake an endowment fund to be raised by their respective graduates."[50] In January 1920, Manchester University in England began "appealing for a further endowment of half-a-million sterling," and the *Spectator* editor "begged the Universities of Oxford and Cambridge to make a new and special appeal to private generosity" along the lines "of the Harvard Endowment Fund."[51] In Germany, too, the academic leaders of Göttingen University hoped to alleviate the university's financial plight after the war by appealing to their American alumni, likely inspired by stories of fundraising in American higher education.[52]

The far-flung influence of HEF was also extended by John Price Jones's efforts to solicit business for his new consulting firm. In fact, Jones wrote a fund-raising manual drawing on the HEF model and sent it to dozens of institutions in higher education across the country. In February 1920, the *New York Times* reported that some 75 colleges and universities in the United States were running campaigns seeking a total of more than $200 million, nearly all based on the HEF template.[53]

Thus, HEF is "tilling the ground for endowment campaigns for other colleges," wrote a prominent Columbia University professor and graduate of the

49. [David M. Little Jr.], "The Harvard Endowment Fund" (typescript), ca. June 1923, HEF Records.

50. Edgar H. Wells to John B. Atkins, November 12, 28, 1919, HEF Records.

51. Quotations are from F. Forbes Adam, Edward Donner, and Henry F. Miers, "The University of Manchester," *Spectator*, January 24, 1920; [Editor], "The University, Manchester," *Spectator*, January 24, 1920.

52. Konrad H. Jarausch, "American Students in Germany, 1815–1914: The Structure of German and U.S. Matriculants at Göttingen University," in *German Influence on Education in the United States to 1917*, ed. Henry Geitz, Jürgen Heideking, and Jurgen Herbst (Washington, DC, 1995), 202.

53. John Price Jones, "How to Conduct Campaigns for Funds for Colleges" (typescript), 1920, JPJ Records; "Universities Ask over $200,000,000," *New York Times*, February 8, 1920.

University of Vermont. "The Harvard Fund will make us ashamed not to do as well for our own colleges when they start their campaigns." Indeed, "we are following in your wake," wrote Princeton president Hibben to Lowell in 1919.[54] This extension of fundraising campaigns throughout higher education during the 1920s was, in many ways, more "democratic" than Yale and Harvard claimed to be in earlier decades. But the romance with "democracy" rapidly faded in the American mind after World War I, so "democratic" terminology was rarely invoked as fundraising drives proliferated throughout higher education.

Campaigns "Dovetail Completely"

Princeton had a lot of catching up to do by the time Hibben began to chart a new financial course for the university in the 1910s. Though a Presbyterian clergyman like his predecessors, Hibben broke new ground in several respects. In theology, he reconciled evolution with theism, in contrast to prior Princeton presidents. Hibben also embraced Darwin in university finance by seeking to advance "the natural growth and expansion of the university . . . in power and influence" amid the evolutionary competition in higher education. And he recognized that money was the key factor in that competition. "Unless we receive immediate adequate financial support," Hibben wrote to alumni, "we will lose that position which Princeton has held so long in the educational world."[55]

In particular, Hibben realized that Princeton's endowment trailed those of its peers significantly, as seen in table 1.1. In 1914, he publicly acknowledged that Princeton needed more endowment rather than continuing to rely on a small group of wealthy alumni and trustees to cover its annual deficits. In 1917, six months after the launch of HEF, Hibben announced a campaign to raise $3 million in endowment to increase faculty salaries.[56] After pausing during the war, the campaign resumed in September 1919 with a new goal of $14 million, apparently to match the HEF goal. Reinforcing the similarity of the two drives, their staffs consulted each other and compared their progress.[57]

54. Thomas Reed Powell to Harvard Endowment Fund, November 6, 1919, HEF Records; Hibben to Lowell, September 24, 1919.
55. Quotations are from "Princeton to Make Entrance Simpler," *New York Times*, February 23, 1919; "Announcement," *Princeton Alumni Weekly*, June 18, 1919, 741. See "Hibben Reconciles Evolution with God," *New York Times*, June 15, 1925.
56. "Princeton Cramped by Yearly Deficit," *New York Times*, January 12, 1914; "Princeton Needs $3,000,000: President Hibben Asks for Increase in Professors' Salary Fund," *New York Times*, January 12, 1917.
57. "Princeton to Raise $14,000,000 Fund," *New York Times*, September 22, 1919. See letters among Edgar H. Wells, Thomas W. Lamont, George A. Brakely, and John Richardson during 1920, HEF Records.

Also like HEF, Princeton's drive struggled to reach its goal, despite receiving more large gifts. Though extending its initial five-month deadline several times, the Princeton drive still had not reached 60 percent of its goal in 1924, after nearly five years. But Princeton, like Harvard, could not fail. In 1925, Princeton therefore declared victory and started a new campaign with a goal of $20 million. Then, because much of the proceeds of earlier drives had gone toward renovating buildings, President Hibben announced a third drive in 1927 recalling the original, unrealized aim to raise "funds to increase the salaries of faculty members."[58]

Meanwhile, Cornell president Schurman in 1919 announced a drive to honor his university's "semi-centennial." Following the HEF template, Cornell aimed to raise $5 million for endowment to support faculty salaries and planned to canvass "in Mexico, Canada, and other countries in which there are twenty-five or more Cornell alumni." In newspapers across the country, President Schurman restated the theme that "the United States pays its ditch diggers more than its college instructors, and its mechanics and trainmen more than its professors."[59]

Schurman also found an opening to associate Cornell closely with Harvard and Princeton, while squeezing out the older and wealthier universities Yale and Columbia due to their presidents' disdain for public canvassing. The Cornell alumni committee enlisted HEF chairman Thomas Lamont to speak at the Cornell kickoff events in Ithaca and Boston and reprinted statements from Lamont's successor, Eliot Wadsworth. In addition, Schurman publicly affirmed the association in the *New York Times*, stating that "the endowment campaigns of Cornell, Harvard, Princeton, and other universities dovetail completely."[60]

In November 1919, Schurman also secured an invitation to join Lowell and Hibben at the Harvard Club in New York City and explain to the 500 attendees "why we are asking for additional endowments at Harvard, Princeton, and Cornell." Significantly, this event occurred in the backyard of Columbia and Yale, and Presidents Butler and Hadley were nowhere to be seen.[61] In 1920, HEF leaders also enlisted Cornell and Princeton representatives in promoting the charitable deduction from income subject to federal taxes.[62]

58. "Commencement Gifts," *New York Times*, June 20, 1924; "$2,250,000 Gifts in Year: Hibben Announces List of Donations at Princeton Alumni Meeting," *New York Times*, June 20, 1927.

59. "The Worst Pinched of All," *[Montana] Anaconda Standard*, September 25, 1919.

60. "Issues Plea for Cornell," *New York Times*, October 19, 1919. See Thomas W. Lamont to Henry S. Pritchett, December 22, 1919, Lamont Correspondence.

61. Quotation is from "Schurman at Harvard Club," *Cornell Alumni News*, November 27, 1919, 111. See "A Boon to Education. Presidents of Three Universities Point Out Value of Endowment Campaigns," *Cornell Alumni News*, November 27, 1919, 111.

62. Thomas N. Perkins to Eliot Wadsworth, May 3, 1920, HEF Records.

Like Harvard and Princeton, Cornell then ambitiously raised its goal to $10 million. In September 1920, when $6 million had been pledged, faculty salaries were increased by 40 percent with much fanfare, as Harvard had done. Also like Harvard and Princeton, Cornell's drive then slowed, partly due to the sharp recession. Rather than limping along, however, the Cornell committee closed the campaign, and in January 1921 the university turned the effort over to its newly formed Cornellian Council. With this step, the university administration assimilated alumni fundraising, just as Harvard had done.[63]

Women's Colleges "Must Go Forward"

Women's colleges faced major barriers in obtaining funding for higher education. Because women "[do] not, as a rule, make and accumulate money, they have difficulty in procuring endowment or adequate revenues" for their educational programs, Charles Eliot observed in *University Administration* (1908). Smith College president Marion Burton (1910–17) repeated this point in letters to prospective male donors in the early 1910s. In addition, when female alumnae married men with large estates, more of the couples' donations went to the husband's alma mater than to the wife's, as Wheaton College found in subsequent decades.[64]

In 1929, the famous journalist Ida Tarbell wrote in *Good Housekeeping* that the combined endowment of "the seven leading women's colleges of the east—Barnard, Bryn Mawr, Mount Holyoke, Radcliffe, Smith, Vassar, Wellesley"—amounted to merely $38 million, while that "of their nearest neighbors among men's colleges" exceeded $280 million. And the gender gap was worsening because donations to the seven women's colleges in the prior year totaled less than $2 million, while those to only five of the men's counterparts came to nearly $26 million.[65]

And when their campaigns succeeded, alumnae of women's colleges sometimes faced accusations that they were greedy and unladylike. In *Ladies Home Journal*, Corra Harris, a reactionary southern journalist who had defended lynching, wrote that alumnae of women's colleges were "ravenous to raise money for . . . enormously rich institution[s]. I know of a small school with an endowment of

63. "The Endowment Fund," *Cornell Alumni News*, September 30, 1920, 3; "The End of the Campaign," *Cornell Alumni News*, December 23, 1920, 155.

64. Charles W. Eliot, *University Administration* (Boston, 1908), 223–24. See Marion L. Burton, letters in "Million Dollar Fund, 1911–1913" files, Burton Files; Linda Eisenmann, email to Bruce Kimball, June 10, 2021, on file.

65. Ida Tarbell, "A Rehearsal for LIFE," *Good Housekeeping* 89 (November 1929): 20.

three million dollars which keeps a flying squadron of . . . lady beggars in the field to collect money for it."[66]

Apart from possessing fewer financial resources, women faced "subordination and segregation" in the leading private universities in the northeastern United States, observed Edwin Slosson.[67] And they fared little better at the coeducational, midwestern, land-grant universities after the turn of the century, when a backlash set in against the educational gains made by women in the late nineteenth century. At Ohio State, for example, most defaulters on student loans were women who predominantly became schoolteachers and could not afford the 6 percent interest charged, particularly if they married and stopped working. Alumnae calls to lower the interest rate for women were rejected by the male trustees of the Ohio Student Loan Association, who proposed to solve the higher default rate by requiring female borrowers to obtain a second guarantor for their loans.[68]

Another financial disadvantage faced by alumnae of many coeducational universities was the lack of facilities for women, such as student unions and gymnasia. For example, Indiana University provided dormitories for men but resisted building them for women, leading the dean of women, Mary Bidwell Breed, to resign in protest in 1906. The lack of facilities forced women who engaged in fundraising to delay seeking endowments for women's programs, in order to appeal for money to build the facilities that the university already provided for men. This happened to the University of Michigan Alumnae Council in the 1920s.[69]

Some leaders maintained, however, that women's colleges could turn these drawbacks to their advantage. Recognizing the smaller resources of women, some wealthy philanthropists were positively disposed toward women's colleges and "may reasonably make larger donations than they otherwise might," wrote Smith president Burton. In addition, the barriers seemed to inspire alumnae loyalty, prompting a much higher percentage of giving by graduates of women's colleges than of men's colleges, noted HEF staff.[70] Perhaps for these reasons, two campaigns run by women's colleges that adopted the HEF template were

66. Corra Harris, "Sob Sister Citizens," *Ladies' Home Journal* 42 (February 1925): 105.
67. Edwin E. Slosson, *Great American Universities* (New York, 1910), 507–8.
68. Ohio Student Loan Foundation, Minutes of Board of Trustees Meeting, June 10, 1932, Ohio State University Archives.
69. Jana Nidiffer, *Pioneering Deans of Women: More Than Wise and Pious Matrons* (New York, 2000), 55–76; Doris Attaway and Marjorie Rabe Barritt, *Women's Voices: Early Years at the University of Michigan* (Ann Arbor, MI, 2000), 1.
70. Marion L. Burton, "To the Members of the Board of Trustees of Smith College" (typescript), July 25, 1911, Burton Files, 6; Wells to Lamont, July 21, 1920.

more successful in reaching their fundraising goal than the contemporaneous drives run by Harvard, Princeton, and Cornell.

At Smith College, President Burton left to become president of the University of Minnesota in 1917, and Harvard English professor William A. Neilson (1917–39) succeeded him. This further strengthened the bonds between Smith and HEF woven by Smith trustee and HEF chairman Thomas Lamont. In fact, Smith became the first client of the new John Price Jones Co. and announced its own campaign in November 1919, along with Cornell. HEF staff carefully tracked the progress of Smith's campaign.[71]

Replicating the "businesslike" organization of HEF, Smith established a New York City headquarters, press bureau, speakers bureau, geographical districts, widespread advertising, a national campaign bulletin, and a training "School" for alumnae leaders. In addition, Smith's drive aimed to raise endowment to increase the "inadequate" salaries of the faculty and to construct buildings. In October 1919 Lamont delivered the keynote address at the "quiet" opening of the campaign and then again in January 1920 at the public launch. Smith's drive thus became "the pioneer" of fundraising campaigns held by women's colleges, according to John Price Jones, who overlooked the precedent set by both Smith and Wellesley in the early 1910s.[72]

Adopting the theme that "Smith Must Go Forward," the campaign embraced the trend of "women . . . taking a more and more active part in the work of the world," in Lamont's words. Nevertheless, Smith's fundraising literature scarcely mentioned the contemporaneous movement to ratify the Nineteenth Amendment authorizing women's suffrage (passed by Congress in June 1919 and ratified in August 1920), surely to avoid controversy. Meanwhile, newspapers relegated news of Smith's campaign to the Society pages because Smith alumnae held social events such as dances, concerts, plays, and bake sales to aid the campaign, illustrated in figure 5.3. But Smith's regular campaign news appeared in the Society's pages as well.[73]

71. "With the College Drives. Harvard Fund $9,763,164—Cornell and Smith Plan Campaigns," *New York Times*, November 16, 1919; Edgar H. Wells to Thomas W. Lamont, July 16, 1920, Lamont Correspondence.

72. Quotations are from Jones, "How to Conduct Campaigns," 3; "Seek Smith College Fund. Alumnae Launch Campaign, for $4,000,000 Endowment," *New York Times*, November 28, 1919; "Smith College Campaign" (1919), JPJ Records.

73. Quotation is from "Smith College Alumnae Hear Thomas W. Lamont," *Boston Globe*, January 13, 1920. See "Smith College Hat Sale," *New York Times*, March 25, 1920; "Spring Programme of Play Dances for the Smith College Fund," *New York Times*, April 2, 1920; "Concert Tonight for Smith College Fund," *Chicago Tribune*, May 18, 1920.

THE SMITH COLLEGE MUFFIN

2 cups white flour
1 cup graham flour
5 teaspoons baking powder
½ teaspoon salt
½ cup sugar

½ cup chopped nuts
½ cup seedless raisins
2 teaspoons cinnamon
grated rind of ½ lemon
1¼ cups cold water

3 tablespoons fat (butter or butter substitutes)

All measurements are level. Mix in a bowl all materials except fats and water. Chop in the fats with two knives. Add the water; mix gently to form a stiff dough. Put dough on a floured board, sprinkle it with a little flour; with rolling pin roll dough about one inch thick, cut out with biscuit cutter. Place muffins on shallow greased pan, bake in moderately hot oven about 20 minutes.

This particularly delicious muffin is to be used in the $4,000,000 campaign for publicity or money-raising in any way that seems practical, such as:

A favor or place card;

Or it may be produced in numbers and sold for the Fund;

Or used at fairs and tea rooms.

Use it in your district in any way that seems most effective to you.

Recipe distributed by

Smith College Fund Headquarters
17 West 47th Street
New York City

Figure 5.3. Muffin Recipe of Smith College Campaign, 1919–20. Courtesy of Smith College Special Collections.

Despite its ambitious goal of $4 million and short timeline ending on June 30, 1920, Smith met both, though just barely. The college had to raise $3.5 million by the deadline in order to receive a conditional grant of $500,000 from the General Education Board (GEB). With one week to go, only $3 million had been pledged, and Smith faced the prospect of losing the GEB grant. Then, ingeniously, the alumnae districts that had fallen short of their quotas made pledges to obtain the needed $500,000. Essentially, these were promises to raise the needed pledges. Nonetheless, the GEB made its grant of $500,000, and the college attained the $4 million goal, at least on paper. Like Harvard, Princeton, and Cornell, Smith declared "Victory," although completing the campaign proved difficult. Three years later, about 11 percent of the $4 million still had not been collected.[74]

Even so, Smith's drive inspired Bryn Mawr, Mount Holyoke, Radcliffe, Simmons, Vassar, and Wheaton, as well as Bedford College for Women in London, to mount similar campaigns in the early 1920s.[75] But the largest and, in some ways, most significant drive was held by Wellesley College to raise $9 million by its semicentennial in 1925: $2.7 million in a "first phase" to endow pay increases for the faculty and $6.3 million more in a "second phase." Starting in November 1920, Wellesley followed the HEF model and retained John Price Jones Co. to manage the campaign.[76]

Characteristic of the women's college drives, Wellesley students and faculty sponsored concerts, plays, bazaars, tea rooms, and other social events to attract gifts. In six months, Wellesley completed the "first phase" with only two large gifts of $100,000 and $130,000, neither from an alumna, apart from a conditional grant from the GEB of $500,000. Wellesley's success, like Smith's, was largely due to the alumnae participation rate of 90 percent, far exceeding that of men's colleges.[77]

Then came the much harder "second phase," aiming for over twice as much—$6.3 million—after the alumnae network had been tapped out. Wellesley therefore scrapped the professional consultants and broad public canvassing and followed Lowell's approach emphasizing "the quiet solicitation of gifts

74. "Four Million Dollar Victory," *Smith Alumnae Quarterly*, July 1920, 249, 250; "The Fund," *Smith Alumnae Quarterly*, November 1923, 50.

75. Robert F. Duncan to Thomas W. Lamont, January 5, 1922, Lamont Correspondence; E. Hildred Carlile et al., "Bedford College for Women," *Spectator*, April 10, 1920; Lewis R. Curzon et al., "The Women's Colleges at Oxford," *Spectator*, January 22, 1921.

76. John Price Jones Corporation, "Tentative Budget for the Wellesley College Semicentennial Fund," ca. September 1920, Wellesley College Archives; "Plans Are Made for Wellesley Drive," *Boston Globe*, November 22, 1920.

77. "Wellesley Fund Goes over Top," *Boston Globe*, June 21, 1921.

from individuals of large wealth." Yet only half of the second phase goal was pledged by 1925. Like Harvard and Princeton, Wellesley slogged on for another five years unwilling to admit defeat, and the college finally reached the announced goal of $9 million in 1930.[78] As in the other extended campaigns, attaining the goal was somewhat illusory because pledges made in the later years or paid in future years would likely have come to the college anyway. Nevertheless, over the course of the 1920s Wellesley replicated the cycle unintentionally introduced by HEF and Lowell at Harvard: a broad national alumni canvass followed by a circumspect appeal to the wealthy, who provided most of the money.

"Voices Bring Endowments" for HBCUs

By 1929, hundreds of colleges and universities across the country were routinely conducting highly organized and publicized, national, long-term drives for endowment. These ranged from appeals to the rabbinic alumni of Hebrew Union College in Cincinnati to calls upon the sorority sisters of women's technical schools in Atlanta.[79] Most often rationalized as support for faculty salaries, the campaigns' success is evidenced by the steady nationwide rise in faculty compensation during the 1920s. After declining annually by 5.3 percent in constant dollars between 1913 and 1919, faculty compensation rose 1.4 percent annually between 1922 and 1930, while consumer prices did not rise at all.[80]

Apart from public drives, colleges and universities continued the traditional practice of quietly soliciting wealthy donors, especially if most alumni were not wealthy and if the general public did not respond enthusiastically to the national appeals. These barriers were higher for HBCUs, whose fundraising received little publicity in major newspapers, compared to the drives of predominantly white institutions. HBCUs therefore had to rely on wealthy white patrons for most of their fundraising.

As of 1870, the literacy rate of African Americans was about 20 percent, and their opportunities for schooling were very limited in subsequent decades. Consequently, as late as 1910, less than 0.1 percent of college-age African Americans were enrolled in courses of study leading to a bachelor's degree or higher, compared to about 3 percent of whites. The vast majority of African American stu-

78. Quotation is from Wellesley College, *Report of the Semi-centennial Fund 1921–1936*, Wellesley College Archives, 6–7. See "Wellesley Fund Has Reached $6,235,000," *Boston Globe*, June 16, 1925.

79. "Among Alumni Answering Alma Mater's Call," *American Israelite*, June 21, 1929; "Sorority Girls Will Give Endowment Fund Dance," *Atlanta Constitution*, October 3, 1926.

80. H. Bowen, *Costs of Higher Education*, 55, 60.

dents in college courses attended 32 "Negro colleges," including 26 in the south, where most African Americans lived. In 1910, these 32 colleges enrolled about 1,130 men and women in college-grade courses of study, as well as another 12,630 students in elementary, secondary, or technical courses of study.[81]

Despite their small enrollment, the "Negro colleges" played a tremendously important role. In the United States, about 3,860 African Americans had earned college degrees by 1910. Of those, about 82 percent had graduated from the Negro colleges since 1865, and the fraction remained constant into the 1920s.[82] Yet the great majority of these colleges lacked any endowment and hovered at the edge of bankruptcy. President Edmund A. Ware (1869–85) of Atlanta University lamented, "I . . . hate to spend so much of my time and strength in begging money! Why can we not secure an endowment . . . and thus relieve me from this disagreeable task of raising money and let me attend to my legitimate business?"[83]

Prior to 1900, philanthropy supporting the education of African American students at all levels came in small amounts and primarily from church organizations, both black and white. In the subsequent two decades, northern white philanthropists began to give substantial sums, primarily to support technical and industrial institutes for African Americans, especially Hampton Institute in Virginia and Tuskegee Institute in Alabama. By 1915, the latter's endowment had grown to $2 million, much larger than any other African American institution of higher education. These white philanthropists—including John D. Rockefeller, Andrew Carnegie, Collis P. Huntington, George Eastman, and J. Pierpont Morgan—did not challenge southern mores or segregation and favored white governance of the HBCUs.[84]

After World War I, most of the industrialists' philanthropy for African American higher education continued to flow to Hampton and Tuskegee. In 1924, following the HEF model, these two technical institutes embarked on a joint campaign managed by John Price Jones Co. to raise $5 million in endowment. The drive featured major publicity events, such as an exhibition in Carnegie Hall in New York City. In 1925, the campaign succeeded due to contributions

81. W. E. B. Du Bois and Augustus G. Dill, *The College-Bred Negro American* (Atlanta, GA, 1910), 14, 46, 100; Thomas D. Snyder, *120 Years of American Education* (Washington, DC, 1993), table 6; *Historical Statistics of the United States*, table Bc523–36.

82. Du Bois and Dill, *College-Bred Negro American*, 14, 46, 100; W. E. B. Du Bois, "The Higher Training of Negroes," *Crisis* 24 (August 1922): 151.

83. "Our Pressing Need," *Bulletin of Atlanta University*, November 1885, 2.

84. Here and below, see Curti and Nash, *Philanthropy*, 169–81; James D. Anderson, *The Education of Blacks in the South, 1860–1935* (Chapel Hill, NC, 1988), 238–78; Marybeth Gasman, *Envisioning Black Colleges: A History of the United Negro College Fund* (Baltimore, 2007), 14–15.

of $1 million from GEB, another $1 million from John D. Rockefeller Jr., and $2 million from George Eastman.[85]

Similarly, the first president of the GEB, William H. Baldwin Jr., focused his personal efforts, and that of the board, on supporting African American industrial schools. Meanwhile, the scholarship and activism of W. E. B. Du Bois advanced the importance of educating African American leaders at liberal arts colleges. "It has been the educated and intelligent of the Negro people that have . . . elevated the mass, and the sole obstacles that nullified . . . their efforts were slavery and race prejudice," argued Du Bois in Darwinian terms, "for what is slavery but the legalized survival of the unfit and the nullification of the work of natural internal leadership? Negro leadership, therefore, sought from the first to rid the race of this awful incubus that it might make way for natural selection and the survival of the fittest."[86]

By 1918, in response to Du Bois's efforts, the GEB began to shift its policy, affirming that it was "highly important that Negro lawyers, Negro clergymen, and Negro business men should enjoy the advantage of academic training." In 1911, Du Bois's study *The College-Bred Negro American* had concluded that only 11 of the "colored colleges" had "a reasonable number of college-grade students," and the GEB decided to focus its efforts on a select few of those 11.[87] Appropriately, the foremost of these was Du Bois's alma mater, Fisk University.

In 1922, white philanthropists' new attention to "academic training" of African Americans prompted the GEB to make a conditional pledge of $500,000 toward the first million-dollar endowment drive for an African American liberal arts college in the south. Fisk University, located in Nashville, undertook this campaign and hired as director William H. Baldwin III, a young, white Harvard graduate and son of the first GEB president. The younger Baldwin had managed the HEF office but declined to follow John Price Jones when he departed to found his consulting business. Aiming to raise $500,000 to match the GEB pledge and reach the goal of $1 million, Baldwin soon determined that a widespread public campaign for Fisk would not reap enough pledges to justify the expense.[88] Ironically, the "democratic" approach to fundraising would not work at, arguably, one of the nation's most "democratic" colleges.

---

85. "Tuskegee's Youngest and Oldest," *Baltimore Afro-American*, November 22, 1924.
86. W. E. B. Du Bois, "The Talented Tenth," in *The Negro Problem* (New York, 1903), 34–35.
87. Quotations are from GEB, *Annual Report 1918–19* (New York, 1819), 55–56; Du Bois and Dill, *College-Bred Negro American*, 17. See Anderson, *Education of Blacks*, 240–50; "Various Questions of Compensation," *Outlook*, April 14, 1920, 636.
88. Cutlip, *Fund Raising*, 269–70.

Instead, Baldwin relied largely on the traditional personal solicitation of wealthy individuals.

But Baldwin did reinstate the public mission of the Fisk Jubilee Singers. Beginning in 1871, this student group had toured cities throughout the northern United States, Canada, and Europe, giving public concerts whose proceeds went to support Fisk. Then, in 1915, Fayette McKenzie (1915–25), a white man, became president of Fisk and established a strict autocratic regime with a dress code and rules of conduct that he had seen previously at the Indian Boarding School in Wyoming and the Ohio Conference of Charities and Corrections. He also directed the Jubilee Singers to give private concerts in the parlors of wealthy people, followed by "passing the hat" for donations. Baldwin considered this practice demeaning and arranged for the Jubilee Singers to resume their public concerts, although they did travel to Windsor Castle in England to give a private concert for the king and queen of England in August 1925, as seen in figure 5.4. By that point, the Fisk campaign had already achieved its goal, and Du Bois proudly announced, "Today Fisk is the best endowed Negro college in America, just as Hampton is the best endowed Negro school."[89]

The success of the Fisk campaign prompted the GEB to make a conditional pledge of $1.5 million in 1928 toward a joint endowment campaign to raise $3.6 million for Spelman College for women and Morehouse College for men in Atlanta. By that point, Spelman and Morehouse were also supporting student music groups that toured northern cities to raise money for their alma mater. For example, in 1930, Josephine Herald and Carol Blanton, students at Spelman, gave piano recitals in Chicago, hosted by the Morehouse-Spelman Alumni Club to meet its quota in the endowment fund drive.[90]

Two years later, the GEB made a conditional grant of $4.2 million to Atlanta University, designating $1.7 million for endowment, $1.5 million for new buildings, and $1 million for a library. Meanwhile, student singing groups from many colleges and industrial schools were touring the North and Midwest. These concert tours amounted to small fundraising drives, since "Voices Bring Endowments," the African American press announced.[91] HBCUs thus participated actively in "the philanthropic decade."

89. W. E. B. Du Bois, "The Dilemma of the Negro," *American Mercury*, October 1924, 183. Anderson, *Education of Blacks*, 238–78; Cutlip, *Fund Raising*, 270. Student protests forced McKenzie out of the presidency in 1925.

90. "Aid Morehouse," *Chicago Defender*, August 23, 1930.

91. "Voices Bring Endowments," *Chicago Defender*, May 28, 1927. See "They Want to Sing $75,000 Worth," *Baltimore Afro-American*, April 13, 1929.

Figure 5.4. Fisk University Jubilee Singers in England on Their Way to Windsor Castle, 1925. Standing left to right: Rev. James A. Myers, Carl Barbour, Henrietta Crawley Myers, Horatio O'Bannon, Ludie Collins. Courtesy of Hulton Deutsch / Corbis Historical / Getty Images.

"As One Ends, Another One Begins"

Later consultants and scholars came to regard mass canvassing as the fundraising standard in higher education.[92] But the fundraising triad created by colleges and universities during the 1920s comprised three modes. Originating in YAF during the 1890s, the first mode constituted annual alumni funds, which proliferated broadly by 1930 and usually provided revenue for current operations.

The second and third modes tended to focus on building wealth for the long term and often alternated cyclically. Without intending to or even cooperating, HEF and President Lowell together had initiated this cycle by raising nearly $27 million for Harvard between 1915 and 1925. In this way, the ubiquitous cycle of incessant fundraising efforts commenced, alternating between comprehensive campaigns and discreet solicitations of wealthy donors by university leaders.

92. Cutlip, *Fund Raising*, 480.

Over the next century, this pattern meant that "campaigns . . . are often continuous. As one ends, another one begins."[93]

In the future scramble for free money, the surviving and winning institutions would be those that successfully and continually employed all three modes of the fundraising triad, depicted in figure 4.3. Indeed, the largest annual totals of gifts and bequests went to the colleges and universities with the largest endowments during the 1920s.[94]

At the same time, the incessant fundraising was already repulsing some observers. In 1926, Mount Holyoke College completed a campaign for $3 million of endowment, and President Mary Emma Woolley (1901–37) announced that the college needed no more. "The entire American population . . . may be grateful to this college," applauded journalist Charles Selden, "for its determination to have no more 'whirlwind campaigns' for cash" and "to take the overworked word 'drive' out of its vocabulary altogether." Indeed, "presidents of other colleges may envy President Woolley her release from being a fundgetter."[95] Whatever the gratitude of the entire American population, Mount Holyoke's endowment would gradually fall behind that of its peers, after the college swore off fundraising.

Fearing that fate, scores of leading colleges and universities enshrined the fundraising triad during the late 1920s, when it became a widespread feature of American higher education. In 1927, for example, members of the American Alumni Council—comprising alumni associations "from all the leading universities"—observed that giving in higher education occurs in three forms." These included "A.) Individual gifts or bequests" resulting from "direct contact . . . between the prospective giver and the President." Also, "B). Campaigns . . . organized on a big scale to reach as many people as possible with a large definite objective." Lastly, "C.) . . . The [Annual] Alumni Fund."[96]

Aided by this emerging triad, the double helix of aggregate wealth and aggregate cost of higher education spiraled upward throughout the formative period of higher education between 1870 and 1930. Remarkably and significantly, this helical spiral prompted scarcely any criticism because enrollment in higher education exploded. The per-student cost therefore did not escalate, as explained in the following chapter.

93. Noah D. Drezner, "Philanthropy and Fundraising in American Higher Education," *ASHE Higher Education Report* 37 (2011): 7.
94. See app. 1 and tables 1.1 and 1.2 in chap. 1.
95. Charles A. Selden, "Goucher Finds Itself," *Ladies' Home Journal* 43 (August 1926): 128.
96. James L. Morrill to George W. Rightmire, October 5, 1928, President George W. Rightmire Papers, The Ohio State University Archives.

CHAPTER 6

Did Cost Escalate
in the Formative Era?

Between 1870 and 1930, the finances of higher education changed profoundly, following new norms established by the wealthiest institutions. Colleges and universities began to believe they were competing for survival in a Darwinian struggle like that engaging industrial and financial enterprises. Amid the rivalry, colleges and universities came to recognize the advantage of accumulating "endowment," understood in its "correct sense" as permanent, productive funds. Increasing this financial capital not only strengthened an institution's autonomy, stability, and flexibility but also indicated its potential to triumph.

During the 1920s, these ideas spread throughout the upper strata of higher education, as Harvard University forged ahead in the race to accumulate endowment by implementing a novel, comprehensive strategy conceived and evangelized by President Charles Eliot (1869–1909). Above all, he proclaimed that unrestricted endowment—which he termed "free money"—is the most valuable kind of wealth. Commensurately, between 1900 and 1930, philanthropists directed the bulk of their gifts to higher education, and most of that went to the endowments of the prosperous colleges and universities. The rich became richer.

A novel triad of fundraising modes in higher education emerged at the same time, illustrated in figure 4.3. The traditional approach of discreetly appealing to wealthy donors continued to generate the largest gifts. But the occasional antebellum lotteries and subscription drives gave way to highly organized, national, multiyear campaigns administered by paid staff. In the 1920s, these two modes began to alternate at wealthy colleges and universities, initiating the perpetual cycle of fundraising campaigns. The third mode—annual appeals to alumni—commenced in the 1890s and provided a steady stream of unrestricted operating revenue while fostering the loyalty of alumni.

All these developments dramatically increased the income of higher education. Although public institutions generally lagged behind private schools in fundraising, the revenue of nearly all public colleges and universities increased significantly during the 1920s. Fed by the expanding GNP, state appropriations swelled, while the 43 percent rise in their enrollments increased tuition revenue at the public institutions during that decade. By 1930, the public and private sectors enrolled about the same number of students, and both sectors were prospering. Indeed, "the year 1928 marked the highpoint of the philanthropic decade," John Price Jones, the leading fundraising consultant, later wrote.[1]

As the income of higher education grew significantly, so too did its expense, the opposite side of the coin, as Eliot conceived. These trends naturally prompt one to ask: How much exactly did the cost to produce higher education rise during the formative era? And did that production cost escalate, that is, rise faster than the cost of living? Scholars then and subsequently found it hard to answer these questions because compiling accurate data about either the cost or the revenue of higher education prior to 1930 is difficult.

To address those questions, this chapter examines data from a cross section of institutions between 1875 and 1930 and arrives at striking conclusions. On the one hand, while the nation's income grew feverishly, the aggregate production cost (and revenue) of higher education rose even faster. The nation made a stupendous investment in colleges and universities, and their aggregate cost escalated rapidly. On the other hand, the per-student cost of higher education rose little more than the price of all commodities. Consequently, higher education became about three times cheaper to produce for each student, relative to the national per-capita income. These findings have great import for the contentious debate about cost escalation that arose later in the twentieth century.[2]

1. See app. 7; Jones, *American Giver*, 15.
2. See Kimball and Luke, "Measuring Cost Escalation," 198–219, for additional discussion and documentation on points in this chapter.

Economic Growth "Unique in Human History"

At the same time that higher education was evolving dramatically during the formative period, American society and culture were changing faster and more profoundly than ever before due, in part, to an economic expansion that was "unique in human history." Between 1870 and 1930, national income, measured by GNP, increased about seven-fold, driven by the nation's rapid industrialization and by immense productivity gains in manufacturing, transportation, and communications.[3] The expansion of the economy coincided with breathtaking demographic shifts resulting from waves of immigration and rapid urbanization. In 1870, the great majority of Americans resided on farms and in small villages. In 1920, the census found that fully half of the nation's 105 million people were living in "urban" communities. In addition, nearly 60 percent of workers or their parents were born outside of the United States, including Andrew Carnegie, one of the richest citizens in the country.[4]

Similar to the hostile reaction against Irish and German immigrants in the 1840s and 1850s, the demographic shifts in the late nineteenth century ignited nativism and xenophobia in many Americans. This reaction was then magnified by the ethnicity of eastern and southern Europeans entering the United States, by the Bolshevik revolution in Russia in 1917, and by the advance of communism in eastern Europe. Further, the rise of unions in manufacturing industries made 1919 "the most-strife-torn year in United States history."[5]

Labor unrest continued early in the 1920s, when unemployment soared to over 19 percent during the sharp recession that followed World War I. These events generated anxiety that fueled the nation's first Red Scare hysteria and led to vilifying immigrants, many of whom had settled in cities. In 1921, Congress enacted the Emergency Immigration Act and, in 1924, the National Origins Act, which severely curtailed immigration by imposing strict quotas. This complex of developments foreshadowed similar events a century later. Meanwhile, new conceptions of virtuous work emerged from the spectacular economic expansion and demographic shifts. In 1870, some 53 percent of Americans made their living in farming, and the prevailing "agrarian myth" idealized the

---

3. Gordon, *Rise and Fall of American Growth*, 1, 185.
4. Keller, *Regulating a New Economy*, 1–10. The census defined "urban" communities as those having a population of 2,500 or more.
5. James R. Green, *The World of the Worker: Labor in Twentieth Century America* (New York, 1980), 68, 94, 120.

yeoman farmer as "the simple, honest, independent, healthy, happy human being."[6]

This Jeffersonian ideal was soon eclipsed by that of the self-made man pursuing opportunity, career, and wealth in the industrial economy. The Gilded Age paragon of success—the industrial capitalist with a grade school education who made a fortune, such as Andrew Carnegie, Cornelius Vanderbilt, and John D. Rockefeller—then faded away. In its place arose the specialization and professionalization of the labor force, driven by advances in science and technology that accelerated the pace of change. By the beginning of the twentieth century, "investment in human capital . . . became supreme," scholars concur.[7] Workers needed education to advance themselves, and the nation's public school systems and higher education expanded rapidly.

The educational and economic developments were thus intimately and reciprocally related. The expansion of school systems and higher education increased human capital in American society, contributing directly to the nation's economic growth. Conversely, the economic expansion provided revenue for school systems and higher education through major increases in philanthropy, public investment, and families' capacity to pay tuition.

The magnitude of this unprecedented nationwide spending on higher education was widely observed but difficult to measure. To improve financial reporting of "what the nation has . . . invested in the work of education," the US commissioner of education hired the prominent statistician Edward Thorndike in 1907.[8] Yet, two decades later, statisticians still could not answer accurately "two questions frequently asked," namely, "How much money is spent for higher education in the United States?" and "How is it spent?"[9]

Even as those questions resounded publicly by 1930, it was impossible to compile accurate and comprehensive financial data for higher education because many colleges and universities were still not issuing accurate financial reports. In 1930, the American Council on Education formed the National Committee on Standard Reports for Institutions of Higher Education. That committee was succeeded by the Financial Advisory Service in 1935, when scholars were still noting

6. Quotations are from Richard Hofstadter, *The Age of Reform: From Bryan to F.D.R.* (New York, 1955), 24, 116. See Lynn Dumenil, *Modern Temper: American Culture and Society in the 1920s* (New York, 1995), 7–11; David J. Goldberg, *Discontented America: The United States in the 1920s* (Baltimore, 1999).

7. Goldin and Katz, *Race between Education and Technology*, 11. See Sean D. Cashman, *America in the Gilded Age*, 3rd ed. (New York, 1993), 81–89; Bruce A. Kimball, *The "True Professional Ideal" in America: A History* (Oxford, 1992), 198–300.

8. US CommEd, *Report [June 30, 1907]*, 2:523.

9. *Biennial Survey of Education 1928–1930*, 2:526.

"discrepancies . . . due to variations in accounting methods" of colleges and universities. The Financial Advisory Service was then discontinued in 1940.[10] The lack of reliable data has meant that cost trends in higher education across the formative period have not been accurately determined or analyzed.

Cost versus Price

As discussed in the introduction, cost and price must be carefully distinguished in studying the finances of higher education. Cost, often called "production cost" by economists, is what colleges and universities spend to produce higher education. "Price" denotes either the announced tuition and fees of institutions or the amount that students actually pay for the education, whether in cash, through loans, or through work-study (or some combination thereof). Through 1930, these two kinds of "price" usually coincided, and colleges and universities received the total revenue that they charged. If a school during the formative era enrolled 1,000 students and charged tuition of $100, then it normally received $100,000, whether the money came from students' pockets, loan funds, or scholarships.

Before 1930, the idea of discounting tuition—crediting some students with "institutional grant aid" so they did not have to pay the full listed tuition—was scarcely contemplated. Indeed, institutional leaders did not seem to conceive of announcing a price and then cutting it for some students but not others. Presidents, deans, and faculties simply resisted increasing tuition if they felt that it would exclude students with few resources or decrease enrollment.[11] Furthermore, discounting tuition was not necessary to recruit students because the capacity of colleges and universities could barely keep pace with the growing number of students flocking to higher education.

In the 1910s and 1920s, the listed tuition started rising, and the growing price of higher education attracted criticism. These fees were never popular, of course, and some students and state residents in prior decades had opposed charging or raising tuition at all. These dissidents had filed lawsuits challenging the authority of public university trustees to set or raise tuition and fees without express authorization from the state legislature or the state constitution. Although these populist suits were largely unsuccessful, more legal challenges were made after 1915 when tuition began rising rapidly. State universities won every case. "By the

---

10. Walter C. Eells, "Income from Endowments," *Journal of Higher Education* 7 (December, 1936): 475. See Ben J. Wattenberg, *Statistical History of the United States from Colonial Times to the Present* (New York, 1976), 365.

11. Eliot, *Annual Report 1904–5*, 23–24. See Bruce A. Kimball and Daniel R. Coquillette, *The Intellectual Sword: Harvard Law School, the Second Century* (Cambridge, MA, 2020), 88–98, 212–15.

end of the 1930s, tuition and fees had become widely accepted at public institutions of higher education in states with and without express legislative or constitutional approval," observes historian Scott Gelber.[12]

Despite the courts' approval, scholars by 1930 began publishing critical studies of the rising undergraduate tuition in the nation.[13] Indeed, between 1910 and 1940, many prominent colleges and universities instituted "skyrocketing tuition charges" and "enormous tuition increases" averaging 206 percent, according to a study published in 2020.[14] But such studies then and now did not account for four factors.

First, colleges and universities had long kept their prices low and steady, leading students and their parents to expect that this pattern would continue. In fact, many schools across the country maintained the same tuition throughout all four decades from 1875 to 1915, including the University of Alabama, the University of Missouri, Earlham College in Indiana, and Harvard University. Also, the price was relatively low, compared to the production cost, because higher education was heavily subsidized by private gifts and state appropriations. Presidents of private universities hesitated to raise their tuition because they faced "formidable competition with a large number of strong state universities in which tuition is free."[15]

Due to this price competition and their traditional charitable association, well-endowed private institutions generally kept their prices low. Johns Hopkins and Stanford charged students nothing or nominal tuition into the 1910s, and less endowed institutions also had to keep their prices low in order to attract students. This background made regular and significant increases in tuition seem unnatural, sparking criticism.

Second, in the opening decades of the twentieth century, inflation forced colleges and universities to break the norm of steady, low fees. The "enormous tuition increases" reported by scholars were calculated in nominal dollars. For example, the 206 percent hike in tuition, mentioned above, amounted to a

12. Scott M. Gelber, *Courts and Classrooms: A Legal History of College Access, 1860–1960* (Baltimore, 2016), 121.

13. See Philip A. Cowen, "The College Tuition Fee in Relation to Current Income" (PhD diss., New York University, 1929); John B. Goodwin, "Trends of Student Fees in Colleges and Universities since 1860" (MS thesis, University of Chicago, 1934); Cavan, "Student and the Financing of the College."

14. Thomas Adam, *College Affordability* (Lanham, MD, 2020), 142, tables 1.1 and 4.3. Cf. John R. Thelin, "Why Did College Cost So Little? Affordability and Higher Education a Century Ago," *Society and Public Policy* 15 (December 2015): 1–5.

15. Eliot, *Annual Report 1906–7*, 16. See US CommEd, *Report [June 30, 1875]*, 738–47; *[June 30, 1916]*, 2:308–19.

102 percent increase in constant dollars between 1910 and 1940. The proportional increase was half as much as reported, after accounting for inflation.

But what warranted even that price increase? The academic studies of rising tuition did not consider, third, the dramatic growth in the production cost of colleges and universities. This was driven by new "elective courses and specialties, . . . more professors . . . and new scientific equipment . . . more buildings . . . heavily increasing the cost of maintenance." Academic advancements drove the additional expenses. In fact, the US commissioners of education repeatedly warned that per-capita spending in higher education was growing too slowly and that colleges and universities needed more revenue to properly educate their students in modern America.[16]

Finally, tuition rose in the early decades of the twentieth century to compensate for the decreasing per-student subsidies provided by state appropriations, gifts, and endowment income. In absolute terms, these subsidies grew, but the production cost and enrollment increased much faster, rising more than six-fold from about 238,000 students in 1900 to about 1.5 million in 1940.[17] The total subsidies did not keep pace with the expanding enrollment and rising production cost of higher education. Tuition and fees therefore had to cover a greater fraction of the aggregate cost. In 1929, a nationwide study of 156 colleges and universities reported that the percentage of production cost paid by tuition and fees held steady during the 1910s and then rose significantly in the 1920s, as seen in table 6.1.

In sum, the perception and criticism of "skyrocketing" tuition between 1910 and 1940 did not account for the long-standing norm that colleges and universities had kept their prices low and increased them rarely and only in small increments. Inflation, rising production cost, and declining per-student subsidies then forced colleges and universities to deviate from that norm. These factors also caused prices to fluctuate and vary significantly across higher education, reinforcing the more fundamental and determinate nature of production cost as a subject of analysis. Production cost also deserved study because it can become a serious problem for society, even if tuition were eliminated and the price of higher education for students fell to zero.

16. Quotation is from "The College Education. Shall It Be Only Rich Man's Luxury? Cost of Tuition Increasing," in *Pandex of the Press*, ed. Arthur I. Street (San Francisco, 1905), 1:488. See US CommEd, *Report [June 30, 1914]*, 1:174–75; *Biennial Survey of Education 1916–1918*, 709–10, 717.

17. *Historical Statistics of the United States*, table Bc523–36.

TABLE 6.1

Aggregate Production Cost Paid by Tuition and Fees at Colleges and Universities Nationwide, 1910–30 (in percentages)

Colleges and universities	Aggregate production cost		
	1910	1920	1930*
109 private institutions[†]	41%	40%	49%
47 public institutions[†]	11%	9%	15%
All 156 institutions[‡]	26%	24%	32%

Source: Computed from data in Philip A. Cowen, "College Tuition Trends," *School and Society* 33 (May 30, 1931): 738–40; Philip A. Cowen, "The College Tuition Fee in Relation to Current Income" (PhD diss., New York University, 1929), 38–45.
* Extrapolated from 1926 figures.
[†] Institutional median.
[‡] Computed by weighting the proportion of enrollments in the public and private sectors.

Kinds of Production Cost

Figure 6.1 sketches the basic conceptual distinctions and relationships pertaining to production cost, price, and subsidies prior to 1930. Aggregate cost refers to the total production cost and comprises both operating expense and capital expense. "Capital" here includes both invested funds and property owned by an institution, and "capital expense" means the cost of buildings, depreciation, opportunity cost, and other dimensions, as explained in appendix 2. The commissioner's reports prior to 1930 often do not list operating expense, but a proxy can be determined by summing the various kinds of current income, nearly all of which went to fund the educational expenses of the institutions before 1930. Additional nuances and distinctions related to cost and price arising after 1945 will be discussed in part II.

Growth in the aggregate cost of higher education is usually salutary for the nation. A democratic society benefits when more people are educated at a higher level because public discussion, social policy, and political decision-making are likely improved. Furthermore, increasing people's intellectual capital often makes them more productive and helps to expand the economy, so raising aggregate spending on higher education normally generates more wealth for society as a whole. Economists Claudia Goldin and Lawrence Katz have estimated that Americans' annual increase in educational attainment raised labor productivity an additional 0.35 percent each year between 1890 and 1970.[18] This annual increase contributed about an additional third to the growth of labor productivity

18. Goldin and Katz, *Race between Education and Technology*, 38–39.

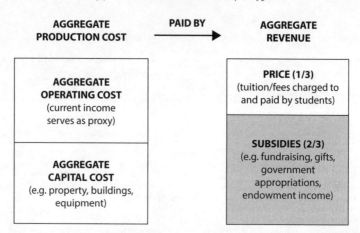

Figure 6.1. Basic Conceptual Relationships among Cost, Price, and Subsidies, 1870–1930.

over the entire span of 80 years, which included most of the formative period of higher education (starting in 1870).

However, rising aggregate production cost of higher education is not always salutary and may become a serious problem for society, depending on the growth rate of the national economy. If the economy expands faster than the aggregate cost, then no problem arises because the fraction of the national income allocated to higher education is shrinking. However, if the aggregate cost of higher education expands faster than the economy, then higher education is consuming an increasing fraction of the national income. This trend, called "cost escalation," can become a serious problem, as is the case with health care today. If such cost escalation continues indefinitely, higher education (or health care) could eventually consume the entire national income, scholars have warned.[19]

But aggregate cost escalation may be justified if enrollment is expanding, because educating more students costs more money. Evaluating aggregate cost escalation therefore depends on whether the number of students is growing faster or slower than that cost. Here arises the critical issue of per-student cost not only in studying national trends but also in comparing schools of different size over time. One must analyze operating expense and capital expense on a per-capita basis by dividing each kind of expense by the number of enrolled students. As the US *Biennial Survey of Education* observed in the 1910s, financial data "lack significance unless per capitas [*sic*] are secured."[20]

19. Christopher Jencks and David Riesman, *The Academic Revolution* (Chicago, 1968), 111; Clotfelter, *Buying the Best.*
20. *Biennial Survey of Education 1916–1918*, 1:711, 716.

If enrollment grows faster than aggregate cost, then the per-student cost declines, and higher education is becoming more efficient. In this case, most scholars agree that escalation of aggregate cost is justified. However, if the aggregate cost of higher education grows faster than the number of students, then the per-student cost to produce higher education is increasing, making it more expensive to educate each student.

Even so, this growing per-student expense might be warranted. Per-student cost justifiably increases if the quality of education is improving, or if more entering students need remediation, or if the cost of goods and services used by colleges and universities grows.[21] In each case, more money is needed to educate each student. But rising per-student cost is generally taken to mean that higher education is becoming less efficient and consuming national income at a faster rate than the number of students is growing. The most worrisome cost escalation therefore occurs when the per-student cost of producing higher education rises faster than either the per-capita national income or the cost of living.

But calculating per-student cost is difficult for a number of reasons. Even counting students is challenging, for example. Enrollment at colleges and universities includes many ambiguous or indeterminate categories: part-time students, summer students, cross-registered students, nondegree candidates, enrollees in different kinds of programs and in different academic levels, and so forth. Which categories should be counted, and how much should each be weighted? Scholars have tried various conversions and given different answers.[22]

"The Difficulties Encountered" in Compiling Data

The data and calculation problems worsen when one looks back in history. Prior to 1930, the most informative and comprehensive data appeared in the annual reports of the commissioner of education and in the biennial surveys of the Bureau of Education. But these reports are riddled with inconsistencies and errors that were incorporated into later sets of pre-1930 financial data, such as *Historical Statistics of the United States* and *Digest of Educational Statistics* produced by the National Center for Education Statistics (NCES).[23] Nevertheless, the pre-1930

21. Charles W. Smith, *Market Values in American Higher Education: The Pitfalls and Promises* (Lanham, MD, 2000), 32–42.

22. See W. Bowen, *Economics of the Major Private Research Universities*, 7, 10, 17n; June O'Neill, *Resource Use in Higher Education: Trends in Outputs and Inputs, 1930 to 1967* (Berkeley, CA, 1971), 3–15; H. Bowen, *Costs of Higher Education*, 4–5, 34, 45, 264–66.

23. See Kimball and Luke, "Measuring Cost Escalation," 198–202; Claudia Goldin, *A Brief History of Education in the United States* (Cambridge, MA, 1999), 15–16.

federal reports and surveys of higher education contain valuable data, though they require careful interpretation.

In 1868, the US Office of Education—headed by the commissioner, located in the Department of the Interior, and known intermittently as the Bureau of Education—began issuing annual reports on the condition of education in the United States. These single volumes included compilations of quantitative data and soon grew to 1,000 pages. By 1889 the information bulked so large that the commissioner started publishing annual reports of two volumes, each consisting of narrative and statistics and exceeding 1,000 pages. By 1915, the work became so overwhelming that the annual report was not completed, and in 1918 the Bureau began issuing the reports in four parts, including a two-volume *Biennial Survey of Education*.[24]

Throughout the formative period, the Bureau operated with a small staff, little money, and no authority to compel schools to report on anything. Not all states and cities gathered data, and when they did, their compilations included different kinds of information in different formats pertaining to different periods. Even determining which institutions to include in "higher education" was debated. Only the staff compiling the annual reports "can understand the difficulties encountered," sighed the commissioner.[25]

Compounding the problems, the Bureau adopted the somewhat perverse policy of dropping a college or university from its lists if the institution failed to report for two years in a row. The Bureau's enumerations of institutions therefore fluctuated and did not reflect how many colleges and universities actually existed. "University statistics are in hopeless confusion," observed Edwin E. Slosson in his classic *Great American Universities* in 1910. The commissioner of education concurred in 1916: "Because of the magnitude, complexity, looseness, and unevenness of our educational systems and the absence of any central administrative agency, it is very difficult to say just what the sum total and average of tendencies for the year have been."[26]

Among the statistical problems, the financial data in higher education remained the least accurate. Colleges and universities had widely divergent bookkeeping practices and policies, which changed over time even at the same in-

24. US CommEd, *Report [June 30, 1889]*, pt. 1, xv; *[June 30, 1916]*, 2:viii; *[June 30, 1918]*, 5; *Biennial Survey of Education 1916–1918*, 2 vols.; Donald R. Warren, *To Enforce Education: A History of the Founding Years of the United States Office of Education* (Detroit, 1974), 91–97.

25. US CommEd, *Report [June 30, 1876]*, xxii. See US CommEd, *Report [June 30, 1885]*, xiv; *[June 30, 1911]*, 2:883; *[June 30, 1895]*, 1:184–85; Frank Blackmar, *The History of Federal and State Aid to Higher Education in the United States* (Washington, DC, 1890), 9.

26. Edwin E. Slosson, *Great American Universities* (New York, 1910), x; US CommEd, *Report [June 30, 1916]*, 1:xvi.

stitutions. Some refused to report their finances out of "super-sensitiveness to unfavorable criticism," noted the commissioner in 1914. Women's colleges, Catholic institutions, and HBCUs were particularly sensitive.[27] But the problems in financial data stemmed fundamentally from the abysmal accounting and bookkeeping of most colleges and universities, which could not report accurate data even if they had wanted to. In 1930, the Bureau of Education lamented, "There is as yet no standard, universally accepted system of financial reporting for institutions of higher learning." All these problems persisted in the following decade.[28]

Through it all, the Bureau's annual reports and biennial surveys continued to present impressively detailed statistical summaries on higher education finances. At the very same time, the Bureau conceded that the summaries were generally incomplete and inconsistent from year to year.[29] These summaries therefore describe different, arbitrary swaths of higher education. They are virtually useless for comparisons over time, but they apparently served as the sources for subsequent compilations of pre-1930 financial data.

Nonetheless, the Bureau's reports and surveys do provide the most comprehensive and informative data on pre-1930 finances, but that information must be compiled selectively institution by institution. This chapter therefore compiles and analyzes data from a cross section of 32 colleges and universities, whose financial data from 1875 to 1930 could be reliably gleaned from the Bureau of Education reports and supplemented by material in the institutions' archives.[30] Listed in table 6.2, the cross section comprises seven relatively large and wealthy eastern universities; eight small, private liberal arts colleges from across the nation; five southern universities; eight midwestern public universities; and four western public universities. One HBCU, two women's colleges, and seven land-grant institutions are included.

To assess cost escalation, data on schools' capital, income, and enrollment are needed, and these three dimensions present analytic challenges and choices, as discussed in appendix 2. In brief, "capital" denotes the wealth of an institution and comprises all of its invested funds and its property. "Income" serves as a proxy for annual operating cost, following the practice of the commissioner of education and subsequent scholars. Finally, enrollment data are needed to calculate the crucial per-student costs. Appendix 3 lists the amounts of capital, income, and

27. Quotation is from US CommEd, *Report [June 30, 1914]*, 1:166. See US CommEd, *Report [June 30, 1883]*, cxli–cxlii; *[June 30, 1907]*, 1:2; *[June 30, 1912]*, 1:97–99.
28. *Biennial Survey of Education 1928–1930*, 2:526. See John D. Millett, *Financing Higher Education in the United States* (New York, 1952), 141.
29. US CommEd, *Report [June 30, 1923]*, 22; *Biennial Survey of Education 1928–1930*, 1:1–8, 2:321–22.
30. App. 2 explains the selection of the 32 schools.

TABLE 6.2
Cross Section of 32 Institutions Studied, 1875–1930

Type of institution	Institutions studied
Large, wealthy eastern universities	Columbia, Cornell, Harvard, <u>Howard</u>, Johns Hopkins, Princeton, Yale
Small, private, liberal arts colleges	Amherst, Baylor, Centre, Earlham, Knox, <u>Smith</u>, <u>Vassar</u>, Wabash
Southern universities	Alabama, Georgia, *Louisiana State*, Vanderbilt, Virginia
Midwestern public universities	Indiana, *Iowa State*, Kansas, Michigan, *Missouri, Nebraska, Ohio State, Wisconsin*
Western public universities*	*California*, Colorado, Oregon, Texas

Notes: Land-grant institutions are italicized. Women's colleges and HBCUs are underlined.
* Oregon (1876), Colorado (1877), and Texas (1883) were opened soon after 1875 and are included to expand the representation of western public universities.

enrollment for each of the 32 institutions in every fifth year over the formative period, in nominal dollars. The aggregate figures are adjusted for inflation in the calculations below.

Massive Escalation of Aggregate Cost, 1875–1930

The aggregate production cost of the cross section of 32 colleges and universities between 1875 and 1930 can be computed from the data in appendix 3. However, analyzing aggregate cost requires data from a consistent set of reporting institutions over the entire period. Adding to the number of institutions over time would arbitrarily inflate the growth of aggregate cost. Consequently, the three public western universities that opened after 1875 must be eliminated, leaving 29 institutions for this analysis.

As indicated in figure 6.1 and explained in appendix 2, two dimensions of production cost must be considered: annual operating expense (represented by current income) and capital expense (based on property and invested funds). After summing those components for the 29 institutions in every fifth year, the totals are deflated into constant dollars to create two aggregate cost indexes—one for income and one for capital. Next, these are compared to the economy-wide index of GNP. Often reported in aggregate terms and well suited to aggregate comparisons, GNP measures the total value of goods and services produced by the citizens of a given country over the course of a year.[31] Table 6.3

31. See app. 2; Richard Sutch, "A Gross National Product and Gross Domestic Product: 1869–1929," in *Historical Statistics of the United States*, 184–91.

TABLE 6.3
Aggregate Production Cost of 29 Colleges and Universities and GNP, 1875–1930
(rounded to billions of constant dollars; 1860 = 1)

Year	Aggregate operating income	Cumulative increase of income	Aggregate capital	Cumulative increase of capital	GNP	Cumulative increase of GNP
1875	1.5	—	17.8	—	5,500	—
1880	1.8	21%	26.1	47%	8,600	56%
1890	4.2	176%	52.4	195%	11,500	109%
1900	8.1	439%	90.8	411%	17,500	218%
1910	18.7	1,137%	148.1	734%	27,600	402%
1920	19.8	1,211%	123.9	597%	35,500	545%
1930	62.9	4,064%	363.7	1,947%	45,200	722%

Source: Data are drawn from appendix 4.

lists the absolute values and percentage increases of the two aggregate cost indexes and GNP in constant dollars for every decade from 1875 to 1930.

Table 6.3 reveals that the aggregate production cost of higher education escalated enormously from 1875 to 1930. The aggregate annual income of the 29 colleges and universities rose more than 4,000 percent, the aggregate capital nearly 2,000 percent, and GNP only 722 percent. Another standard of comparison, often used by economists, is the compound annual growth rate (CAGR). Over the entire period, the corresponding CAGR was 7.0 percent for total income, 5.6 percent for total capital, and 3.9 percent for GNP.[32] By either measure, the aggregate cost of higher education rose much faster than the national income during this period.

It is remarkable that the growth of aggregate income and aggregate capital of higher education significantly outpaced GNP during this period of unprecedented economic expansion in the United States. One major reason was the increase in quality, evident in the introduction of laboratory and graduate work, according to Commissioner of Education William T. Harris. In addition, the demand for postsecondary education grew enormously between 1875 and 1930 due to additional requirements for expertise and academic credentials to work in offices, business, teaching, medicine, law, engineering, and other professions. In fact, the total number of colleges and universities more than doubled, and the number of regular students in higher education rose over 13 times.[33]

32. See app. 5 for calculations of CAGR over different periods.
33. US CommEd, *Report [June 30, 1889]*, pt. 1, lvii; US CommEd, *Report [June 30, 1875]*, xxv; *Biennial Survey of Education 1928–1930*, 2:2–6. See Geiger, *History of American Higher Education*, 518–19.

Apart from demand, another reason for the aggregate cost escalation was the growing supply of funding: the nation's remarkable economic growth made more revenue available to invest in higher education. One major source of revenue was public funds supplied by taxes. The federal government subsidized land-grant colleges and universities directly and indirectly through the first Morrill Act of 1862, the Hatch Act of 1887, the second Morrill Act of 1890, and the Smith-Lever Act of 1914. State legislatures, though sometimes grudgingly, also increased their funding for public colleges and universities. In 1912, the US Office of Education reported that "practically every state" was providing "larger funds than in the preceding year" to higher education. In 1920, statistician Mabel Newcomer reported that "the cost of public education in the United States . . . increased much faster from 1910 to 1920 than in any preceding ten-year period since 1870."[34]

In addition, new revenue streamed in from private philanthropy, fed by the economic growth. Already in 1890, before Andrew Carnegie and John D. Rockefeller weighed in, Commissioner Harris applauded the "generous endowments of institutions of learning by rich men," including "our Johns Hopkinses, Tulanes, Peabodys, Purdues, Licks, Drexels, Clarks, and Stanfords," who were contributing an "annual average of $10,000,000 . . . to various forms of higher education."[35] Coupled with the government subsidies, this private philanthropy permitted many colleges and universities to make "extraordinary expenditures" for capital and operations, as the Office of Education reported in 1897 and continued to extoll through the 1910s.[36]

The trend was amplified after World War I, when fundraising in higher education blossomed during the 1920s. Despite the "financial stringency" imposed by the Panics of 1893 and 1907, the First World War, the recession of 1920, and the stock market crash of 1929, both the aggregate operating expense and the aggregate capital of higher education increased remarkably between 1875 and 1930.[37]

Per-Student Cost Becomes Cheaper, 1875–1930

And what happened to the historical per-capita production cost, which became the great concern in the second half of the twentieth century? For this analysis, all

34. US CommEd, *Report [June 30, 1912]*, 1:83; Mabel Newcomer, *Financial Statistics of Public Education in the United States 1910–1920* (New York, 1924), 3.

35. US CommEd, *Report [June 30, 1889]*, pt. 1, lvii.

36. US CommEd, *Report [June 30, 1897]*, pt. 2, 1651. See also US CommEd, *Report [June 30, 1912]*, 1:40; *[June 30, 1913]*, 1:21.

37. Quotation is from US CommEd, *Report [June 30, 1896]*, pt. 2, 1924–25.

32 institutions in the cross section can be included because adding the per-student figures of the three western universities opening after 1875 does not inflate the per-capita cost of the entire cross section. Here again, two dimensions of production cost must be considered: operating expense and capital expense. For this pre-1930 analysis, capital expense includes building construction, depreciation, equipment, furnishings, maintenance, and supplies, as explained in appendix 2.

Adding these two dimensions, deflating them to constant dollars, and dividing by the number of students yields the cost per student, which undulated significantly in the formative era. Nevertheless, over the entire period, the per-student production cost rose only 27 percent in constant dollars—little more than the price of commodities. Between 1875 and 1930, a historical Commodities Price Index rose 17 percent, as seen in table 6.4.

Table 6.4 also reveals that national income, or gross domestic product (GDP), grew much faster than either the price of commodities or the per-capita cost of higher education. Often reported in per-capita terms, GDP measures the total value of the goods and services produced by citizens or noncitizens within the borders of a country in a given year.[38] Between 1875 and 1930, per-capita GDP increased more than 20 times as much as the price of commodities and 12 times as much as the per-student cost of higher education.[39] In 1930, Americans, on average, had a great deal more income to spend on higher education and other goods and services than they did 55 years earlier.

The point is even more striking in proportional terms, as seen in table 6.4. In 1875, the per-student production cost of a year of college consumed the average annual GDP of more than three people. In 1930 a year of college education consumed the average GDP of about one person. Between 1875 and 1930, higher education had become about three times cheaper to produce for each student, relative to per-capita GDP.

Why Did Per-Student Production Cost Become Relatively Cheaper?

In the 1960s, scholars and policy makers began to worry about the escalating per-capita cost of higher education. But this type of cost escalation was not a concern between 1870 and 1930. The per-student cost rose relatively little during this period compared to commodity prices or per-capita GDP. In fact, in the

38. Richard Sutch, "A Gross National Product and Gross Domestic Product: 1869–1929," 184–91. Yet GDP may understate economic growth because the goods and services measured by GDP overlook new products that are adding wealth to the economy. See Gordon, *Rise and Fall of American Growth*, 9–11.
39. The corresponding CAGRs are 0.44 percent for per-student cost, 0.29 percent for Commodities Price Index, and 2.69 percent for GDP. See app. 5.

TABLE 6.4
*Cumulative Change in Production Cost per Student Compared to GDP and Commodities
Price Index, 1875–1930 (in constant dollars; 1860 = 1)*

Year	Production cost per student	Cumulative change in production cost per student	GDP per capita	Cumulative change in GDP per capita	Cumulative change in commodities price index
1875	596	—	170	—	—
1880	671	13%	205	21%	−16%
1885	851	43%	205	21%	−28%
1890	581	−3%	208	22%	−28%
1895	553	−7%	200	18%	−39%
1900	566	−5%	246	45%	−29%
1905	556	−7%	299	76%	−24%
1910	691	16%	385	126%	−11%
1915	663	11%	398	134%	7%
1920	363	−39%	860	406%	107%
1925	607	2%	804	373%	47%
1930	758	27%	734	332%	17%

Source: Data are drawn from appendix 6 and *Historical Statistics of the United States*, table Cc125–37.

early twentieth century, commissioners of education feared that the per-capita expense of higher education was growing too slowly and that colleges and universities lacked sufficient revenue to meet the needs of students.[40]

Widely acknowledged during the formative era, the fundamental reason that per-student cost did not rise appreciably was that the number of students exploded. Between 1875 and 1930, the total number of colleges and universities more than doubled from 577 to 1,409, and the number of their regular students rose over 13 times from about 82,700 to about 1,086,000.[41]

To be sure, per-student cost fluctuated significantly during the formative era, depending on the circumstances. Between 1875 and 1885, the per-student cost jumped 43 percent to a peak of $851 in constant dollars. In this early decade, public and private universities were opening and expanding with abundant resources and capacity and were not yet overwhelmed by students. Prominent among these institutions were fledgling land-grant universities, represented by the seven identified in table 6.2.

40. US CommEd, *Report [June 30, 1914]*, 1:174–75; *Biennial Survey of Education 1916–1918*, 709–10, 717.
41. US CommEd, *Report [June 30, 1875]*, xxv; *Biennial Survey of Education 1928–1930*, 2:2–6.

After 1885, postsecondary enrollment accelerated, particularly in the professional schools and vocational programs at universities, as discussed in appendix 2. Colleges and universities could not expand fast enough to accommodate the throngs of students, and per-student production cost fell between 1885 and 1905. In 1902, the commissioner's annual report noted that many colleges and universities were overcrowded. In 1904, Commissioner Harris lamented that investment in higher education, particularly in facilities, was falling behind the burgeoning number of students. Confirming these points, the capital cost per student in constant dollars plummeted after 1885 and never caught up to the initial amount of $366 in 1875, finishing at $334 in 1930.[42] Students enrolled faster than colleges and universities could construct buildings to accommodate them.

Because the per-student capital cost fell behind, the small rise in per-student production cost to $758 between 1875 and 1930 came entirely from the growth in operating expense (current income) after 1895. But that small rise was inadequate. In 1921, the Bureau of Education doubted that per-student income "has kept pace with the necessarily increasing cost of giving students a college education."[43] Even if the enrollment had remained the same, colleges and universities were going to spend more to provide education because of advances in knowledge and academic specialization. Given the sharp rise in enrollment, colleges and universities needed even more revenue to educate more students, as knowledge rapidly expanded and new academic disciplines emerged.

Hiking tuition was not the solution, due to the "well known fact that income derived from fees received from students forms only about one-third of the total income" in higher education, remarked the Bureau of Education repeatedly.[44] Confirmed by table 6.1, that customary fraction meant that conceivable tuition increases could not supply the required revenue. Colleges and universities needed more in subsidies.

Additional state funding helped the public institutions, though this was often unreliable. Commissioner Harris observed in 1903 that public colleges and universities had to make "constant appeals to sometimes unfriendly legislatures . . . for current support." Because tax levies had been fixed "long ago" and enrollment had grown "so rapidly," state revenue "has not kept pace with the . . . expenditures rendered necessary" in postsecondary education, Harris wrote. In the

---

42. See app. 6; US CommEd, *Report [June 30, 1902]*, 1:657; *[June 30, 1904]*, 2:1428.
43. *Biennial Survey of Education 1916–1918*, 1:709–10.
44. US CommEd, *Report [June 30, 1904]*, 2:1428. See *Biennial Survey of Education 1916–1918*, 1:717.

state of Washington, for example, legislative appropriations lagged far behind enrollment growth at the University of Washington. Hoping to slow the growth, the regents stopped advertising the university, while the university held classes in attics, cellars, and outbuildings.[45]

The rapid expansion of public sector enrollment compounded the problem of "unfriendly legislatures." New kinds of public institutions arose, such as junior colleges. In fact, more than half of the 408 new colleges founded in the 1920s were junior colleges. In addition, women's enrollment expanded dramatically, rising to 47 percent of all college students by 1920, and 90 percent of women attended coeducational institutions, which were predominantly public. The public sector expansion also resulted because private institutions began to cap their enrollments and introduce selective admissions during the 1920s, rather than accept all qualified students, as they had in the past. Consequently, by 1930 the state colleges and universities had grown enormously and enrolled about the same number of students as the private sector, though numbering only about one-third of the private institutions.[46]

Meanwhile, the "stunning industrial productivity" that had "made the United States the dominant world economic power" in the 1920s ignited a frenzy of higher education fundraising in each mode of the triad presented in figure 4.3.[47] While this phenomenon occurred predominantly in the private sector, the leading public universities also participated, as described in earlier chapters. Nevertheless, though revenue increased dramatically in the late 1920s, the per-student cost of higher education rose only 27 percent over the entire formative era.

At the same time, the aggregate cost of higher education soared steeply, as described above. Table 6.3 shows that aggregate operating income rose more than 4,000%, higher education capital nearly 2,000%, and GNP only 722% in the cross section of 29 colleges and universities between 1875 and 1930.[48] The staggering size of this aggregate cost escalation is demonstrated by comparing it with the ensuing 50 years from 1930 to 1980. In those five decades, scholars and policy makers began to "assert that higher educational costs have been out of control" and decried what they considered "the explosive growth of higher educational costs," stated economist Howard Bowen. But the CAGR of 7.0% for

45. US CommEd, *Report [June 30, 1903]*, 1:xii. See Gelber, *Courts and Classrooms*, 119.
46. *Historical Statistics of the United States*, table Bc523–36; *Biennial Survey of Education 1928–1930*, 2:2, 322. See Lynn D. Gordon, *Gender and Higher Education in the Progressive Era* (New Haven, CT, 1990); Goldin and Katz, *Race between Education and Technology*, 262; Kimball and Coquillette, *Intellectual Sword*, 175–77.
47. Quotation is from Dumenil, *Modern Temper*, 6.
48. US CommEd, *Report [June 30, 1896]*, pt. 2, 1924–25.

the aggregate operating income between 1875 and 1930 *exceeded* that of 6.5% between 1930 and 1980.[49]

In sharp contrast to the fears about so-called "out-of-control" costs expressed during the second half of the twentieth century, scholars and policy makers in the formative era applauded the even faster growth in the aggregate expense of higher education. Many more students were being educated, and knowledge was advancing. At the same time, European observers began to admire "higher education in the United States," given "how rich the universities are there, and how the dollars flow in to endow them and maintain them in a splendid condition."[50] Whether the wealth, cost, and price of higher education actually grew "out of control" after 1930, what forces and factors drove them, and how they were explained, are the questions addressed in part II.

49. App. 5; H. Bowen, *Costs of Higher Education*, 34–35.
50. Gabriel Compayré, "Higher and Secondary Education in the United States [in translation]," in US CommEd, *Report [June 30, 1896]*, pt. 2, 1157.

THE GOLDEN AGES, 1930–2020S

CHAPTER 7

Depression, 60/40 Rule, and Cost-Disease Theory, 1930s–1960s

After the formative era ended in about 1930, higher education struggled financially, and scholars began to publish more research on wealth, cost, and price of higher education. As state appropriations, philanthropy, and investment returns plummeted during the Great Depression, colleges and universities responded to the declining subsidies by reducing their production cost and generally holding the price level. The Darwinian competition for revenue and wealth slowed in the 1930s and then ground to a halt in the 1940s, due to the upheaval wrought by World War II. After 1945, the flood of returning veterans funded by the Servicemen's Readjustment Act (1944) continued to depress that competition because this "G.I. Bill" brought prosperity to virtually all colleges and universities. Meanwhile, the exploding enrollment drove the per-student cost of higher education lower in the late 1940s.

When the flood of veterans ebbed in 1951, the feverish competition for revenue and free money resumed, while fundraising, state appropriations, and tuition rates increased rapidly. In the 1950s and 1960s, two new, important sources of revenue and wealth emerged: mammoth federal grants or contracts and aggressive investing of endowment portfolios. The latter took the form of a new 60/40 rule of portfolio management: 60 percent invested in equities and 40 percent in fixed-income securities. The wealthiest private and public institutions led the way in both respects, just as they had in fundraising innovations.

The rapid expansion of the postwar economy, the torrent of federal grants and contracts, and the dramatic rise of the stock market during the 1950s and 1960s have led scholars to name these two corpulent decades a "golden age" of higher education. It was a time when new academic programs and new colleges and universities sprouted like mushrooms and established ones waxed ever larger. Funding was available for any decent research project, and a faculty job awaited every new PhD.[1]

Meanwhile, the terms of analyzing production cost in higher education also changed significantly in the 1950s and 1960s. Most federal grants and contracts funded staff, programs, and facilities for medical, defense, and scientific research that was not directly related to students' education. Studies of higher education cost therefore began to distinguish the rapidly growing "non-educational" expenses from the "institutional costs that properly can be ascribed to the education of students." But distinguishing "educational and non-educational expenditures" was subject to interpretation, and the financial data sets presented serious "technical problems" in assigning expenses to the categories. These problems made higher education costs "notoriously hard to interpret" over the next 50 years.[2]

Nevertheless, by any measure, the production cost of higher education soared alongside the influx of new revenue in the 1950s and 1960s. Money went out as fast as it came in, unless channeled into endowment. This golden age culminated in the late 1960s with dolorous warnings that the cost of higher education was escalating out of control. Just at that point, two economists at Princeton University famously diagnosed the problem. Higher education had contracted a "cost disease," a contagion that originated early in the Industrial Revolution. Due not to any fault of the colleges and universities, their per-student cost had escalated inexorably for a century, these economists said.

Declining Cost, 1930s

In October 1929, the stock market crashed, and the United States entered the deepest and longest economic recession in its history. Initial signs of improve-

1. See Freeland, *Academia's Golden Age*.
2. Quotations are from H. Bowen, *Costs of Higher Education*, xiv, 4–9, 37–39, 150–51.

ment appeared in 1931, but most economists agree that the Federal Reserve System and President Herbert Hoover (1929–33) failed to do enough to increase the domestic money supply and stimulate consumer demand. This weak response led to a second phase of decline starting with a vicious deflationary cycle in 1932 that overwhelmed Hoover's cautious remedies, such as the Reconstruction Finance Corporation, and left the nation in disarray. Between 1929 and 1932, US industrial production fell 46 percent, wholesale prices 32 percent, and international trade 70 percent, while 20 percent of banks failed. Unemployment rose six-fold, the worst increase in the Western world. These conditions led, in the election of 1932, to Democratic control of Congress, the overwhelming victory of President Franklin D. Roosevelt (1933–45), and his proclamation of a "new deal for the American people."[3]

Roosevelt's New Deal created whole new legal and regulatory worlds in so-called "alphabet agencies," many of which strengthened the monetary system and financial markets, such as the Federal Deposit Insurance Corporation in 1933 and the Securities and Exchange Commission in 1934. The Democrats expanded their congressional majorities in the 1934 midterm election, enabling them to pass a flurry of legislation with little resistance. The ensuing "Second New Deal" created more new agencies, such as the Federal Reserve Board and the Works Progress Administration in 1935. Conservative Republicans were horrified by the expansion of the federal government wrought by the New Deals. But the alphabet agencies restored public trust in banks, financial markets, and the entire monetary system and relieved the anxiety felt by many Americans about securing fair employment, surviving natural disasters, and growing old, although people of color were excluded from many of those relief efforts.

Meanwhile, "colleges and universities weathered the Depression far better than most other institutions," notes historian Roger Geiger.[4] Higher education fared relatively well because postsecondary enrollment often expands during periods of high unemployment, although colleges and universities certainly did not prosper. The average per-student educational cost fell by nearly 4 percent in constant dollars between 1929 and 1939, owing partly to the sharp decline in philanthropy, endowment income, and state appropriations. Some public university presidents who had previously considered public fundraising to be

---

3. See Robert S. McElvaine, *The Great Depression, 1929–1941*, rev. ed. (New York, 2009); Anthony J. Badger, *The New Deal: The Depression Years, 1933–1940* (New York, 1989); Keller, *Regulating a New Economy*; Dona Cooper Hamilton and Charles V. Hamilton, "The Dual Agenda of African American Organizations since the New Deal: Social Welfare Policies and Civil Rights," *Political Science Quarterly* 107 (1992): 440.

4. Geiger, *History of American Higher Education*, 507–8.

inappropriate for their institutions, such as George Rightmire at Ohio State University, changed their mind when faced with severe cuts by state governors in the 1930s.[5]

Gifts and grants to higher education dropped precipitously, bottoming out in 1933 at less than half of the amount pledged annually during the 1920s. A few institutions attempted fundraising drives in the mid-1930s, but these anomalies were less ambitious and successful than a decade earlier, including Harvard's campaign in honor of its tricentennial in 1936. As a result, the largest gifts to higher education were usually bequests, which came primarily to the oldest and best-endowed institutions with elderly, wealthy alumni.[6]

But even some of those institutions struggled. New buildings burdened Yale University with maintenance costs that weakened the university financially as the Depression deepened. Its endowment income declined more than 20 percent; gifts to the Yale Alumni Fund fell by 85 percent, and the university had trouble collecting pledges made during its drives in the 1920s. The university started cutting expenses in 1931, and enrollment dropped by almost 1,000 students in four years. Pressed for tuition revenue, Yale admitted over 100 undergraduates with deficient academic qualifications in 1933, and more than one-third of those soon flunked out.[7] Columbia University also struggled, as discussed in chapter 5.

Many schools with fewer resources fared even worse during the Depression. Some that depended heavily on tuition tried to raise it steeply, although that threatened enrollment. The treasurer of Rollins College in Florida argued for this approach, citing the "law of the survival of the fittest."[8] Meanwhile, per-capita endowment at women's colleges lagged far behind that of men's colleges, according to a study of 108 single-sex colleges in 1935. The endowment per student ratio of the 67 women's colleges was half that of the 41 men's colleges.[9]

HBCUs faced even higher barriers. The Great Depression had hit farmers earlier and harder than Wall Street or manufacturing industries. By 1931, the agricultural South was much worse off than the industrial North, and most

5. H. Bowen, *Costs of Higher Education*, 38, 45; Benjamin A. Johnson, "Fundraising and Endowment Building at a Land Grant University during the Critical Period, 1910–1940" (PhD diss., The Ohio State University, 2013), 208–365.

6. R. Keith Kane and Dana Doten, "The Case for Endowment," *Harvard Alumni Bulletin*, November 24, 1951, 214; Jones, *American Giver*, 16–20, 70; Scott M. Cutlip, *Fund Raising in the United States: Its Role in America's Philanthropy* (New Brunswick, NJ, 1965), 486–88.

7. George W. Pierson, *Yale: The University College, 1921–1937* (New Haven, CT, 1955), 661n2; Gaddis Smith, "Life at Yale during the Great Depression," *Yale Alumni Magazine* 73 (November–December 2009): 1–5.

8. Quoted in Cavan, "Student and the Financing of the College," 9.

9. Walter C. Eells, "Educational Research and Statistics: Endowments in American Colleges and Universities," *School and Society* 41 (1935): 270.

African Americans lived in the South, worked on farms, and already earned far less on average than whites. The distribution of proceeds from the second Morrill Act of 1890 had greatly shortchanged "the Negro land-grant colleges" throughout the South. Several private HBCUs closed because their graduates could not afford to support them during the Depression. The survivors were forced to continue their appeals to wealthy white industrialists, who did not envision political or social equality for African Americans.[10]

Cost Still Falling, 1940s

As the United States struggled to emerge from the Depression, storm clouds gathered across the world. After invading mainland China in 1937 and French Indo-China in 1939, Japan attacked Pearl Harbor, Hawaii, on December 7, 1941. The next day, the United States declared war on Japan, and Germany and Italy reciprocated on the following day. American colleges and universities began to empty, as students and faculty left in droves to aid the war effort. The aggregate production cost of higher education therefore fell sharply, and the per-student cost rose dramatically. Colleges and universities limped along with skeletal staff and enrollments.

HBCUs were particularly hard-hit, and in 1943 President Frederick D. Patterson of the Tuskegee Institute in Alabama; economist William J. Trent; and Mary McLeod Bethune of the National Youth Administration conceived a way to attract philanthropy for HBCUs. Emulating the model of mass giving pursued by the successful March of Dimes drives, they proposed organizing a coordinated public appeal so donors would not be forced to choose among individual HBCUs. The famous United Negro College Fund was born, and the 18 member colleges retained the John Price Jones consulting firm to assist in 1943.[11] Figure 7.1 reveals that the Fund grew rapidly over the next decade.

In June 1944, the prospects for higher education began to brighten when President Roosevelt signed the G.I. Bill. This legislation provided generous benefits for returning soldiers to pursue postsecondary education, although African Americans were once again shortchanged. In order to secure the votes of southern congressmen, the sponsors of the bill did not expressly prohibit racial discrimination and allowed local officials and college administrators, rather than

10. John W. Davis, "The Negro Land-Grant College," *Journal of Negro Education* 2 (1933): 312–28; James D. Anderson, *The Education of Blacks in the South, 1860–1935* (Chapel Hill, NC, 1988), 238–78.
11. Marybeth Gasman, *Envisioning Black Colleges: A History of the United Negro College Fund* (Baltimore, 2007), 20–23.

Figure 7.1. Presidents of the Colleges and Universities Belonging to the United Negro College Fund at Their Ninth Annual Convocation Held in Philadelphia in 1952. *Seated left to right in the first row*: Florence M. Read, Spelman College (Atlanta, GA); Harry V. Richardson, Gammon Theological Seminary (Atlanta, GA); Richard V. Moore, Bethune-Cookman (Daytona Beach, FL); M. S. Davago, Huston-Tillotson (Austin, TX); Benjamin E. Mays, Morehouse College (Atlanta, GA); Frederick D. Patterson, Tuskegee Institute (Tuskegee, AL); James P. Brawley, Clark College (Atlanta, GA); David D. Jones, Bennett College (Greensboro, NC); Rufus E. Clement, Atlanta University (Atlanta, GA). *Standing left to right in the second row*: John H. Lewis, Morris Brown College (Atlanta, GA); Charles S. Johnson, Fisk University (Nashville, TN); James A. Colston, Knoxville College (Knoxville, TN); W. R. Strassner, Shaw University (Raleigh, NC); Milton K. Curry Jr., Bishop College (Marshall, TX); Horace Mann Bond, Lincoln University (Lincoln University, PA); J. S. Scott, Wiley College (Marshall, TX); D. R. Glass, Texas College (Tyler, TX); A. D. Gray, Talladega College (Talladega, AL); Hollis F. Price, LeMoyne College (Memphis, TN). *Standing left to right in the third row*: William J. Trent Jr., Livingstone College (Salisbury, NC); E. C. Peters, Paine College (Augusta, GA); Alonzo G. Moron, Hampton Institute (Hampton, VA); J. A. Bacoats, Benedict College (Columbia, SC); Raymond Pace Alexander, Philadelphia Councilman; C. A. Kirkendoll, Lane College (Jackson, TN); Harold L. Trigg, St. Augustine's College (Raleigh, NC); Hardy Liston, Johnson C. Smith University (Charlotte, NC); M. Lafayette Harris, Philander Smith College (Little Rock, AR). Courtesy of Department of Special Collections and University Archives, W. E. B. Du Bois Library, University of Massachusetts Amherst.

federal officials, to administer the program and distribute the benefits. As a result, in many states, relatively little funding went to HBCUs or to African American veterans, particularly those wishing to attend out-of-state schools.[12]

Notwithstanding this racial inequity, the small stream of students entering colleges and universities during the early 1940s swelled to a broad river after 1944 due to the G.I. Bill. Three times more veterans took advantage of the benefits than had been predicted. By 1947, 1.1 million veterans were enrolled in colleges and universities, and the G.I. Bill ultimately funded some 2 million soldiers returning from World War II. Between 1945 and 1950, the veterans helped to boost total enrollment in higher education from about 1.7 million to 2.3 million.[13]

The unprecedented scope of this federal financial aid was a great boon to colleges and universities. Scurrilous for-profit institutions jumped at the chance to exploit the G.I. Bill, as would happen every time government aid programs for higher education expanded. While generally offering substandard programs, the for-profits inflated their enrollments and profits by 300 percent during the postwar years, although the non-profit schools received a much larger share of the money because they enrolled many more students. Within the non-profit domain, the public and private sectors enrolled about the same number of students during the 1940s, and near the end of that decade the G.I. Bill paid about 56 percent of total student fees in private colleges and universities and 67 percent in public ones. The private institutions generally had higher fees, but the Veteran's Administration paid the out-of-state tuition rate for all students on the G.I. Bill, inflating tuition revenue at public institutions as well.[14]

Meanwhile, the surge of new and returning students meant that the per-student educational cost of higher education declined rapidly. With enrollments and tuition revenue increasing and per-student cost falling, the overcrowded colleges and universities prospered. In Cambridge, Harvard University enjoyed "the most favorable situation in our history in regard to student aid," stated President James B. Conant (1933–53), because "approximately three quarters of the students in the University were receiving financial assistance, primarily in the form of allowances under the G.I. Bill." By 1950, the party was ending. Conant reported that the proportion of Harvard students supported by the G.I. Bill had fallen from about 75 percent in 1947 to about 10 percent in 1950. At that

12. Hillary Herbold, "Never a Level Playing Field: Blacks and the G.I. Bill," *Journal of Blacks in Higher Education* 6 (1994): 104–8; Suzanne Mettler, *Soldiers to Citizens: The G.I. Bill and the Making of the Greatest Generation* (New York, 2005).
13. See app. 7.
14. Angulo, *Diploma Mills*, 59; Roger L. Geiger, *Research and Relevant Knowledge: American Research Universities since World War II* (New York, 1993), 13–15, 40–41, 195–96.

point, the average per-student cost began to climb across higher education, although the wave of returning Korean War veterans between 1951 and 1953 provided another, smaller surge of enrollment that briefly arrested the increase in per-student cost.[15]

A Golden Age for Higher Education, 1945–70

Bolstered by the G.I. Bill, new and renewed sources of funding over the next two decades propelled American higher education to global leadership and produced what scholars have described as a "golden age." The wellspring of the financial torrent coursing into higher education was the booming economy. The "unique" century of American economic growth that had begun in the 1870s culminated in the 1950s and 1960s. After the Depression, the wartime manufacturing boom and the postwar opening of markets to the United States (the only nation with an intact industrial base) reignited the economic growth.[16]

GNP rose about 250 percent in nominal dollars between 1949 and 1969, and family income grew, permitting many more students to enroll in higher education, as seen in appendix 7. Driven by rising enrollments and tuition hikes (largely postponed under the G.I. Bill), tuition income at non-profit colleges and universities grew more than 11 times: from $395 million to $4.4 billion between 1950 and 1970. State governments, flush with rising tax revenues, increased their appropriations for higher education nearly 12 times: from $492 million in 1950 to $5.8 billion in 1970.[17]

Beyond the rapid growth of tuition revenue and state funding, the flourishing economy inspired ambitious fundraising in the early 1950s. New tax incentives prompted corporations to donate to higher education, while inheritance tax laws encouraged charitable giving through bequests. And it remained true "that nine-tenths of the money is normally contributed by one-tenth of the donors." Schools with ties to the wealthiest individuals therefore continued to receive the most and the largest gifts and bequests. Overall, annual donations to higher education increased more than seven-fold, from $240 million to $1.86 billion between 1950 and 1970.[18]

---

15. James B. Conant, *Annual Report of the President of Harvard University 1948–49*, 18–19. See W. Bowen, *Economics of the Major Private Research Universities*, 19; H. Bowen, *Costs of Higher Education*, 38, 45.

16. Quotations are from Twentieth Century Fund, *Funds for the Future*, 3; H. Bowen, *Costs of Higher Education*, 35; Gordon, *Rise and Fall of American Growth*, 1–3, 285.

17. Freeland, *Academia's Golden Age*, 92–93, 70–120. Here and below these figures are in nominal dollars, unless otherwise indicated.

18. Quotation is from Kane and Doten, "Case for Endowment," 214–15. See Jones, *American Giver*, 25, 60–64; Cutlip, *Fund Raising*, 486–88.

Another large infusion of revenue came from federal legislation that authorized massive, general funding of higher education after the Soviet Union launched *Sputnik 1* in 1957. Congress responded the following year by passing the National Defense Education Act, which provided generous financial aid for students in higher education, including those in professional and graduate programs. This was followed in 1963 by the Higher Education Facilities Act, supporting construction and renovation of buildings at non-profit colleges and universities. Next came the Higher Education Act of 1965, authorizing grants and federally insured, low-interest loans for students, along with other aid designed to strengthen the financial resources of colleges and universities.

Still another large infusion of revenue came from grants and contracts for research. In the 1940s, scientists and leaders at the Carnegie Institute of Technology, MIT, Harvard, and California Institute of Technology persuaded Presidents Roosevelt and Harry Truman (1945–53) to support "the all-important decision to award federal funds directly to campus-based scientists" at established universities, rather than to independent research institutes. As a result, huge federal grants and contracts flowed to universities for basic and applied research, primarily in defense, medicine, and advanced natural sciences. By the mid-1960s, the federal government was providing 70 percent of all external grant funding to higher education. At the same time, private foundations shifted their focus away from building endowments and toward funding university research, and the Ford Foundation became the largest source of research dollars outside of the natural sciences.[19]

This massive growth in grant funding has led some scholars to argue that new research universities overturned "the hegemony of traditional elites." But only 20 universities received about half of all the federal research monies during the 1960s, and "there was little movement in and out of this select group," historian Richard Freeland observes.[20] It is more accurate to say that the enormous infusion of grant funding reinforced the hegemonic elite, whose membership expanded but actually constituted a smaller fraction of higher education.

That fraction decreased because the total number of degree-granting colleges and universities nearly quintupled from about 800 to about 4,000 in the century between 1920 and 2020. In the 1920s, the 39 wealthiest colleges and universities with the largest endowments—listed in tables 1.1 and 1.2—constituted about

19. Quotation is from Freeland, *Academia's Golden Age*, 73. See John T. Wilson, *Academic Science, Higher Education, and the Federal Government, 1950–1983* (Chicago, 1983), 1–42.
20. Quotations are from Graham and Diamond, *Rise of American Research Universities*, 5–6; Freeland, *Academia's Golden Age*, 91.

4 percent of the schools. The "hegemony" would actually constitute a smaller fraction a century later. In 2020, the wealthiest 100 colleges and universities—about 2 percent—owned nearly 80 percent of the permanent funds in higher education. And those 100 included all 63 members of the Association of American Universities (AAU), comprising the leading research universities in the country that also receive the bulk of the grant funding from the federal government and private foundations.[21]

During the "Golden Decade of the 1960s," therefore, certain flagship public universities and a flock of newly endowed private universities joined the "traditional elites."[22] This relatively small group established grant getting as another significant revenue stream in higher education. However, while grant money contributed to universities' income and expense, most of it did not directly support the "educational" expense. In fact, grant getting began to drain universities' resources in subsequent decades, as the amount of overhead paid by grantors fell dramatically. Chasing grants also began to cost schools and scholars their autonomy and flexibility, as foundations shifted their aims from endowing programs and professorships to stipulating the kinds of research projects that they would fund. Scholars relinquished control of their own research agendas in order to obtain research grants.

In any event, the revenue growth during "this golden age of financial support" was unprecedented in higher education. So too was the spending, just as Harvard president Charles Eliot (1869–1909) had prescribed. Institutions should spend all their revenue, he maintained, and roll any surplus into endowment or use it to expand existing programs and develop new ones that would justify requests for more revenue. This is how certain universities would survive and triumph, while building the greatest higher education system in the world. And the biggest economy, because endowing higher education endowed the human capital of the nation. At the same time, it remained true during this golden age, as during the formative era, that, in American higher education, "predominantly the haves . . . garnered the fruits of economic growth."[23]

21. NACUBO, *Endowment Study 2020*; Association of American Universities, "Three Leading Research Universities Join the Association of American Universities" (Washington, DC, 2019); *Historical Statistics of the United States*, table Bc510–22.

22. Graham and Diamond, *Rise of American Research Universities*, 5–6.

23. Quotations are from Freeland, *Academia's Golden Age*, 92–93; Geiger, *To Advance Knowledge*, 40.

How to Measure Endowment?

Interest in accumulating endowment persisted during the four decades from 1929 to 1969, notwithstanding the Depression, World War II, the G.I. Bill, and massive increases in state subsidies, tuition revenue, and research grants. In fact, these developments underscored the benefits of permanent funds in enhancing the autonomy, stability, and flexibility of a college or university over the long term. The social and political upheavals and the vacillations of tuition revenue and public funding magnified the importance of free money, prompting the declaration in 1951 that endowment was "the Rock of Gibraltar of American higher education."[24]

In the 1920s, the growth of endowment began to attract scholars' interest, which intensified in the next decade because the Great Depression posed a serious threat to investment portfolios. In the early 1930s, studies of the management, income yields, and distribution of endowments across higher education started to appear. Since the US Office of Education did not publish data on these topics, early studies of endowments asserted that "no really comparable statistics" could be compiled owing to the "many ways of reporting endowment income and the principal of endowment."[25]

Indeed, variation and indeterminacy had characterized endowment reporting in America from the very beginning. Harvard College had the longest and most complete record of investments in the nation, beginning in 1643. Its earliest investments include 12 legacies received in the seventeenth century and 45 bequests made during the eighteenth century. But evaluating and managing these assets was no easy feat. In the colonial period, when a gift to what we now call an endowment was received by a college, the treasurer had to record, or "book," its value as a new permanent fund. But this "book value" was usually difficult to determine. Gifts to the university came as land, buildings, bonds, notes, monies, and other assets. In addition, different currencies circulated in the colonies and fluctuated in value, including pounds sterling, colonial paper, bank notes, and even wampum. The different currencies alone forced the Harvard treasurer to keep three different sets of accounts at times.[26]

24. Kane and Doten, "Case for Endowment," 212.

25. Arthur R. Seass, *Endowment Income and Investments, 1926–35* (Washington, DC, 1937), 1–2. See Struthers Wood et al., *Trusteeship of Endowment Funds* (New York, 1932); John D. Russell and Floyd W. Reeves, *The Management of Endowment Funds* (Chicago, 1933); Eells, "Educational Research and Statistics," 263–72; Lloyd R. Steere, *Administration of Endowment Funds* (Chicago, 1936).

26. William H. Claflin Jr., "Our Endowment: Its Vital Importance to the University," *Harvard Alumni Bulletin*, May 31, 1940, 1081; Paul C. Cabot and Leonard C. Larrabee, "Investing Harvard Money," *Harvard Alumni Bulletin*, May 12, 1951, 628.

The problem of determining the value of endowment funds persisted through the nineteenth century. When a "munificent individual" donated midwestern lands to Dartmouth College in 1856, the president and treasurer went on a personal tour to Illinois, Wisconsin, and Michigan to inspect the tracts and determine their value.[27] This was prudent. Colleges relying on distant land agents to assess and sell real property were often cheated, as many state schools learned when they liquidated their federal lands granted to them through the Morrill Act of 1862, which endowed public universities in each state.

Even a personal inspection was fraught, due to "the difficulty of arriving at an accurate estimate of the value of lands situated . . . where prices are constantly changing," wrote the Dartmouth treasurer. Nevertheless, he and the president determined "the aggregate value of the western lands" to be about $12,000, which would "form an endowment sufficient to meet the highest anticipation" for the gift, "if this estimate should be realized." Although the treasurer booked the gift at the value of $12,000, this proviso raised the specter of "market value": how much the asset could actually fetch if sold.[28]

Thus, accounting for the value of endowment assets was difficult and imprecise, even for highly competent treasurers. Book value might differ significantly from market value, which varied widely owing to local conditions and to booms and busts in the economy. Treasurers at nearly all colleges and universities therefore carried forward the book values of permanent funds and assets until the 1960s, when the practice began to be criticized as old-fashioned and amateurish.[29]

But treasurers before and during the formative era of higher education normally had no staff and shouldered numerous responsibilities, including collecting tuition, room rents, and other fees from students; paying faculty and staff; and negotiating contracts with outside vendors and paying their invoices while ensuring the quality of their goods and services. For these treasurers to continually adjust market values for all the assets booked in their accounts would have been onerous, fruitless, and likely misleading.

In any event, these treasurers certainly understood and accounted for market value in managing their endowment portfolios, for they customarily pooled the separate endowment funds of their institution in order to invest the entire pool together. Developing one overall investment strategy for the entire pool was

27. David Blaisdell, *Annual Report of the Treasurer of Dartmouth College*, July 1857.
28. Blaisdell, *Annual Report*, July 1857.
29. Trevor Arnett, *College and University Finance* (New York, 1922), 29–30; Seass, *Endowment Income*, 1; Williamson, *Funds for the Future*, 103.

more manageable and effective than investing each permanent fund separately. Consequently, after an asset's value was booked (and sold), the treasurers added the receipts to the investment pool. Two pages in the earliest printed treasurer's report of Williams College reveal how this pooling worked in 1870, as seen in figure 7.2.

The page on the right lists the original, booked values of the permanent funds in the college's endowment pool. The page on the left lists the current values of the investments in the pool comprising those funds. Note that the total current value of the college's investment pool ($205,000+) far exceeded the total original value ($153,000+) of the constituent funds. In other words, the market value of the invested pool had risen far above the book value of the constituent funds—at least until the next economic panic or recession, when the market value might well plummet.

At the end of the fiscal year, the treasurer had to distribute the earnings from the investment pool to the beneficiary of each permanent fund. Here arose a significant and pervasive problem. How much income should be distributed to an older theology professorship fund booked at, say, $10,000 in 1810 and to a recent science professorship fund booked at, perhaps, $10,000 in 1865? The market value of the older permanent fund had certainly appreciated. Should the older theology professorship receive more income than the newer science professorship? If so, how much?

Having the oldest permanent funds in the United States, Harvard wrestled with this problem for at least 150 years. From the early 1800s (if not earlier) to the mid-1900s, the treasurer distributed investment income to the designated beneficiary of each fund based on its original book value, regardless of its market value. If the total investment pool earned 4 percent, then the old theology professorship and the recent science professorship were each credited with 4 percent of their respective book value of $10,000. However, this solution effectively depreciated the permanent fund of the older theology professorship, whose market value had grown over time and greatly exceeded its book value of $10,000. As a permanent fund aged, it was depreciated. Beyond the inequitable depreciation, this approach led to another bedeviling problem.[30]

Because the market value of the investment pool had risen well above the book value of the constituent funds, there was residual investment income left after the distribution of 4 percent. For example, in the case of Williams College

30. See Bruce A. Kimball and Daniel R. Coquillette, *The Intellectual Sword: Harvard Law School, the Second Century* (Cambridge, MA, 2020), 565–68.

INVESTED FUNDS OF WILLIAMS COLLEGE, JUNE 1, 1870.

BONDS AND STOCKS—U. S. AND STATE.

U. S. 6-81, 6 per ct. gold,	$ 6,000 00
U. S. 5-20, 6 per ct.	24,200
U. S. R. R. 6 per ct. currency,	7,000
Mass. 6 per ct.	10,000
Texas, 7 per ct. gold,	2,000 00
	$49,200 00

BANK STOCK.

National Bank, North America, Boston, 9 per ct.	$1,400 00	
National Bank, Phoenix, Hartford, 9 per ct.	2,900	
National Bank, North Adams, 10 per ct.	3,600 00	
		7,900 00

RAILROAD STOCKS.

Naugatuck,	$ 3,000 00	
Cayuga & Susquehanna,	480	
Troy & Boston, (not paying),	3,000	
Pittsburg, Fort Wayne & Chicago,	20,000 00	
		26,480 00

RAILROAD BONDS.

Troy & Boston,	7 per ct.	$3,000 00	
Detroit & Milwaukee,	7 per ct.	4,435	
Warren, N. J.,	7 per ct.	200	
Chicago & Northwestern,	7 per ct.	1,000	
Reading & Columbus,	7 per ct.	2,000	
Cedar Rapids, "	7 per ct.	30,000 00	
			40,635 00
Williamstown Aqueduct Co., 8 to 10 per ct.			800 00
D. D. Field Bond, 6 per cent.			25,000 00

NOTES.

Mortgage do., 7 3-10 int.	$19,566 48	
" 7 int.	11,285 31	
" 6 int.	8,932 37	
		39,784 16
Notes on Personal Sec. and Col. 7 int.	$9,500 00	
Notes given for subscriptions,	6,000 00	
		15,500 00
		$205,299 16

Figure 7.2. Market Value and Book Value of Williams College Invested Funds, 1870.
Source: [Treasurer,] *Invested Funds of Williams College June 1, 1870* (Williamstown, MA, 1870), 2–3. Courtesy of Williams College Special Collections.

FUNDS INCLUDED IN THE FOREGOING AND SPECIALLY APPROPRIATED.

General Fund to aid Indigent Students,	$17,432 57	
Alumni Fund to aid Indigent Students,	10,100	
Sundry Scholarships,	9,800 00	
		$37,332 57

PROFESSORSHIPS.

Jackson Fund, Professor of Natural Theology,	$14,000 00	
Morris Professor of Rhetoric,	10,000	
Memorial Professor of Astronomy,	25,000	
Walker Professor of Natural History,	25,000	
President's Fund,	30,000 00	
		104,000 00
Mrs. A. Lawrence, Library and App.	$5,000 00	
Jonathan Phillips, Library,	5,000 00	
		10,000 00
Williams Festival Fund, (Jackson)		2,000 00
		$153,332 57

Figure 7.2. (continued)

in 1870, the 4 percent return on the invested pool of $205,000 amounted to $8,200 of income received. And the 4 percent distributed to the constituent funds with a total book value of $153,000 was $6,120. What happened to the residual income of $2,080 that was not distributed? Not at all trivial, this leftover amount nearly equaled the salaries of two professors at the time.

Harvard's governing board, the Corporation, answered this question by transferring the residual income to an unrestricted fund under its control. The transfers started near the beginning of the nineteenth century, if not earlier, and surely distressed members of the Corporation. In 1842, 1866, 1876, and 1908, the president and the treasurer of the university earnestly discussed how to solve it. But no one could figure out a solution, so the hand-wringing continued, as did the transferring. Over time, this practice gradually depreciated the value of all endowment funds and transferred the amount of that depreciation to the unrestricted reserve fund controlled by the Corporation.

The Harvard Corporation finally addressed the problem in 1929, after the stock market ran up during the 1920s. The treasurer was directed to mark up the book value of all the university's endowed funds by 10 percent in a weak attempt to approximate their market value. This turned out to be terrible timing. The market value of the investment pool fell dramatically during the Great Depression, so the Corporation reversed itself in 1939 and wrote down the value of all the endowed funds by 10 percent.[31] This reversal, occurring at the university with the oldest and most reliable investment records in the nation, demonstrates why scholars who began studying endowments in the 1930s could compile "no really comparable statistics" on endowments across the country.

Finally, in the 1960s, the Harvard Corporation began to transfer the capital appreciation in its reserve funds back to the permanent funds of the constituent units from which the appreciation originally came, although this transfer did not fully compensate for the historical depreciation. Then, in 1970, the treasurer shifted the accounting of Harvard's portfolio to market value.[32] Other colleges and universities soon followed, demonstrating the increased attention to measuring endowment size. Coincidentally or not, this shift coincided with the first

31. *Annual Report of the Treasurer of Harvard University 1938–39*, 333.

32. Seass, *Endowment Income*, 1–2. See Walter C. Eells, "Income from Endowments," *Journal of Higher Education* 7 (1936): 477; Charles R. Sattgast, "The Administration of College and University Endowments" (PhD diss., Teachers College, Columbia University, 1940), 7; *Annual Report of the Treasurer of Harvard University 1969–70*, 5.

public reporting of largest endowments by the *Chronicle of Higher Education*. To maintain book value would have dramatically understated a school's permanent funds and lowered its ranking in the race for acquired wealth.

Shifting Investment Strategy, 1900s–1960s

Beginning in the colonial period, college trustees and treasurers had three distinct aims when investing their permanent funds: ensure stable income, safeguard the principal, and maximize earnings. Amid the financial vagaries before 1800, colleges emphasized the first two conservative aims and invested their permanent funds largely in mortgages, promissory notes, and real estate that could be rented or farmed. Early in the nineteenth century, this conservative approach persisted, although bonds began to replace other kinds of investments because "bonds were easier to buy and sell, and their value could be determined with less difficulty than personal notes, short-term industrial paper, or real estate."[33]

Over the nineteenth century, most private colleges and universities gradually shifted their investments from mortgages, notes, and real estate into government and corporate bonds, along with a small amount in corporate stocks, especially in railroads, utilities, and banks, as a hedge against inflation. In the first three decades of the twentieth century, the relatively risky investing in corporate stocks expanded somewhat, but it rarely reached 20 percent by 1929, even in the most aggressive portfolios. Meanwhile, public colleges and universities, especially land-grant institutions, remained much more conservative, investing predominantly in long-term bonds and mortgages.[34] Of course, there were many exceptions, such as Columbia University, which invested primarily in Manhattan real estate.

The stock market crash and ensuing Great Depression naturally made investors even more skeptical about equities during the 1930s. Colleges and universities pulled back from stocks and emphasized the conservative aims of minimizing fluctuation in annual income and safeguarding the endowment principal far more than the aim of maximizing income. The 1930s studies of endowments therefore found that investment income from endowments dropped in every sector of higher education. Even so, schools with larger endowments had higher rates

33. Cabot and Larrabee, "Investing Harvard Money," 628–29. See Seass, *Endowment Income*, 7; Sattgast, "Administration of College and University Endowments," 1, 71–89.

34. Arthur J. Klein, *Survey of Land Grant Colleges and Universities* (Washington, DC, 1930), 86–122, 258; Stanley King, *A History of the Endowment of Amherst College* (Amherst, MA, 1950), 108; Williamson, *Funds for the Future*, 76, 103.

of return, increasing their lead over less endowed colleges and universities during the 1930s.[35]

For example, one study of private colleges and universities between 1922 and 1934 found that the average annual return was 5.1 percent for the 20 largest endowments and 4.8 percent for the rest. Over those 12 years, this small annual difference increased the value of the 20 largest endowments by 3.5 percent more than the smaller endowments. Another study of endowments of public and private colleges and universities across the northern United States between 1929 and 1936 reached a similar conclusion. Scholars at the time attributed the greater return from the endowments of wealthier colleges and universities to "more competent investment service and advice enjoyed by the boards of trustees."[36] The rich could access and afford better advice.

The economy began expanding in the 1940s and accelerated thereafter, notwithstanding occasional brief downturns. Between 1950 and 1965, one standard index of the stock market rose almost 9 percent annually, after adjusting for inflation. Wealthier institutions continued to receive "more competent investment service and advice," and their advisors urged them to invest more aggressively in equities than had ever been the case in American higher education. The aggressive approach during these critical two decades resulted in even higher rates of return that further widened the wealth gap among institutions of higher education.[37] Here again, the university with the largest endowment led the way, not by banking the biggest gifts but by breaking new ground in the strategy of cultivating wealth.

The 60/40 Rule, 1950–65

In 1924, Paul C. Cabot, scion of a Boston Brahmin and Harvard family, opened State Street Investment Corporation, the first operating mutual fund in the country. While pioneering and designing mutual funds, Cabot developed new techniques to analyze prospective investments in companies, and his firm was hugely successful. In 1948, President Conant appointed Cabot treasurer of Harvard. By the time he retired in 1965, Cabot was considered the "dean" of "university money managers," according to the *Institutional Investor*.[38]

35. Walter C. John, *Higher Education 1930–36* (Washington, DC, 1938), 17; Trevor Arnett, *Observations on the Financial Condition of Colleges and Universities in the United States* (New York, 1937), 28–36; Joseph H. Cain, *College and University Investments and Income, 1925–41* (Washington, DC, 1942), 2.

36. Quotation is from Eells, "Income from Endowments," 477, 479. See Sattgast, "Administration of College and University Endowments," 2–10, 71–89; Seass, *Endowment Income*, 3–9.

37. Twentieth Century Fund, *Funds for the Future*, 4–19.

38. Chris Welles, "Paul C. Cabot: Harvard's Distinguished Ex-Treasurer Talks about Managing Endowments Today," *Institutional Investor*, September 1967, 19. See Editor's Note, "Investing Harvard Money," *Harvard Alumni Bulletin*, May 12, 1951, 628n.

Cabot acquired this reputation by rapidly introducing three innovations aligned with the three long-standing goals of portfolio management in higher education. First, aiming to ensure stable income, Cabot broke the convention of distributing investment earnings to the university's departments and units in the year that income was received. Instead, in 1951 Cabot began to channel some of the investment earnings into a new reserve fund that he called "quasi-endowment," with the goal of reserving a full year's worth of investment income. This reserve fund allowed him to set a prudent rate of income distribution a year in advance, to guarantee that distribution, and to reduce income fluctuation. With this assurance, departments could plan their budgets for the following year without fiscal uncertainty. By 1959, Cabot had fully funded Harvard's new reserve fund.[39]

This first breakthrough led directly to Cabot's second innovation, which maximized earnings. The historical convention of distributing investment earnings when received had impelled treasurers to invest conservatively in order to ensure stable income. Building the reserve fund guaranteed stable income, enabling Cabot to make riskier and more profitable investments. In addition, the new regulatory agencies established during the New Deal bolstered the integrity of the US monetary system and financial markets. Furthermore, at the State Street Investment Corporation, Cabot had studied how stocks provide greater return than fixed-income securities, though with greater volatility. For example, between 1920 and 1992, the inflation-adjusted return was almost 7 percent for stocks, 2 percent for bonds, and about 0.5 percent for US Treasury bills (first offered in 1920). Over the same period, the asset value varied by 5.4 percent for stocks, 4.5 percent for bonds, and 2.8 percent for Treasury bills.[40]

Altogether, the new reserve fund, the strengthened financial regulation, and the greater historical return of equities prompted Cabot to invest more of Harvard's endowment portfolio in stocks than had been done previously in American higher education. This development resembled the move of college treasurers to invest in fixed-income securities following the appearance of reliable bonds early in the nineteenth century.

In the early 1930s, Harvard had acquired some common stocks at their low point, and subsequent appreciation drove the fraction of equities in its investment portfolio from 12 percent in 1932 to 35 percent in 1941. Further appreciation during the wartime economic boom pushed that fraction to nearly 49 percent of

---

39. Cabot and Larrabee, "Investing Harvard Money," 632.
40. Williamson, *Funds for the Future*, 31. Figures are based on 10-year rolling averages.

the portfolio during the 1940s. Conventional wisdom in portfolio management called for harvesting those windfall gains and retrenching to a conservative position by buying bonds. But in 1948 Cabot went in the opposite direction, increasing Harvard's exposure in common stocks. By 1951, he had deliberately boosted equities to 54 percent of the investment pool, and then to 59 percent in 1952. Thus emerged the 60/40 proportion of stocks to fixed-income securities, a new approach to "sound investing" that eventually became standard.[41]

Cabot's riskier strategy broke the norms of portfolio management in higher education at the time, making Harvard "among the most aggressive of university investors in the late 1940s and early 1950s," according to George Putnam, who had founded another hugely successful mutual fund investment firm in 1937. Yet the great majority of colleges and universities, including wealthy ones, hesitated to follow Cabot's lead. In the 1940s, the Yale treasurer established a rule of investing half as much in stocks as in fixed-income securities and maintained this 33/67 rule into the 1960s. Meanwhile, Princeton's investing became more aggressive, but MIT and Columbia refrained. Public colleges and universities and less endowed private institutions also hung back because aggressive portfolios entailed more volatility in endowment return and principal, at least in the short run.[42]

Finally, to safeguard the principal and mitigate volatility, Cabot made a third innovation of widely diversifying the stock portfolio. He spread Harvard's equity allocation across 175 different corporations in a range of industries, the *Institutional Investor* marveled. Such diversification was unparalleled. For example, the University of Rochester also adopted aggressive portfolio management in the 1950s and 1960s, investing 65 percent of its portfolio in equities. While outperforming almost every other university in the country, Rochester's portfolio held the stock of just 27 companies, leaving it highly vulnerable and precipitating a decline in the 1970s.[43]

Cabot's three innovations, along with initiating the shift in portfolio accounting from book value to market value in 1970, as mentioned above, positioned Harvard and the other wealthy universities that followed its lead to benefit from

---

41. George Putnam, "Sound Investing: A Brief Comparison of the Financial Policies of Five Eastern Universities," *Harvard Alumni Bulletin*, May 9, 1953, 629; Cabot and Larrabee, "Investing Harvard Money," 629; Lucie Lapovsky, "Critical Endowment Policy Issues," *New Directions for Higher Education* 140 (Winter 2007): 102; Kenneth E. Redd, "Forever Funds," *Business Officer Magazine*, November 2015, 1.

42. Quotation is from Welles, "Paul C. Cabot," 19. See Putnam, "Sound Investing," 628–30; Williamson, *Funds for the Future*, 76; Fishman, "What Went Wrong," 207.

43. Chris Welles, "University Endowments: Revolution Comes to the Ivory Tower," *Institutional Investor*, September 1967, 19; Kip McDaniel, "The Ivory Tower's Origin Myth," *Institutional Investor*, April 14, 2017, 1–5.

the rising stock market between 1950 and 1965. Over that period, one general index of common stock prices rose 380 percent, while Harvard's common stock portfolio rose 473 percent.[44]

Modern Portfolio Theory

In the early 1950s, while Cabot was drawing on three decades of experience in portfolio management at State Street Investment Corporation, a young PhD student at the University of Chicago independently developed a theory explicating and validating the latent principles that Cabot was employing. In 1952, two years before completing his dissertation in economics, Harry Markowitz published a seminal paper that proposed what became known as modern portfolio theory and led to his winning the Nobel Prize in economics in 1990.[45]

College treasurers had, for centuries, prioritized avoiding risk and ensuring stable return when investing their endowment portfolios. Markowitz's first insight was to show that the amount of return on an investment is highly correlated with the level of risk. Assuming greater risk yields greater return over time. But how could one gauge the risk in order to compare it to the potential return? Markowitz maintained, second, that "risk," in its popular sense, was actually the degree of variance—the volatility—of an asset's value over time. And risk could be measured by the historical volatility of an investment's return, specifically by the variance in the historical mean of an asset's returns.

Third, Markowitz proposed that risk, or volatility, in an investment portfolio could be managed by diversifying the investments so that their variations counterbalance each other. Declines in one asset would be offset by gains in another. "A portfolio with sixty different railway securities, for example, would not be as well diversified as the same size portfolio with . . . dissimilar industries," Markowitz wrote. If done properly, this "diversification . . . leads to efficient portfolios," in which risk and return are closely correlated. In addition, Markowitz developed formulas to explain and validate his "expected returns–variance of returns rule," which produced efficient portfolios through diversification.[46]

Although Markowitz did not address higher education portfolios in his groundbreaking article, modern portfolio theory was perfectly suited to endowments. Their long timeline permits a higher tolerance for volatility, and their

44. Seymour E. Harris, *Economics of Harvard* (New York, 1970), 351–70.
45. Harry Markowitz, "Portfolio Selection," *Journal of Finance* 7 (1952): 77–91. See Harry Markowitz, *Portfolio Selection: Efficient Diversification of Investments* (New York, 1959); Alan Lavine, "Still Diversified: Harry Markowitz, Father of Modern Portfolio Theory," *Financial History*, Fall 2011, 17–19.
46. Markowitz, "Portfolio Selection," 77, 89.

large size affords a greater capacity for diversifying the holdings. An endowment portfolio can afford to include and hold a broad range of bonds and stocks and cash them in when their price rises. Modern portfolio theory—coupled with Cabot's practical guideline of investing 60 percent in diverse equities—would rationalize and encourage "a new aggressive approach to endowment management" that scholars identified in later decades.[47]

Cost Escalation, 1949–69

These historical developments aligned with President Eliot's strategy. Invoking him explicitly in the early 1950s, Harvard financial officers emphasized the importance of permanent funds and urged that endowment be "free" in Eliot's two senses: unrestricted both in purpose and in the kind of investment. Furthermore, as Eliot had insisted, Cabot issued clear and accurate financial reports that were made public. In fact, Cabot issued the "first popular yet comprehensive report on the management of the University's investments," and Harvard published companion articles on the same subject.[48]

Finally, Harvard financial officers in the early 1950s followed Eliot in emphasizing Harvard's insatiable "monetary need." There was never a surplus. Expenses rose with revenue. New, improved, and expanded programs required more spending, and anything left over went into financial capital to support them. Even as its lead over the endowments of all other universities widened, Cabot announced that Harvard "has outgrown its investments," given that the fraction of annual production cost covered by Harvard's endowment income had fallen from about one-half in 1915 to about one-quarter in 1950 owing to the growth of the student body, faculty, programs, and facilities.[49]

Cabot therefore faced a problem that he considered unprecedented—"how to dispel the idea that 'Harvard is so rich it does not need any money'" (although President A. Lawrence Lowell [1909–33] had tried to dispel the same perception in the 1910s).[50] Furthermore, Cabot and his colleagues believed that all of higher education faced a financial crisis in the early 1950s, notwithstanding the infusion of financial aid through the G.I. Bill.

47. Fishman, "What Went Wrong," 209. See Ryan, "Trusting U," 169.
48. Quotation is from Kane and Doten, "Case for Endowment," 211. See Kane and Doten, "Case for Endowment," 212–14; Cabot and Larrabee, "Investing Harvard Money," 628; Putnam, "Sound Investing," 629.
49. Cabot and Larrabee, "Investing Harvard Money," 631, 634.
50. Cabot and Larrabee, "Investing Harvard Money," 632. See Lowell, *Annual Report 1909–10*, 22–23.

"Not since the Civil War . . . has there been such concern over the future of our universities," they said. "Bankruptcy . . . is predicted almost daily in . . . the press . . . by many spokesmen for the universities." In fact, these predictions also echoed those from a generation earlier in the 1920s, when fundraising campaigns had warned of universities going "bankrupt."[51]

Hyperbole and historical amnesia aside, these alarms about financial stress throughout higher education in the early 1950s were justified. The per-student educational cost of all colleges and universities had declined significantly during the 1930s and 1940s. Indeed, by 1950 "higher education was clearly underfinanced," according to the most thorough study of cost trends in the 1930s and 1940s.[52]

Then, during "the golden years of the 1950s and 1960s," these cost trends reversed. In those two decades, aggregate annual spending on higher education grew nearly 520 percent, while GNP rose about 130 percent and the Consumer Price Index 58 percent, all in constant dollars.[53] In these aggregate terms, higher education therefore experienced tremendous cost escalation because the aggregate production cost of higher education increased much faster than either the cost of living or the nation's income. This escalation meant that the aggregate spending on higher education was consuming an increasing fraction of the national income.

The escalating aggregate cost during the "golden years" approximated that between 1880 and 1910, as seen in table 6.3. Unlike that earlier period, however, the rising aggregate cost alarmed policy makers and scholars in the 1960s. For example, in 1968 sociologists Christopher Jencks and David Riesman warned that "if we extrapolated current trends [in cost] sufficiently far unto the future, the entire GNP would be devoted to higher education." And this was true. The fraction of GNP devoted to aggregate annual spending on higher education grew from 1 percent in 1949 to 2.6 percent in 1969.[54]

But there was something even more alarming about the production cost of higher education during "the golden age" of the 1950s and 1960s. The per-student cost increased much faster than the Consumer Price Index or per-capita GNP.[55] Table 7.1 quantifies this striking development, which was unprecedented, as seen by comparing table 6.4.

51. Quotations are from Kane and Doten, "Case for Endowment," 212, 215; Thomas W. Lamont to Peter G. Gerry, December 22, 1920, Lamont Correspondence.

52. H. Bowen, *Costs of Higher Education*, 53.

53. H. Bowen, *Costs of Higher Education*, 35, 39, 46.

54. Christopher Jencks and David Riesman, *The Academic Revolution* (Chicago, 1968), 111n. See H. Bowen, *Costs of Higher Education*, 35.

55. Carnegie Commission on Higher Education, *The More Effective Use of Resources* (New York, 1972), 4.

TABLE 7.1
Change in Per-Student, Educational Cost of Higher Education, 1929–69 (in percentages)

Time period	Change in per-student educational cost*	Change in consumer price index	Change in GNP per capita
1929–39	−35%	−17%	+13%
1939–49	−45%	+72%	+37%
1949–59	+374%	+23%	+29%
1959–69	+269%	+29%	+18%

Source: Entries calculated in constant dollars from data in H. Bowen, *Costs of Higher Education*, 35–45, 258–61.
*Adjusted by Howard Bowen for changes in the distribution of students by educational level, with more advanced students weighted more heavily. These adjustments effectively decrease the per-student educational costs.

The remarkable per-student cost escalation in the 1950s and 1960s was entirely new. During the formative era of American higher education, per-capita national income had increased much faster than per-student educational cost, as explained in chapter 6. That trend continued through the turbulent 1930s and 1940s, as seen in table 7.1. Therefore, during the 80 years from 1870 to 1950, the per-student educational cost of American colleges and universities had not escalated at all. In the 1950s and 1960s, for the first time, it was costing vastly more to produce higher education for each student, relative to the growth of national income and the cost of living.

Cost-Disease Theory

As the per-student cost continued to escalate dramatically near the end of the "golden age," scholars, policy makers, and leaders in higher education began looking for reasons to explain the alarming phenomenon. An acclaimed explanation originated in the mid-1960s, when William J. Baumol, an economist at Princeton, published an elegant thesis that came to be known as the cost-disease theory. In 1966, he and a younger colleague at Princeton, William G. Bowen, applied the theory to explain the "economic emergency in the performing arts" resulting from expenses rising faster than revenue.[56] In the following year, Baumol published what is considered the first statement of the theory, although he did not employ the term "cost disease" at that time.[57]

56. William J. Baumol and William G. Bowen, *Performing Arts—the Economic Dilemma* (New York, 1966), 3.
57. William J. Baumol, "Macroeconomics of Unbalanced Growth: The Anatomy of Urban Crisis," *American Economic Review* 57 (1967): 415–26.

Cost-disease theory begins with a fundamental distinction between manu-facturing (goods-producing) industries and personal-service industries. In the former, "labor is primarily an instrument . . . for the attainment of the product"; in the latter, "the labor is itself the end product," Baumol stated.[58] In addition to treating labor as the end, rather than the means, of production, personal-service industries involve a "handicraft—or in-person—attribute."[59] Defined primarily by these two attributes, personal-service industries include "most no-tably, health care, education, legal services, welfare programs for the poor, po-lice protection, sanitation services, repair services, the performing arts, restau-rant services, and a number of others," Baumol wrote in 1993.[60]

That fundamental distinction between the two kinds of industries has impor-tant implications for production cost, according to cost-disease theory. Over time, goods-producing industries have increased their productivity, or output per labor hour, due to advances in labor-saving technology and organization. During the nineteenth century, for example, mechanized looms made textile production faster and cheaper per hour of manual labor. Between 1908 and 1927, the development of assembly-line production permitted the Ford Motor Com-pany to cut the cost—and then the price—of the Model T automobile from 150 percent of the average annual wage of an American worker to 33 percent of that annual wage.

In contrast, the productivity of personal-service industries is "stagnant." The "handicraft—or in-person—attribute" prevents these industries from increas-ing their productivity. A service provider today must spend the same amount of time to deliver the service as in the past. "The live performing arts" are the ex-emplar. "Whereas the amount of labor necessary to produce a typical manu-factured product has constantly declined since the beginning of the industrial revolution, it requires about as many minutes [to perform a Shakespeare play] . . . as it did on the stage of the Globe Theatre."[61]

Yet compensation in service industries must keep pace with that in the goods-producing sector in order to recruit and retain service workers. The per-service labor cost in service industries will therefore rise inexorably, while the per-product

58. Baumol, "Macroeconomics of Unbalanced Growth," 416.

59. Baumol, *Cost Disease*, 22. See William J. Baumol and S. A. B. Blackman, "How to Think about Rising College Costs: A Primer for Planners about Higher Education's 'Cost Disease' and Its Future Effects," *Planning for Higher Education* 23 (1995): 3.

60. William J. Baumol, "Social Wants and Dismal Science: The Curious Case of the Climbing Costs of Health and Teaching," *Proceedings of the American Philosophical Society* 137 (1993): 624.

61. Quotations are from Baumol, "Social Wants and Dismal Science," 624; Baumol and Bowen, *Performing Arts*, 162, 164.

labor cost in productive industries declines. Since that rising per-service labor cost must be absorbed in the total production cost of service industries, the "costs in the personal services industries move ever upward at a much faster rate than the rate of inflation" or than the price of manufactured goods in the economy.[62] The cost of a live performance, such as a concert, becomes ever more expensive relative to the cost of a cotton shirt or an automobile.

In 1968, William Bowen, who later became president of Princeton University and then the Andrew W. Mellon Foundation, applied cost-disease theory to higher education in a noted study sponsored by the Carnegie Commission on Higher Education.[63] William Bowen argued that professors must still meet the same number of students in the classroom and read and grade the same number of papers in order to provide high-quality education as they did a century earlier. This stagnant productivity of professors constitutes a "productivity problem" that causes the production cost of higher education to escalate, because professors' wages must keep pace with workers making productivity gains in other industries. "If the salary of the typical faculty member does increase at an annual rate of 4 percent, so that his living standard improves along with the living standard of the auto maker, [and] if output per man-hour in the education industry remains constant, it follows that the labor cost per unit of educational output must also rise 4 percent per year," William Bowen maintained.[64]

This reasoning followed the cost-disease theory precisely, and William Bowen presented evidence to validate this explanation for "the seemingly inexorable tendency for institutional cost per student . . . to rise faster than costs in general over the long term." And though he studied only "major private research universities," Bowen posited that "much of the analysis" applies to all of higher education—"public as well as private institutions, and to colleges as well as universities."[65]

Flaws in Method and Evidence

Cost-disease theory, sketched in figure 7.3, predicts that the per-student cost of higher education will escalate especially during periods of rising productivity

62. Baumol, *Cost Disease*, xvii–xvii. See Baumol and Bowen, *Performing Arts*, 171.
63. Both William Bowen and Howard Bowen, who were not related, were influential economists of higher education and university presidents, and both are discussed extensively in part II of this book. Their first names are therefore frequently used in order to help the reader follow the discussion.
64. W. Bowen, *Economics of the Major Private Research Universities*, 3, 15.
65. W. Bowen, *Economics of the Major Private Research Universities*, 1, 3, 13, 15.

| INDUSTRY TYPE | TECHNOLOGY EFFECT | LABOR COST | PRODUCTION COST |

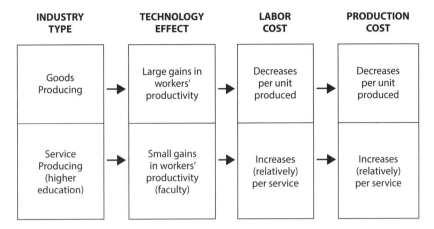

Figure 7.3. Cost-Disease Theory of Escalating Per-Student Cost of Higher Education, 1968.

and economic growth, because the labor costs of goods-producing industries fall markedly. If this held true historically, then the per-student cost of higher education should have escalated significantly between 1875 and 1930, when productivity in the United States grew prodigiously. Indeed, per-student cost escalation should have prevailed in higher education "since the Industrial Revolution . . . in the eighteenth century," wrote Baumol.[66] But the evidence presented in chapter 6 and earlier in this chapter contradicts these propositions.

Indeed, during the entire span of 80 years from 1870 to 1950, the per-student educational cost of colleges and universities in the United States did not escalate, as seen in tables 6.4 and 7.1. Per-student cost escalation in higher education was a new phenomenon that occurred only in the two decades before William Bowen's 1968 study. Hence, those two decades likely exercised a recency effect that fostered the cost-disease theory in higher education. In any event, one must closely examine the method and evidence with which Bowen "documented the seemingly inexorable tendency for institutional cost per student . . . to rise faster than costs in general over the long term."[67]

William Bowen's 1968 study examined "major private research universities" during the years from 1905 to 1966. Like most subsequent scholars, he distinguished educational expenses from non-educational expenses in order to study

66. Baumol, *Cost Disease*, 5.
67. Quotation is from W. Bowen, *"Cost Disease,"* 3. For further discussion and documentation about the following, see Kimball and Luke, "Historical Dimensions of the 'Cost Disease,'" 29–55.

the costs that are characteristic of higher education.[68] For example, the cost of oil is non-educational, because the service of education does not directly require oil and because many other industries use oil as well. A correlation between the costs of oil and higher education would not, therefore, explain why the cost of higher education is rising *faster* than other industries, unless one showed that higher education required more oil than all other industries for some reason.

Relying on surveys and data sets from the US Office of Education beginning primarily in 1955, William Bowen isolated "educational expenses" by setting aside capital expenditures, university hospitals, "sponsored research," all overhead and indirect costs, student aid, and "auxiliary" expenses for "dormitories, dining halls, athletics, etc." In this way, he arrived at "direct expenditures on instruction and departmental research," consisting "mainly of faculty salaries charged to the regular departmental budgets."[69]

William Bowen's data for the years between 1955 and 1966 came from Chicago, Princeton, and Vanderbilt universities, which he considered "representative" of major private research universities and whose per-student educational cost was "typical" of such intuitions, he stated. To extend "the Historical Record of Cost per Student" earlier than 1955, he calculated the average per-student educational cost of the three "representative" universities back to 1905 and then compared the "Chicago-Princeton-Vanderbilt Average" to an economy-wide cost index. William Bowen found that "between 1905 and 1966" the three universities' average, per-student, educational cost "increased twenty-fold, whereas our economy-wide cost index increased between three- and four-fold." He therefore concluded that significant cost escalation in higher education occurred in the set of representative universities between 1905 and 1966 and that their faculty salaries had driven the per-student, educational cost increase.[70] His numbers confirmed these conclusions and the cost-disease explanation.

This method had a number of serious flaws, however. The first concerned the sources. William Bowen did not cite or, apparently, consult the reports and surveys of the US commissioner of education prior to 1955 or the numerous extensive studies of educational costs that began in the 1920s.[71] Furthermore, he

---

68. H. Bowen, *Costs of Higher Education*, 6–10; Getz and Siegfried, "Costs and Productivity," 286–87; Michael S. McPherson and Morton O. Shapiro, "Issues of Cost and Price in Higher Education: Observations on Needed Data and Research," in NCES, *Study of College Costs and Prices*, 75.
69. W. Bowen, *Economics of the Major Private Research Universities*, 5, 6n, 17n, 32.
70. W. Bowen, *Economics of the Major Private Research Universities*, 2, 9–10, 17–19, 63–64.
71. See, e.g., Thomas F. Kane, "University Problems: Uniform Methods of Calculating the Per Capita Cost of Education," *Proceedings of the National Association of State Universities* 19 (1921): 53–68; Floyd W. Reeves, "Finance and Business Management in Institutions of Higher Education," *Review of Educational Research* 2 (April 1932): 116–33.

drew the pre-1955 data from institutional sources at Princeton, Chicago, and Vanderbilt without providing the specific sources or their locations. There is no way for scholars to evaluate the figures or replicate the study.

The second problem concerned missing data and William Bowen's attempt to fill in the gaps. He had a complete set of data starting in 1905 only from his own university, Princeton, while Vanderbilt's data began in 1910 and Chicago's in 1948. He tried to compensate for these lacunae by equating the early values he had with those he lacked. He assumed that the growth of Vanderbilt's educational expense before 1910 was the same as Princeton's, and that Chicago's educational expense prior to 1948 was the same as Princeton's and Vanderbilt's average. But this assumption was precisely what the study was trying to determine: the average of the three "representative" institutions. Hence, his attempt to compensate for the missing data presupposed his result: the value of the "Chicago-Princeton-Vanderbilt Average" prior to 1948.[72]

Third, even if William Bowen had had complete data for the three universities, they were not representative. He assumed that universities "representative" in the period 1955–66 were also "typical" during the prior 50 years. While Chicago was a major research university by 1905, Princeton had only a small graduate program prior to 1948 and was considered an "aberration" among major research universities. Vanderbilt did not become heavily invested in graduate research until 1950, when it was admitted to the AAU. Only Chicago was "typical" of major research universities prior to 1948.[73] Yet the two unrepresentative universities—Princeton and Vanderbilt—supplied all of the data prior to that year.

Although William Bowen claimed to study "major private research universities" during the years from 1905 to 1966, he actually studied only one, Chicago, and had no data for that institution prior to 1948. Furthermore, his sample was unrepresentative not only of major private research universities but even more of the rest of higher education—public and private, colleges and universities, research focused or not—to which he applied "much of the analysis."

Finally, there was the critical problem of reductive and circular reasoning. Like other scholars in the late twentieth century, William Bowen distinguished between "instructional costs" and non-educational costs. The latter typically include expenses for buildings, land, teaching hospitals, sponsored research, financial aid, student services, public service, administrative overhead, and auxiliary

72. See W. Bowen, *Economics of the Major Private Research Universities*, 2, 9–18, 63–64.
73. On Princeton, see Geiger, *To Advance Knowledge*, 201. Geiger did not include Vanderbilt among research universities between 1900 and 1940.

enterprises, such as dormitories, dining halls, athletics, security, and bookstores. And distinguishing and compiling these costs are fiendishly complicated and disputed.[74]

Avoiding that problem, William Bowen defined educational expenditures in extremely narrow terms. He included only "direct expenditures on instruction and departmental research," which consisted "mainly of faculty salaries."[75] In this way, he tailored educational cost to fit closely faculty salaries. He therefore studied primarily service workers' compensation in order to validate the cost-disease hypothesis that service workers' compensation drives the production cost of higher education. The reasoning was circular, and other possible costs and causes were not considered.

The Cost-Disease Shield

Despite its flaws, William Bowen's 1968 study was widely invoked over the next five decades. Many scholars cited it as proof that per-student cost escalated throughout the twentieth century in all of higher education and that the cost-disease theory explained the escalation. Furthermore, Baumol and Bowen had shown the cost disease to be unpreventable and incurable, it was said. Personal-service industries cannot contain their rising cost. Their lower productivity and growing relative consumption of national income stem from an intrinsic technical aspect of their nature. And *"there is nothing in the nature of this situation to prevent educational cost per unit of product from rising indefinitely at a compound rate."* Baumol and Bowen emphasized this statement in 1966, and Bowen repeated it in 1968.[76]

Hence, cost-disease theory had a clear exculpatory implication. In a personal-service industry, "the tendency for costs to rise . . . is neither a matter of bad luck nor mismanagement," affirmed Baumol and Bowen in 1966.[77] "Though it is always tempting to seek some villain to explain such cumulative cost increases, there is no guilty party here," wrote Baumol in 2012. "The cost increases are not caused by criminal neglect, incompetence, or greed, but rather . . . the essentially irreducible quantity of labor entailed."[78]

74. H. Bowen, *Costs of Higher Education*, xiv, 37–39, 150–51; W. Bowen, *"Cost Disease,"* 4; Getz and Siegfried, "Costs and Productivity," 296–97; Clotfelter, *Buying the Best*, 51.
75. W. Bowen, *Economics of the Major Private Research Universities*, 6n; see also 5–10, 17n, 32.
76. W. Bowen, *Economics of the Major Private Research Universities*, 15. See Baumol and Bowen, *Performing Arts*, 168–69.
77. Baumol and Bowen, *Performing Arts*, 162.
78. Baumol, *Cost Disease*, 26, 92.

Cost-disease theory thus shielded higher education from blame for its rising production cost. The theory would subsequently be cited to justify and defend, partly or implicitly, the increasing cost, as well as the soaring price of higher education. Meanwhile, after a decade of rampant inflation in the 1970s, another economist, Howard Bowen, forged a different theory that seemed to hold higher education responsible for its rising cost and that some would wield as a sword to attack the rising cost and price of higher education.

CHAPTER 8

Stagflation, Total Return, and Revenue-Cost Theory, 1965–80

After the soaring US stock market reached its peak in the late 1960s, the nation slipped into a recession in the early 1970s, as the enormous cost of the Vietnam War and the Great Society programs of President Lyndon B. Johnson (1963–69) impacted the domestic economy. Then came a decade of "stagflation," that is, stagnant growth and steep inflation coupled with high unemployment. Amid this economic malaise, the Ford Foundation sponsored a series of studies proposing accounting and legal modifications that resulted in three important changes in the management of endowment portfolios by 1975.

First, colleges and universities began to embrace "total-return" investing, which treats capital gains, along with dividends and interest, as part of the annual return of invested endowment. Second, trustees, who had personal, fiduciary responsibility for investment decisions, were permitted to delegate that responsibility to professional investment advisors. Lastly, those two changes resulted in the management of endowment portfolios becoming much more aggressive, as treasurers, trustees, and the new advisors actively encouraged heavy investment in riskier common stocks. This new strategy, though initially penalized in the 1970s, would thereafter yield massive returns in the large, long-term portfolios of higher education endowments.

Meanwhile, the aggregate production cost of higher education rose rapidly, although the per-student cost fell because enrollment grew much faster than the aggregate cost. Higher education therefore became more efficient. But institutions were forced to raise their prices in order to compensate for inflation and for declines in their subsidies and ancillary income—gifts, endowment income, and government grants, contracts, and appropriations—resulting from the economic stagflation. Most students paid nearly all the tuition and fees they were charged, whether through savings, loans, work-study, or funded scholarships, because the practice of discounting tuition was just beginning. Conversely, colleges and universities received nearly all the revenue from the price that they charged.

The year 1970 also initiated fundamental, long-term shifts in both the economy and the education system of the United States. The nation's century-long economic expansion began to slow, and the CAGR of labor productivity fell by about half over the next 50 years, as compared to the prior five decades. Concurrently, educational attainment in America started to decelerate, after having led the world since 1900. The high school completion rate leveled off after 1970, and the growth rate of college completion began to fall behind other developed nations, despite the rising enrollment in higher education.

At the very end of this difficult decade, economist Howard Bowen (no relation to William Bowen) published a book that made two fundamental contributions to the analysis of cost trends in American higher education. This new study provided robust evidence challenging cost-disease theory and proposed a "famous" new theory to explain the rising production cost of higher education.[1] Howard Bowen's revenue-cost theory and William Bowen's cost-disease theory subsequently became the two primary theoretical explanations for cost escalation in higher education that scholars subsequently debated.

Financial Headwinds, Capital Gains, and "Endowment Funds," 1965–75

In 1965, the stock market boom began to fade. Over the next five years, the annual yield dropped to merely 1.5 percent, while bonds lost over 6 percent of their value in constant dollars, according to standard indexes. Things worsened during the early 1970s, when the oil crisis of 1973 hit amid a deep recession.

---

1. Quotation is from Frans van Vught, "Mission Diversity and Reputation in Higher Education," *Higher Education Policy* 21 (2008): 169.

Stocks lost almost 8 percent of their value, and bonds gained less than 1 percent annually. These problems were compounded by steep inflation that exceeded 9 percent in 1975 and 13 percent in 1980.

More significantly, the year 1970 marked a fundamental economic turning point after a century of robust growth. The nation began to face stiff global competition from Japan and West Germany, whose industrial sectors had finally recovered from the Second World War and whose products, especially cars, challenged the quality and price of American manufacturing. Long-productive American factories began to close, and the so-called Rust Belt emerged in the northern, industrialized United States. During the 1970s, American economic growth therefore started to slow and remained sluggish through the 2010s. Notwithstanding a brief upsurge between 1996 and 2004, the CAGR of labor productivity fell by almost half—from nearly 3 percent during the period 1920–70 to 1.6 percent during the period 1970–2014.[2]

Part of the reason for declining labor productivity was a leveling off in educational attainment, which had contributed significantly to prior economic growth. The high school completion rate, having climbed steadily from 10 percent of adults in 1900 to 80 percent in 1970, plateaued over the next 45 years. Enrollment in postsecondary education did continue to expand dramatically, but this increase did not keep pace with the growth rate of college completion in other developed nations. The US rank in growth rate of college completion fell from first in 1950 to no higher than 15th by 2013, partly due to the fact that the United States had a larger base of college graduates. As a result, the contribution of educational attainment to labor productivity in America gradually shrank after 1970.[3]

Meanwhile, starting in the late 1960s, the expenses of even the wealthy colleges and universities began outrunning their revenue, a trend exacerbated by stagflation in the 1970s. For example, Yale University was already strapped for revenue in 1965. One reason was that Yale had been "running one of the most backward endowment funds" in portfolio management, guided by "a succession of conservative, banking-oriented, investment committee chairmen on the trustees," according to the *Institutional Investor*. This problem of relatively low investment returns was compounded by the ambitious and expensive academic reforms undertaken by Kingman Brewster Jr., who became provost in 1961 and

2. Williamson, "Background Paper," 4, 25–27; Gordon, *Rise and Fall of American Growth*, 523.
3. App. 7; Gordon, *Rise and Fall of American Growth*, 16, 499, 513, 625; Goldin and Katz, *Race between Education and Technology*, 2–39. The college completion rate of those aged 25–29 increased from 10 percent in 1966 to 20 percent in 1990 and 32 percent in 2013.

president in 1963. Yale therefore faced a severe budget crunch in 1966. To make ends meet, the new Yale treasurer, William Halsey, brilliantly and somewhat desperately committed "the radical deed" of treating capital gains as endowment income, along with the traditional income streams of dividends and interest.[4]

Halsey's strategy came to be called "total return," which nearly all treasurers and trustees considered heresy at this point. Although Paul Cabot at Harvard had pioneered the policy of investing 60 percent of endowment portfolios in common stocks, most of these equities were sought for dividend income, which often exceeded the return from bonds through the mid-1960s. Those dividend-earning "value" stocks had less prospect of increasing their price than did "growth" stocks, which paid small or no dividends but offered much greater return in capital appreciation over time if the company did well. Most sophisticated investors combined both kinds of equities in their portfolios. But growth stocks were volatile and presented several problems for endowment portfolios in the 1960s.

First was simply the greater risk assumed by treasurers and trustees, who worried that their portfolio performance would be jeopardized. In addition, most financial officers believed that the "landmark decision" in the Massachusetts court case *Harvard College v. Amory* (1830) bound them to invest conservatively. This decision announced the rule that trustees of private trusts were not legally liable for poor investment performance so long as the trustees had invested as would "a prudent man."[5] Many financial officers in higher education believed that investing in volatile growth stocks did not meet the "prudent" standard.

Third, treasurers and trustees believed that *Harvard College v. Amory* (1830) required them to return capital appreciation into the endowment principal, rather than distribute capital gains as investment income. Hence, even if they invested successfully in riskier growth stocks, they could not harvest any more revenue until they traded the stocks for "prudent" investments. Growth stocks were thus deemed unproductive in generating income in the short run.

Finally, investing in growth stocks actually decreased the annual return on endowment because the amount devoted to such stocks was unavailable to invest in assets that annually yielded larger, more secure dividends. Treasurers and trustees who dared to invest in growth stocks would therefore be penalized for

---

4. Quotations are from Chris Welles, "University Endowments: Revolution Comes to the Ivory Tower," *Institutional Investor*, September 1967, 52, 54. See Williamson, *Funds for the Future*, 75–76.

5. Quotations are from Williamson, "Background Paper," 106–7; Harvard College v. Amory, 26 Mass. 446, 465 (1830).

risk-taking because the annual income of their endowment in the short run would trail that of their peers who invested conservatively.[6]

But Yale needed revenue. In his 1965–66 annual report, Treasurer Halsey set aside all these reservations and argued that the conventional definition of "income" as dividends and interest was too narrow. Capital gain was simply another kind of income, and favoring value stocks that produced high dividends in the short run sacrificed the larger gains that growth stocks provided in the long run. Treasurers and trustees therefore must include growth stocks in order to manage their portfolios prudently. Otherwise, the endowment would lose the opportunity to grow, and "the future would be prejudiced," wrote Halsey.[7]

In the late 1960s, his revolutionary annual report, amplified by the stature of Yale and its long-standing conservative approach to investing, became required reading for treasurers and trustees, who circulated it widely.[8] Without mentioning Harry Markowitz or modern portfolio theory, Halsey's report incorporated their central principles: that risk and return are highly correlated, that risk in the short run actually means volatility over the long run, and that diversifying assets mitigates the degree of risk without sacrificing greater return.

Halsey's report also heralded a decade of rethinking and transforming the management of endowment portfolios. Starting in 1970, "endowment funds" once again became a hot topic in the United States, while the formerly popular terms "permanent funds" and "productive funds" slid into disuse, as graphed in figure 8.1.

This 1970 inflection point in the discussion about "endowment funds" coincided with the *Chronicle of Higher Education* publishing its very first list of the values and returns of the largest endowments. The *Chronicle* genteelly listed the colleges and universities in alphabetical order, rather than by endowment size or yield. But that inaugural list nevertheless fired the starting gun of a public race for endowment rank. In the succeeding years, the *Chronicle* began publishing annual lists of "Grants, Gifts, and Bequests" and then ranked lists of endowments after 1974, when NACUBO began annually compiling endowment values. From that point, the Grand Prix race for endowment size and annual yield attracted ever more spectators across higher education and throughout the nation over the next 50 years.[9]

6. Williamson, "Background Paper," 106–16.
7. William Halsey, *Annual Report of the Treasurer of Yale University 1965–66*, 7–8.
8. Welles, "University Endowments," 56.
9. "College Endowment Funds: Their Performance in 1969," *Chronicle of Higher Education*, May 4, 1970; "Grants, Gifts, and Bequests," *Chronicle of Higher Education*, October 15, 1973, April 8, 1974, April 19, 1974, April 28, 1975; NACUBO, "1974 NACUBO Investment Question-

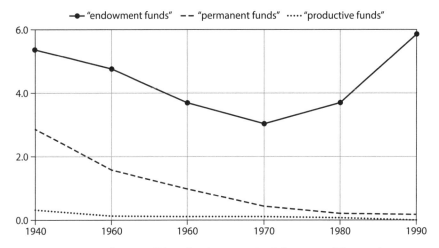

Figure 8.1. Historical Usage of Term "Endowment Funds," 1940–90. This graph presents the frequency of the phrases among the total words in English-language books published in the United States in a given year and digitized by Google as of 2019. Each line is defined by the frequencies calculated for 10-year moving averages in decennial years. Values on the *y*-axis are hundred-thousandths of a percent. *Source:* Google Ngram website (https://books.google.com/ngrams). Graph created by Sarah M. Iler.

The Ford Foundation Push for Aggressive Investing, 1966–72

Following Halsey's 1965–66 annual report, organizations such as the American Council on Education and the Association of Governing Boards of Universities and Colleges began planning seminars and conferences on endowment performance. The *Institutional Investor* announced that "university magazines are starting columns on portfolio management. Professors are making studies." Endowment performance "is now the hot topic at monthly trustee meetings. It's all anybody talks about these days."[10]

Amid all the seminars, conferences, and publications, the most deliberate and influential agency was the Ford Foundation, guided by its new president, McGeorge Bundy, the former national security advisor to President John F. Kennedy (1961–63). In 1967, Bundy criticized conservative portfolio management, which "has cost our colleges and universities much more than imprudence or excessive risk-taking." Raising the average annual return merely by 1 percent on

naire Endowment Market Value . . . of 145 Responding Institutions" (typescript; Washington, DC, 1974); Kenneth Redd to Sarah M. Iler, February 26, 2021, email on file.

10. Welles, "University Endowments," 2. See William F. Massy, *Endowment: Perspectives, Policies, and Management* (Washington, DC, 1990).

the collective endowment of higher education would yield an "increased return to our colleges and universities [of] $120 million a year," he wrote.[11] Here Bundy echoed the iconoclastic exhortation of Harvard president Charles Eliot, who urged in 1869 that colleges should never "sit down contentedly" on their investments, mortgages, and bonds but "be always seeking . . . to make a quarter of a per cent more." With Bundy's mandate, the Ford Foundation began underwriting studies and initiatives that encouraged financial officers in higher education to invest more aggressively.[12]

In 1968, the Ford Foundation sponsored its first study, which was conducted by Dartmouth finance professor J. Peter Williamson and Dartmouth treasurer John F. Meck. In their survey of 30 well-endowed colleges and universities, Williamson and Meck found that the financial officers worried most about how to justify investing in growth stocks and harvesting capital gains. This 1968 survey became the background paper for a signal report issued by the Ford Foundation's Advisory Committee on Endowment Management in 1969. This report encouraged financial officers across higher education to maximize the total return—both capital appreciation and annual yield in dividends and interest—from endowment portfolios. In effect, the report drew on modern portfolio theory to justify investing endowment portfolios more aggressively.[13]

Still, many financial officers balked at the total-return strategy, believing that legal and accounting rules prohibited them from treating capital gains as income. Also, trustees were barred from delegating investment decisions to professional financial managers who could expertly evaluate riskier and higher-return investments. Even if treasurers were willing to gamble on growth stocks, they could not rely on experts or count the gains if the gamble paid off. Why try at all? To address these presumed barriers, the Ford Foundation commissioned a concurrent study led by William L. Cary, a Columbia University law professor and former chairman of the Securities and Exchange Commission.[14]

11. McGeorge Bundy, *Annual Report of the President of the Ford Foundation* (New York, 1967), 7–8. See Williamson, "Background Paper," 113; Bevis Longstreth, *Modern Investment Management and the Prudent Man Rule* (New York, 1986), 152–57.

12. Charles W. Eliot, "Inaugural Address . . . October 19, 1869," in *Educational Reform: Essays and Addresses* (New York, 1901), 33. See Thomas E. Blackwell and Ralph S. Johns, "College Endowment Funds: A Consideration of Applicable Accounting and Legal Principles," *NACUBO Professional File* 1, no. 2 (May 1970).

13. Advisory Committee on Endowment Management, *Managing Educational Endowments: Report to the Ford Foundation* (New York, 1969); Williamson, "Background Paper," 111; Ryan, "Trusting U," 169–71.

14. Williamson, "Background Paper," 117–18; Jason R. Job, "The Down Market and University Endowments: How the Prudent Investor Standard in the Uniform Management of Institu-

In *The Law and the Lore of Endowment Funds,* Cary found "no substantial authority under existing law" to support the barriers and essentially dismissed them. In fact, treasurers and trustees had long misconstrued the "landmark decision" of *Harvard College v. Amory* (1830). Harvard College had not been found guilty of imprudent investing. Rather, Harvard was defending its own conservative policy by suing the trustees of a private trust for aggressively investing in risky corporate stock. The court ruled against Harvard and laid down the "prudent man" standard to sanction investment in corporate stock, which the court considered "the exercise of reasonable prudence and discretion."[15] Guided not by the court's decision but by their own conservative mindset and aversion to risk, college financial officers subsequently decided to "sit down contentedly" on their mortgages and bonds, contrary to Eliot's exhortation in 1869.

In addition, Cary addressed capital gain. Contrary to the view prevailing among treasurers and trustees, he maintained that colleges and universities may legally treat the capital appreciation of their endowments differently than do private trusts. The reason is that the beneficiary of a trust's current income often differs from the ultimate beneficiary of a trust's principal. For example, a private trust often provides current income to a spouse until death, at which point the principal passes to another person or entity. In such a case, harvesting capital gain for the current beneficiary would deprive the ultimate beneficiary. Therefore, private trusts must treat capital gain differently than the annual yield in dividends and interest.

But, with college endowments, the school receiving the current income is normally the beneficiary of the principal, so these endowments are not legally analogous to private trusts. Instead, endowments resemble the invested reserves of business corporations, which receive the total return—both annual yield and capital appreciation—from their investments. Colleges and universities are therefore entitled to do so as well. Furthermore, corporations may rely on external, professional investment managers, and colleges and universities may do the same, Cary concluded.[16]

After these studies in the late 1960s authorized financial officers to invest more aggressively, the Ford Foundation provided the means through a grant to

tional Funds Act Does Not Yield Prudent Results," *Ohio State University Law Review* 66 (1995): 574–76; Ryan, "Trusting U," 171–76.

15. Quotations are from William L. Cary and Craig R. Bright, *The Law and the Lore of Endowment Funds* (New York, 1969), 7, 16, 33; *Harvard College,* 26 Mass. 446, 460, 465.

16. Cary and Bright, *Law and the Lore,* 7, 16, 33. See John F. Meck, "Total Return and College and University Investments, a Comment," *NACUBO Professional File* 1, no. 6 (December 1970): 5–8; Ryan, "Trusting U," 171–76.

establish the Common Fund in 1971. Guided by counsel from Williamson and Meck, this fund pooled the endowments of colleges, universities, and independent schools, particularly smaller endowments, so they could retain professional investment managers to provide guidance for more aggressive investing. More than 70 colleges, universities, and independent schools enlisted in the first year.[17]

Large, wealthy institutions generally followed on their own. For example, in 1974 Harvard founded the Harvard Management Co., the first investment management company wholly owned and independently operated by a university. That same year, NACUBO undertook its first examination of college and university endowments, including their rates of return and asset allocations. NACUBO's annual report became the largest and most widely used survey of higher education endowment performance, and the number of reporting institutions grew from 145 in 1974 to about 800 by 2020.[18]

Meanwhile, the Ford Foundation's efforts came to fruition in 1972, when the National Conference of Commissioners on Uniform State Laws—advised by Meck and Cary, among others—drafted and approved the Uniform Management of Institutional Funds Act (UMIFA). This model statute—*"recommended for enactment in all the states"*—codified the Ford-supported developments of the prior six years. UMIFA permitted annual spending of a portion of capital gains (without depreciating the historical value of endowment gifts) and subsumed "total return" within the 1830 standard of "prudence." In addition, UMIFA recognized the trustees' right "to delegate investment management of institutional funds."[19] Without explicitly mentioning modern portfolio theory, this model statute, like the entire Ford initiative, relied on that theory. By 1975 at least 16 states had enacted a version of UMIFA.[20]

Some higher education financial officers attributed these important reforms in portfolio management between 1966 and 1972 to the more sophisticated acumen of contemporary managers and investors. Their forebears, it was said, were somewhat naive or ignorant in the nineteenth century—a period "long before people began to think in terms of diversified portfolios and the risk and

17. Quotation is from Twentieth Century Fund, *Funds for the Future*, 15. See Williamson, *Funds for the Future*, 55.

18. Kenneth E. Redd, "Forever Funds," *Business Officer Magazine*, November 2015, 1; NACUBO, *Endowment Study 2019*.

19. National Conference of Commissioners on Uniform State Laws, *Uniform Management of Institutional Funds Act . . . Recommended for Enactment in All the States* (Chicago, 1972), secs. 2 and 6. While authorizing the spending of capital gains, sec. 2 did not label that spending as "income" because this term would have required other changes in accounting rules.

20. Williamson, "Background Paper," 36–37, 107–9.

return characteristics of those portfolios."[21] But these concepts, later synthesized and validated mathematically by Markowitz in modern portfolio theory, had been familiar to treasurers and trustees since the 1600s. No less significant than increasing acumen was the introduction of reliable bonds in the early 1800s and the federal regulation of the monetary system and financial markets established a century later during the New Deal. These developments enabled college and university investors to obtain reliable data and assess future performance of equities with some confidence.

The Total-Return Trap and the Spending Rule Problem, 1970s

The golden age of the 1950s and 1960s may have exercised a recency effect on total-return investing, just as happened with cost-disease theory. In 1968, cost-disease theory was applied to higher education at the end of the only two decades of sharply rising per-student educational cost since 1870. Similarly, the Ford Foundation spurred aggressive investing at the close of the two decades with the largest returns on endowments since 1870. Plunging into total return in 1970 was like starting to buy stocks at the top of the market. In fact, it was almost a trap, for the economy entered a decade of stagflation.

In 1974, the Task Force on College and University Endowment Policy, established by the Twentieth Century Fund, recognized the trap. "The great bull market of the 1960s lured many colleges and universities to adopt aggressive investment policies," the Task Force reported. "The debacle in the stock market" followed, and many colleges and universities saw "large profits turn into severe losses." The *New York Times* reported that "Universities Flunk Investing," a theme echoed by various pundits.[22] In 1974, endowments lost over 11 percent of their value on average, as seen in table 8.1. Aggressive portfolios, such as those of Harvard and Dartmouth, dropped by nearly a third in that year alone. Yale University reported no growth in its endowment from 1967 to 1978 even though it received $100 million in gifts. One Yale administrator remarked hyperbolically that "Yale will not go public" before the year 2000, but "after that, I would not like to say." In response, the investing policy at many schools "became conservative, forsaking growth for income."[23]

21. Williamson, *Funds for the Future*, 69. See Keller, *Regulating a New Economy*, 200–208.

22. Twentieth Century Fund, *Funds for the Future*, vii; John A. Allan, "Universities Flunk Investing," *New York Times*, September 24, 1972.

23. Quotations are from Angela Stent, "Harvard and Yale and Their Money," *Change* 9 (November 1973): 12; Twentieth Century Fund, *Funds for the Future*, vii. See Ryan, "Trusting U," 172.

TABLE 8.1

Average Annual Investment Returns of Large College and University Endowments, 1968–80
(net of external management fees and expenses)

Fiscal year	Average annual return	Inflation rate	Number of schools reporting
1967–68	4%	4%	71
1968–69	4%	6%	71
1969–70	*	6%	—
1970–71	*	4%	—
1971–72	*	3%	—
1972–73	*	6%	—
1973–74	–11%	11%	145
1974–75	12%	9%	144
1975–76	10%	6%	142
1976–77	5%	7%	148
1977–78	3%	8%	144
1978–79	11%	11%	147
1979–80	12%	14%	198

Source: Data for 1968–70, as reported in *Chronicle of Higher Education*, May 4, 1970; data for 1974–80, from Kenneth E. Redd, "Forever Funds," *Business Officer Magazine*, November 2015, table 1.
* Neither NACUBO nor the *Chronicle of Higher Education* collected endowment values for these years. Kenneth E. Redd to Sarah M. Iler, February 26, 2021, email on file with the author.

Plummeting endowment values and investment returns prompted great concern about the "spending rule," that is, how much a school pays out annually from its endowment. If the endowment earns only 1 percent in a given year, should a school pay out the traditional 4 percent in revenue or anything at all? In an oft-cited article in 1974, Yale economist and future Nobel laureate James Tobin analyzed the spending rule. "The trustees of an endowed institution are the guardians of the future against the claims of the present. *Their task is to preserve equity among generations*," Tobin wrote. "They want to know, therefore, the rate of consumption from endowment which can be sustained indefinitely."[24] In these words, Tobin famously formulated the principle in economics that came to be called "intergenerational equity." Spending endowment income in the present should not deprive future generations of endowment income.[25]

24. James Tobin, "What Is Permanent Endowment Income?," *American Economic Review* 64 (1974): 427–28 (emphasis added).
25. In order to achieve the desired financial sustainability, many schools subsequently derived their spending rules from the complex, mathematical formulas developed in David S. P. Hopkins and William F. Massy, *Planning Models for Colleges and Universities* (Stanford, CA, 1981).

While encouraging "a university to consume *recurrent* capital gains," Tobin therefore "defended a low-risk portfolio strategy." He recommended that financial officers in higher education "put enough of the endowment into bonds and high-dividend stocks so that . . . no securities need to be bought or sold to meet the formula definition of income, and the university is insulated from fluctuations of capital values."[26] In contrast to the Ford Foundation push toward total return, Tobin thus proposed a relatively conservative spending rule for an endowment portfolio. Many financial officers shared or followed Tobin's approach and even retreated from total return altogether.

The Twentieth Century Fund, an independent research foundation, then jumped in to halt the retreat. Trying to bolster confidence in the new, aggressive approach to portfolio management, the fund enlisted a dozen financial officers from well-endowed private colleges and universities to form the Task Force on College and University Endowment Policy. This task force commissioned Peter Williamson, coauthor of the initial 1968 Ford study, to prepare a noted background paper explaining the rapid developments that had taken place over the prior decade. In 1975, the Task Force issued its own report encouraging endowed colleges and universities to align themselves with the total-return approach to portfolio management. While cautioning "against an extremely aggressive policy of investing," the Task Force emphatically urged colleges and universities to "*look to the total return of the endowment in evaluating its performance*" and avoid "*artificial distinctions between 'income' and 'principal.'*"[27]

At the same time, the Task Force recognized that less endowed colleges and universities faced significant difficulties in seeking total return from their portfolios. "Shifting from a fixed-income portfolio to a portfolio strong in equities, particularly in growth stocks, generally reduced the level of income yield (that is, interest and dividends)." Consequently, institutions making this shift "faced an immediate reduction" in return from their portfolios, Williamson wrote. The challenge was "to bridge the trough" in the short term, he said.[28]

But less endowed colleges and universities simply could not afford to build the bridge because they could not sacrifice a penny of secure current income for the sake of investing in possibly larger, but volatile, future returns. In addition, deeply conservative financial officers held back as a matter of principle. Such institutions

26. Quotations are from Tobin, "What Is Permanent Endowment Income?," 427–28 (emphasis in the original). See Carnegie Council on Policy Studies in Higher Education, *Three Thousand Futures: The Next Twenty Years for Higher Education* (New York, 1980), 10–14.

27. Quotations are from Twentieth Century Fund, *Funds for the Future*, 12, 16 (emphasis in the original). See Williamson, "Background Paper," 21–199.

28. Williamson, "Background Paper," 114.

therefore missed the booming stock market recovery in the 1980s, and the gap between the lesser endowed and the richly endowed schools widened further.

Falling Per-Student Cost and Rising Price

From the late nineteenth century through the 1940s, revenue from tuition and fees had paid about one-third of the aggregate production cost of higher education. After 1950, the aggregate production cost exploded owing largely to the burgeoning income from federal grants and contracts. But those mainly involved non-educational cost, and revenue from tuition and fees still covered about one-third of educational cost, depending on the era and the sector of higher education. The other two-thirds of the revenue pie constituted a subsidy composed of slices of gifts, fundraising proceeds, foundation grants, endowment income, and federal, state, and local appropriations.[29] Consequently, the tuition price of non-profit higher education was never a markup over production cost, as in for-profit business, although this basic fact has sometimes been overlooked even in scholarly analysis.[30] More broadly, failure to recognize the subsidy often confounded public and political discussion about tuition price and production cost over the five decades between 1970 and 2020.

In the 1970s, the subsidy slices of the revenue pie shrank owing to the economic woes associated with stagflation. Investment income from endowment portfolios decreased because the return on every domestic asset class trailed inflation. Tax revenue fell, as the economic woes fostered an anti-tax movement that was epitomized by the passage of Proposition 13 in California (capping real estate tax increases) in 1978. Middle-class families joined the movement as inflation pushed them into higher marginal tax rates intended for the rich and caused their take-home income to decline by 2 percent annually in constant dollars between 1973 and 1981, sowing the seeds of resentment against wealthy elites and their institutions.[31] Reductions in federal, state, and local appropriations followed, while fundraising inevitably struggled, even as the United Negro College Fund announced its most successful and enduring theme—"A Mind Is a Terrible Thing to Waste"—in 1972.

29. Table 6.1; US CommEd, *Report [June 30, 1904]*, 2:1428; *Biennial Survey of Education 1916–1918*, 1:717; Philip A. Cowen, "The College Tuition Fee in Relation to Current Income" (PhD diss., New York University, 1929); Cavan, *Student and the Financing of the College*; Weisbrod, Ballou, and Asch, *Mission and Money*, 298–99; College Board, *Trends in College Pricing 2020*, 22–23.

30. William Nordhaus, "Baumol's Diseases: A Macroeconomic Perspective," *B[erkeley] E[lectronic] Journal of Macroeconomics* 8, no.1 (2008): 4.

31. Swensen, *Pioneering Portfolio Management* (2000), 41; Dominic Sandbrook, *Mad as Hell: The Crisis of the 1970s and the Rise of the Populist Right* (New York, 2011), 281–82.

When their subsidy shrinks, colleges and universities have two options to pay their expenses: decrease production cost to fit the smaller revenue pie, or enlarge the revenue slice of tuition and fees to compensate for the smaller subsidy slices. The production cost did not diminish. In fact, the aggregate cost of higher education rose dramatically at the annual rate of 2.6 percent in constant dollars between 1969 and 1976. This aggregate cost increase—though less than occurred in government, hospitals, or elementary and secondary education—exceeded that in goods-producing industries and in many service industries. The combination of falling revenue and rising aggregate expense in the early 1970s was sometimes called "the new depression in higher education."[32] Aggregate expense increased for a good reason: students were flocking to colleges and universities. Thus, although aggregate cost rose, the per-capita cost of higher education declined because enrollment doubled between 1965 and 1980. Per-student cost therefore fell at an annual rate of nearly −0.4 percent in constant dollars between 1969 and 1978. In fact, the decrease in per-student cost during this period exceeded that during the Great Depression.[33]

Thus, tuition soared in the 1970s not only to compensate for inflation. Colleges and universities had to raise their prices in constant dollars because they had many more students to educate and because the subsidy slices of the revenue pie were shrinking. A fierce debate therefore ensued over several questions: Who shoulders the tax burden of subsidizing higher education? And who are the students attending and benefitting from the subsidy, particularly at public universities? What policies should be adopted to answer those questions fairly in the future? In 1969, a landmark study of the California public system of higher education, usually considered the best in the nation, surprisingly concluded that the system was highly regressive. Taxes from low- and middle-income families disproportionately paid the public subsidy, and students from wealthier families disproportionately received the benefits because they attended the highest tier of the system with the greatest subsidy, the University of California campuses.[34]

In 1973, the Carnegie Commission on Higher Education released a broader study confirming that general pattern nationally and issuing two recommendations. Government support for higher education should be capped so that a student's price would gradually rise, on average, from 17 percent to 33 percent

---

32. H. Bowen, *Costs of Higher Education*, 47; see also 35–45.

33. App. 7; Earl F. Cheit, "Plight of the Colleges," *New York Times*, January 10, 1972; Earl F. Cheit, *The New Depression in Higher Education* (New York, 1971). See H. Bowen, *Costs of Higher Education*, 35–45.

34. W. Lee Hansen and Burton A. Weisbrod, *Benefits, Costs and Finance of Public Higher Education* (Chicago, 1969).

of per-student production cost in public higher education. Then, to offset that increase for low-income families, direct federal grant aid to students should be increased and distributed based on income. The more conservative Committee for Economic Development responded shortly thereafter, proposing that the student's price rise to 50 percent of per-student production cost. The Carnegie Commission rejoined in 1974.[35] Notwithstanding the continuing debate over the regressive policies, the *New York Times* reported in 1978 that "many readers are convinced that rising college costs are squeezing out the children of middle-class income families in favor of the rich, who can afford to pay what they must, and the poor, who are eligible for government scholarships."[36]

But middle-class income had actually grown faster than the price of attending college, the *New York Times* also observed. According to the Congressional Budget Office, between 1967 and 1976 the median income of families with college-age children rose slightly faster than the tuition and fees of higher education.[37] Nevertheless, students and parents who were paying higher prices and facing tax-bracket creep did not feel relief, nor did colleges and universities, even though per-student cost was declining. Everyone's anxiety was rooted in the changed economic conditions: prosperity in the 1960s had given way to stagflation in the 1970s that increased schools' dependence on tuition. In the late 1970s, complaints grew louder as rising inflation and tax-bracket creep dragged on middle-class incomes, which could not keep pace with higher education price increases.

Research into the rising production cost of higher education therefore intensified. In 1972, Congress established the National Commission on the Financing of Postsecondary Education. In 1975, statistician D. Kent Halstead at the US Office of Education created the Higher Education Price Index, which subsequently became a standard measure of the cost of operations in higher education.[38] Culminating the research into the rising cost of higher education during the 1970s, the Carnegie Council on Policy Studies in Higher Education sponsored a major study by economist Howard Bowen that appeared in 1980.

35. Carnegie Commission on Higher Education, *Higher Education: Who Pays? Who Benefits? Who Should Pay?* (New York, 1973); Carnegie Commission on Higher Education, *Tuition: A Supplemental Statement to the Report* (New York, 1974). See William Zumeta et al., *Financing American Higher Education in the Era of Globalization* (Cambridge, MA, 2012), 66–71.

36. "What Middle-Class Tuition Squeeze?," *New York Times*, March 28, 1978.

37. Edward B. Fiske, "Less Able to Pay, or Just Less Willing?," *New York Times*, June 4, 1978.

38. National Commission on the Financing of Postsecondary Education, *An Informational Brief* (Washington, DC, 1973); D. Kent Halstead, *Higher Education Prices and Price Indexes* (Washington, DC, 1975), i–iii.

"Colleges Raise All They Can—and Spend All They Raise"

Having served successively as president of Grinnell College, University of Iowa, and Claremont Graduate University, Howard Bowen in 1980 published *The Costs of Higher Education: How Much Do Colleges and Universities Spend per Student and How Much Should They Spend?* In two respects, this work challenged the cost-disease theory proposed by William Bowen in 1968.

On the one hand, Howard Bowen presented contrary evidence. Based on the authority of William Bowen's study, "it is widely believed that the costs of higher education per student have increased steadily over many years" and that the trend is "inevitable," observed Howard Bowen. However, in contrast to William Bowen's partial figures from Princeton, Vanderbilt, and Chicago, broad data from NCES revealed that "instructional costs per student have not risen steadily year after year" in higher education, stated Howard Bowen. Rather, "they have held steady or declined over long periods."[39] The findings in chapter 6 support this conclusion.

On the other hand, Howard Bowen proposed an alternative to cost-disease theory. Over the next 40 years, these two interpretations became recognized as the "only two basic theories" that "warrant consideration" in explaining cost escalation in higher education.[40] Variations of these two theories are sometimes identified under different names or without citing either Bowen, but these two predominate throughout the literature on higher education cost.

Howard Bowen named his interpretation the "revenue theory of cost," which has not been fully understood or explained, despite its prominence. The fundamental reason is that his "extraordinarily thoughtful book" is maddeningly incoherent.[41] The book comprises four disjunct parts. The first constitutes a brief introductory chapter, which presents a provocative account of his theory in seven pages. The last three parts address successively long-term cost trends from 1929 to 1978, a cross section of 268 representative institutions in 1976–77, and "what higher education *should* cost."[42] Howard Bowen did not clearly explain the relationships among these three parts or their connection to his new theory, which is mentioned only twice in the 240 pages after the brief introduction. The reader

---

39. H. Bowen, *Costs of Higher Education*, 29, 37.

40. Breneman, "Essay on College Costs," 14.

41. Quotation is from Dennis P. Jones, "Cost Analysis and the Formulation of Public Policy," in NCES, *Study of College Costs and Prices*, 48.

42. Quotations are from H. Bowen, *Costs of Higher Education*, 199.

is left to puzzle how the abundant quantitative data in the last three parts prove or even relate to his theory.[43]

Howard Bowen's initial, provocative account set forth his "theory" by enumerating five "laws" that govern the expenses of colleges and universities:

1. The dominant goals of institutions are educational excellence, prestige, and influence. . . .

2. In quest of excellence, prestige, and influence, there is virtually no limit to the amount of money an institution could spend for seemingly fruitful educational ends. . . .

3. Each institution raises all the money it can. No college or university ever admits to having enough money. . . .

4. Each institution spends all it raises. . . .

5. The cumulative effect of the preceding four laws is toward ever-increasing expenditure.[44]

Howard Bowen thus reversed the conventional assumption that the "cost of higher education . . . is determined by the needs of institutions." Rather, he maintained, "there is no precise need that can be objectively defined and defended" because "the true outcomes in the form of learning and personal development of students are on the whole unexamined and only vaguely discerned." Consequently, "if . . . revenues are increased, then costs will rise. But they will rise because revenues grew, not merely because of newly perceived needs."[45] Hence, critics and proponents subsequently summarized Howard Bowen's theory in the following aphorism: "Colleges raise all they can—and spend all they raise." This has been called "Bowen's famous law of higher education."[46]

Both proponents and critics subsequently interpreted that initial, provocative account as the full expression of Howard Bowen's theory. But those seven pages do not fully explain the theory because the last three parts of the book are filled with implicit qualifications, clarifications, and emendations. For example, Howard Bowen's qualified endorsement of cost-disease theory, his view of "spending" on endowments, and his treatment of non-educational cost are usually overlooked or misunderstood.

43. H. Bowen, *Costs of Higher Education*, 17–24, 150–51, 227.
44. H. Bowen, *Costs of Higher Education*, 15, 19–20.
45. H. Bowen, *Costs of Higher Education*, 16, 20.
46. Quotations are from John R. Thelin and Richard W. Trollinger, "Forever Is a Long Time: Reconsidering Universities' Perpetual Endowment Policies in the Twenty-First Century," *History of Intellectual Culture* 9 (2011): 3; Vught, "Mission Diversity," 169.

Also, in his brief, provocative version of the theory, Howard Bowen states that it applies to the educational spending of individual institutions in the "short run." He never explains whether or how his theory relates to the long-term cost trends "for the entire American system of higher education," addressed in the last three parts of the book.[47] Consequently, several close readings of the entire book are required to piece together a full, coherent account of Howard Bowen's view. This full account, presented below, is termed the "revenue-cost theory" in order to simplify syntax and to distinguish this interpretation from the truncated version in Howard Bowen's first chapter.

Revenue-Cost Theory

To develop a full, coherent account of Howard Bowen's theory, it is helpful to start by explaining his interpretation of cost-disease theory, which had appeared a dozen years earlier and rapidly gained adherents. According to both critics and proponents, Howard Bowen is said to "dismiss" cost-disease theory.[48] But a careful reading of his discussion reveals that he actually endorses the cost-disease theory with two important qualifications.

First, Howard Bowen observed, as have other economists, that some "service industries" do improve their labor productivity, contrary to cost-disease theory. "For example, the performing arts use recordings, films and videotapes to reach large audiences." Similarly, sanitation trucks with mechanical arms have improved the productivity of sanitation workers. Howard Bowen therefore denied that cost-disease theory explains cost escalation in all service industries. Instead, he endorsed cost-disease theory as it applies to "a subgroup of the service sector, the *professional industries*," which require the personal application of expertise to clients. "Higher education is one of these," he stated.[49] This explicit, qualified endorsement has generally been overlooked.

Second, Howard Bowen demonstrated that, in the "professional industry" of higher education, the service costs "have not risen steadily year after year" but "have held steady or declined over long periods." In fact, the cost-disease thesis holds only for "the golden years of the 1950s and 1960s," when faculty compensation and per-student educational cost escalated together, as evident in table 8.2. Howard Bowen thus implied that this relatively brief but influential golden age

47. H. Bowen, *Costs of Higher Education*, 18; see also 14–17, 227.
48. See Robert B. Archibald and David H. Feldman, "Explaining Increases in Higher Education Costs," *Journal of Higher Education* 79 (2008): 277–78.
49. H. Bowen, *Costs of Higher Education*, 30–32 (emphasis in the original). See Gordon, *Rise and Fall of American Growth*, 13, 173, 190.

TABLE 8.2

CAGR of Faculty Compensation and Educational Cost per Student, 1930–78
(based on constant dollars)

Time period	CAGR of per-student educational cost*	CAGR of faculty compensation
1930–50	−0.4%	+0.3%
1950–70	+3.2%	+3.1%
1970–78	−0.36%	−0.5%

Source: Calculated from data in H. Bowen, *Costs of Higher Education*, 45, 74.
*Adjusted by Howard Bowen for changes in the distribution of students by educational level, with more advanced students becoming more expensive. See H. Bowen, *Costs of Higher Education*, 115.

contributed to a recency effect, or presentism, that resulted in William Bowen's claim about historical cost escalation in American higher education being "widely believed."[50]

Save those qualifications, Howard Bowen endorsed significant tenets of cost-disease theory: that "most of the current educational expenditures are paid out as compensation," that educational cost trends are "powerfully influenced by levels of faculty and staff compensation," and that "the relationship between cost-per-student and faculty compensation is a close one," as demonstrated by table 8.2.[51] But even this correlation does not demonstrate that faculty compensation drives educational cost upward over the long run—or even at all—as cost-disease theory posits. In this fashion, Howard Bowen approved cost-disease theory with qualifications.

Beyond this qualified endorsement of cost-disease theory, Howard Bowen raised three larger questions: Why does revenue continue to flow to a professional industry whose production cost keeps rising? What is the role of non-educational expenses, which still have to be paid by colleges and universities? What limits the spending of colleges and universities on educational and non-educational costs? In considering these larger questions, Howard Bowen essentially subsumed cost-disease theory into a more complex and comprehensive framework.

Three Questions

First, why does society persist in spending more on a professional industry whose production cost continually rises? This question lies beyond the ken of cost-

50. H. Bowen, *Costs of Higher Education*, 29, 37.
51. H. Bowen, *Costs of Higher Education*, 47, 55, 74, 137.

disease theory, which offers no answer. Yet the industry could shrink, or deteriorate, or simply close altogether. Howard Bowen argued that a professional industry can remain competitive in recruiting and employing its professionals only "if it is able to raise enough money to finance increases in wages and salaries. . . . The critical factor that determines the result is the amount of money the industry is able to raise."[52]

That critical factor is governed by "social attitudes toward the value of higher education," Howard Bowen repeatedly maintained. These "public attitudes" must include the shared belief that higher education confers collective benefits, particularly "an opportunity for all youth" to advance themselves, as well as "economic productivity and national power." These attitudes then create "societal demands for higher education" that elicit the continuing revenue from society.[53]

For example, the golden age of the 1950s and 1960s "was a special episode when the nation wished to improve as well as expand higher education and deliberately provided the money to make possible a big increase in unit cost," he asserted. In particular, "a national consensus was reached that . . . academic compensation rates were so low that they failed to attract and hold faculty and staff of adequate capability." As a result, "the nation set out to raise academic pay scales," and "compensation in higher education improved steadily in the 1950s and 1960s."[54] Public attitudes create societal demand that generates more revenue to pay for rising production cost.

Second, what role is played by non-educational expenses, which colleges and universities still have to pay? Howard Bowen focused much of his attention on educational cost, as economists have generally done since 1950. The reason for this focus is that "the effects upon costs of factors extraneous to education may be removed and trends in costs related to the education of students may be identified," he stated. But distinguishing educational and non-educational costs presents significant conceptual problems, and sorting available cost data into these categories presents challenging "technical problems." Failing to reach consensus on solving these problems, scholars began to favor the categories of "educational and general expenses," "administrative and support expenses," and "auxiliary enterprises," which Howard Bowen also employed.[55] Nevertheless,

52. H. Bowen, *Costs of Higher Education*, 32.
53. H. Bowen, *Costs of Higher Education*, 18, 32, 58.
54. H. Bowen, *Costs of Higher Education*, 46, 53.
55. Quotations are from H. Bowen, *Costs of Higher Education*, xiv–xv, xx, 6, 37–46, 131, 143, 151. See Darrell L. Lewis and Halil Dundar, "Costs and Productivity in Higher Education:

identifying "educational" cost—the cost to produce the education—remains the salient issue, given that costs unique to higher education must explain why the total cost of higher education rises faster than other goods and services.

But what if non-educational cost escalates in higher education faster than in other industries for some reason? Then, non-educational cost would not be "extraneous." Here again, nothing can be learned from cost-disease theory, which sets aside non-educational expenses. Cost-disease theory does not consider whether schools are adding administrators, lawyers, counselors, coaches, or other staff or increasing their salaries faster than in other industries.

Although cost-disease theory excludes these non-educational costs, they are significant. Non-educational cost amounts to no less than 40 percent of aggregate cost if educational cost is considered to include student services, scholarships and fellowships, and a prorated share of operations, maintenance, overhead, and capital expenses, as Howard Bowen broadly defined it. And non-educational cost soars to about 66 percent of aggregate cost if educational cost includes only instruction and departmental research, as William Bowen narrowly defined it.[56]

Furthermore, non-educational cost grew much faster than educational cost during the period from 1930 to 1978, as revealed in table 8.3. This faster growth suggests that non-educational cost deserves attention because it must still be paid by colleges and universities. And faculty compensation cannot explain the faster growth of non-educational spending because this spending, by definition, does not include that compensation.

Due to its significance and faster growth, Howard Bowen addressed non-educational cost, while maintaining that "the faculty is the necessity of higher education, comparable to food and housing for families," and non-educational costs concern the "less important objects." He found that colleges and universities exhibit behavior that "every economist knows: successive increments of expenditure are devoted to successively less important objects." Furthermore, this rule applies not only to educational expense but particularly to non-educational expense.[57]

The distinctive spending on "less important objects" in higher education occurs in three ways, according to Howard Bowen. One is building "a more opulent physical plant." Another is adding to reserve funds or endowment. Third, and most costly, is that, "as institutions become more affluent, the numbers of

Theory Evidence, and Policy Implications," in Paulsen and Smart, *Finance of Higher Education*, 134–37.

56. Percentages calculated from H. Bowen, *Costs of Higher Education*, 6, 35–37, 257–59.

57. H. Bowen, *Costs of Higher Education*, 130, 143.

TABLE 8.3
CAGR of Educational and Non-educational Costs per Student, 1930–78
(based on constant dollars)

Time period	CAGR of educational cost	CAGR of non-educational cost
1930–50	−0.4%	+1.3%
1950–70	+3.2%	+3.7%
1970–78	−0.36%	+0.3%
1930–78	+1.3%	+2.1%

Source: Calculated from data in H. Bowen, *Costs of Higher Education*, 35, 38, 258–61.

administrative and nonprofessional staff increase more than the numbers of faculty. The fruits of growing affluence lie more largely in additional administrative and professional staff than in additional faculty." The result is "overlays of administrators, secretaries, clerks, assistants, counselors, office equipment, travel, stationary, supplies."[58]

To prove this point, Howard Bowen cited a study of 68 public midwestern colleges and universities. As "discretionary revenue" rose, the study found "declining percentages spent on instruction" and "increasing administrative costs by the institution's administrative officers." Hence, these 68 schools exhibited an "administrative expense bias," the study concluded. In his examination of 268 representative institutions in the second part of his book, Howard Bowen likewise identified an administrative expense bias in both the educational and non-educational domains.[59] Other studies also demonstrated that at the largest public university system in the country, the University of California, wages for administrative and staff positions had risen "at a higher compound annual rate . . . than faculty salaries" between 1950 and 1970.[60]

The phenomenon that "as institutions become more affluent, the numbers of administrative and nonprofessional staff increase" can be seen, for example, in the growth of alumni affairs and fundraising that was first harnessed by universities in the 1920s, as discussed in chapter 4. As staff in this area generated more and more revenue for colleges and universities, their numbers, facilities, and expenses grew tremendously. In 1974, the Council for the Advancement and Support of

58. H. Bowen, *Costs of Higher Education*, 137, 150, 151.
59. Walter W. McMahon and Charles T. Strein, *University as a Non-profit Discretionary Firm* (Urbana, IL, 1979), 1–2. See H. Bowen, *Costs of Higher Education*, 140.
60. Frederick E. Balderston, "Cost Analysis in Higher Education," *California Management Review* 17 (1974): 102. See Frederick E. Balderston, *The Varieties of Financial Crisis* (Washington, DC, 1971), 13–16.

Education (CASE) was founded. Over the next 50 years, its membership grew to 85,000 members, as CASE became the leading consortium of alumni, development, and "advancement" officers. By 2020, every college and university in the country employed, on average, over 20 CASE "professionals working in alumni relations, advancement services, communications, fundraising and marketing."[61] Some schools employ many more than 20 CASE professionals, some less. But every college and university in the country employs a significant number of such non-educational professional staff, proportional to its size. Though set aside by cost-disease theory, the growth of this type of non-educational cost demonstrates the central thesis of Howard Bowen's revenue-cost theory: more revenue generates more non-educational cost that requires more revenue.

Limit to Spending?

Third, Howard Bowen asked, what limits the spending of colleges and universities on educational and non-educational costs? "Sometimes educators argue that [spending] is determined by the needs of institutions," he stated. But "most educators" believe "that needs are almost unlimited and that almost every department or function could put additional funds to good use." In short, the needs of colleges and universities for more revenue are limitless, according to Howard Bowen.[62]

As with hospitals, churches, charities, and other philanthropic organizations, no spending limit exists partly because educators believe altruistically that their work is "so vital to human welfare that no effort or resources should be spared," Howard Bowen stated. This altruistic belief "means that the services rendered to each client should be as perfect and complete as possible." But, in his view, self-interest also motivates workers in colleges and universities. Although trustees, administrators, faculty, and staff in higher education "generally share the goals of excellence, prestige, and influence," these "aspirations are always tinged with the personal ambitions of the administrators and professional workers involved," particularly when facing "the competition of other colleges and universities."[63] This coupling of altruistic aspiration and personal ambition was recognized and analyzed by other noted scholars, such as Robert Zemsky and William Massy, in subsequent decades.[64]

---

61. See app. 9; Council for Advancement and Support of Education, *Reimagining CASE 2017–2021* (Washington, DC, 2016), 5.
62. H. Bowen, *Costs of Higher Education*, 16, 135.
63. H. Bowen, *Costs of Higher Education*, 14, 20–21.
64. William F. Massy and Robert Zemsky, "Faculty Discretionary Time: Departments and the 'Academic Ratchet,'" *Journal of Higher Education* 65 (1994): 1–21; William F. Massy, *Reengi-*

Spurred by altruism, self-interest, and competition, "there is virtually no limit to the amount of money an institution could spend," Howard Bowen wrote. As a result, "each institution raises all the money it can" and "spends all it raises." Hence, "an institution's educational cost . . . is determined . . . by the revenue available," he concluded. Higher education provides no "incentives leading to parsimony or efficiency" and "no guidance . . . that weighs costs and benefits in terms of the public interest." In particular, "the economic principle of equi-marginal returns is not considered," Howard Bowen stated. According to this principle, "the final dollar spent for higher education should yield a return equal to the final dollar spent for health services, national defense, elementary education, environmental improvement, private family consumption, or any other purpose."[65]

In sum, revenue-cost theory, sketched in figure 8.2, proposes that "social and public attitudes" about the benefits of the "professional industry" of higher education create "societal demand" that determines the amount of its revenue. This income pays for aggregate costs, which can be divided into educational and non-educational domains. In the educational domain, the production cost is driven by faculty compensation, per cost-disease theory, but also by the expansion of programs and facilities and an administrative expense bias. In the non-educational domain, the productive cost is driven by the expansion of "less important" programs and facilities, as well as an administrative expense bias.[66]

Due to the altruistic wish to improve human welfare by increasing value and excellence and to the desire to compete for prestige and influence, both the educational and non-educational domains identify "ever-expanding 'needs'" that shape the "social and public attitudes" stimulating "societal demand."[67] Revenue therefore grows in the form of tuition, gifts, grants, and other subsidies that support the continual expansion of aggregate cost. Wealth growth and cost growth are thus mutually reinforcing and spiral ever upward.

Revenue-cost theory also has a normative implication. Howard Bowen adjudged that colleges and universities are insatiable, especially affluent schools. "No college or university ever admits to having enough money and all try to increase their resources without limit," he wrote. "Each one operates with a sort of hunting license which enables it to gather funds wherever it can find them and to obtain the maximum amount possible."[68]

neering the University: How to Be Mission Centered, Market Smart, and Margin Conscious (Baltimore, 2016), 1–38.

65. H. Bowen, *Costs of Higher Education*, 17–21.
66. H. Bowen, *Costs of Higher Education*, 130, 143.
67. H. Bowen, *Costs of Higher Education*, 36.
68. H. Bowen, *Costs of Higher Education*, 19–20, 22.

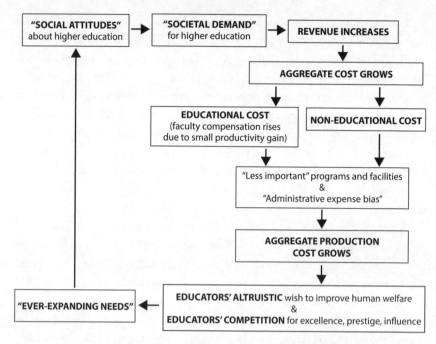

Figure 8.2. Revenue-Cost Theory of the Professional Industry of Higher Education, 1980. Based on H. Bowen, *Costs of Higher Education*.

Furthermore, Howard Bowen maintained that additional spending yields diminishing returns in benefits—partly because the additional revenue is directed not to the instructional faculty but to "less important objects" and to "administrative costs by the institution's administrative officers" in both the educational and non-educational domains. Finally, Bowen proposed that these tendencies increase with wealth. "The more affluent institutions apply their incremental expenditures to successively less important purposes. Families and, to some extent, profit seeking businesses, behave in the same way."[69]

The normative implication of revenue-cost theory contrasts sharply with that of the exculpatory shield of cost-disease theory. Though described as "the supreme defender of higher education and the supreme optimist about its future," Howard Bowen forged a critical sword in *The Costs of Higher Education* that critics began to wield over the next three decades.[70] The appearance of revenue-cost theory in 1980 thus coincided with a turning point in public esteem for higher education.

69. H. Bowen, *Costs of Higher Education*, 151; see also 16, 130, 143, 150.
70. Quotation is from Clark Kerr, foreword to H. Bowen, *Costs of Higher Education*, xi–xii.

For a century, the wealth, aggregate cost, and price of higher education had increased inexorably along with the American economy, accompanied by highly approving "social attitudes toward the value of higher education." During the 1970s, small doubts began to arise about whether higher education still contributed to fulfilling the American Dream of socioeconomic opportunity. The economic malaise, the resulting populist anger at lagging middle-class family income, and the implicit elitism of higher education initiated a shift in "public attitudes" toward colleges and universities and their steadily rising price, soaring aggregate cost, and widely publicized competition for bigger endowments and fundraising campaigns. In the 1980s, a wave of resentment swelled, as the financial practices and policies of colleges and universities that Howard Bowen posited in revenue-cost theory began to be recognized.

CHAPTER 9

Wealth, Cost, and Price Ignite Resentment, 1980–2008

By the 1970s, higher education in the United States led the world, and its development over the prior century had brought tremendous benefits to the nation. Noted scholars celebrated the resulting economic expansion, technological advancements, educated citizenry, and socioeconomic mobility, relative to other nations.[1] Consequently, higher education contributed enormously to the public good in America, although some minority groups, especially people of color, faced daunting barriers in accessing higher education. Nevertheless, public criticism began to smolder in the 1970s and ignited in the 1980s. By 1990, observers said that higher education was rapidly catching "the health care system" as the institution most "criticized by the public today."[2] Public resentment burned brighter, though intermittently, in the 1990s and 2000s.

---

1. Martin Trow, "American Higher Education: Past, Present and Future," *Studies in Higher Education* 14 (1989): 5–22.
2. Thomas Langfitt, "The Cost of Higher Education: Lessons to Learn from the Healthcare Industry," *Change* 22 (1990): 8. See Robert Zemsky and William Massy, "Cost Containment," *Change* 22 (1990): 16–22.

This ire was fueled by a number of factors. One was the populist anti-elitism that contributed to the 1980 election of President Ronald Reagan (1981–89). Another was the declining rate of economic growth coupled with the increasing concentration of wealth in a small fraction of the population, which deflated the financial prospects of middle-class families. But the most direct factor was the combination of rising wealth, price, and production cost of many colleges and universities, especially the richest ones, which sparked "public criticism" and congressional hearings by 1987.[3]

In the 1990s and 2000s, these factors were magnified. In particular, the "discordance" between skyrocketing tuition and growing institutional wealth—both soaring endowment values and oversubscribed fundraising campaigns—stoked public resentment. Furthermore, the growing "wealth gap," or stratification, among colleges and universities fed the public rancor, especially as that gap widened into a chasm when another breakthrough in portfolio management yielded huge returns for the tiny fraction of schools that owned the largest endowments.[4]

Indeed, despite the success of fundraising and portfolio management by the wealthiest schools through the 1980s, 1990s, and 2000s, most colleges and universities felt they were gaining little ground financially. The steep climb of listed tuition added little to their revenue. In the public sector, price increases barely compensated for decreases or slow growth of government subsidies. In the private sector, the growing practice of tuition discounting deflated the value of price hikes. In the end, raising their price merely enabled most colleges and universities to pay their bills, while at the same time incurring public rancor and prompting congressional inquiries. Many schools were struggling, not flourishing.

Slowing Economy and the "Golden Age Redux"

Compared with other developed nations, the growth rate of both educational attainment and labor productivity slowed in the United States after 1970. These two compounding factors then retarded American economic growth, apart from a resurgence between 1996 and 2004 that many analysts attributed to the digital revolution in information technology.[5] If true, that revolution likely contributed

3. Peter Likins, "Colleges Must Rethink Their Goals and Priorities in an Era of Tight Budgets and Public Criticism," *Chronicle of Higher Education*, May 9, 1990; Scott Jaschik, "House Panel Eyes Plans to Tax Colleges on Some Income," *Chronicle of Higher Education*, November 4, 1987; Freeland, *Academia's Golden Age*, 418.

4. Quotations are from Sarah E. Waldeck, "The Coming Showdown over University Endowments: Enlisting the Donors," *Fordham Law Review* 77 (2009): 1795.

5. Gordon, *Rise and Fall of American Growth*, 15, 319, 499, 523. See Stephen D. Oliner and Daniel E. Sichel, "The Resurgence of Growth in the Late 1990s: Is Information Technology the Story?," *Journal of Economic Perspectives* 14 (2000): 3–22.

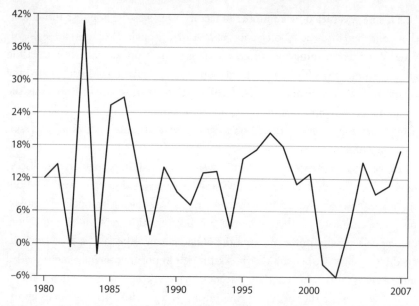

Figure 9.1. Average Annual Returns of College and University Endowments, 1980–2007 (net of external management fees and expenses). *Source:* Data drawn from *2009 NACUBO-Commonfund Study of Endowments*; Kenneth E. Redd, "Forever Funds," *Business Officer Magazine*, November 2015, table 1.

to the prosperity enjoyed by the top tiers of higher education in the 1990s and 2000s.

In fact, the year 1980 marked the beginning of a "Golden Age Redux" for that upper echelon.[6] For almost three decades thereafter, until 2008, the mean of the average annual returns of endowments reporting to NACUBO exceeded 11 percent. But portfolios rode a terrifying rollercoaster to reach this remark- able overall return, as seen in figure 9.1. Nevertheless, at the end of the ride in 2007, 76 schools owned what came to be called "mega-endowments" (exceeding $1 billion), and 18 schools had endowments surpassing an incredible $5 billion.[7]

Attention to endowment therefore pervaded higher education, regardless of the financial capital of any given school. In 2000, the development office of Utah State University, having $77 million in permanent funds and ranked 339 in the NACUBO survey, described how "the annual endowment standings published

6. Graham and Diamond, *Rise of American Research Universities*, v.
7. Kenneth E. Redd, "Forever Funds," *Business Officer Magazine*, November 2015, table 1; NACUBO, *Endowment Study 2007*.

in the *Chronicle of Higher Education* are greeted with . . . much interest in university board rooms. . . . University trustees and administrators regularly review quarterly endowment earnings reports and investment portfolios. That's how important the endowment is to a university."[8]

Contributing to the prosperity was energetic fundraising in each of the three modes that became customary by 1930 and continued apace throughout the twentieth century. In fact, colleges and universities were repeatedly urged to continue fundraising and to direct the proceeds into endowment as much as possible.[9] Wealthy colleges and universities needed these reminders because, by 2000, their portfolios were yielding such bountiful returns that fundraising seemed outmoded, so far as increasing endowments was concerned. University of Michigan president James J. Duderstadt (1988–96), among others, observed that wealthy schools had shifted their focus from "gifts to growth," that is, from fundraising to portfolio management.[10]

Indeed, this shift in emphasis might have seemed prudent for all of higher education. In 2006, for example, college and university endowments grew by almost 18 percent on average, and only about one-fifth of that growth came from gifts and bequests. But this small fraction reflected the preponderance of permanent funds owned by the wealthiest schools and the returns that they received. The vast majority of colleges and universities had endowments under $10 million, and fully half of their endowment growth came from gifts and bequests. These less endowed institutions could not afford to cease asking for money, a report from the Commonfund Institute warned in 2006. And the wealthiest institutions did not stop anyway. In 2006, over 25 schools were running capital campaigns with goals of $1 billion or more. Three universities were each seeking more than $3 billion in their drives.[11] Notwithstanding these campaigns, begging for money contributed less to increasing the endowments of the wealthiest institutions because another new kind of investing had emerged, yielding unprecedented returns for schools that could afford to adopt it.

8. Utah State University, Development Office, "Priorities: Endowment" (ca. 2000), on file with the author.

9. Williamson, *Funds for the Future*, 9–10, 15–16; Swensen, *Pioneering Portfolio Management* (2000), 36–44; (2009), 35–42.

10. Quotation is from Humphreys, *Educational Endowments*, 18. See James J. Duderstadt, *Testimony before the U.S. Senate Committee on Finance*, 109th Cong., 1st sess. (December 5, 2006).

11. Lucie Lapovsky, "Critical Endowment Policy Issues," *New Directions for Higher Education* 140 (Winter 2007): 100–101; Fred Rogers and Glenn Strehle, *Sources of Endowment Growth at Colleges and Universities [Commonfund Institute]* (Wilton, CT, 2006), 2; Brennen Jensen, "Three Universities Seek $3-Billion or More," *Chronicle of Philanthropy*, October 12, 2006, B18.

"Alternative Assets" Emerge at Yale

As more and more newspapers and magazines broadcast the rankings of endowment and institutions in the 1990s and 2000s, two subjects dominated the academic and policy literature about endowments: "The first is portfolio management. . . . The second is the appropriate spending rule."[12] Analyses of the former focused on the tactics of more aggressive investing, which had gradually spread throughout higher education and culminated in the "Yale Model" or the "Endowment Model of Investing" (EMI).[13]

Through 1990, about 20 percent of endowed colleges and universities still clung to the conservative approach to portfolio management that predominated in the early twentieth century. These timid schools dared not adopt even the 60/40 rule, let alone total return. Instead, they invested primarily in domestic bonds and spent only the yield of dividends and interest. Leading financial officers in higher education regarded this approach as hopelessly outdated and ironically imprudent owing to the loss of long-term gains and endowment growth.[14]

During the 1990s, these laggards finally adopted the 60/40 rule, which had become customary in portfolio management. But that convention included three variants of investing the 60 percent component of equities. The conservative option was to put the stocks solely in large American corporations, the moderate variant was to invest in both foreign and domestic corporations, and the aggressive version was to adopt total-return investing by purchasing growth stocks in smaller domestic and international companies, whose appreciation could be harvested as annual return.[15]

Although that aggressive variant of total-return investing had stumbled out of the gate in the early 1970s, it gained ground in portfolio management during the 1980s and gradually took the lead in the 1990s, as NACUBO, the Common Fund, the Association of Governing Boards of Universities and Colleges, and other organizations hosted dozens of management seminars and conferences urging colleges and universities to invest more aggressively. In response, the

---

12. Henry Hansmann, "Why Do Universities Have Endowments?," *Journal of Legal Studies* 19 (1990): 8. See Harold R. Christensen and Elizabeth L. Rankin, "Do College Endowments Matter? The Case of Educational Spending," *Southwestern Economic Review* 30 (2003): 35–42.

13. Ryan, "Trusting U," 172; Fishman, "What Went Wrong," 215.

14. Williamson, "Background Paper," 114; Swensen, *Pioneering Portfolio Management* (2000), 32.

15. Lapovsky, "Critical Endowment Policy Issues," 102; Redd, "Forever Funds"; Humphreys, *Educational Endowments*, 11–12; Ryan, "Trusting U," 169.

membership of the Common Fund, which afforded smaller endowments the opportunity to adopt total return, grew to 1,200 schools in 1992.[16] In that same year, the American Law Institute issued the *Third Restatement of Trusts*, which reinforced the trend toward aggressive investing. This updated account of trust doctrine defined "prudent investing" in terms of modern portfolio theory and loosened the standard of risk by applying it to a trust's entire portfolio rather than each investment. By the following year, 34 states had adopted some form of the Uniform Management of Institutional Funds Act (UMIFA). By 2006, the number of adopting states had grown to 48.[17]

In 2007, the National Conference of Commissioners on Uniform State Laws drafted and approved a more liberal successor to UMIFA—the Uniform Prudent Management of Institutional Funds Act (UPMIFA). This act, like its predecessor, endorsed the principles of modern portfolio theory but went further by eliminating the requirement that a school continually preserve the original value, or "historic dollar value," of a permanent fund. By permitting the principal to lose value, this change meant that a permanent fund could be invested in more volatile assets. By 2012, 49 states had adopted some form of UPMIFA.[18]

Meanwhile, the scope of total-return investing expanded to include "alternative assets" through the pioneering work of David Swensen, the chief investment officer of Yale University. After earning his PhD in economics under James Tobin at Yale and working on Wall Street, Swensen returned to New Haven in 1985 to manage Yale's endowment. At that time, Yale's portfolio had a moderate profile, which Swensen revolutionized over the next two decades by applying the principles of modern portfolio theory and designing the Yale Model or EMI.[19]

According to modern portfolio theory, risk and return are highly correlated; assuming greater risk leads to greater return over time. The investor's goal is to create an "efficient" portfolio, such that "for a given risk level no other portfolio produces a higher return" and "for a given return level, no other portfolio exhibits lower risk," in Swensen's words. The key to balancing the risks and returns is

16. Williamson, *Funds for the Future*, 55; Vartanig G. Vartan, "Market Place: Tending Assets for Colleges," *New York Times*, May 24, 1985.

17. American Law Institute, *Restatement (Third) of Trusts* (Minneapolis, 1992), sec. 90; Max M. Schanzenbach and Robert H. Sitkoff, "The Prudent Investor Rule and Market Risk: An Empirical Analysis," *Journal of Empirical Legal Studies* 14 (2017): 135.

18. National Conference of Commissioners on Uniform State Laws, *Uniform Prudent Management of Institutional Funds Act, Drafted, Approved and Recommended for Enactment in All the States* (Chicago, 2006), sec. 4; Fishman, "What Went Wrong," 219.

19. Ryan, "Trusting U," 172; Fishman, "What Went Wrong," 215. Swensen died in May 2021. See Juliet Chung and Dawn Lim, "David Swensen, Yale Endowment Chief Who Changed the Course of Institutional Investing, Dies at 67," *Wall Street Journal*, May 6, 2021.

to properly diversify the portfolio.[20] In designing EMI to accomplish this, Swensen relied on three fundamental insights.

Anticipated by the formation of index mutual funds in the 1970s, Swensen's first insight was to see that all expert investors can effectively apply the principles of modern portfolio theory in efficient markets, like those of publicly traded securities, including stocks and bonds. Due to the abundance and validity of information, as well as governmental oversight and regulation, all expert investors can diversify their assets effectively, making these markets "brutally competitive" and resulting in "efficiently priced" securities. In fact, no expert investor can significantly and consistently outperform others in efficiently priced markets. If one expert obtains relatively large gains, others will soon find them.[21]

A corollary is that professional "active management" provides little benefit to an experienced investor in efficiently priced markets. Novice investors do gain from professional advice about publicly traded securities. But active management rarely benefits the experienced investor because the returns are marginally higher, at best, and the margin of larger gain is usually consumed by the fees charged by professional active managers.

Swensen's second insight was to recognize that the opportunity to apply modern portfolio theory with greatest advantage lay outside of efficient markets. He therefore aimed to construct efficient portfolios in "less efficient" markets. Located "outside of established markets," these less efficient markets are usually "private markets" in which nontraditional, "alternative assets" are traded. Private markets are "less efficient" because information is harder to find and compile, conditions change rapidly, regulation is weak, and asset value is often opaque or difficult to calculate.

In the Yale Model, or EMI, these "alternative assets" fall into three classes: absolute return, private equity, and real assets. "Absolute return" means "exploiting inefficiencies in pricing marketable securities," as hedge funds do. Such inefficiencies arise in corporate mergers, distressed companies, short selling, futures, derivatives, and so forth. Exploiting the inefficiencies requires complicated financial instruments, highly sophisticated mathematical techniques, and extremely robust and timely data. "Private equity" includes venture capital investments in small, infant companies, as well as buying and selling companies. Finally, "real assets" consist of material assets, such as real estate, petroleum,

---

20. Swensen, *Pioneering Portfolio Management* (2009), 104. See Harry Markowitz, "Portfolio Selection," *Journal of Finance* 7 (1952): 77, 89.

21. Quotations here and in the following two paragraphs are drawn from Swensen, *Pioneering Portfolio Management* (2009), 7–8, 54, 76–77, 207, 245–46.

timber, and other natural resources. These three classes of alternative assets, often leveraged with borrowed money that can multiply gains and losses dramatically, yield "uncomfortably idiosyncratic investment portfolios" that appear extremely risky according to "conventional wisdom."[22]

Swensen's third fundamental insight was to see that alternative assets require "active management" by expert advisors. Though unprofitable in efficient markets, "active management" is necessary in less efficient markets because success requires delicately balancing the volatility of the investments in changing conditions over time. Achieving the balance requires "tools ranging from the technical rigors of modern finance to the qualitative judgments of behavioral science," as well as detailed knowledge of developments across the globe, in local markets, and within individual companies.[23]

The expertise required for active management is extremely specialized and expensive. Given this, some wealthy universities established their own internal investment office to manage endowment, as at Brown, Cornell, Pennsylvania, and Texas. Other universities formed their own management company, as did Harvard, Stanford, and Duke. A few relied on an in-house staff that selected outside managers and served "as a manager of managers," as at Yale. By 2013, more than 80 percent of the institutions reporting to NACUBO employed outside managers to invest their endowment.[24]

Whatever the organization of active management, colleges and universities must engage paid portfolio managers, whose annual compensation of several million dollars and possible conflicts of interest frequently sparked criticism on campuses in the 1990s and 2000s. But that outsized compensation paled in comparison to the tens of millions that university investment managers could earn at external firms. As endowment returns climbed astronomically in 2006 and 2007, portfolio managers played musical chairs. Each year, a third of investment managers at universities left their jobs for more lucrative investing positions in outside firms, while others who had previously departed returned to universities.[25]

Meanwhile, the performance of Yale's endowment portfolio under Swensen was superlative, even compared with other college and university endowments that earned "seemingly limitless gains" during the 1990s and 2000s. As of 2007, Yale's endowment had outperformed virtually all others over the previous 5-, 10-,

22. Swensen, *Pioneering Portfolio Management* (2009), 7–8, 112–17, 180–82.

23. Swensen, *Pioneering Portfolio Management* (2009), 8, 76–77, 207, 245–46.

24. Humphreys, *Educational Endowments*, 21. See Swensen, *Pioneering Portfolio Management* (2009), 305–14; Fishman, "What Went Wrong," 234–35.

25. Weisbrod, Ballou, and Asch, *Mission and Money*, 132; Swensen, *Pioneering Portfolio Management* (2009), 305–14.

and 20-year periods. Even during the dot-com stock collapse in 2001–2, Yale's "risky" portfolio had posted a mean positive return of 5 percent, while the average annual return on all college and university endowments was almost negative 5 percent.[26] EMI thus triumphed in the best of times and the worst, ushering in yet another golden age. And Swensen was universally regarded as "one of the world's truly great investment professionals."[27]

Alternative Assets Enter the Mainstream

As early as 1988, the Common Fund had established an affiliated corporation to help schools with smaller endowments invest in alternative assets.[28] Nevertheless, many colleges and universities hesitated to do so in the 1990s, partly because this alluring, alternative dimension seemed so novel and untried. But was it really? Portfolios of the colonial colleges had necessarily and regularly included certain alternative assets, particularly in real estate, which Swensen considered well suited to active management.[29] Even after the advent of reliable bonds in the early nineteenth century, some college and university leaders greatly enriched their institutions by investing in and actively managing such alternative assets.

One such leader was Ezra Cornell, who was planning a university in the mid-1860s, soon after the first Morrill Act (1862) granted federal lands to the states, which were to sell the land and use the proceeds to endow universities. After intense political infighting, the New York State legislature agreed to confer its windfall on Ezra's infant university, which would open for classes in 1868. To select their land granted under the Morrill Act, some states relied on agents in distant territories and were swindled into taking fallow lands. But Ezra shrewdly provided active management for this real asset. Though aged and infirm, he made an exhausting trip by wagon throughout the Midwest and personally selected prime timber and farm lands in Minnesota, Wisconsin, and Kansas for New York State's land grant.[30]

Then came the matter of managing volatility in an inefficient market. As state after state selected its federal grant and dumped it on the market, the price

---

26. Quotation is from Ryan, "Trusting U," 161–62. See Swensen, *Pioneering Portfolio Management* (2009), 1–2.

27. Charles D. Ellis, foreword to Swensen, *Pioneering Portfolio Management* (2009), ix.

28. Williamson, *Funds for the Future*, 55.

29. Swensen, *Pioneering Portfolio Management* (2009), 207.

30. This paragraph and the following rely on Paul W. Gates, *The Wisconsin Pine Lands of Cornell University* (Ithaca, NY, 1943); Richard J. Cotter, *"True and Firm": Biography of Ezra Cornell* (New York, 1884), 215–27; Carl L. Becker, *Cornell University: Founders and the Founding* (Ithaca, NY, 1943), 39, 89–118.

of land fell precipitously, as did Cornell's grant, which was booked at $500,000 in 1865. But Ezra put up collateral to allow his university to hold the lands without selling, and the grant appreciated rapidly, even through the Panic of 1873. When Cornell's land-grant endowment was finally sold in the 1880s and 1890s, the university netted over $5 million—10 times the original book value. This amount vastly exceeded the proceeds received by every other state for its federal grant. In fact, Cornell's proceeds equaled $115 million in 2020 dollars. Furthermore, if invested at an average yield of merely 3 percent over the ensuing 130 years, Cornell's federal land grant endowment would amount to $5.4 billion in 2020 dollars. Ezra thus vaulted his namesake university into the first tier of older, wealthy universities in the nation. As Swensen wrote 140 years later in 2009, "high quality investment management makes a difference!"[31]

Despite such precedents, the average allocation to alternative assets in college and university portfolios remained small through the 1990s. That allocation began to increase in the 2000s and became a major component in the 2010s, as seen in table 9.1.

Institutions with the largest endowments invested much more heavily in alternative assets. As of 2006, domestic stocks and bonds constituted 57 percent of the average portfolio of colleges and universities, but only 26 percent of the portfolios of the four wealthiest private universities: Yale, Harvard, Stanford, and Princeton. Conversely, the average portfolio invested about 19 percent in alternative assets, while the portfolios of Harvard, Yale, Stanford, and Princeton invested 61 percent on average. Yet Swensen maintained that, due to their diversification, the latter portfolios were statistically less risky than the average

TABLE 9.1
Average Investment Allocation of College and University Endowments,
1974–2020 (in percentages)

Kind of asset	1974	1994	1997	2006	2014	2020
Fixed income, cash	39%	43%	31%	24%	22%	21%
Equities	60%	55%	63%	57%	50%	49%
Alternative assets	<1%	2%	6%	19%	28%	30%

Sources: Lucie Lapovsky, "Critical Endowment Policy Issues," *New Directions for Higher Education* 140 (Winter 2007): 102–3; Kenneth E. Redd, "Forever Funds," *Business Officer Magazine*, November 2015, fig. 2; *NACUBO Endowment Study 2006*; *NACUBO Endowment Study 2020*.
Note: Averages are calculated by weighting institutions equally.

31. Swensen, *Pioneering Portfolio Management* (2009), 2.

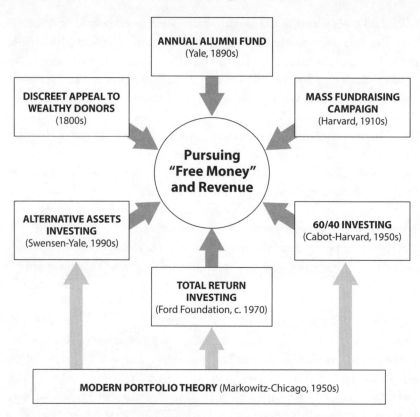

Figure 9.2. Six Modes of Building Wealth in Higher Education, 1870–2020.

portfolio.[32] Led by the wealthiest institutions, investing in alternative assets became a sixth mode of building free money in higher education between 1870 and 2020, as depicted in figure 9.2.

Spending Rules and Intergenerational Equity

In addition to portfolio management, academic and policy literature about endowments focused on the spending rule in the 1990s and 2000s. This guideline, set independently by each college or university, determines the amount that the school spends annually from its endowment income. Federal tax law requires private foundations to distribute annually no less than 5 percent of their endowment value. But this rule does not apply to higher education, and each school determines its own annual payout. Since the early nineteenth century, most institutions had typically spent in the range of 4–5 percent of their endowment value annually,

32. Swensen, *Pioneering Portfolio Management* (2009), 127–28.

based on a rolling average of that value over about four years in order to smooth the spending over time. This norm continued into the twenty-first century.[33]

Nothing might seem more technical and duller than setting spending rules. But these guidelines indirectly generated great controversy and inflamed public opinion about higher education. The reason was that the payout affects endowment size. Historically, colleges and universities set their spending rules guided by the tenet of harvesting as much income as possible while preserving the endowment principal. Running down the endowment value was not only foolish but unethical because it violated the principle of intergenerational equity, as James Tobin explained in 1974.[34]

Setting the spending rule too high and drawing too much income benefitted the current generation of students, faculty, and administrators but deprived future generations of equal benefit. Under the necessarily "prudent" approach to investment from the early 1800s through the 1940s, the normal payout of 4–5 percent was justified because most portfolios in higher education were dominated by fixed-income securities, mortgages, and rented properties. Returns averaged around 6–7 percent, though fluctuating in economic booms and busts.

After 1950, the meaning of "prudence" in portfolio management changed rapidly and dramatically. Investing 60 percent in stocks became the norm for large endowments in the 1950s and 1960s, followed by "total-return" policies in the 1970s and 1980s. These developments in portfolio management generated much bigger returns, although many endowed colleges and universities refrained from aggressive investing. For these hesitant institutions, the normal payout continued to make perfect sense both financially and ethically.

But the wealthy institutions that invested more aggressively began to see much higher returns, which drove the annual average return of all college and university endowments to unprecedented heights. Between 1974 and 1989, the mean of the annual average returns was an astronomical 12.4 percent.[35] Yet the spending rule of 4–5 percent persisted across higher education, even at the wealthiest institutions. Not only was it the safe, customary convention, but who knew how long the high returns would continue? And portfolios were riding a roller coaster, as seen in figure 9.1. Even under the total-return approach to portfolio management, colleges and universities expected to realize average returns of only 8–9 percent

33. Williamson, *Funds for the Future*, 30; Weisbrod, Ballou, and Asch, *Mission and Money*, 139; American Council on Education, *Understanding College and University Endowments* (Washington, DC, 2014), 5, 10.

34. James Tobin, "What Is Permanent Endowment Income?," *American Economic Review* 64 (1974): 427–28.

35. Redd, "Forever Funds," table 1.

and to set aside about 4 percent to cover both management fees and inflation. Due to this expectation, the traditional 4–5 percent payout made sense even for wealthy schools that were innovating in portfolio management.

But there was another reason to maintain the traditional spending rule. Competition over endowment size intensified dramatically after endowment rankings were first published in 1970. When returns were averaging 12.4 percent, spending only 4–5 percent meant that an endowment would grow 4 or 5 percent per year, after accounting for expenses and inflation. At that rate, an endowment doubled in value about every 15 years owing to investment growth alone, apart from new additions and gifts. And large endowments that were aggressively invested grew faster than all others both because their return was higher and because their principal was bigger. Schools with large endowments were winning the public competition and widening their lead by adhering to the traditional spending rule. The long-standing wealth stratification in higher education grew more extreme.

Low Spending Rules Spark Controversy

Harvard president Charles Eliot (1869–1909) had urged colleges and universities to create surpluses and invest them in endowments in order to strengthen the institutions for the long run. Without citing Eliot, Howard Bowen in 1980 recognized this behavior of maintaining low payout rules and accumulating endowment. Plowing investment returns back into endowment was simply another form of spending, Howard Bowen wrote. Having "spent" their investment returns by reinvesting them, schools then asked for more revenue.[36] This was a key proposition of the revenue-cost theory.

Without referencing either Eliot or Howard Bowen, Henry Hansmann, a Yale law professor and economist, attacked this tactic of endowment accumulation in an often-cited article in 1990. In the prior decade, aggressive portfolio management had yielded astronomical returns, and permanent funds had grown rapidly in higher education largely due to reliance on the traditional spending rule. Without mentioning Yale's contemporaneous turn to alternative assets under Swensen, Hansmann attacked this vast accumulation and the conservative spending rule that effected it.[37]

Hansmann's attack basically turned around Tobin's famous principle of intergenerational equity. Writing amid the stagflation of the early 1970s, Tobin warned universities against setting the spending rate too high. At the end of the

---

36. H. Bowen, *Costs of Higher Education*, 16, 150–51.
37. Hansmann, "Why Do Universities Have Endowments?," 3–42. Swensen later rebutted Hansmann extensively. Swensen, *Pioneering Portfolio Management* (2000), 45–50; (2009), 43–48.

prosperous 1980s, Hansmann addressed the opposite case. Setting the spending rate too low would "cause the real value of the endowment to increase over time," he asserted. This result would shortchange the current generation and profit later generations. Hansmann thus employed Tobin's principle of intergenerational equity but flipped its application, although Hansmann did not frame his argument in this way and has been said to reject the intergenerational principle altogether. In any event, Hansmann argued that the 1980s generation had been inequitably shortchanged and that annual payouts should increase under the total-return regime of portfolio management.[38]

Hansmann's prominent article did have serious weaknesses. Using data almost exclusively from Yale, he treated that university as typical of all endowed institutions. He also trivialized or ignored the justifications of autonomy, stability, and flexibility, while describing endowments as "financial reserves" for difficult times. In addition, Hansmann did not account for the greater income generated for future generations by the endowment accumulated through a lower spending rule. Thus, he effectively ignored the fundamental rationale for having endowment in the first place. After all, a growing endowment will "furnish a continuous and growing contribution to the budget of an institution" in the long run, as Peter Williamson emphasized in 1993, implicitly replying to Hansmann. Finally, although Hansmann's gravamen was the accumulation of huge endowments, his essay seemed to question the need for endowment at all, as suggested by its title, "Why Do Universities Have Endowments?"[39]

Nevertheless, Hansmann's attack on low spending rules gained attention as the average annual return of higher education endowments remained strong between 1990 and 2007, despite the fluctuations seen in figure 9.1. Over that period, the mean of the annual average returns exceeded 10 percent, and the number of mega-endowments (with more than $1 billion) grew to 76 by 2007. Articles in the *Chronicle of Higher Education* and other outlets echoed Hansmann's argument against low spending rules and endowment accumulation.[40]

But little changed, despite the "tremendous pressure for universities—particularly wealthy universities—to increase endowment spending," according

38. Hansmann, "Why Do Universities Have Endowments?," 10, 14–15; Tobin, "What Is Permanent Endowment Income?," 427. Compare Fishman, "What Went Wrong," 202n; Henry Riggs, "Boards Should Reconsider What They Mean by Intergenerational Equity," *Chronicle of Higher Education*, August 5, 2005.

39. Quotation is from Williamson, *Funds for the Future*, 11. See Hansmann, "Why Do Universities Have Endowments?," 3, 9, 22, 31–32.

40. Redd, "Forever Funds," table 1. See Henry Hansmann, "Bigger Is Not Necessarily Better," *Chronicle of Higher Education*, May 28, 2004; Mark B. Schneider, "Endowments Can Become Too Much of a Good Thing," *Chronicle of Higher Education*, June 2, 2006.

to legal scholar Sarah Waldeck. Repeated studies between 2000 and 2008 found that nearly all endowed colleges and universities were still spending annually about 5 percent of their endowment value. The astronomical returns and seemingly tightfisted payouts led Waldeck to predict a "Coming Showdown over University Endowments."[41]

Declining Subsidies, Rising Price

Debate about tuition and fees in higher education intensified between 1980 and 2008 because the list price of higher education ascended dramatically. During the 1970s, tuition and fees had risen steeply in nominal dollars but increased little in constant dollars. Then, in the 1980s, "tuition and fees began to grow much more rapidly than consumer prices," observed a College Board study of college pricing. Over that decade, the average tuition and fees increased 41 percent at public colleges and 64 percent at private institutions in constant dollars. Meanwhile, middle-class incomes plateaued. During the 1980s, the average annual tuition at Ivy League institutions, for example, rose from about one-quarter to about one-half of the median American family income.[42]

During the 1990s, prices continued to soar. Listed tuition and fees climbed 51 percent at public four-year colleges and 34 percent at private colleges in constant dollars. Consequently, "as the twenty-first century begins, institutions of higher education find themselves under intense scrutiny and criticism," wrote economist Robert Toutkoushian. Nevertheless, colleges and universities kept raising their price. During the 2000s, listed tuition and fees rose 61 percent at public colleges and 29 percent at private colleges in constant dollars.[43] Some scholars even suggested that public financial aid programs for students induced colleges and universities to raise their prices, while others rebutted that suggestion.[44]

Outrage about climbing prices erupted primarily at public colleges and universities. There were three reasons. First, in the 1990s and 2000s, tuition and fees rose nearly twice as much at public schools as at private schools in constant dol-

---

41. Quotations are from Waldeck, "Coming Showdown over University Endowments," 1799, 1814. See NACUBO, *Endowment Study 2008*; College Board, *Trends in College Pricing 2012*, 27–28.

42. Quotation is from College Board, *Trends in College Pricing 2003*, 3. See College Board, *Trends in College Pricing 2000*, 7; Ehrenberg, *Tuition Rising*, 7.

43. Robert K. Toutkoushian, "Trends in Revenues and Expenditures for Public and Private Higher Education," in Paulsen and Smart, *Finance of Higher Education*, 11. Figures are calculated from data in College Board, *Trends in College Pricing 1999*, 11; *2009*, 9.

44. Evelyn Brody, "Charities in Tax Reform: Threats to Subsidies Overt and Covert," *Tennessee Law Review* 66 (1999): 697, 710; Michael S. McPherson and Morton O. Schapiro, "Issues of Cost and Price in Higher Education: Observations on Needed Data and Research," in NCES, *Study of College Costs and Prices*, 78.

lars. In addition, many more students were affected by the larger increase. Enrollment in public four-year schools expanded tremendously and nearly doubled
that in private schools, as of 2007.[45] Finally, public schools could be pressured
effectively by politicians. When the Claremont Colleges hiked tuition, Califor-
nians rolled their eyes. When California state universities raised their prices,
students held demonstrations, and government bodies held hearings. Thus, public colleges and universities raised tuition faster, enrolled most of the students,
and were directly subject to political pressure.

Even so, public schools that raised their price did not increase their total revenue. As explained earlier, price in higher education is not set by a markup
over cost and covers much less than half of the production cost. The rest of the
revenue comes primarily from federal, state, and local subsidies, which declined
relative to other revenue sources of public colleges and universities. Between 1988
and 2001, the proportion of aggregate revenue that public four-year colleges and
universities received from federal, state, and local appropriations fell from
54 percent to 41 percent in constant dollars—a decline of about 1 percent per
year on average.[46]

Prominent economists, such as Michael McPherson and David Breneman,
therefore testified that public colleges and universities had been raising tuition
in the 1980s and 1990s not in order to increase their revenue but to compensate
for shrinking subsidies. In fact, between 1980 and 2000, the burden of paying
the cost of public colleges and universities underwent "a steady shift . . . away
from the taxpayer and toward the student."[47] This shift reflected the policy announced by President Reagan's budget director, David Stockman, in 1981: "If
people want to go to college bad enough, then there is opportunity and responsibility on their part to finance their way through the best way they can."[48] By
this view, higher education was a private commodity, not a public good improving the nation's economy and polity.

Despite economists' testimony, the general public and most students and
their families still did not understand the basic relationships among price, cost,
and subsidy in higher education, sighed the president of the American Council

45. App. 7; College Board, *Trends in College Pricing 1999*, 11; *2009*, 9; Weisbrod, Ballou, and
Asch, *Mission and Money*, 295.

46. Weisbrod, Ballou, and Asch, *Mission and Money*, 298–99.

47. Breneman, "Essay on College Costs," 16. See McPherson and Schapiro, "Issues of Cost
and Price," 76; Ronald G. Ehrenberg, ed., *What's Happening to Public Higher Education? The Shifting Financial Burden* (Baltimore, 2006).

48. Quoted in Edward B. Fiske, "Beyond Cutbacks, What's U.S. Goal in Education?," *New
York Times*, December 13, 1981.

on Education in 2008. Demonstrating the problem, the College Board's annual public report *Trends in College Pricing* did not address the "subsidy" and explain its role in paying for part of the production cost of higher education until 2008. During the 2000s, meanwhile, federal, state, and local subsidies to public four-year institutions fell from about 70 percent to 58 percent of per-student revenue in constant dollars. Tuition and fees largely made up the difference. However, only in 2018 did the College Board's annual public report on college pricing begin to highlight and document changes in such "subsidies."[49]

Raising and Discounting Tuition

For the first time in 40 years, Princeton University did not raise tuition in 2007. Such restraint was rare. The wealthiest private colleges and universities had steadily increased their prices, even while their endowments swelled. Consequently, critics of rising tuition often pilloried these schools.[50] Yet resentment over the tuition of elite, wealthy institutions seems misdirected, like complaining about the high price of luxury cars.

Students from rich families could afford to pay the high price, and more than half of the students at the premier, private institutions like Stanford, Princeton, Brown, and Pennsylvania came from families in the top 10 percent of wealth in the United States. Meanwhile, students from families with small means received financial aid. In 2006–7, Harvard announced that students from families earning under the median family income of $60,000 in the United States would pay nothing to attend, and students whose parents earned under $180,000 a year would pay no more than 10 percent of their family's annual income in tuition.[51] The disadvantaged students therefore came primarily from middle- and upper-middle-class families. For them, admission to a premier, private university was a privilege, and attending was a choice. Any students admitted to Princeton could surely attract offers of a free ride from another college or an excellent honors program at a public university.

Still, the price increases of the wealthiest colleges and universities deserved public resentment, because those increases compelled lower-ranked and lesser-

49. Molly Corbett Broad, "Endowments Are Both Vital and Misunderstood," *Chronicle of Higher Education*, November 21, 2008; College Board, *Trends in College Pricing 2008*, 2; *2012*, 24; *2018*, 27.

50. Karen W. Arenson, "Tuition Steady at Princeton; Other Fees Rise," *New York Times*, January 22, 2007; Gordon, *Rise and Fall of American Growth*, 500; Weisbrod, Ballou, and Asch, *Mission and Money*, 222.

51. Nina Munk, "Rich Harvard, Poor Harvard," *Vanity Fair* 51, no. 8 (August 2009): 106; Kevin Carey, "The Creeping Capitalist Takeover of Higher Education," *Huffington Post*, April 1, 2019; Scott Jaschik, "Faculty Want to Know: Is Stanford Letting in Too Many Wealthy Students?," *Inside Higher Ed*, February 16, 2021.

endowed private schools to raise their tuition. The latter institutions had to do so in order to pay for the same amenities that the elite schools provided. In addition, replicating the price of Princeton implied that lower-ranked schools matched the quality of Princeton, just as the quality of luxury cars is often measured by their price. It was therefore widely understood that "if the better-endowed institutions slow down their rates of tuition growth, so eventually will the lesser-endowed, selective private institutions," stated economist Ronald Ehrenberg.[52]

In addition to public rancor, another big problem confronted the lower-ranked, lesser-endowed private schools that raised their price to approximate Princeton's. Students were often unwilling to pay Princeton's tuition to attend a lower-ranked, private school, particularly if a lower-priced, public university beckoned. Squeezed between the wealthy, private elites and less expensive public institutions, most lower-ranked private schools ended up heavily discounting tuition. This approach differed from awarding aid that was funded by endowment income or gifts or external grants of some kind. Tuition discounting occurred when a school simply "remitted," or cut, the tuition that it charged in order to induce a particular student to enroll, whether due to that student's merit or financial need. Tuition discounting thus resulted in differential pricing; students simultaneously enrolled at the same school paid very different prices, just as airlines charge very different prices for seats in the same class on the same flight.

Schools often subsumed both tuition discounts and funded aid under the term "institutional grant aid," and students generally could not tell the difference. In either case, the "net price"—the amount the student actually paid to the institution for attending (including savings, loans, and work-study)—was the same.[53] But the distinction between tuition discounts and funded aid was critical to a school, because its "net tuition revenue"—how much it actually received to cover the student's attendance—differed significantly.

In the case of a student awarded funded aid, the school received all the revenue for its listed price. The funded aid covered the difference between the list price and the "net price" that the student paid, and the school's net tuition revenue equaled what it charged. In the case of discounted tuition, however, the school did not receive the revenue from its discount. The school's net tuition revenue equaled the student's net price: the listed tuition minus the discount. If a student received both

52. Ehrenberg, *Tuition Rising*, 266.
53. College Board, *Trends in College Pricing 2003*, 1, 14–15.

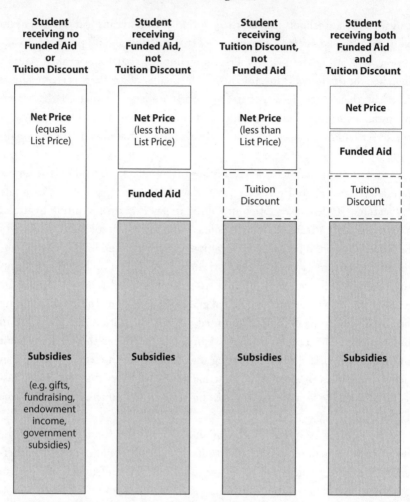

Figure 9.3. Components of Revenue Covering Educational Production Cost, 1980–2020.
Note: White boxes represent total amount of List Price, announced by Institution. Net
Price equals amount paid by student from savings, loans, or work-study. White boxes
with solid borders represent components of Net Tuition Revenue received by Institution.

funded aid and a tuition discount, then the net tuition revenue equaled the student's funded aid and the student's net price. The school still did not receive the
total revenue of its listed price, as illustrated in figure 9.3.

Although tuition discounts mattered greatly to less endowed institutions, the
huge endowments of the wealthiest schools effectively permitted them to fund
all their student aid. Leaders of these schools who studied educational finance
sometimes did not appreciate the significance of tuition discounting, which they

regarded as a kind of revenue transfer. Their different perspective muddied the data about tuition discounting, as did the refusal of many schools to report the sometimes embarrassing data of how much they had to cut their price in order to recruit students. These factors likely contributed to the fact that the College Board did not distinguish between "net price" and "net tuition revenue" until its 2020 pricing study.[54]

Enrollment Management Tool

Historical evidence of tuition discounting, even of the idea, is hard to find before 1970. At state colleges and universities prior to 1960, providing scholarships or free tuition for defined classes of students, such as veterans or future schoolteachers, became widespread, though sometimes disputed and challenged in court. But remitting tuition to individuals apparently did not occur, for this practice would have smacked of favoritism.[55] Nor did private schools consider announcing a price and remitting tuition to some individuals and not others. Instead, they simply refused to raise tuition if they feared that higher tuition would exclude students of lesser means. Indeed, during the Great Depression and the 1940s, raising tuition at all was widely felt to damage a school's reputation or to exploit the students or the G.I. Bill subsidy. Discounting seems not to have occurred, at least as an institutional policy.[56]

In the 1950s and 1960s, tuition spiked dramatically at private colleges and universities, propelled by per-student cost escalation during those two decades. At the same time, intense competition for survival and success resumed among colleges and universities and sowed the seeds of tuition discounting that sprouted in the 1970s and branched out in the 1980s. Tuition discounting then began to transform financial aid into "an enrollment management tool" that served three purposes: recruiting stellar students, diversifying the student body, and maintaining full enrollment.[57]

---

54. College Board, *Trends in College Pricing 2003*, 1; *2020*, 22. See William G. Bowen and David W. Breneman, "Student Aid: Price Discount or Educational Investment?," *Brookings Review* 11 (Winter 1993): 28–31; Michael S. McPherson and Morton O. Schapiro, *The Student Aid Game: Meeting Need and Rewarding Talent in American Higher Education* (Princeton, NJ, 1998); Weisbrod, Ballou, and Asch, *Mission and Money*, 77–101.

55. Scott M. Gelber, *Courts and Classrooms: A Legal History of College Access, 1860–1960* (Baltimore, 2016), 123–33.

56. For example, no consideration of tuition discounting is presented in Katharine T. Kinkead, *How an Ivy League College Decides on Admissions* (New York, 1961).

57. Quotation is from Lucie Lapovsky, "Institutional Financial Health: Tuition Discounting and Enrollment Management," in NCES, *Study of College Costs and Prices*, 65, 71. See Williamson, *Funds for the Future*, 1.

Again, evidence is elusive and usually must be gleaned from institutional records. But one early example at the law schools of Harvard and Yale suggests how tuition discounting slowly evolved at intensely competing private institutions.[58] During the 1950s and 1960s, these two law schools reshaped their financial aid policies in order to help them attract the best students. Prior to 1950, neither law school gave much attention to financial aid. Less than 10 percent of the students received aid; amounts were small and distributed during the academic year and heavily based on exam results. Financial aid had nothing to do with recruitment.[59]

In the early 1950s, competition to enroll stellar students intensified, and escalating tuition prompted more applicants to request financial aid. Harvard shifted its financial aid policy to target admitted applicants by offering them aid upon acceptance. For the first time, admittees could weigh financial aid when making decisions about which law school to attend. In the late 1950s, the Yale law dean recognized the threat and responded, as evident in the recollection of law professor Alan Dershowitz, who was admitted to both Harvard and Yale law schools in 1961. "The deciding factor" for Dershowitz in choosing Yale was that the school offered him "a small scholarship and a loan."[60]

In the early 1960s, realizing that they were losing funded admittees to Yale, the Harvard law faculty decided to award more full-tuition scholarships in order "to increase the attractiveness" of Harvard. These awards were entirely funded by annual alumni gifts or endowed funds reserved for scholarships. The law school therefore did not lose any tuition revenue, and tuition discounting had not begun, although the financial aid was aimed at recruitment. Finally, in 1967–68, Harvard Law School raised its total scholarship aid to $611,000, and about 7 percent came from remitted "tuition" according to a faculty report. This is the first allusion to tuition discounting in this historical record of financial aid at these two schools competing intensely for superlative students.

This discount was very small. Based on the school's list price, the discount amounted to only about 1 percent of total potential tuition revenue. (In other

58. Here and below, see Bruce A. Kimball and Daniel R. Coquillette, *The Intellectual Sword: Harvard Law School, the Second Century* (Cambridge, MA, 2020), 88–98, 212–15, 313, 616–19.

59. Wesley A. Sturges, *Annual Report of the Dean of Yale Law School 1949–50*, 21. The following draws on [Andrew L. Kaufman, Chair,] Memorandum to the Faculty from the Financial Aids Committee [Cambridge, MA, ca. March 1970], typescript on file, 2–6, 17–21, app. 2.

60. Alan M. Dershowitz, Oral History conducted by Daniel R. Coquillette with Andrew Klaber, October–November 2009, typescript on file. See Eugene V. Rostow, *Annual Report of the Dean of Yale Law School 1957–59*, 36; *1959–62*, 45.

words, the net tuition revenue was 99 percent of the potential tuition revenue.) From this threshold of 1 percent, the discount rate ascended inexorably at many colleges and universities over the next 50 years. Meanwhile, the exact amount of discounts often remained obscure because published financial data from colleges and universities rarely distinguished their tuition discounts from their funded aid.

From such scattered starts in the 1960s, the average discount rate was estimated to have grown close to 20 percent of tuition revenue at private colleges and universities during the economic stress of the 1970s. Then, the discount rate rose nearly to 30 percent during the 1980s, reaching almost 50 percent at some schools and transforming financial aid into the "enrollment management tool" with three aims.

Recruiting academic stars likely emerged first chronologically, as suggested in the account of the two law schools above. The second enrollment management goal of tuition discounting—diversifying the student body in terms of gender, race, and social class—became prominent in the 1980s.[61] Over the next two decades, colleges and universities competed to maintain full enrollment—the third goal of tuition discounting.

In 1994, NACUBO launched an annual Tuition Discounting Study, and in 2000 established a Tuition Discounting Advisory Committee. Based on a survey of 276 private colleges and universities, the NACUBO committee found that, during the 1990s, the fraction of students receiving "institutional grant aid" had climbed to 79 percent, and the percentage of tuition covered by "institutional grant aid" had grown to 48 percent. Although the meaning of that term was ambiguous, the survey implied that "institutional grant aid" meant primarily tuition discounting and concluded that "published tuition has increased much more than net tuition."[62]

During the 2000s, the College Board's annual pricing studies estimated that students' net price—what they actually paid from savings, loans, and work-study—fell to 45 percent of the list price at private four-year institutions. The 55 percent difference was attributed to "institutional grant aid."[63] The meaning of this term still remained ambiguous because the data of the College Board, the

61. Williamson, *Funds for the Future*, 1.
62. Quotation is from Lapovsky, "Institutional Financial Health," 58–60. See David W. Breneman, James L. Doti, and Lucie Lapovsky, "Financing Private Colleges and Universities: The Role of Tuition Discounting," in Paulsen and Smart, *Finance of Higher Education*, 475; NACUBO, *The 2019 NACUBO Tuition Discounting Study* (Washington, DC, 2020).
63. College Board, *Trends in College Pricing 2009*, 11.

NCES, and NACUBO did not and could not accurately distinguish tuition discounts from funded aid. "Institutional grant aid" sometimes meant funded aid, sometimes "tuition remission," and sometimes both. The fundamental problem was that only a few hundred private colleges and universities reported this sensitive data precisely, and tuition remission at public institutions was scarcely studied at all.[64]

In any event, no authority doubted that tuition discounting became a serious problem between 1980 and 2008. The list prices of colleges and universities rose higher and higher, while many schools, particularly in the private sector, received proportionally less and less net revenue from the price increases.[65]

Production Cost Growth

Analyzing production cost in higher education grew even more complicated after 1980. The fraught distinction between educational and non-educational costs became more problematic, particularly for schools that received large government or foundation grants supporting major research projects. How much of a given project was "educational" and contributed directly to students' education? How much contributed indirectly, and how should that be measured? By 2008, a major study of higher educational finances, funded by the Spencer Foundation, largely ignored the distinction between educational and non-educational costs, while explaining how new kinds of revenue and costs exacerbated the analytical problems.[66]

For example, the University and Small Businesses Patent Procedures Act (1980) removed the prohibition on patenting research supported by any federal grant money. Subsequently, higher education revenue from research activity, patents, and licensing significantly increased. How much of this revenue and its associated costs directly contributed to the education of students? In addition, distinguishing costs was complicated by the plethora of published institutional rankings, which expanded dramatically after the *U.S. News & World Report* issued its first in 1983. A number of schools responded by spending to improve

64. See College Board, *Trends in College Pricing 2020*, 22, 23n; National Center for Education Statistics, "Student Financial Aid Glossary," in *Integrated Postsecondary Education Data System Survey Components* (accessed February 2021); NACUBO, *2019 NACUBO Tuition Discounting Study*; Lapovsky, "Institutional Financial Health," 71.

65. See "Tuition and Fees, 1998–99 through 2020–21," *Chronicle of Higher Education*, May 21, 2021.

66. Weisbrod, Ballou, and Asch, *Mission and Money*, also tends to vitiate the non-profit/for-profit distinction in higher education. See 1–8, 70–76.

their standings in the rankings even when the expenditures did not affect their educational quality. Was this spending educational or not?[67]

Furthermore, college athletics exploded into a huge business, as historian John Thelin has chronicled. Widespread debates over the role of "scholar-athletes" exemplified the murky relationship between educational and non-educational costs in this domain. Finally, the for-profit sector of higher education saw "tremendous" growth, as its full-time enrollment climbed from 73,000 in 1980 to 912,000 in 2006, an increase of more than 1,100 percent. In this sector, the distinction between educational and non-educational was particularly vexed.[68]

A compounding difficulty in assessing production cost between 1980 and 2008 lay in long-standing "gaps and inconsistencies" in the financial data that prevented an accurate longitudinal analysis.[69] The problem worsened in 1995, when the Financial Accounting Standards Board stopped requiring private institutions to employ the long-established conventions of fund accounting. This change made it "impossible to compare the financial status of public and private institutions" after 1995 or to "examine trends . . . for private institutions" before and after 1995, as Robert Toutkoushian has observed.[70]

Notwithstanding these data problems, many concluded that "higher education costs started to get out of control" in the 1980s, when a study of over 2,000 schools found that per-student "educational and general expenditures" grew 2.5 percent annually above inflation.[71] Then, the per-student production cost leveled off in the 1990s and 2000s, although some scholars continued to express "growing concern about the rising costs of higher education."[72] Over the entire 46-year duration of the Higher Education Price Index from 1961 to 2007, the aggregate production cost of higher education certainly did escalate above the cost

67. Weisbrod, Ballou, and Asch, *Mission and Money*, 51, 111–12, 155–57, 189–90.

68. See John R. Thelin, *Games Colleges Play: Scandal and Reform in Intercollegiate Athletics* (Baltimore, 1996), 179–204; John R. Thelin, "A New Deal for Students as Athletes," *Inside Higher Ed*, April 6, 2021; Weisbrod, Ballou, and Asch, *Mission and Money*, 27, 251–59.

69. Quotation is from Olson, "Cost Effectiveness," 196. See National Research Council, *Improving Measurement of Productivity in Higher Education*, ed. Teresa A. Sullivan et al. (Washington, DC, 2012).

70. Toutkoushian, "Trends in Revenues and Expenditures," 18. See Robert B. Archibald and David H. Feldman, "Explaining Increases in Higher Education Costs," *Journal of Higher Education* 79 (2008): 293n8.

71. Quotation is from Getz and Siegfried, "Costs and Productivity," 261, 300. See William F. Massy, "Improving Productivity in Higher Education: Administration and Support Costs," *Capital Ideas* 6, no. 1 (1991): 2–3.

72. Quotation is from Darrell L. Lewis and Halil Dundar, "Costs and Productivity in Higher Education: Theory Evidence, and Policy Implications," in Paulsen and Smart, *Finance of Higher Education*, 137. See Archibald and Feldman, "Explaining Increases," 277–79.

of living. But the enrollment in higher education ascended steeply as well, as seen in appendix 7, so the increase in aggregate cost did not prove that per-student cost had escalated "over the long term," as some scholars who favored cost-disease theory asserted.[73]

Resentment Ignites and Burns Intermittently

During the 1970s, few suggested that colleges and universities were gouging students, even though tuition climbed dramatically in nominal dollars. Most Americans blamed stagflation, rather than higher education, for the tuition increases. Articles in the *New York Times* maintained that complaints from middle-income families about price increases amounted to whining and that "colleges can certainly use all the money they can get."[74] In 1978, Congress considered more than 50 bills proposing ways to help middle-class families pay tuition. Higher education was the victim, not the villain.[75]

Howard Bowen's *The Costs of Higher Education* marked a turning point in 1980 by suggesting that higher education bore responsibility for rising production cost. Whether or not this book was a catalyst, the growth of institutional wealth, cost, and price sparked resentment about higher education thereafter. By 1987, Congress was flooded with "criticisms of higher education's quality and cost," and congressional staffers reported "a negative impression about the university community. . . . They've got a real education job to do overcoming it." Tacking away from its approach in the 1970s, Congress therefore formulated proposals to tax the earnings of colleges and universities from ancillary ventures, such as bookstores, computer stores, and applied research.[76]

Some scholars have attributed the genesis of these attacks to a conservative backlash against the "liberal" values of higher education during the administration of President Reagan. And it was true that spokesmen for that conservative reaction assailed "our greedy colleges," particularly Reagan's secretary of education William Bennett (1985–88).[77] But, during the 1990s and 2000s, public ire was stoked primarily by the "discordance" between skyrocketing tuition in constant dollars and the incessant announcements of huge investment returns,

73. W. Bowen, *"Cost Disease,"* 3. See Swensen, *Pioneering Portfolio Management* (2009), 34.
74. John A. Allan, "Universities Flunk Investing," *New York Times*, September 24, 1972. See Fred M. Hechinger, "Another Cry for Help: Colleges," *New York Times*, December 19, 1971; Earl F. Cheit, "Plight of the Colleges," *New York Times*, January 10, 1972; "What Middle-Class Tuition Squeeze?," *New York Times*, March 28, 1978.
75. Edward B. Fiske, "Less Able to Pay, or Just Less Willing?," *New York Times*, June 4, 1978. See Steven V. Roberts, "Tax Credit Fervor Rises with Tuitions," *New York Times*, June 21, 1978.
76. Quotations are from Jaschik, "House Panel Eyes Plans," A34.
77. William Bennett, "Our Greedy Colleges," *New York Times*, February 18, 1987.

soaring endowment values, and oversubscribed fundraising campaigns, as well as "a growing institutional wealth gap" in higher education.[78] By the beginning of the twenty-first century, the public "outrage" prompted "intense scrutiny and criticism" of higher education.[79]

In 1997, Congress created the National Commission on the Cost of Higher Education to examine the cause of spiraling tuition. In 1998, Congress directed the NCES "to conduct a new study of higher education costs paid by institutions and prices paid by students and their families."[80] Yet despite such studies of cost escalation in higher education, Stanford professor and vice president of business and finance William Massy observed in 2003 that "little has been learned about how to contain it."[81]

Although the outrage temporarily abated after the dot-com stock collapse of 2001–2, Congress soon resumed its inquiries into tuition increases at highly endowed colleges and universities. In 2006 and 2007, the US Senate Committee on Finance held hearings, led by Republican senator Charles E. Grassley of Iowa. By 2008, broad public dissatisfaction with the financial activities of higher education prompted a bipartisan inquiry by Grassley and Democratic representative Peter Welch of Vermont, who had assumed the seat vacated by Senator Bernie Sanders. Grassley and Welch convened a round table of higher education leaders to discuss "Maximizing the Use of Endowment Funds and Making Higher Education More Affordable."[82]

Some scholars meanwhile maintained that the expense/endowment ratio is the most accurate gauge of a school's wealth. By this standard, in 2006 Harvard was ranked 17th in the country, Yale 21st, and Stanford 58th, owing to their huge expenses in medical centers and scientific research. The wealthiest institution in the country was, in fact, Grinnell College, located in Iowa, Grassley's home state.[83]

Encouraged by many critics, congressional inquiries in 2006, 2007, and 2008 also threatened the federal subsidies and tax benefits in all of higher education. These included the tax-free status of income earned from educational activities and from investments, the right to issue tax-exempt bonds to finance educational activities, and donors' ability to deduct gifts to higher education. Also

78. Waldeck, "Coming Showdown over University Endowments," 1795.
79. Ehrenberg, *Tuition Rising*, 8; Toutkoushian, "Trends in Revenues and Expenditures," 11.
80. Quotation is from abstract in NCES, *Study of College Costs and Prices.*
81. Massy, *Honoring the Trust*, 39.
82. Broad, "Endowments Are Both Vital and Misunderstood."
83. Waldeck, "Coming Showdown over University Endowments," 1795, 1799–1805; Weisbrod, Ballou, and Asch, *Mission and Money*, 143–44; "Report Card on Tax Exemptions and Incentives for Higher Education: Pass, Fail, or Need Improvement?," *Hearing Before the U.S. Senate Committee on Finance*, 109th Cong. 97 (December 5, 2006).

scrutinized were tax benefits to citizens that strengthened the demand for higher education, such as the Helping Outstanding Pupils Educationally tax credit and the Lifetime Learning tax credit, as well as tax deductions or exemptions for contributions to 529 education accounts, state prepaid tuition plans, employer-provided educational assistance, and student loan interest.[84]

Amid these gathering storm clouds, the double helix of wealth growth and cost growth continued its upward spiral, intermittently drawing price higher. The overall market value of college and university endowments in the NACUBO survey for 2006–7 grew more than 18 percent (including fundraising and investment returns). In that year, for example, Grinnell's growth in market value was 17 percent, and the college announced a 13 percent tuition increase for the 2007–8 academic year.[85] This typical and tone-deaf combination of huge investment returns and tuition hikes further inflamed the anger of critics, who wanted to force the wealthiest colleges and universities to stop increasing tuition, if not begin cutting it.

The approach of Grinnell, the wealthiest school in the country by some measures, epitomized the financial evolution of colleges and universities.[86] They had become "small capitalistic enterprises" competing intensely for students, prestige, and excellence in a large marketplace, according to the director of the Center of Studies in Higher Education at the University of California. The schools resembled "living organisms . . . in an ecological system—competitive for resources, highly sensitive to the demands of the environment, and inclined, over time, through the ruthless processes of natural selection, to be adaptive to . . . their environment."[87] Yet competition in that marketplace did not work to "promote internal efficiency" and reduce cost and price, as would normally be expected.[88] Instead, schools' key adaptive behavior was to reinforce the helical relationship between aggregate wealth and aggregate cost.

84. Waldeck, "Coming Showdown over University Endowments," 1797–98.

85. Jane Norman, "Grassley to Colleges: Use Riches for Tuition," *Des Moines Register*, January 21, 2008; Herbert A. Allen, "Gold in the Ivory Tower," *New York Times*, December 21, 2007; Broad, "Endowments Are Both Vital and Misunderstood," A32; Weisbrod, Ballou, and Asch, *Mission and Money*, 143–44.

86. Janet Lorin, "Buffett Chides College for Not Cutting Tuition as Endowment Grew," *Bowling Green Daily News*, May 3, 2016.

87. Trow, "American Higher Education," 11–13.

88. William F. Massy, "Markets in Higher Education: Do They Promote Internal Efficiency?," in *Markets in Higher Education: Rhetoric or Reality?*, ed. Pedro Teixeira et al. (Boston, 2004), 3–35. See Sheila Slaughter and Gary Rhoades, *Academic Capitalism and the New Economy: Markets, State, and Higher Education* (Baltimore, 2009); Robert Zemsky and Susan Shaman, *The Market Imperative: Segmentation and Change in Higher Education* (Baltimore, 2017).

CHAPTER 10

What Is the Real "Cost Disease"?
1980s–2020s

In the opening decades of the twenty-first century, the wealth-cost double helix continued to spiral upward, followed by price and student debt. These last two topics dominated public and policy discussion but remained mercurial, because price and debt were derivative and subject to subsidies, discounts, and external forces that varied adventitiously. Meanwhile, scholarship concerning wealth growth focused on portfolio management, spending rules, and the impact of fluctuating endowment returns. Within higher education, leaders celebrated both endowment growth and fundraising success and regarded the competition for more revenue as inevitable and largely beneficial. All these subjects are addressed in the next chapter.

This chapter examines cost growth, which continued to receive a great deal of scholarly attention early in the twenty-first century. Conceptual analysis focused primarily on the cost-disease and revenue-cost theories, although scholars' preference between the two theories shifted significantly. In addition, their long-standing approval of the helical relationship between wealth growth and cost growth began to fade, after prevailing throughout the twentieth century.

Cost-Disease Theory Predominates, 1968–2000

Applying cost-disease theory to higher education in 1968, William Bowen argued that professors' stagnant productivity causes the labor cost of higher education per unit of production to rise faster than the labor cost in other industries where workers make productivity gains. Because professors' wages must keep pace with workers in other industries, the labor cost rises faster in higher education.[1] Consequently, the overall production cost of higher education, like other service industries, escalates above both the production cost of goods-producing industries and the cost of living, as sketched in figure 7.3. Soon after 1968, studies of higher education finance began to invoke cost-disease theory authoritatively, and they continued to do so for decades, usually while referencing William Bowen or his senior colleague, William Baumol.[2]

Economists and other scholars favored cost-disease theory not only because it subtly exculpated higher education but primarily because most other studies of cost growth were "non-theoretical and directly empirical, often resulting in a laundry list of contributing factors."[3] For example, the rising cost of technology or unfunded government mandates or new regulations often appeared on the lists. Though certainly contributing to cost growth in higher education, such factors impact other industries as well, or are somewhat adventitious, and therefore cannot explain why the per-student production cost of higher education rises faster than the cost of living over the long term. Cost-disease theory thus gained favor among economists because it offered a "behavioral foundation," permitting researchers "to frame . . . a testable hypothesis."[4]

At the same time, William Bowen's 1968 study became a virtual palimpsest, as his explanation of cost-disease theory was overwritten and misconstrued. For example, the theory was said to address the price rather than production cost

1. Additional discussion and documentation of the following are found in Kimball and Luke, "Historical Dimensions of the 'Cost Disease.'"

2. See G. Richard Wynn, "Inflation in the Higher Education Industry," *NACUBO Professional File* 6, no. 1 (1975): 2; Edward B. Fiske, "How Tuition Costs Are Set: An Education in Itself," *New York Times*, May 14, 1987; Williamson, *Funds for the Future*, 7–8; Swensen, *Pioneering Portfolio Management* (2000), 35; (2009), 34; Gordon, *Rise and Fall of American Growth*, 13, 173; Christopher P. Loss, "Can Endowments Save Higher Education?," *HistPhil* (blog), March 27, 2017.

3. Breneman, "Essay on College Costs," 14. See Getz and Siegfried, "Costs and Productivity," 261–67; Olson, "Cost Effectiveness," 217–30.

4. Robert B. Archibald and David H. Feldman, "Explaining Increases in Higher Education Costs," *Journal of Higher Education* 79 (2008): 269, 281. See Darrell L. Lewis and Halil Dundar, "Costs and Productivity in Higher Education," in Paulsen and Smart, *Finance of Higher Education*, 47–49, 63–73.

of higher education, or aggregate cost rather than per-student cost, or the compensation of all employees rather than just the service providers, the faculty. Furthermore, virtually all studies that properly invoked cost-disease theory took for granted that William Bowen's study definitively proved how and why per-student cost in higher education had escalated during the first two-thirds of the twentieth century. No scholar apparently scrutinized William Bowen's evidence or method, and his 1968 study became the unquestioned locus classicus in the financial literature that predisposed analyses in the late twentieth century to affirm cost-disease theory.

Indeed, through the 2010s, William Baumol applauded the reliance on cost-disease theory and maintained that his predictions and those of William Bowen were "fully borne out." In a summative book in 2012, Baumol fairly crowed that "our predictions . . . may well be the longest valid forecast ever to emerge from economic analysis."[5] Less effusively, William Bowen also continued to endorse his 1968 study and became interested in how information technology could reduce the faculty labor cost and therefore the production cost of higher education. Lecturing on the subject at Stanford University in 2012, William Bowen stated that his "detailed examination of . . . the University of Chicago, Princeton and Vanderbilt between 1905 and 1966" had validated cost-disease theory and "documented the seemingly inexorable tendency for institutional cost per student . . . to rise faster than costs in general over the long term."[6]

Meanwhile, the definition of "service" industry began to appear fluid and indeterminate. For example, the US Bureau of Economic Analysis (BEA) classified dozens of industries as "service industries," including airlines, railroads, long-distance trucking, radio, television, hotels, motels, dwelling rentals, sanitation services, and electric, gas, and water utilities, among others.[7] Thus, several of the BEA "service industries" did not fit the central criteria posited by Baumol: that the labor is "the end product" and involves "handicraft—or in-person" work.[8] Conversely, the paradigmatic service industries identified by Baumol and William Bowen—higher education and performing arts—were

---

5. Quotations are from William J. Baumol, "Social Wants and Dismal Science: The Curious Case of the Climbing Costs of Health and Teaching," *Proceedings of the American Philosophical Society* 137 (1993): 623–24; Baumol, *Cost Disease*, xix.

6. W. Bowen, *"Cost Disease,"* 3.

7. See, e.g., US Bureau of Economic Analysis, Department of Commerce, *Price Indexes for Personal Consumption Expenditures by Type of Product* (Washington, DC, 2015), table 2.4.4.

8. William J. Baumol, "Macroeconomics of Unbalanced Growth: The Anatomy of Urban Crisis," *American Economic Review* 57 (1967): 416; Baumol, *Cost Disease*, 22.

outliers on the BEA list. In addition, some service industries that Baumol considered typical (e.g., restaurants) were not so classified by the BEA at times.[9]

In 2008, some economists who endorsed the application of cost-disease theory to higher education suggested that the BEA classification "may seem strange." They therefore treated Baumol's criteria and classification as the norm, although they also suggested their own modification that cost-disease theory applied to "personal service industries that use highly educated labor."[10] Ironically, their modification fit perfectly Howard Bowen's analysis, which they rejected, in defining service industries as "professional industries." In any event, the definition of "service industry" appeared fluid, and this indeterminacy opened cost-disease analysis to the circular reasoning of redefining "service industry" in order to fit the desired conclusion.

This circularity can be seen in the evolution of Baumol's own criteria over time. In the late 1960s, Baumol and Bowen had maintained that stagnant labor productivity in service industries causes their total productivity to stagnate and then their production cost to escalate above the cost of living. Service industries necessarily become stagnant industries, according to cost-disease theory. But Baumol's indeterminate and evolving definition of "service industry" led him, in subsequent decades, to identify service industries by their stagnant growth. The argument that service industries necessarily become stagnant industries then became circular because the service industries were initially identified by their stagnant growth.[11]

Similarly, some cost-disease analyses tended to tailor the total production cost in service industries to fit closely the labor cost of the service workers. William Bowen did this in the 1968 study by treating higher education production cost as "direct expenditures on instruction and departmental research" consisting "mainly of faculty salaries." Defined narrowly in this way, higher education production cost is virtually equated with service workers' pay, and the total production cost must necessarily be closely correlated with that labor cost. The argument that labor cost drives total production cost in the service industry of higher education therefore becomes circular because it relies on the initial, narrow definition of total production cost.[12]

---

9. William J. Baumol and William G. Bowen, *Performing Arts—the Economic Dilemma* (New York, 1966), 162–64; Baumol, "Social Wants and Dismal Science," 624–25.
10. Quotations are from Archibald and Feldman, "Explaining Increases," 281, 287.
11. Kimball and Luke, "Historical Dimensions of the 'Cost Disease,'" 38–43.
12. Quotations are from W. Bowen, *Economics of the Major Private Research Universities*, 6n. See Kimball and Luke, "Historical Dimensions of the 'Cost Disease,'" 38–43.

Turning Point for Cost-Disease Theory, 2000

The preference of economists and public commentators for cost-disease theory as an explanation for the rising cost in American higher education began to wane at the end of the twentieth century. Testifying before Congress in 1996, economist David Breneman gave equal billing to both cost-disease theory and revenue-cost theory, while noting that it was difficult to test either theory. In 2000, Breneman stated that these were the "only two basic theories" about higher education cost escalation that "warrant consideration," and he went further to suggest that cost-disease theory "has not proved convincing to most policymakers."[13] Other scholars began to adopt Breneman's view.[14]

In the early twenty-first century, the waning influence of cost-disease theory became evident when some prominent economists endorsed the theory but accorded it little weight. Instead, they affirmed the tenets of revenue-cost theory without mentioning or citing Howard Bowen, although his work was certainly known to any scholar writing on higher education cost by 2000. Thus, early in the twenty-first century, scholars continued deferring respectfully to William Bowen's theory while actually favoring the tenets of Howard Bowen without mentioning him.

For example, a major book published in 2000 by Ronald Ehrenberg of Cornell University offered an approving, three-page account of William Bowen's cost-disease theory. Ehrenberg then devoted the rest of his long book to an interpretation entirely consistent with revenue-cost theory, without referencing Howard Bowen. In their pursuit of "maximizing value" and excellence, Ehrenberg wrote, higher education leaders "seek out all the resources that they can get their hands on and then devour them." Thus, "cost increases at selective private colleges and universities are driven by the desires of these institutions to be the very best. . . . In our increasingly winner-take-all society, each institution . . . strives to maintain or improve its position, rather than to reduce its costs." Every college and university is therefore "engaged in the equivalent of an arms race of spending to improve its absolute quality and . . . its relative stature in the prestige pecking order. . . . No institution will unilaterally reduce its rate of growth of spending—to do so would invite reduced prestige."[15]

13. Breneman, "Essay on College Costs," 14.
14. Olson, "Cost Effectiveness," 228–29; Roger L. Geiger, *Knowledge and Money: Research Universities and the Paradox of the Marketplace* (Stanford, CA, 2004), 59, 278n7.
15. Ehrenberg, *Tuition Rising*, 5–6, 11, 265, 277–78.

Likewise, in a major study published in 2008, Northwestern University economist Burton A. Weisbrod and his colleagues listed William Bowen's 1968 book among "important studies on the economics of higher education." But they never discussed cost-disease theory, and their analysis aligned closely with the revenue-cost theory. By their account, universities act like for-profit enterprises, competing to maximize their revenue and spending profligately on non-educational costs, which includes depositing money in reserves. In fact, "the American college . . . was and is always revenue hungry, taking money from the government . . . and from any other available source." Indeed, "the insatiable quest for resources" and "the importance of competition" dominate "the higher education industry," which is becoming "increasingly competitive," while "college and university administration has increased enormously."[16] Here was another echo of Howard Bowen, though Weisbrod never mentioned or cited his work, let alone including it among "important studies on the economics of higher education."

Similarly, in 2012 William Bowen himself invoked Cornell University economist Robert H. Frank, who discussed "cost disease" in a *New York Times* editorial. But Frank erroneously cited cost-disease theory as an explanation for "tuition growth" rather than production cost. Then, while naming Baumol and William Bowen, Frank argued that "the escalating competition for academic prestige" caused universities to "spend in pursuit of elite status." Here again were the lineaments of revenue-cost theory, without referring to Howard Bowen, although the *Times* editor wrote the accurate headline "The Prestige Chase Is Raising College Costs."[17]

Economists' continued deference to cost-disease theory in the 2000s and 2010s coincided with their curious neglect of the growing number of adjunct faculty in higher education. The central claim of cost-disease theory is that the "productivity ratio"—output over compensation—of faculty in higher education does not grow. One way to increase that ratio is to "raise the numerator" of faculty output, as William Bowen stated. Information technology and online learning have often been proposed to achieve this.[18] But little consensus has been reached because "good teaching requires intensive interaction between teacher and student" and "cannot be made more efficient without impairing the process," in the words of David Swensen.[19]

16. Weisbrod, Ballou, and Asch, *Mission and Money*, 4n, 18, 29, 33–34, 39–37, 311.

17. Robert H. Frank, "The Prestige Chase Is Raising College Costs," *New York Times*, March 10, 2012. See W. Bowen, *"Cost Disease,"* 4.

18. Quotations are from W. Bowen, *"Cost Disease,"* 6.

19. Swensen, *Pioneering Portfolio Management* (2009), 34–35. See Jack E. Triplett and Barry P. Bosworth, "Productivity Measurement Issues in Services Industries: 'Baumol's Disease' Has Been Cured," *FRBNY Economic Policy Review*, September 2003, 23.

The other way to improve the "productivity ratio" of faculty is "to lower the denominator" by reducing compensation cost.[20] This outcome can be achieved by hiring low-paid, adjunct or short-term faculty instead of more expensive, long-term, tenure-line faculty. And such hiring has advanced rapidly over the past three decades, prompting a great deal of criticism and debate.[21] Yet economists who invoke or support cost-disease theory have neglected this well-known trend, perhaps seeking to avoid the implication that cost-disease theory warrants the "adjunctification of the professoriate." Or, as Joshua Kim has suggested, the "adjunctification" trend is neglected because it tends to disprove cost-disease theory, given that the cost of higher education is still escalating despite adjunctification, while the growth rate of administrators' salaries has outpaced the growth of faculty salaries.[22]

In any event, scholars in the twenty-first century became increasingly willing to sublimate or challenge "Baumol's cost-disease orthodoxy" as the sole or primary explanation for rising cost in higher education. Indeed, in the 2010s it almost became fashionable in some quarters to discredit cost-disease theory, even as the theory continued to be misconstrued, as described above.[23] In addition, other scholars challenged the application of cost-disease theory to health care, the other major field to which Baumol increasingly applied cost-disease theory.[24] Cost-disease theory was losing support.

Revenue-Cost Theory Ascends, 2000–2020

Whereas William Bowen's cost-disease theory rapidly attracted adherents in the decades after its appearance in 1968, Howard Bowen's analysis received less

20. W. Bowen, *"Cost Disease,"* 6.

21. Karen Thompson, "Marginalized near the Center: Part-time Faculty and the Need to Reform and Refinance the University," *Anthropology of Work Review* 15 (1994): 18–20; Gwendolyn Bradley, "Contingent Faculty and the New Academic Labor System," *Academe* 90 (January–February 2004): 28–31; Herb Childress, *The Adjunct Underclass: How America's Colleges Betrayed Their Faculty, Their Students, and Their Mission* (Chicago, 2019).

22. Joshua Kim, "Baumol's Cost Disease Orthodoxy," *Inside Higher Ed*, November 12, 2017. See Andrew Erwin and Marjorie Wood, *The One Percent at State U: How Public University Presidents Profit from Rising Student Debt and Low-Wage Faculty Labor* (Washington, DC, 2014); Allana Akhtar and Taylor Borden, "15 College Presidents Who've Been Paid Millionaire Salaries," *Business Insider*, September 15, 2020.

23. Kim, "Baumol's Cost Disease Orthodoxy." See Michael Maiello, "Diagnosing William Baumol's Cost Disease," *Chicago Booth Review*, May 18, 2017; Preston Cooper, "The Exaggerated Role of 'Cost Disease' in Soaring College Tuition," *Forbes*, May 10, 2017; Andrew Gillen, "Does the Baumol Effect Explain Rising College Costs?," *Education Text*, July 18, 2019.

24. Akinwande Atanda, Andrea K. Menclova, and W. Robert Reed, "Is Health Care Infected by Baumol's Cost Disease? Test of a New Model Using an OECD Dataset," *Health Economics* 27 (2018): 832–49; Akinwande Atanda and Robert Reed, "Not Evidence of Baumol's Cost Disease," *International Journal for Re-views in Empirical Economics* 4 (2020): 1–10.

attention and favor following its publication in 1980. Then, as public criticism about higher education finances swelled in the 1990s, scholars and commentators began to pay heed to Howard Bowen's theory, along with Henry Hansmann's critical view in 1990 that "universities compete" to accumulate "the largest endowment."[25] Nevertheless, revenue-cost theory, sketched in figure 8.2, was often dismissively equated with "the conventional wisdom" that colleges and universities "have no . . . interest in minimizing costs."[26] Even scholars who endorsed this conventional wisdom preferred cost-disease theory as an explanation for cost escalation.[27]

The resistance to analyze closely or even to cite Howard Bowen's theory stemmed partly from its "unfavorable" implications about higher education. Then, in the mid-1990s, there emerged a roseate interpretation that construed the theory to mean: "because of the . . . striving for excellence motivating all research universities, there is no limit to the amount of money that a thriving creative institution usefully can spend." Reinterpreted to sanction the insatiable need for more revenue in higher education, revenue-cost theory gradually became "one of the most frequently cited explanations for rising expenditures."[28]

Resistance to Howard Bowen's theory also stemmed from his book's incoherence, which led many commentators to address only the truncated, introductory statement of the theory.[29] His brief, provocative account—that educational spending "is determined by the amount of revenues currently available"—appeared tautological, as Howard Bowen himself acknowledged. And several scholars, including Breneman, noted this seemingly circular reasoning, which also appeared to invert cause and effect.[30] This putative circularity resulted, in part, because Howard Bowen sublimated his view that revenue generation for higher education depended fundamentally on public attitudes and societal demand.

25. Henry Hansmann, "Why Do Universities Have Endowments?," *Journal of Legal Studies* 19 (1990): 37–38.

26. Paul T. Brinkman, "Higher Education Cost Functions," in *The Economics of American Universities: Management, Operations, and Fiscal Environment*, ed. Steven A. Hoenack and Eileen L. Collins (Albany, NY, 1990), 109; Getz and Siegfried, "Costs and Productivity," 261.

27. Getz and Siegfried, "Costs and Productivity," 265; Williamson, *Funds for the Future*, 19, 40–41.

28. Quotations are from Clotfelter, *Buying the Best*, 34–35. See Edward P. St. John and Michael B. Paulsen, "The Finance of Higher Education," in Paulsen and Smart, *Finance of Higher Education*, 553–54; Massy, *Honoring the Trust*, 39–40.

29. See Larry L. Leslie and Gary Rhoades, "Rising Administrative Costs: Seeking Explanations," *Journal of Higher Education* 66 (1995): 210.

30. Quotation is from H. Bowen, *Costs of Higher Education*, 18. Breneman, "Essay on College Costs," 15; Robert K. Toutkoushian, "Trends in Revenues and Expenditures for Public and Private Higher Education," in Paulsen and Smart, *Finance of Higher Education*, 14–15; Massy, *Honoring the Trust*, 40.

In addition, resistance to revenue-cost theory was fed by obvious evidence that seemed to refute it. On the one hand, some scholars asserted that colleges and universities do not "maximize" their revenue because elite private schools could charge much higher tuition than they do. But others pointed out that elite schools that raise their price exorbitantly in the short run would alienate donors and students and threaten public subsidies, reducing their revenue in the long run.[31] On the other hand, it was said that schools do not maximize their spending because many put revenue in reserve funds or endowment. But Howard Bowen considered this practice to be another way to consume, or "spend," revenue. His valid point was that schools never refuse or return revenue.[32]

Above all, many economists discounted Howard Bowen's view because they believed that he offered "little in the way of theory" to explain cost escalation. They maintained that revenue-cost theory was not generalizable to other industries (though Howard Bowen did suggest that his theory applied to health care). Critics also said that Howard Bowen merely described practices in higher education and did not identify a cause, or "objective function," of spending behavior that could be framed "as a testable hypothesis."[33] Instead, he merely identified "incentives" and "motivations" of higher education leaders, and those could scarcely be tested.[34] Though some scholars in other fields preferred such "alternative explanations . . . to economic theory," many economists continued to neglect revenue-cost theory even when they endorsed "the basic insight expressed by Howard Bowen."[35]

After the turn of the century, Howard Bowen's "extraordinarily thoughtful book" began to be extolled as a "classic book on the costs of higher education," sometimes without even mentioning cost-disease theory explicitly.[36] Scholars

31. Brinkman, "Higher Education Cost Functions," 110. Compare Gordon C. Winston and David J. Zimmerman, "Where Is Aggressive Price Competition Taking Higher Education?," *Change* 32 (July/August 2000): 10–17; Archibald and Feldman, "Explaining Increases," 270–75.

32. Brinkman, "Higher Education Cost Functions," 110; Geiger, *Knowledge and Money*, 10. Compare H. Bowen, *Costs of Higher Education*, 19–20, 130, 147–50.

33. Quotations are from Clotfelter, *Buying the Best*, 35; Archibald and Feldman, "Explaining Increases," 269, 281.

34. Quotations are from St. John and Paulsen, "Finance of Higher Education," 554; William F. Lasher and Deborah L. Greene, "College and University Budgeting," in Paulsen and Smart, *Finance of Higher Education*, 511. See Lewis and Dundar, "Costs and Productivity," 74.

35. Quotations are from Sarah E. Waldeck, "The Coming Showdown over University Endowments: Enlisting the Donors," *Fordham Law Review* 77 (2009): 1799; Breneman, "Essay on College Costs," 15.

36. Quotations are from Dennis P. Jones, "Cost Analysis and the Formulation of Public Policy," in NCES, *Study of College Costs and Prices*, 48; Lewis and Dundar, "Costs and Productivity," 43. See John R. Thelin and Richard W. Trollinger, *Philanthropy and American Higher Education* (New York, 2014), 97; Andrew R. Dorantes and Justin R. Low, "Financial Crisis Management in Higher Education," *Journal of Education Finance* 42 (2016): 190.

and executives of major universities writing on higher education finance in the 2000s shifted from emphasizing cost-disease theory and ignoring Howard Bowen's view to gradually elevating the latter. This progression was apparent in the publications of William F. Massy, professor and vice president of business and finance at Stanford University.[37] It was also evident in the works of D. Bruce Johnstone, professor and chancellor of the State University of New York system.[38]

Over the course of 50 years, discussion about the two economic theories thus shifted remarkably within commentary on higher education finance. The cost-disease theory of William Bowen predominated between 1970 and the late 1990s. Then, the revenue-cost theory of Howard Bowen emerged prominently between the late 1990s and 2020, while the cost-disease theory continued to be invoked but deemphasized.[39] The shift occurred even though the full dimensions of revenue-cost theory, set forth in chapter 8, had not been fully explicated.

In 2011, economist Robert E. Martin observed the shift. While "the cost disease argument makes considerable sense," Martin wrote, it does not explain "why cost increases in higher education have significantly outpaced cost increases in the rest of the service sector." Instead, "the root cause" lies in "the network of incentives" identified by Howard Bowen, which lead "to a revenue-to-cost spiral in higher education." Indeed, Martin ironically suggested that Howard Bowen had identified and explained the real "cost disease" in American higher education.[40]

Origin and Extension of Revenue-Cost Theory

Explaining this shift in preference away from cost-disease theory and toward revenue-cost theory requires solving two historical puzzles. First, when and how did the policies and practices identified by revenue-cost theory arise? Howard Bowen and subsequent commentators did not probe its origins or consider whether colleges and universities acted that way prior to 1929, the starting point of the large data sets on which they relied. Second, how did those policies and

---

37. Compare William F. Massy, "Budget Decentralization at Stanford University," *Planning for Higher Education* 18, no. 2 (1989): 39–55; William F. Massy, "Improving Productivity in Higher Education: Administration and Support Costs," *Capital Ideas* 6, no. 1 (1991): 2–12; Massy, *Honoring the Trust*, 39–47, 139–40, 307; William F. Massy, "Collegium Economicum: Why Institutions Do What They Do," *Change* 36 (2004): 27–35.

38. Compare D. Bruce Johnstone, "Higher Education and Those 'Out of Control Costs,'" in NCES, *Study of College Costs and Prices*, 29; Johnstone, "Financing Higher Education," 312–13, 320, 329–31.

39. See, e.g., George P. Purcell Jr., "An Econometric Estimate of Baumol and Bowen Expenditures at Texas Public Universities Following Tuition Deregulation" (PhD diss., University of Texas at Austin, 2015).

40. Robert E. Martin, *The College Cost Disease: Higher Cost and Lower Quality* (Northampton, UK, 2011), 2, 17, 110, 179.

practices spread throughout higher education, since Bowen related the theory only to individual institutions in the "short run"?[41]

The solution to the first puzzle lies in the free-money strategy of Harvard president Charles Eliot. His singular, prescriptive strategy closely matches Howard Bowen's theory. The emergence of that strategy evidences and explains the historical origin of the behavior that Howard Bowen theorized.[42]

The congruence between free-money strategy and revenue-cost theory appears, first, in their common affirmation that colleges and universities have an altruistic desire to be "serviceable to a rapidly changing society, provide for the wants of the new generations, and . . . serve their communities best." Second, this altruism prompts and warrants insatiable financial "needs." In his free-money strategy, Eliot urged universities "to spend every year all their income" and run a deficit while avoiding a surplus. Deficits justify asking for more revenue to improve existing programs and facilities and to establish new ones. A university must never stop building and growing, and its financial needs are therefore insatiable, he maintained.[43]

Likewise, Howard Bowen observed that colleges and universities have "ever-expanding 'needs,' " and, as revenue increases, the needs do not diminish but grow. Hence, "as institutions become increasingly affluent, they rarely reject additional funds. . . . Rather, they are likely to allow enrollments to grow, take on new and expensive educational programs, expand their research and public service activities, add physical plant."[44]

Third, while altruism drives a school's financial needs, it is also true that "reputation ranks high among the purposes of most institutions," stated Bowen. This self-interest prompts "formidable competition" among both private universities and "a large number of strong State universities," in Eliot's words. According to both free-money strategy and revenue-cost theory, institutional leaders believe that the outcome of the competition to meet needs and elevate reputation depends on acquiring more revenue and financial capital.

---

41. H. Bowen, *Costs of Higher Education*, 18, 27, 29.

42. Further discussion and documentation on the following are found in Bruce A. Kimball, "The Rising Cost of Higher Education: Charles Eliot's 'Free Money' Strategy and the Beginning of Howard Bowen's 'Revenue Theory of Cost,' 1869–1979," *Journal of Higher Education* 85 (2014): 886–912.

43. Eliot's quotations and points here and in the following three paragraphs are drawn from Charles W. Eliot, "Inaugural Address . . . October 19, 1869," in *Educational Reform: Essays and Addresses* (New York, 1901), 27; Eliot, *Annual Report 1881–82*, 51; *1895–96*, 43; *1902–3*, 53; *1905–6*, 52–58; *1906–7*, 16; *1907–8*, 29–30.

44. Bowen's quotations and points here and in the following three paragraphs are drawn from H. Bowen, *Costs of Higher Education*, 14–16, 20–21, 36, 147, 150–51.

Fourth, endowment plays a key role in sustaining the spiral of wealth growth and cost growth. Endowment provides the vehicle both to consume surplus revenue, which justifies the insatiable need for more revenue, and also to increase future revenue. Eliot urged every college or university to direct as much current revenue as possible, including any surplus, into endowment, and Bowen maintained that accumulating endowment is a significant form of spending for wealthy institutions. But they disagreed on the merit of treating endowment as a repository of surplus funds. Howard Bowen disapproved, while Eliot recommended the practice because permanent invested funds confer the benefits of autonomy, stability, and flexibility to a university. Notwithstanding that disagreement on the merits, both recognized the tactic.

Lastly, Howard Bowen's attention to non-educational costs echoed Eliot's advocacy of fungible revenue. Eliot shrewdly welcomed restricted gifts for "such comprehensive purposes as salaries, retiring allowances, scholarships, administration, and service in the Gymnasium, Chapel, Library, or Dining Hall." After the 1950s, economic analyses of cost escalation in higher education set aside such costs, considering them "non-educational." But Eliot argued that revenue for "comprehensive" or auxiliary expenses was essentially fungible because it freed up resources that the university could redirect to educational purposes. All money is green, and the analytical distinction between educational and non-educational expenses is chimerical. Eliot's interest in fungibility thus matches Bowen's attention to non-educational cost, especially the "administrative expense bias," which contributes to aggregate cost and has to be paid somehow.

In sum, the fundamental congruence between Eliot's strategy and Howard Bowen's theory appears in their positing a helical relationship between revenue growth and cost growth. Each reinforces the other in higher education, creating an upward spiral that draws prices higher intermittently. The behavior that Howard Bowen theorized in 1980 thus originated in Eliot's free-money strategy during the late nineteenth century.

The second historical puzzle is to explain how the policies and practices identified by revenue-cost theory spread throughout higher education. The solution lies in the historical proliferation of Eliot's free-money strategy. Throughout his tenure from 1869 to 1909, Eliot publicly advocated this strategy, which Harvard successfully pursued. In the 1910s and 1920s, other prominent universities began to adopt it during the first national fundraising campaign, which advertised the strategy amid the Darwinian competition for excellence, prestige, and influence. Many colleges and universities framed their needs in terms of "*providing larger salaries and increasing the number of the teaching staff*," as the president of Smith College wrote in 1911.[45] Such appeals confirm the strong correlation between faculty compensation and educational cost that William Bowen identified and that Howard Bowen subsumed into revenue-cost theory.

Already in 1920, some 75 colleges and universities were "following in [Harvard's] wake," as Princeton president John Hibben wrote to Harvard's president at the outset of Princeton's first endowment fund campaign.[46] In the subsequent decade, women's colleges, HBCUs, and public universities followed the wealthy private universities. After the Depression and World War II, the free-money strategy spread horizontally across the stratum of wealthy colleges and universities that joined "the hegemony of traditional elites."[47]

In the "golden age" of higher education between 1950 and 1970, the strategy multiplied vertically through the strata of many more colleges and universities that felt they were becoming affluent. This proliferation of financial policy exemplified the tendency of colleges and universities to replicate the norms of elite institutions. Almost every college and university expanded its programs, created an annual alumni fund, conducted a national fundraising drive, started an endowment fund, invested its portfolio more aggressively, or declared that it had ever more "needs" requiring additional revenue. By 2000, virtually every college and university in the nation had a "How to Donate" link on the landing page of its website. The strategy had become the financial common sense in higher education.

In 1980, economist Howard Bowen codified in revenue-cost theory the free-money strategy that Eliot formulated a century earlier and that had become the conventional wisdom of how to operate a successful college or university during the twentieth century. In the early twenty-first century, revenue-cost theory therefore came to be seen as the more adequate account of rising production cost in higher education, not only because of the flaws in cost-disease theory but also because revenue-cost theory fit the financial practices and policies of higher education that had come to predominate since the end of the formative era.

45. Quotation is from Marion L. Burton, "To the Members of the Board of Trustees of Smith College," June 25, 1911, Burton Files (emphasis in the original).
46. John G. Hibben to A. Lawrence Lowell, September 24, 1919, Lowell Records.
47. Graham and Diamond, *Rise of American Research Universities*, 5–6.

CHAPTER 11

Steady Price, Rising Debt, Widening Wealth Gap, 2009–2020s

Following the "Golden Age Redux" that extended from 1980 to 2008, the upward-spiraling, wealth-cost, double helix dipped sharply downward, as all subsidies to higher education from endowment earnings and public sources plummeted during the Great Recession of 2008–9.[1] Public criticism therefore abated, although total-return investing in alternative assets came under fire. Endowments recovered by 2014 and prospered during the late 2010s. The real costs of aggressive portfolio management were the austerity measures imposed on college and university communities, including students, staff, and faculty.

At the same time, the average net price of undergraduate tuition held steady in constant dollars across higher education during the 2010s. This largely unrecognized trend happened because colleges and universities cut their production costs, discounted tuition, and increased funded aid, as investment yields and public subsidies recovered.

1. Quotation is from Graham and Diamond, *Rise of American Research Universities*, v.

Despite the steady net price, undergraduate debt grew rapidly due primarily to two factors. Students' overall expense—including room, board, clothing, books, technology, travel, entertainment, and other ancillary charges—increased in constant dollars with the cost of living. Second, the resources of most students diminished because the income of middle-class families plateaued in the four decades after 1980 in constant dollars and trailed increases in the cost of living. Many college students therefore had to borrow to pay the larger expense that families could not cover. As a result, the nation's cumulative student debt rose steeply to more than $1.5 trillion by 2020.[2] Following the medieval precedent, it seemed time for universities to begin issuing a "license-to-beg" to middle-class students so they could finance their education.

Simmering public outrage over the seeming contradiction between rising student debt and the successful fundraising and growing endowments of elite, wealthy schools led Congress to impose a retributive excise tax on the investment earnings of the largest endowments in 2017. But this attack on the investment earnings of about 30 private schools did nothing to address the rising debt of the nearly 20 million students across the nation, most of whom were enrolled in for-profit or state schools.

During the pandemic beginning in 2019, the pattern of the Great Recession initially seemed to recur. The double helix dipped, because subsidies were expected to fall and colleges and universities sent students home and refunded some of their payments. Harvard experienced its first two, consecutive years of declining revenues since the Great Depression of the 1930s. Again came announcements of austerity measures imposed on faculty, staff, and communities.[3]

But unlike earlier decades when public criticism declined in tandem with the double helix, that resentment did not abate during the pandemic. Little sympathy for higher education could be heard, indicating how far public esteem had fallen since the 1970s. Calls to cut tuition and spend endowments grew louder and more frequent, particularly as staggering endowment returns were reported in 2021. Some even began to doubt the value of in-person education or higher education altogether.[4]

In addition to rising student debt and growing endowments, the stratification of colleges and universities into tiers of institutional wealth fueled criticism

2. Adam Looney, et al., "Who Owes All That Student Debt?," *Policy 2020 Brookings Institution*, January 28, 2020. This chapter addresses undergraduate debt, the focus of public anger.
3. Harvard University, *Financial Report, Fiscal Year 2021* (Cambridge, MA, 2021), 3.
4. Chad Wellmon, "The Crushing Contradictions of the American University," *Chronicle of Higher Education Review*, April 22, 2021.

of higher education, especially of the richest schools. This widening stratification, long viewed favorably as evidence of vigorous competition contributing to quality, sparked anger in the twenty-first century because it mirrored and reinforced the growing wealth inequality in the nation, and vice versa. In fact, the wealth tiers of higher education hardened, much like the socioeconomic strata within the United States. The wealth advantage of the higher castes made it extremely difficult for colleges and universities in a lower caste to ascend.

Colleges and universities continued to compete fiercely for position within their tier, but few rose above or fell below it because all were employing the customary six modes of pursuing revenue that had developed over the prior 130 years, illustrated in figure 9.2. Consequently, the wealth advantage of a higher tier sealed off those below. The Darwinian competition was no longer a contest across higher education, even though schools jousted for more "value" or "quality" or "excellence," as well as prestige, within their caste.

A Golden Age Ends and Another Begins

In about 2013, enrollment nationwide peaked at 21 million students, who attended some 4,700 degree-granting colleges and universities. Both totals declined through the end of the decade owing primarily to the demise of for-profit schools, whose proprietors typically abandon higher education during lean times. Students may also have begun to recognize that the return on investment from degrees earned at for-profit schools was significantly less than from degrees of non-profit schools.[5] By 2020, the total number of degree-granting colleges and universities fell below 4,000. Within that group, the number of non-profit schools held steady at about 3,300 during the 2010s, as seen in appendix 8.

About one-quarter of the non-profit, degree-granting schools reported endowment data to the annual NACUBO endowment study, and these permanent funds remained highly concentrated. In 2020, nearly 80 percent of the endowed wealth in higher education belonged to 100 colleges and universities, about 3 percent of the non-profit colleges and universities. In the twenty-first century, Harvard continued to head the list of the 10 wealthiest universities in the nation (or, for that matter, in the world). Four other private institutions (Yale, Princeton, Stanford, and MIT) and four public universities or systems (California, Michigan, Texas, and Texas A&M) consistently rotated among the other nine spots.[6] Various aspirants occupied the tenth seat.

5. Michael Itzkowtz, *Which College Programs Give Students the Best Bang for Their Buck?* (Washington, DC, 2021). See Angulo, *Diploma Mills.*
    6. See app. 9.

Due to the benefits of institutional autonomy, stability, and flexibility, well-endowed schools create "a superior educational environment" and "a margin of excellence," stated David Swensen. Consequently, "endowment size correlates strongly with institutional quality" and with "reputational capital" or prestige. Indeed, "even modest endowments make a significant difference," Swensen noted. All colleges and universities without endowments therefore "aspire to have one," observed the former president of Mercy College in New York.[7]

In 2000, mindful of this strong correlation among financial capital, academic quality, and reputation or prestige, Swensen published the first edition of *Pioneering Portfolio Management*, soon "recognized as the best book ever written on managing institutional investment portfolios." In the following year, the stock market plunged, as the dot-com bubble burst. After the crash, as before, Swensen and his pioneering investment strategy in alternative assets contributed "more to strengthen our educational and cultural institutions than anyone else on our planet," it was said. Endowments soared during the recovery, and Swensen sent his second edition of *Pioneering Portfolio Management* to the publisher in 2008.[8] The following year witnessed "the nation's most severe financial crisis since the Great Depression."[9]

During fiscal year 2008, higher education endowments lost on average 3 percent of their value. Although the largest portfolios declined less than smaller endowments, 2008 was a bad year for every school. Then came the debacle in fiscal year 2009, when higher education endowments fell on average nearly 19 percent and the largest portfolios that were heavily invested in alternative assets plummeted even further. The Harvard, Yale, and Stanford endowments each dropped nearly a third, and the 76 mega-endowments (valued at over $1 billion) lost more than a fifth of their value on average. To pay their bills and avoid selling their volatile assets at a steep discount, several well-endowed institutions were forced to borrow money, costing them even more. A great deal of public recrimination and controversy followed, and some schools sued their portfolio managers, including the University of Minnesota and DePauw University.[10]

7. Quotations are from Lucie Lapovsky, "Critical Endowment Policy Issues," *New Directions for Higher Education* 140 (Winter 2007): 99; Swensen, *Pioneering Portfolio Management* (2000), 23, 323; (2009), 17, 22, 323.

8. Quotations are from Charles D. Ellis, foreword to Swensen, *Pioneering Portfolio Management* (2009), ix, xvi.

9. Fishman, "What Went Wrong," 203.

10. Goldie Blumenstyk, "Market Collapse Weighs Heavily on College Endowments," *Chronicle of Higher Education*, February 6, 2009; College Board, *Trends in College Pricing 2012*, 27; Fishman, "What Went Wrong," 203–5, 231–32; Ryan, "Trusting U," 162.

Inevitably, aggressive portfolio management came under attack. Pundits maintained that schools' greedy and risky overreaching had earned its just deserts. Some wags begged Swensen not to issue a third edition of *Pioneering Portfolio Management*. Other critics, with hindsight, tried to break "the curse of the Yale Model" or even challenged modern portfolio theory itself.[11] Censuring mainly the heavy investing in alternative assets, their critique addressed a number of points.

Some called for revising the "prudence" standard of *Harvard College v. Amory* (1830) yet again. That decision—originally condoning risk, then understood to discourage risk for the next 140 years, and finally said to sanction risk through UMIFA (1972)—was now reinterpreted to mean moderating risk after all. Furthermore, critics said, the Endowment Model of Investing (EMI) relied on "exotic derivatives" created in the "shadow banking system" and entailed "exposure to illiquid assets" that "posed significantly greater short-term risks than expected." In addition, "over-compensated finance officers" and trustees with "conflicts of interest" encouraged EMI and placed excessive confidence in statistical models to determine and manage levels of risk.[12]

Swensen had carefully addressed all these points in *Pioneering Portfolio Management*. In fact, he explicitly warned that, under EMI, "the average endowment faces a nearly 20 percent probability of a disruptive . . . decline in operating budget support" and a "more than 50 percent long-run likelihood of losing one-half of endowment purchasing power" at some point.[13] But Swensen's preemptive rebuttals gave little comfort when the disruptive recession actually hit.

In any event, investment performance ultimately validated EMI because endowments recovered rapidly, much as they had after the dot-com bust. Already in fiscal year 2011, endowment assets in higher education climbed out of the chasm to their prerecession value of fiscal year 2006. After a small setback in 2012, endowments made up their lost gains by posting strong returns in 2013 and 2014. Over the four decades since the advent of "total return"—from 1974 to 2014—the mean of the average annual return of endowments was nearly 12 percent.[14] This was the best 40 years of portfolio performance in the history of American higher education!

11. Rock Ferri, "The Curse of the Yale Model," *Forbes*, April 16, 2012; Peter Conti-Brown, "Scarcity amidst Wealth: The Law, Finance, and Culture of Elite University Endowments in Financial Crisis," *Stanford Law Review* 63 (2011): 699–749.

12. Humphreys, *Educational Endowments*, 4, 11–24, 40. See Ryan, "Trusting U," 169–74, 185–86; Fishman, "What Went Wrong," 226, 233.

13. Swensen, *Pioneering Portfolio Management* (2000), 34; (2009), 33.

14. College Board, *Trends in College Pricing 2012*, 27; Kenneth E. Redd, "Forever Funds," *Business Officer Magazine*, November 2015, table 1.

Aggressive investing had worked. Although some critics recommended moderating risk in the future, they also conceded that total-return investing and EMI produced greater returns than previous approaches to portfolio management. Consequently, modern portfolio theory "remains, as it should, the fundamental approach to portfolio investing," even in the eyes of critics.[15]

Despite this consensus, the investment success raised another important reservation. The superlative investment performance between 1974 and 2014 resulted from employing the new, aggressive investing strategies. But colleges and universities, including the wealthiest, still clung to the historical spending rule of about 5 percent that was at least two centuries old. Money was coming in at a faster rate than it was going out, resulting in rapid accumulation of endowment. The evident contrast between their eagerness to adopt novel, aggressive portfolio management in order to increase their wealth and their reluctance to raise their historical, conservative spending rule made the wealthiest schools appear miserly.

Meanwhile, alumni, friends, and advocates repeatedly warned that the rising list price in higher education, particularly in the private sector, was being driven by the tuition hikes of the wealthiest elite colleges and universities, which arguably did not need more tuition revenue.[16] This damage to their reputation exacted a cost in public esteem that led to a day of reckoning.

Collateral Damage

Between 1974 and 2014, portfolio values and returns validated aggressive, total-return investing because the gains more than offset the losses, smoothing average performance over time. But volatility impacted more than portfolio performance. Each "disruptive . . . decline" inflicted widespread collateral damage on colleges and universities. The loss of endowment income forced schools to impose austerity measures, including "cutting budgets, firing staff, and deferring new projects, which disrupted essential college and university functions." Even when faculty and staff were not fired outright, many were furloughed or lost pay raises or retirement benefits; students lost services for which they had paid; and donors saw the value of their gifts decline.[17] This collateral damage raised two important questions about investment policy and spending rules apart from the validity of EMI.

15. Fishman, "What Went Wrong," 201, 228–29; Ryan, "Trusting U," 164, 180–84.

16. Ehrenberg, *Tuition Rising*, 266; Robert H. Frank, "The Prestige Chase Is Raising College Costs," *New York Times*, March 10, 2012.

17. Fishman, "What Went Wrong," 229–30, 243–46. Here and below, see Humphreys, *Educational Endowments*, 4, 7, 11–16, 25, 31, 54–62.

First, how should cash reserves be invested? In the aftermath of the Great Recession, criticism of EMI focused primarily on liquidity. Alternative assets are generally illiquid: they are difficult to sell on short notice without losing money. With respect to collateral damage, however, the issue was less liquidity than the kinds of funds invested. Not only permanent funds but also reserve funds, building funds, and cash balances were invested in alternative assets. The rent money was put at risk.

To be sure, leaving the rent money in safe, low-yielding investments may sacrifice potential earnings. In 1993, riding the wave of total return, Dartmouth finance professor Peter Williamson urged trustees to harvest "the earning power of cash balances," which offer "even more potential for increasing revenue . . . than through better management of endowment."[18] Taking this to an extreme a decade later, Harvard president Lawrence Summers (2001–6) aggressively invested building funds, cash balances, and reserves in alternative assets, as did executives at other wealthy institutions. When the recession began and the rent came due, the illiquid assets could not be sold without taking huge losses. Harvard therefore issued bonds for $2.5 billion in order to fund its current operations and uphold its contractual obligations.[19]

Harvard treasurer Paul Cabot, who had created the university's reserve fund and stocked it with a year's income in the 1950s, surely turned over in his grave, as did Yale economist James Tobin. Both had urged universities "to put enough . . . into bonds and high-dividend stocks so that . . . no securities need to be bought or sold to meet the formula definition of income, and the university is insulated from fluctuations of capital values." In contrast to Harvard, Yale, Stanford, and many other universities, Boston College had followed this advice, and its conservatively managed reserve funds enabled the school to meet most of its financial obligations throughout the Great Recession, thereby avoiding the need to unload illiquid assets or to borrow heavily.[20]

If university leaders do put the rent money at risk, then they face a second question: how should periodic collateral damage influence the calculation of return and the spending rule? One searches in vain through the literature on portfolio management for mention of restitution for collateral damage that oc-

18. Williamson, *Funds for the Future*, 1.

19. Humphreys, *Educational Endowments*, 37–38, 54; Elias J. Groll and William N. White, "Harvard to Borrow $480 Million to Fund Capital Projects and Refinance Debt," *Harvard Crimson*, January 9, 2010; Nina Munk, "Rich Harvard, Poor Harvard," *Vanity Fair* 51, no. 8 (August 2009): 106–48.

20. James Tobin, "What Is Permanent Endowment Income?," *American Economic Review* 64 (1974): 427. See Humphreys, *Educational Endowments*, 25.

curs during the inevitable downturns in endowment yields. Instead, analysis of investment return and spending rules is confined to the topics of maintaining or growing endowment value and operating income. For example, Swensen's discussion of "Yale's elegant spending rule" did not address the cost of collateral damage resulting from the inevitable "disruptive . . . decline in operating budget support" that he anticipated.[21]

The literature on portfolio management consistently calculates investment return and spending rules "net of management fees," but no calculations are ever made "net of collateral damage." If a school invests its reserve funds, building funds, and cash balances aggressively in order to maximize return, then the calculation of spending from returns should include the cost of restitution to those in the university community who suffered financial losses—lost jobs, pay, or benefits—during the inevitable downturns in investment yields. Like the fees for active management, the cost of collateral damage incurred by the inevitable downturns is an expense of investing reserve funds aggressively. If the calculation of investment return and spending rules is not made "net of collateral damage," then sufficient reserves ought to be set aside "so that . . . the university is insulated from fluctuations of capital values," in Tobin's words. Otherwise, the schools and the portfolio managers in higher education shirk responsibility for the collateral damage that their aggressive investing inflicts.

Price, Debt, and a Perfect Storm

While endowment income rode a frightful but profitable roller coaster, several factors combined to create a perfect storm of price, debt, and public ire for higher education after the Great Recession of 2008–9.

Subsidies fell. The recession ravaged "state budgets, current giving, and the ability of many families to cover the . . . costs of a college education."[22] Over the decade from 2008 to 2018, federal, state, and local per-student subsidies grew in absolute amounts but declined proportionally from about 64 percent to 55 percent of the revenue in higher education. HBCUs, many of which are primarily state funded, lost more subsidies than did predominantly white institutions.[23]

21. Swensen, *Pioneering Portfolio Management* (2009), 29–30, 33–34.
22. Johnstone, "Financing Higher Education," 314, 326.
23. College Board, *Trends in College Pricing 2020*, 20–23; Ronald Roach, "Report: Funding, Institutional Support Lacking for Historically Black Public Colleges," *Diverse Issues in Higher Education*, May 7, 2014; Douglas Belkin, "Maryland, Black Colleges Settle Suit," *Wall Street Journal*, March 25, 2021.

List prices rose. To compensate for the proportional decline of subsidies, many colleges and universities raised their tuition and fees, though more slowly, chastened by the Great Recession. Between 2010 and 2020, listed tuition and fees increased, on average, about 16 percent in constant dollars at both public and private four-year institutions. These publicized hikes naturally spawned widespread complaints, particularly when announced by the wealthiest schools.[24]

Net price remained flat. Suffering public resentment for tuition hikes might have been worth it, if schools realized more revenue. But they did not, and many had to trim their budgets. The reason was that the average undergraduate net price plateaued between 2006 and 2020 in constant dollars. After deducting funded aid and tuition discounts from the list price, the average annual net price of tuition and fees over those 14 years held steady at about $15,900 in constant dollars at private, non-profit, four-year colleges and about $3,200 in constant dollars for in-state students at public colleges.[25]

Nevertheless, students' overall expense grew, although they were not paying more for the educational production cost of colleges and universities. The price of ancillary expenses—room, board, clothing, books, technology, travel, entertainment, and so forth—climbed in constant dollars along with the cost of living. Meanwhile, the income of middle-class families had fallen behind the cost of living for three decades. Students were borrowing to make up the difference that families could no longer pay.[26]

Student debt therefore rose steeply. By 2019, it reached $1.5 trillion, and the House Committee on Financial Services held hearings on the issue, while some experts projected that if current trends continue student debt will reach $3 trillion by 2030. "The American higher education system is a gigantic debt-producing machine with no one at the controls," observers complained.[27]

This syndrome caused serious damage. Economists warned that the diminishing affordability of higher education for the middle class was slowing the

24. American Council on Education, *Understanding College and University Endowments* (Washington, DC, 2014), 3; College Board, *Trends in College Pricing 2020*, 13, 18–19.

25. American Council on Education, *Understanding College and University Endowments* (Washington, DC, 2014), 3; College Board, *Trends in College Pricing 2020*, 13, 18–19. These figures are calculated in constant 2020 dollars.

26. Ehrenberg, *Tuition Rising*, 6–8; Johnstone, "Financing Higher Education," 322–26.

27. Quotation is from Kevin Carey, "What About Tackling the Causes of Student Debt?," *New York Times*, November 18, 2020. See Majority Staff, "A 1.5 Trillion Crisis: Protecting Student Borrowers and Holding Student Loan Servicers Accountable," Memorandum to Members, US House of Representatives Committee on Financial Services, Hearing, September 5, 2019; Lorna Collier, "College Costs," *CQ Researcher*, October 25, 2019, 1–29.

growth of labor productivity and the American economy.[28] Sociologists revealed the resulting financial strain and emotional stress on middle-class families, who were becoming "downwardly mobile" and watching their children's career prospects erode.[29]

Colleges and universities were dismayed. The vast majority were losing subsidies and cutting or capping expenses just to break even. They were not pocketing more college tuition. But undergraduates had to borrow more, and everyone was blaming higher education. It was a perfect storm.

As in the dot-com bust of 2001–2, the precipitous losses of endowment value in 2008–9 temporarily quelled the criticism, which was primarily aimed at wealthy, elite colleges and universities. When the economy and endowment began to recover, the angry drumbeat started again. In 2014, Michigan representative David L. Camp, chairman of the House Ways and Means Committee, proposed a flat excise tax of 1 percent on the investment earnings of about 60 highly endowed, private colleges and universities. In 2015, law professor Victor Fleischer called on Congress to legislate a minimum spending rule of 8 percent in order to "stop universities from hoarding money."[30]

In that same year, the Oversight Subcommittee of the House Ways and Means Committee held hearings to consider various options: setting a spending rule for higher education endowments, taxing endowment investment earnings, and taxing certain debt-financed investments often employed by EMI. The subcommittee also considered rolling back the charitable deduction for gifts to endowments, which had been critical to fundraising in higher education ever since the very first major campaign a century earlier.[31]

In 2017, the congressional assault on the revenue and endowments of elite colleges and universities succeeded some 30 years after it began under President Reagan. Enacted under President Donald J. Trump (2017–21), the Tax Cuts and Jobs Act (TCJA) imposed a 1.4 percent excise tax on net annual investment income of private, non-profit colleges and universities with more than $500,000

28. Goldin and Katz, *Race between Education and Technology*, 7–8; Gordon, *Rise and Fall of American Growth*, 16, 23, 285, 499–521.

29. Caitlin Zaloom, *Indebted: How Families Make College Work at Any Cost* (Princeton, NJ, 2019); Joe Pinsker, "Why College Became So Expensive and What That Has Meant for America's Middle-Class Families," *Atlantic*, September 3, 2019; Simon Kuper, "How the Middle Class Became Downwardly Mobile," *Financial Times*, April 29, 2021.

30. Victor Fleischer, "Stop Universities from Hoarding Money," *New York Times*, August 19, 2015. See Sarah E. Waldeck, "The Coming Showdown over University Endowments: Enlisting the Donors," *Fordham Law Review* 77 (2009): 1830.

31. Molly F. Sherlock, et al., "College and University Endowments: Overview and Tax Policy Options," *Congressional Research Service Report* (December 2, 2015), 1, 19.

of endowment per student. About 30 schools were subject to the tax, although the number fluctuated annually with endowment values and several institutions would not divulge whether they were subject to TCJA.[32]

This excise tax was all about optics. It had nothing to do with addressing the problem of students' debt because the great majority of students incapacitated by debt had attended for-profit or state colleges whereas the 30 targeted schools were private non-profits and had the most generous financial aid policies and resources. What TCJA demonstrated was the severe public resentment of the wealthy elite leaders of higher education. Politicians scored points by skewering those schools, such as Harvard, whose reported excise tax in 2019 was almost $50 million, and Stanford, which reportedly paid $43 million in 2020.[33]

A Golden Age Ends, and a "Golden Era" Begins

As the impact of TCJA was still being assessed, the pandemic beginning in 2019 forced colleges and universities to suspend residential education and refund room and board fees, as well as tuition in some cases. In addition, the economy began to contract, and state subsidies and endowment yields were projected to drop sharply. Schools announced many of the same austerity measures they had taken during the Great Recession: furloughing employees, freezing hiring and salary increases, suspending retirement contributions, cutting athletics teams, slashing undergraduate majors, and halting admissions to some doctoral programs.[34]

So strong had become the animus against wealthy universities that, rather than eliciting sympathy, this collateral damage of the pandemic inflamed public resentment. Faculty wrote to the *New York Times* that "rich colleges can afford to spend more."[35] Humorists satirized the explanations of university presidents as to "why we cannot simply use funds from our endowment to tide us

32. Scott Jaschik, "House Panel Eyes Plans to Tax Colleges on Some Income," *Chronicle of Higher Education*, November 4, 1987; Tax Brookings Institution Tax Policy Center, "What Is the Tax Treatment of College and University Endowments," *Tax Policy Briefing Book*, May 2020.
33. Rick Seltzer, "$50 Million Tax Bill for Harvard," *Inside Higher Ed*, October 25, 2019; Rick Seltzer, "How Much Are Most Colleges Paying in Endowment Tax?," *Inside Higher Ed*, February 18, 2020.
34. Megan Zahneis, "More Doctoral Programs Suspend Admissions. That Could Have Lasting Effects on Graduate Education," *Chronicle of Higher Education*, September 28, 2020; Andrew Spear, "Colleges Slash Budgets in the Pandemic, with 'Nothing Off-Limits,'" *New York Times*, October 26, 2020.
35. Paul F. Campos, "Rich Colleges Can Afford to Spend More. They're Acting Like They Exist to Protect Their Endowments, Instead of the Other Way Around," *New York Times*, June 6, 2020.

over."[36] Critics even tried to show that the EMI golden goose returned lower yields than would have resulted from simply following the "60/40 rule" between 1961 and 2019, along with, presumably, firing all the portfolio managers.[37]

The pandemic crisis also threatened the life of a number of schools across the nation. During the same week in March 2021, both Becker College in Massachusetts, which began granting degrees in 1887, and Mills College in California, founded in 1852, announced they would close due to financial stress from the pandemic, after struggling financially for years. Many other colleges serving primarily students of color, such as Bloomfield College in New Jersey, founded in 1868, also edged near the precipice.[38] Meanwhile, the American Council on Education estimated that the pandemic cost the country's colleges and universities more than $120 billion and urged Congress to earmark additional funds for higher education in the federal financial relief package.[39]

In 2020, the average endowment yield of 1.8 percent, though the lowest in five years, was better than expected and enabled several universities to rescind the Draconian cuts announced earlier. And NACUBO emphasized that endowment income had enabled colleges universities to minimize the cuts.[40] In 2021, aggressive portfolio management produced astonishing endowment growth for the rich schools: Vanderbilt, 58 percent; Bowdoin, 53 percent; Notre Dame, 51 percent; Duke, 50 percent; Carnegie Mellon and Boston College, 49 percent; Virginia, 45 percent; Minnesota, 41 percent; Washington University in St. Louis, 61 percent. Another "golden era" was dawning.[41]

But this new "golden era" only seemed to inflame the animus toward the wealthiest universities. Buried in the federal pandemic relief bill (CARES Act)

36. Quotation is from President Sarah C. Mangelsdorf et al., "Responding to the Financial Challenges of the COVID-19 Pandemic," University of Rochester, April 15, 2020, on file with the author. See Stephen Wood, "A University President Responds to Those Who Have Suggested the School Should Dip into the Endowment," *McSweeney's*, May 15, 2020.

37. Dennis Hammond, "A Better Approach to Systematic Outperformance? 58 Years of Endowment Performance," *Journal of Investing*, August 2020, 13.

38. Emma Whitford, "Becker College Will Close," *Inside Higher Ed*, March 20, 2021; Elizabeth L. Hillman, "A Message from Mills President," Oakland, CA, March 17, 2021, on file with the author; Emma Whitford, "Without Financial Help, Bloomfield College Risks Closure," *Inside Higher Ed*, October 20, 2021.

39. Deirdre Fernandes, "Harvard Endowment Posts Strong Returns," *Boston Globe*, September 29, 2020.

40. Emma Whitford, "Endowment Returns Tumble," *Inside Higher Ed*, February 19, 2021; Juliet Chung and Eliot Brown, "University Endowments Mint Billions in Golden Era of Venture Capital," *Wall Street Journal*, September 29, 2021; NACUBO, "In Year Punctured by Pandemic, Higher Education Endowments Provide More Than $23 Billion to Support Students, Mission," in NACUBO, *Endowment Study 2020*.

41. NACUBO, *Endowment Study 2021*; Juliet Chung and Eliot Brown, "University Endowments Mint Billions in Golden Era of Venture Capital," *Wall Street Journal*, September 29, 2021.

was a provision prohibiting the colleges and universities subject to the TCJA excise tax from using relief funds to defray their pandemic-related expenses. Once again, the wealthiest schools were singled out and then coerced into returning the small amount of federal relief funds that they did receive.[42] Demonstrating the public ire, politicians gained favor with their constituents by stiffing elite, wealthy schools.

Stratification and Wealth Inequality

Higher education, particularly the leading wealthy schools, thus came under assault on several fronts. One legion attacking the free money of colleges and universities marched under the banner of populist anti-elitism that motivated supporters of politicians who had targeted the schools since the 1980s. The fervor and ranks of the populists swelled as wealth inequality not seen since Andrew Carnegie's era resurged in the United States.[43] Although higher education was not targeted in the late nineteenth century, the growing wealth inequality in the American population between 1980 and 2020 generated anger at higher education, particularly the elite schools, for two reasons.

On the one hand, the national wealth inequality was implicated in the rising student debt crisis that fostered resentment against higher education. Returns from invested capital that enriched wealthy Americans grew faster than the wages of the middle-class, who owned relatively little invested capital. This long-term trend worsened during the 2010s when American corporations spent more than $6 trillion to buy back their own shares, sharply driving up the price of equities. The stock-owning wealthy grew richer, widening the gap between themselves and the middle class, whose wages stagnated or trailed the cost of living.[44]

Middle-class families and students then had to borrow ever larger sums to pay the overall expense of higher education, which rose with the cost of living. Middle-class parents and children assumed staggering debt to pay for higher education, which they naturally considered "a gigantic debt-producing machine." But the average net price of tuition and fees at both public and private schools remained level in constant dollars after 2006, as discussed above. The

42. Kery Murakami, "Wealthier Colleges and Universities Targeted in COVID Relief Bill," *Inside Higher Ed*, April 6, 2020; Michael Stratford, Bianca Quilantan, and Juan Perez Jr., "Elite Colleges Back Away from Rescue Cash amid Criticism of Endowments," *Politico*, April 22, 2020.

43. Matthew Stewart, *The 9.9 Percent: The New Aristocracy That Is Entrenching Inequality and Warping Our Culture* (New York, 2021).

44. Thomas Piketty, *Capital in the Twenty-First Century*, trans. Arthur Goldhammer (Cambridge, MA, 2014), 304–76; Carter C. Price and Kathryn Edwards, "Trends in Income from 1975 to 2018," RAND Education and Labor Working Paper, September 2020, 1–11; "Measuring the 1%; Inequality," *Economist*, November 20, 2019, 23–26.

debt problem resulted from the stagnant income of middle-class Americans, who did not profit from the returns of invested capital that drove the concentration and unequal distribution of wealth in the nation.

On the other hand, the wealth inequality among Americans fueled populist anger at higher education because that inequality was reflected and reinforced by the concentration of endowment and the wealth stratification of colleges and universities. In the same way that the invested capital of the rich grew while middle-class wages stagnated, so too did the schools with large endowments harvest high investment returns and mammoth fundraising campaigns, leaving the rest of colleges and universities straggling behind. The wealth inequality in the American population seemed interwoven with the wealth stratification in higher education.

Indeed, it has not been recognized that the endowment concentration in higher education during the decades after 1990 actually exceeded the capital concentration in the US population. In 1990, the wealthiest 1 percent of colleges and universities owned about 58 percent of the total endowments of American higher education, while the wealthiest 1 percent of American households owned about 42 percent of all households' invested capital. Between 1990 and 2020, the concentration of household capital approached, but did not catch, the concentration of endowment in higher education. In 2020, the wealthiest 1 percent of colleges and universities owned about 54 percent of the total endowment of American higher education, while the wealthiest 1 percent of American households owned about 53 percent of households' total invested capital, as seen in table 11.1.

In the populist view, the primary vehicle of social mobility for middle-class youths for the prior 150 years had become, for many, an anchor around their necks that plunged them deeply into debt. Meanwhile, a small number of gilded academic citadels admitted a few select students, primarily from elite families, into membership in the top 1 percent of American society. "The country's best colleges are an overpriced gated community whose benefits accrue mostly to the wealthy," critics said. The scandals of wealthy parents buying admission to elite schools, which came to light in 2019, validated this assessment.[45] In addition, the historical admissions preference of elite schools for "legacies"—the children of alumni—created a back door that further eroded social mobility and strengthened the

45. Kevin Carey, "The Creeping Capitalist Takeover of Higher Education," *Huffington Post*, April 1, 2019. See John R. Thelin, "An Embarrassment of Riches: Admission and Ambition in American Higher Education," *Society* 56 (2019): 329–34.

TABLE II.I

Comparison of Top Tier of Higher Education Endowments and Household Capital in the United States (in nominal dollars)

	Endowment*			Household capital†		
Year	Total (billions)	Billions owned by richest 1%	Proportion owned by richest 1% of schools	Total (trillions)	Trillions owned by richest 1%	Proportion owned by richest 1% of households
1990	59.9	34.6	58%	5.2	2.2	42%
2000	241.2	134.2	56%	13.9	6.3	45%
2010	327.8	187.4	57%	18.6	8.8	47%
2020	647.5	349.5	54%	46.6	24.8	53%

Sources: Figures calculated from NACUBO, "Final Endowment Market Values—Fiscal Years 1974 to 2020," *Historic Endowment Data*, accessed April 2021; "Distributional Financial Accounts: Distribution of Household Wealth in the U.S. since 1989," *US Federal Reserve* (2021), accessed April 2021.
* Not including life income funds, which would likely increase the percentage.
† Investments in corporate equities, mutual funds, and private businesses, but not real estate, which would likely increase the percentage.

interrelation between higher education stratification and America's wealth inequality.[46]

Dura lex, sed lex

Populists and American workers were not alone in these complaints. A legion of academic and social critics also reviled the mounting student debt, the accumulating endowment, and the widening wealth stratification in higher education. They alleged that this wealth gap reinforced inequality in the United States; that the stratification was inequitable within higher education; that the continued accumulation of permanent funds provided diminishing benefit and increasing waste, particularly through the "administrative expense bias"; and that the pursuit of wealth corrupted the pursuit of knowledge. Thus, the stratification seemed to contravene fundamental values that colleges and universities had long espoused, values that justified the pursuit of wealth to begin with.

Analyzing these critiques historically begins by recalling that colleges and universities commenced the pursuit of free money near the end of the nineteenth century with the ultimate goal to "serve their communities best" by expanding

46. Richard D. Kalenberg, ed., *Affirmative Action for the Rich: Legacy Preferences in College Admissions* (New York, 2010).

knowledge, culture, and the economy.[47] To achieve that goal, schools entered a Darwinian competition for survival and success that appeared natural and necessary at the time.

The second historical point is that the contest was rationalized by the "law of competition," quintessentially expressed by Andrew Carnegie.[48] Like industrial corporations of the time, a college or university deserved to survive and to win by virtue of the "ability and energy" of its leaders, faculty, staff, students, and alumni. Their "peculiar talent" and hard work would attract and generate resources that, carefully saved and invested, would aid their successors. In this way, the gradually emerging disparity "between the palace of the [university] and the cottage of the [struggling college]" would be justified. Institutions rising to the top would deserve their place by virtue of their merit and effort.

Third, since the late nineteenth century, the wealth stratification of American higher education seemed natural, necessary, and warranted. Hence, it "is not to be deplored, but welcomed as highly beneficial," in Carnegie's words. Granted, "the law of competition . . . may be somewhat hard" for a Becker College or a Mills College or a struggling HBCU, and "rigid castes are formed." But the law "ensures the survival of the fittest," so each institution is made stronger by the competition, and higher education is fortified and improved overall. Indeed, many scholars considered wealth stratification both the cause and the consequence of producing the best system of higher education in the world. The competitive, ceaseless pursuit of free money supported the ceaseless pursuit of knowledge, and almost every commentator affirmed the strong correlation between wealth, excellence, and prestige. The published ranking systems of the "best" colleges and universities presupposed this correlation when they began to appear in the 1980s.

Finally, membership in that top stratum of colleges and universities was perduring. Nearly all of the wealthiest 4 percent of schools during the 1920s (numbering 39) remained in that rank a century later.[49] As the total number of colleges and universities grew over time, the absolute number in the wealthiest 4 percent increased (amounting to 132 in 2020). And the new members rarely fell out of that tier once they had joined.[50] The best-endowed colleges and universities had remarkable staying power. The rich remained rich, due not only to their talent and hard work but also to certain advantages conferred by wealth.

47. Eliot, *Annual Report 1905–6*, 54–55.
48. Quotations below are from Carnegie, *Gospel of Wealth*, 1–6.
49. See tables 1.1 and 1.2.
50. See app. 9.

Highest Caste Perdures

Already in the 1920s, scholars began to note reasons for the constancy of the highest caste, and those reasons have persisted and multiplied during the past century. First, large endowments consistently earned higher rates of return than small endowments, and their larger base increased the absolute return even more. The NACUBO list of endowments for 2021 reveals the point today. The percentage of growth generally decreases as one scrolls down the list, with some exceptions that are usually explained by the receipt of a major gift at lesser-endowed schools.[51]

Large size permitted greater risk and more aggressive investment, and wealthy schools normally received more expert advice, both because they could afford it and because their trustees often had contacts in financial circles. Think of the Smith College president consulting trustee and financier Thomas Lamont in the 1910s, and of Joseph Rosenfield recruiting investor Warren Buffett for the board of Grinnell College in 1968. Similarly, economist and alumnus William Bowen served on the board of Denison University in the 1990s when it surpassed its famous neighbors Oberlin College and Kenyon College in endowment per student.[52]

Second, if well-endowed schools were injured financially, then their prestige and capital facilitated borrowing to staunch the bleeding, as Harvard did under President Summers. In contrast, for example, HBCUs historically paid more in underwriting fees to issue tax-exempt bonds, compared to similar, predominantly white schools, let alone elite wealthy schools, like Harvard.[53] This greater capacity to recover from downturns and thus to take risks compounded the advantage that larger endowments earned from higher rates of return over the past century.

Third, schools with large endowments had more success in fundraising. Over the past century, 90 percent of donations to higher education usually came from about 10 percent of donors, and wealthy individuals, who could afford large

51. NACUBO, *Endowment Study 2021.*

52. Redd, "Forever Funds," 4–5; Lapovsky, "Critical Endowment Policy Issues," 100–102; Hammond, "Better Approach," exhibit 10; Janet Lorin and Katherine Chiglinsky, "Buffett Reveals 'Outrageous Acts' That Lifted College Endowment," *Economic Times,* May 2, 2019; Linda Fathauer, "The Methodology of Archival Research in Endowment Data for Oberlin College, Kenyon College, and Denison University 1970–2000" (PhD qualifying exam, The Ohio State University, 2016).

53. Casey Dougal et al., "What's in a (School) Name? Racial Discrimination in Higher Education Bond Markets," University of Houston Law Center Institute for Higher Education Law and Governance Publication, February 4, 2016, 1.

gifts, generally graduated from the wealthier schools. Hence, endowment size was strongly correlated with annual revenue from gifts. One study in 2008 found that "each added $100 million of endowment is associated with an additional $2 million of increased donations in a single year."[54]

Prosperous donors gave to their alma mater not only out of altruism or gratitude, but also because "the donor benefits in some way from the act of giving" to a wealthy alma mater, economists have argued. Wealthy alumni of elite institutions received the benefit of burnishing their own brand by keeping their alma mater strong, and they gained public recognition and accolades, often including their name on a building or center.[55] The nouveau riche, who did not attend the elite schools but still donated to them, receive some of these same benefits, including the opportunity to perpetuate their name, like Gordon McKay at Harvard, noted in chapter 2.

These points also explain the remarkable finding that wealthy schools spent less per dollar raised to attract donations than did less endowed schools.[56] Also, highly endowed schools directed a larger proportion of gifts to their endowment. Not living hand to mouth, rich schools could afford to urge donors to give either free money or a restricted permanent fund that "poses no real restrictions on the institution."[57] In other words, the wealthy schools routinely applied Eliot's fungibility tenet.

In sum, wealthy schools received more donations, spent less to obtain them, and allocated more of them to endowment. These advantages increased their financial capital, which they invested more aggressively and expertly to earn larger rates of return that produced even more in absolute terms due to the larger size of their endowments. And if wealthy schools stumbled when taking more risk, they paid less to recover without fearing they would close down. All these factors explain their wealth advantage and perduring membership in the highest caste.

While reinforcing the wealth stratification of higher education, these advantages also reveal the interrelation between that stratification and the national wealth inequality. In fact, the proportion of donations coming from "mega-gifts"

54. Weisbrod, Ballou, and Asch, *Mission and Money*, 123. See Heather Joslyn, "Campaign Fever: Fundraising Drives Are Getting Bigger and More Numerous," *Chronicle of Philanthropy*, April 2, 2019.

55. Jessica Holmes, "Prestige, Charitable Deductions and Other Determinants of Alumni Giving: Evidence from a Highly Selective Liberal Arts College," *Economics and Education Review* 28 (2009): 19.

56. Ehrenberg, *Tuition Rising*, 46.

57. Quotation is from Ronald G. Ehrenberg and C. L. Smith, "The Sources and Uses of Annual Giving at Selective Private Research Universities and Liberal Arts Colleges," *Economics of Education Review* 22 (2003): 227.

to colleges and universities rose in the 2010s, while the fraction coming from smaller alumni gifts fell. Fundraising drives became more ambitious and succeeded spectacularly, like Harvard's $9.6 billion campaign completed in 2019. But a rising proportion of the money came from a shrinking fraction of donors.[58] In the early twenty-first century, fundraising became less "democratic," reversing the development of a century earlier, when the double helix arose.

These trends were demonstrated by Michael Bloomberg's donation of $1.8 billion to Johns Hopkins University in 2018. This gift, the largest ever made to one school, came from a multibillionaire, went to his alma mater, and was designated for the endowment. Though generous and aimed to support financial aid, Bloomberg's enormous gift cost him less than the annual income that he earned from his net worth of some $59 billion in 2020. Bloomberg's gift therefore strengthened Johns Hopkins's place within the top 1 percent of endowed schools, without jeopardizing Bloomberg's place within the top 1 percent of wealthiest Americans, while burnishing his own pedigree and providing him with large tax deductions.[59]

Bloomberg's gift thus typified the interrelation of higher education stratification and America's wealth inequality, as well as the continuity of both. Barring catastrophe, schools in the early twenty-first century became locked within their stratum. They competed intensely within that caste, but they rarely rose above or fell below it, because nearly all schools practiced the customary six modes of acquiring wealth so far as they could, and greater resources imparted advantages that sealed off a higher tier from those below.[60] Converse College (with $73 million of endowment) would never overtake Carleton ($890 million), nor Marquette ($690 million) surpass Notre Dame ($12 billion), nor the University of Houston system ($1 billion) catch the University of Texas system ($32 billion), although all six of these were among the wealthiest 15 percent of the 3,300 degree-granting, non-profit institutions in the country in 2020.[61]

Whatever one thinks of Carnegie's "law of competition," that law no longer justified the pursuit of free money even on its own terms. The Darwinian competition for victory across higher education became moot early in the twenty-first century.

58. Mike Scutari, "Mega-Gifts Are Rising and Alumni Giving Is Shrinking, Which Means What Exactly?," *Inside Philanthropy*, April 2017; Joslyn, "Campaign Fever," 1–9.
59. Arthur M. Hauptman, "Bloomberg's Gift and the Role of Endowments," *Inside Higher Ed*, January 17, 2019; Paul Basken, "US Colleges' Billion-Dollar Question: Is Philanthropy Worth the Cost?," *Times Higher Education*, April 29, 2021.
60. See fig. 9.2; Juliet Chung and Dawn Lim, "How Brown University's Endowment Quietly Became Tops in Ivy League," *Wall Street Journal*, October 10, 2020.
61. NACUBO, *Endowment Study 2020*.

Plato's Descent, Perseveration, and History

During the formative period of higher education from 1870 to 1930, the nation's income grew feverishly, and the United States made a gigantic investment in colleges and universities, as both aggregate revenue and aggregate production cost of higher education ascended rapidly. But enrollment grew just as fast, so per-student production cost rose slowly—scarcely more than the price of all commodities. The combination of soaring national income and steady per-student production cost meant that higher education became about three times cheaper to produce for each student, relative to the national per-capita income between 1870 and 1930.

At the same time, colleges and universities commenced a Darwinian struggle to survive and succeed by deliberately increasing both their revenue and their expenses, emulating the competition among industrial corporations. The growth of aggregate wealth and the growth of aggregate cost therefore reinforced each other in higher education, forming a double helix that began to spiral upward, drawing price behind them. The conviction spread that each school and all of higher education would grow stronger and more beneficial if wealth growth and cost growth reinforced each other.

This conviction underlay a novel, financial strategy formulated by Harvard president Charles Eliot and adopted by colleges and universities during the formative era. A key tenet of Eliot's new strategy was that a university's financial needs are insatiable. That precept suited a new ethos in American higher education. During the formative period, academic culture shifted from what has been called collegiate, "oratorical" mores, devoted to transmitting received knowledge and inculcating civic virtue, to "philosophical" mores enshrining ceaseless academic inquiry and the unending pursuit of knowledge. Whereas the former view emphasized conservation and moral formation, the latter implied that the pursuit of wealth must never end because the pursuit of knowledge must always continue.[1]

Adhering to Eliot's "free-money" strategy, Harvard in 1920 first attained the lead in financial capital that it would not relinquish thereafter. Encouraged by the Rockefeller-funded GEB, hundreds of colleges and universities in the ensuing decade began to appreciate the institutional benefits of autonomy, stability, and flexibility conferred by "endowment," which they came to understand in its "correct sense" of permanent, productive funds. At the same time, many colleges and universities adopted a novel triad of complementary modes of fundraising to increase their revenue: the annual alumni fund; the national, multiyear fundraising campaign; and the traditional, discreet appeal to wealthy donors.

During the Great Depression and World War II, the fundraising and competition for revenue naturally subsided, and the helical upward spiral of wealth growth and cost growth slowed. The trend reversed in the late 1940s when the G.I. Bill released a torrent of federal dollars into all colleges and universities. As soon as that abated, a tsunami of federal appropriations, grants, and contracts flooded into higher education during the 1950s and 1960s. But most of this new revenue funded staff, programs, and facilities for medical, defense, and scientific research that was not directly related to students' education. The intense competition to acquire more revenue and wealth to cover educational costs therefore recommenced, and colleges and universities revived the three modes of fundraising, and began to devote new effort to managing their endowment portfolios.

Relying on the principles of modern portfolio theory, articulated and validated by Harry Markowitz at the University of Chicago in the early 1950s, the wealthiest schools adopted increasingly aggressive investment strategies. First came the 60/40 rule during the 1950s and 1960s, then total return in the 1970s,

---

1. See Bruce A. Kimball, *Orators and Philosophers: A History of the Idea of Liberal Education* (New York, 1986).

nurtured by the Ford Foundation. The new investment strategies culminated with alternative assets, pioneered by David Swensen at Yale in the late 1980s and 1990s. The returns from these three investing innovations were supplemented by expanding revenue from government appropriations, grants, and contracts. As a result, the aggregate production cost of higher education rose dramatically.

Scholars began sounding the alarm about this growing cost in the 1950s and 1960s, although rising aggregate cost was not necessarily detrimental. But the per-student cost increased much faster than the cost of living over those two consecutive decades for the first time since the 1870s. This troublesome development led two economists at Princeton, William Baumol and William Bowen, to propose the "cost-disease" theory in the late 1960s. This theory purported to explain why the per-student production cost of higher education had supposedly escalated not only throughout the twentieth century, but even since the beginning of the Industrial Revolution. Despite conceptual and empirical weaknesses, the elegant cost-disease theory was embraced by many scholars over the next four decades.

Meanwhile, after the woeful stagflation of the 1970s, the continuing proliferation and institutionalization of the free-money strategy prompted economist Howard Bowen in 1980 to propose an alternative explanation for the rising production cost in higher education. By that point, American higher education was acclaimed for profoundly benefitting the national economy, polity, and culture, and was recognized as the best in the world, led by the wealthiest, elite colleges and universities. Nevertheless, Howard Bowen's revenue-cost theory implied significant criticism of schools' insatiable appetite for money.

In the 1980s and 1990s, competition among both private and public schools continued to drive the wealth-cost double helix upward. At the same time, the American economy began to stall, and esteem for the wealthiest, elite institutions of higher education started to ebb. An undercurrent of criticism welled up in the press, the public, and political circles, as subsidies for higher education declined, middle-class incomes lagged, and student debt grew. At the same time, wealth inequality resurged in the United States, reminiscent of Andrew Carnegie's era. Yet colleges and universities in the 2000s and 2010s incessantly sought more revenue and relished their "increasingly competitive" ethos.[2]

Schools that depended heavily on tuition struggled to make ends meet, and many analysts considered their search for more revenue both understandable

2. Weisbrod, Ballou, and Asch, *Mission and Money*, 39–57. See Swensen, *Pioneering Portfolio Management* (2000), xiii, 9, 323; (2009), xiii, 10, 17.

and justified. What began to attract strong criticism, even resentment, were the wealthiest institutions, which acted "like cookie monsters searching for cookies," as some of their leaders applauded, seemingly oblivious to the growing public disfavor. Rich colleges and universities must and do "seek out all the resources that they can get their hands on and then devour them." According to this approving view, these wealthy insatiable schools seek more money in order "to improve [their] absolute quality and . . . relative stature in the prestige pecking order."[3]

Meanwhile, colleges and universities became stratified into "rigid castes" of wealth, to use Carnegie's term. Schools jousted fiercely within their caste, aspiring to ascend dramatically or fearing a precipitous fall. But the wealth advantage of a higher stratum sealed off those below, with very few exceptions. This development stoked public resentment because the stratification in higher education seemed to resemble and reinforce the growing wealth inequality in the American population and vice versa. Consequently, the Darwinian competition for money and dominance throughout higher education effectively became pointless after 150 years. Why then does it continue?

More importantly, how is the competition for revenue and wealth related to the aims of higher education? What does all this analysis and behavior concerning money say about the fundamental purposes of higher education? These are the crucial questions.

Plato's Descent and the Pursuit of Wisdom

The classic treatise written about those purposes is Plato's *Republic*, a work as much about higher education as political theory. Furthermore, Plato's treatise deserves attention because he, not coincidentally perhaps, addressed the same three aims most often cited in the current literature to explain the ongoing pursuit of revenue and wealth in American higher education.

In the early twenty-first century, some maintain that higher education aims predominantly to increase its "value," "absolute quality," or "excellence." By this view, acquiring more revenue and wealth serves that lofty goal. Others assert that the ceaseless pursuit of money is primarily driven by the competitive aim to maintain standing in "the prestige pecking order" or "the positional arms race in higher education," in the phrase of economist Gordon Winston.[4] Still

3. Ehrenberg, *Tuition Rising*, 11, 265, 277. See Weisbrod, Ballou, and Asch, *Mission and Money*, 39–57; Swensen, *Pioneering Portfolio Management* (2000), xiii, 9, 323; (2009), xiii, 10, 17.
4. Gordon C. Winston, "The Positional Arms Race in Higher Education" (working paper, Washington, DC, April 2000), ED 474–73. See Ehrenberg, *Tuition Rising*, 11, 265, 277; William F.

others—including critics and prominent leaders, such as former Harvard president Derek Bok (1971–91)—have suggested that higher education is now so consumed by commercial efforts to profit financially that its dominant aim seems simply to increase its revenue and wealth.[5]

In the *Republic*, Plato identified and analyzed these same three aims of polity and higher education over two millennia ago. Indeed, he maintained that they form three tiers of a descending hierarchy from the best constitution to the worst: from one guided by love of wisdom, to one guided by love of honor (conferred by winning a contest), to one guided by love of money.[6] Which of Plato's constitutions now rules American higher education—particularly the elite, wealthy colleges and universities—given the assertions of their leaders, critics, and scholars that any one of the three governs?

Consider the first and highest possibility: commitment to seeking and advancing wisdom. In the twenty-first century, prominent scholars and leaders of higher education have justified the insatiable need for more revenue because it furthers the "quality," the "excellence," or the "value" of colleges and universities. Without debating the precise meaning of these terms, let us grant that these goods do contribute to learning and, broadly, to wisdom in Plato's terms. By this rationale, today's persistent search for more revenue and wealth in higher education is consistent with Plato's best constitution.

But resources are limited, and other non-profit, beneficent institutions require them. This limitation prompts the question, how much quality, excellence, or value results from additional revenue received by higher education? In other words, one must consider what Howard Bowen called "the economic principle of equi-marginal returns," sometimes termed "effective altruism" today. Does each additional dollar spent on higher education increase its quality, excellence, and value as much as a dollar spent on other beneficial institutions with a broad public mission? Like everyone working in "hospitals, churches, schools, museums, and . . . governmental agencies," people laboring in higher education believe that their work is "so vital to human welfare that no effort or resources should be spared," wrote Howard Bowen. Given that resources are limited, he asked whether increasing the revenue and wealth of institutions outside of higher

---

Massy, "Collegium Economicum: Why Institutions Do What They Do," *Change* 36 (2004): 27–35; William F. Massy, *Reengineering the University: How to Be Mission Centered, Market Smart, and Margin Conscious* (Baltimore, 2016), 1–38.

5. Derek Bok, *Universities in the Marketplace: The Commercialization of Higher Education* (Princeton, NJ, 2003); Christopher Newfield, *Ivy and Industry: Business and the Making of the American University, 1880–1980* (Durham, NC, 2003).

6. We are grateful to philosopher Randall Curren for suggesting this analogy.

education might contribute more quality, excellence, or value to human welfare.[7]

It is tempting to dismiss the premise of limited resources and this question of equi-marginal return in a nation that spends trillions of dollars on the military. But, even conceding that point, the issue remains germane within the field of education. Does each additional dollar spent on higher education increase educational quality, excellence, or value as much as a dollar spent on preschool education? And within higher education, does each additional dollar spent on elite, wealthy colleges and universities increase their quality, excellence, and value—Plato's "wisdom"—as much as a dollar spent on less endowed and less prestigious institutions?

Consider the plight of liberal arts colleges, many of which closed between 1970 and 2020 due to financial problems. Indeed, the future of all but the wealthiest was endangered, alarming many in higher education.[8] In 2021, a survey reported that three-quarters of provosts expect many more liberal arts colleges to expire in the coming decade. Meanwhile, many colleges and universities that did survive the dot-com bust of 2001–2, the Great Recession of 2008–9, and the pandemic starting in 2019 drastically cut or closed their humanities programs or departments, including Ohio Wesleyan, Chatham College, and many public universities.[9]

According to Carnegie's "law of competition," many of these liberal arts colleges and even liberal arts disciplines appear increasingly unfit to survive. Nor would that law permit subsidizing these colleges and disciplines with "indiscriminate charity" because "those worthy of assistance, except in rare cases, seldom require assistance."[10] Meanwhile, most wealthy colleges and universities claim to support the liberal arts disciplines that the unfit and expiring colleges and programs provided and that, arguably, Plato endorsed as guides to wisdom, such as the discipline of philosophy. Therefore, donating funds to the wealthy colleges and universities to preserve their liberal arts seems consistent with a constitution guided by wisdom and with Carnegie's law of competition, taken together.

7. H. Bowen, *Costs of Higher Education*, 21.

8. David W. Breneman, *Liberal Arts Colleges: Thriving, Surviving, or Endangered?* (Washington, DC, 1994); Robert Zemsky, ed., *The Nation's Liberal Arts Colleges in an Age of Universities* (Philadelphia, 1995); Michael S. McPherson and Morton O. Schapiro, "The Future Economic Challenges for the Liberal Arts Colleges," *Daedalus* 128 (Winter 1999): 47–75.

9. Eliza Gray, "Are Liberal Arts Colleges Doomed?," *Washington Post Magazine*, October 21, 2019; Scott Jaschik, "Provosts Face the Pandemic," *Inside Higher Ed*, April 26, 2021.

10. Carnegie, *Gospel of Wealth*, 16–17.

Here enters the economic principle of equi-marginal return. Where would, say, an additional $10 million of funds yield the most quality, excellence, and value? Would that happen at a wealthy liberal arts college, like Pomona, with an endowment of $2.3 billion, or at Guilford College, the oldest coeducational liberal arts college in the South, with an endowment of $73 million? Similarly, HBCUs historically faced great disadvantages, such as in the inequitable distribution of federal land-grant monies, the advent of fundraising campaigns, the access to New Deal programs, the dispensing of G.I. Bill benefits, and the issuing of tax-exempt bonds, to name a few. Due to the overlapping financial challenges, traditional liberal arts disciplines are being phased out at some HBCUs.[11] Would an additional $10 million advance wisdom more at Pomona or at an HBCU with a small endowment?

This question is not speculative, as demonstrated by the Bloomberg philanthropies' recent gift of $20 million to Princeton University to endow the Emma Bloomberg Center for Access and Opportunity. This Bloomberg Center will provide support for first-generation and low-income students at Princeton and funds for research on how schools can support such students, which will be disseminated to other colleges.[12] To be sure, this Bloomberg gift is designed to advance both wisdom and social justice. But the tangible benefits flow largely to Princeton, as do similar donations that add to the revenue of elite wealthy universities to support their students and found research centers funding their scholars.

The equi-marginal question is whether this $20 million will do more for first-generation and low-income students at Princeton, with an endowment of nearly $27 billion, than at Tougaloo College, an HBCU, with an endowment of about $10 million, founded in 1871 and still serving predominantly first-generation and low-income students in Mississippi. Indeed, it seems ironic that Princeton researchers will instruct Tougaloo about how to support first-generation and low-income students. This irony suggests that the Bloomberg Center does not meet the equi-marginal return standard of maximizing the advance of wisdom in the republic. Indeed, in many cases, the donations, wealth accumulation, and spending at wealthy colleges and universities fall short of that standard. Hence, these activities are not warranted by the pursuit of wisdom guided by Plato's best constitution.

11. Cornel West and Jeremy Tate, "Howard University's Removal of Classics Is a Spiritual Catastrophe," *Washington Post*, April 19, 2020.
12. Melissa Korn, "Princeton Gets $20 Million from Bloomberg Philanthropies toward Diversity," *Wall Street Journal*, April 19, 2020.

In contrast, a positive example might be found in the pledge by the University of Pennsylvania in 2020 to contribute $100 million to the Philadelphia School District. Paid over 10 years, Pennsylvania's contribution will go toward renovating "aging school buildings" that the district could not afford to fix. Though owning endowment of nearly $15 billion, Pennsylvania could surely use the $100 million to enhance its own quality, excellence, and value. But the $100 million likely supplies more equi-marginal return for the kindred, needful Philadelphia School District.[13] A cynic might dismiss such a contribution by a wealthy university as a self-serving effort to burnish its local reputation. Yet, even by this cynical view, Pennsylvania's contribution deserves a place no lower than the next tier on Plato's hierarchy.

Honor, Prestige, and Reputational Capital

Over the past half century, virtually all colleges and universities, especially the wealthiest, entered "the positional arms race in higher education." The prize was honor or prestige, sometimes called "reputational capital."[14] In order to advance or preserve their standing, schools sought more revenue and wealth, and the positional arms race therefore became "an arms race of spending."[15] The pursuit of revenue and wealth thus served the aim of improving a school's reputation, prestige, and honor, the second tier in Plato's descent.

However, this aim seems belied by the fact that colleges and universities have misconstrued prestige and honor and miscalculated reputational capital. Indeed, their understanding of this aim is insular, counterproductive, and shortsighted. Discussion of the "reputation race" in higher education has addressed prestige primarily in terms of academic reputation, while viewing financial capital and reputational capital as strongly correlated. More money means more academic prestige for a school, hence the endless published rankings of endowment. "The bigger the endowment, the stronger the academic reputation of the university," commentators affirm.[16]

But this insular understanding of prestige and honor is ultimately counterproductive. As their endowments grew enormously, colleges and universities in

13. "Penn Pledges $100 Million to the School District of Philadelphia," *Philadelphia Free Press*, November 18, 2020.

14. Henry Hansmann, "Why Do Universities Have Endowments?," *Journal of Legal Studies* 19 (1990): 27; Swensen, *Pioneering Portfolio Management* (2000), 323.

15. Ehrenberg, *Tuition Rising*, 277–78.

16. Quotations are from Frans van Vught, "Mission Diversity and Reputation in Higher Education," *Higher Education Policy* 21 (2008): 169; Utah State University, Development Office, "Priorities: Endowment," (ca. 2000), on file with the author.

the wealthiest tier began to appear greedy, and their reputation in the polity and society turned malodorous. Though having the most financial and reputational capital in academic terms, the wealthiest schools' reputation for civic virtue declined in the twenty-first century. This decline certainly contributed in 2017 to what had been unimaginable for over a century: Congress targeted the crown jewels of American higher education with the retributive TCJA excise tax.

The insular focus on the "reputation race" within academe was not only counterproductive but also shortsighted. Intending to enhance their academic reputation, the wealthiest schools grew their own financial capital at the expense of their reputational capital in civic virtue. Yet acting more generously in the polity and broader society in the short term often would have cost less than the pilloried schools will eventually be compelled to expend under TCJA. Sharing their cookies in the short run would save them in the long run.

Many recent examples could be cited, including controversies over the University of Chicago Medical Center and its Level 1 trauma center in the 2000s; the University of Michigan tuition hike during the pandemic of 2019, immediately after completing "the most successful fundraising campaign in its history"; and Yale University's parsimony in helping the city of New Haven even as it reveled in David Swensen's superlative portfolio management in recent decades.[17] These universities' reluctance to share their wealth with their local communities hurt their reputation (or did not improve it) and cost them money (or did not save what they intended).

Calculating the monetary cost of improving or damaging the public reputation of a college or university is difficult. But the $10 million paid annually by Pennsylvania is little less than the cost incurred or revenue gained (at the expense of the universities' public reputation) in the examples of Chicago, Michigan, or Yale cited above. And the potential cost is much larger. The TCJA excise tax reportedly cost Harvard $50 million in 2019 and Stanford $43 million in 2020. The amounts are higher for 2021.

And no one considers these payments virtuous. In contrast, the initiative of the University of Pennsylvania to contribute $10 million in cash annually to the Philadelphia schools—also helping the university indirectly—gained appreciation

---

17. Quotation is from University of Michigan, "Victors for Michigan Campaign: Final Results," *Michigan News*, February 2019. See Lisa Schencker and Ese Olumhense, "University of Chicago's New Trauma Center Opens, with Cautious Optimism," *Chicago Tribune*, April 30, 2018; Calder Lewis and Arjun Thakker, "Days after Rejecting University Budget, Regents Approve Tuition Increase in Special Meeting," *Michigan Daily*, June 30, 2020; Hilary Burns and Craig M. Douglas, "Death, Taxes and Ivory Towers: A Story about Yale University and the Untenable Ties to Its Hometown of New Haven, Connecticut," *Business Journals*, May 6, 2021.

and honor for the university. Philadelphia's mayor, school board president, and school superintendent publicly proclaimed, "We are thrilled to have this very generous gift from the University of Pennsylvania."[18] No such proclamations for schools' paying the TCJA excise tax have yet been published.

Had the 30 institutions subject to TCJA voluntarily begun two decades ago raising their spending rate and sharing their soaring endowment income with kindred, needful educational institutions—HBCUs or struggling liberal arts colleges or schools in local communities—their reputational capital in civic virtue would have increased and the rationale and political support for TCJA declined. And the monies would likely have been spent more economically and effectively than will the tax revenue.

The "reputation race" in higher education therefore does not seem to fit Plato's constitution guided by the desire for honor and prestige. The wealthiest, elite schools apparently do not understand the relationship between their honor and prestige and their search for revenue and wealth. If they did, then the calculations of endowment return and spending rules would include expenses to enhance their reputation in civic virtue, as those calculations now include the fees for active management (and should include the cost of collateral damage).

Without that calculation, the schools' celebrated high returns on large endowments actually detract from their reputational capital in terms of civic virtue. To state the point finely, a wealthy college or university would enhance its broader reputation in the long run by coupling its annual announcement of investment return with a statement of how much of that return the school is going to spend directly on specific, civic or social endeavors. And wealthy colleges and universities would do well to require that the *Chronicle of Higher Education* do the same in its annual rankings of endowments. The competition for endowment growth would then be linked to a competition for spending on civic virtue.

Avarice and Perseveration

At the bottom of Plato's descent is the constitution guided by avarice, the love of money. And it often seems that wealthy colleges and universities adore their endowments, carefully protecting them and nurturing their growth. Although the benefits of autonomy, stability, and flexibility warranted accumulating financial capital in the past, rich schools today "are acting like they exist to protect

18. "Penn Pledges $100 Million to the School District of Philadelphia," *Philadelphia Free Press*, November 18, 2020.

their endowments, instead of the other way around," law professor Paul Campos opined in the *New York Times* in 2020.[19] Thus, wealthy schools might be pursuing free money out of avarice. But who are the greedy persons who profit? The fundraising and capital wealth do not enrich the faculty and staff, most of whom could earn much more in business (even though presidents' salaries have risen dramatically).[20] Avarice cannot explain the pursuit of money.

In sum, the upward spiral of the wealth-cost double helix of higher education today does not seem guided by any of Plato's three constitutions, notwithstanding the affirmations of leaders, alumni, scholars, and critics that the wealthiest colleges and universities aim at the three goals of money, prestige, or value and excellence. If not, then what else could explain this behavior?

The history of the past 150 years suggests another explanation. Over the century from the 1870s through the 1970s, colleges and universities persistently followed the "law of competition" and pursued wealth with the ultimate aims of improving higher education, serving the nation, and advancing knowledge. And they successfully built the best higher education system in the world.[21] Raising money and spending it on themselves worked spectacularly, while equimarginal return and civic virtue took care of themselves.

Then, between 1980 and 2020, vociferous public criticism of higher education began to grow. At the same time, the wealth stratification of higher education hardened, permitting less and less movement between castes of higher education as the aggressive investment regimes took hold. The historical rationale of seeking to triumph in the Darwinian competition therefore withered away. Likewise, the Platonic rationales of pursuing wisdom or prestige could not bear scrutiny.

The historically rooted, free-money strategy prescribed by Eliot and described in Howard Bowen's revenue-cost theory continued of its own inertia in the late twentieth century. By that point, the strategy had become the common sense of how a successful college or university should operate—indeed, must operate—manifested in the six modes of acquiring revenue. In the early twenty-first century, relentless persistence in driving upward the wealth-cost spiral transformed into

19. Paul F. Campos, "Rich Colleges Can Afford to Spend More," *New York Times*, June 6, 2020.

20. Andrew Erwin and Marjorie Wood, *The One Percent at State U: How Public University Presidents Profit from Rising Student Debt and Low-Wage Faculty Labor* (Washington, DC, 2014); Allana Akhtar and Taylor Borden, "15 College Presidents Who've Been Paid Millionaire Salaries," *Business Insider*, September 15, 2020; Linda Blackford, "UK Trustees Give Shocking, Tone-Deaf Raise to an Already Highly Paid UK President," *Lexington Herald Leader*, December 15, 2021.

21. Martin Trow, "American Higher Education: Past, Present and Future," *Studies in Higher Education* 14 (1989): 5–22; Freeland, *Academia's Golden Age*, 419.

perseveration: repeating the behavior over and over after losing sight of the original reason. Displacing the goals, the methods of acquiring money are running on autopilot, and this perseveration is reinforced by the competition.

The perseveration predominates higher up the pecking order, where the anxious competition for revenue and wealth intensifies. Schools that might be considered most confident of their status—members of the AAU, for example—are constantly looking over their shoulder, checking their revenues against the AAU metrics and other AAU members' performance, as executives push department chairs and program directors to raise more money. Competing intensely to obtain larger grants, hold ever larger fundraising drives, and post the highest endowment returns (driven by aggressive investing whose volatility they alone can afford), the wealthy schools are thrilled to publicize those returns, unaccountably neglecting the price they pay in public and political resentment, as list prices rise and student debt grows.[22]

In Plato's terms, these crown jewels of American higher education have apparently forgotten their true nature and foundational purposes, particularly in strengthening democracy. Indeed, their insatiable need and competitive pursuit of wealth and prestige has eclipsed the important ways that higher education has historically benefited democracy: training in citizenship and civic virtue, inculcating appreciation for expertise, enhancing the expression and contest of ideas, and, particularly, fostering social mobility.[23]

History and Hope

The fundamental point of this history is that the financial practices and policies of higher education are not derived from nature or necessity or "common sense." They arose for specific purposes in particular circumstances that have now changed. Yet, after a century of salutary growth, the wealth, cost, and price in American higher education have culminated over the past four decades in amnesia and perseveration, spawning disfavor and resentment, if this brief history is convincing.

And if this account is persuasive, then historical evidence and interpretation may contribute an important perspective on higher education finances in the United States today, alongside economic analysis, policy studies, and sociological research. This contribution is valuable because we need to summon all our learning in order to understand these complex financial issues.

22. Juliet Chung and Eliot Brown, "University Endowments Mint Billions in Golden Era of Venture Capital," *Wall Street Journal*, September 29, 2021.
23. See Ronald J. Daniels, *What Universities Owe Democracy* (Baltimore, 2021).

As this book goes to press, higher education endowment returns have recently "boomed," fundraising drives have reported "a record amount," and tuition and fees have climbed.[24] In 2022, however, these indices have begun to decline, as their undulation continues. Perhaps we are in for a brief precipitous downturn like the recession of 2008–9, or an extended period of stagflation as in the 1970s, or even a deep malaise like the Great Depression of the 1930s. In any event, this brief history suggests that higher education will soon recover, and the wealthiest colleges and universities will resume driving the wealth-cost double helix, designed and instituted in the formative era, spiraling upward, intermittently pulling price higher.

A more beneficial and pathbreaking outcome seems nowhere on the horizon, and it is not the province of a historian to propose visions for the future. But it is worth noting that a remarkably small group of about 10 persons have the capacity to set a new course for the fleet of colleges and universities. These are the presidents of the wealthiest private universities who meet regularly and could agree to steer their vessels in a new direction.

They could, for example, agree to freeze their tuition for five years or modify their spending rules and distribute some of the proceeds to needful schools of all kinds. Everyone knows that this group effectively sets the parameters for colleges and universities, and such a breathtaking move would reset the norms for the entire fleet and reshape public opinion.

In addition, the 63 provosts of the public and private AAU institutions, who convene regularly as a genteel club in idyllic settings, could agree to a truce in their competition for revenue and prestige. They could, for example, dictate to grantors collaborative standards by which they would apply and accept grants. After all, the grantors need the AAU universities as much as vice versa. The AAU provosts could also create their own collaborative standards of institutional quality rather than complying with the competitive benchmarks of popular magazines. Again, the rest of the fleet would follow their lead.

To be sure, it seems unlikely that these 73 powerful leaders will begin to think cooperatively about how they can strengthen all of higher education and its contribution to our democratic republic rather than competitively about how to sustain and elevate the rankings of their individual schools. But one can hope.

---

24. Emma Whitford, "College Endowments Boomed in Fiscal Year 2021, Study Shows," *Inside Higher Ed*, February 18, 2022; Mike Scutari, "'A Perfect Storm.' Higher Ed Institutions Raised a Record Amount in the 2020–21 Fiscal Year." *Inside Philanthropy*, February 16, 2022; Jon Marcus, "Inflation Is Coming to College Campuses. Prepare to Pay More." *Hechinger Report*, February 6, 2022.

Wealth, cost, and price are reaching a crisis point amid a cacophony of criticism even from the strongest proponents and friends of higher education. Nevertheless, one must expect that the highest caste of colleges and universities will continue their scramble to grab all the cookies they can and leave it to Congress to rein in the free-for-all.

That is a dismaying prospect, and surely not what Charles Eliot had in mind. Even Andrew Carnegie and John D. Rockefeller knew better than to it leave it to Congress to determine the philanthropic distribution of their wealth. Recent experience confirms the point for higher education.

So we are left with merely the hope that the current 73 "captains of erudition" can rise at least to the level of the robber barons of old in foresight and generosity, that is, enlightened self-interest. The bar is low, and the hope is modest. But it seems the best we can do, given the amnesia and perseveration that prevail.

APPENDIX I

Largest Average Annual Total of Gifts and Bequests Received by Colleges and Universities, 1920–30 (in thousands of nominal dollars)

TABLE AI.I

Institution type	Largest average annual total of gifts and bequests, 1920–30						
Private universities	Yale 9,072	Harvard 8,303	Chicago 4,516	Columbia 3,226	Johns Hopkins 3,029	Cornell 1,905	Princeton 1,653
State universities	California 1,759	Minnesota 970	Iowa 391	Texas 279	Illinois 276	Rutgers 249	Cincinnati 80
Small colleges	Williams 719	Wesleyan 509	Bowdoin 331	Lafayette 326	Carleton 277	Antioch 200	Beloit 199
Women's colleges	Wellesley 795	Smith 653	Vassar 488	Mount Holyoke 327	Bryn Mawr 311	Radcliffe 263	Barnard 180

Source: Data drawn from Jones, *American Giver*, 72–73.

Explanation of the Cross Section of Institutions and Analytic
Categories of Capital, Income, and Enrollment, 1875–1930

In the year 1875, 577 colleges and universities reported to the US Office of Education. From that base year through 1930, the commissioner's annual reports and individual schools' archives supplied adequate financial data in every fifth year for only about 60 institutions. In some cases, it was necessary to interpolate financial figures.[1] From those 60, a cross section of 32 institutions was identified based on region, type, size, and student population, as listed in table 6.2. For each of the 32 institutions, data were collected on income, capital, and enrollment, and all three dimensions present analytic challenges and choices.

"Income" serves as a proxy for production cost because the Bureau of Education generally reported revenue and not expenses prior to 1930. In addition, operating income serves as an approximation of the "educational expenses" that later scholars began distinguishing from "non-educational expenses" after about 1950. Prior to 1930, "non-educational" expenses were minimal compared to the post-1950 era, as discussed in chapter 7.

Data on "enrollment" are needed to calculate the critical per-student production costs. But determining the number of students is not straightforward because the kinds of enrollment multiplied over time, including summer, correspondence, extension, "irregular," and military drill students. Fortunately, their numbers were relatively small prior to 1930, so this study does not count those part-time categories.

More problematic are the "preparatory students," who were numerous prior to 1900, especially during the decades after an institution opened. The definition of this population varied across institutions, and the associated income, or expense, was rarely stipulated. Due to this analytic difficulty, institutions that had adequate financial data but enrolled a large proportion of "preparatory" students for decades after

1. For further discussion and documentation, see Kimball and Luke, "Measuring Cost Escalation," 202–4; Kimball and Luke, "Historical Dimensions of the 'Cost Disease,'" 45–48.

their opening, such as Oberlin College, were eliminated from the cross section. But institutions that had adequate financial data and a large preparatory enrollment that steadily diminished after their opening, such as the University of Nebraska and the University of Colorado, were included. In these cases, preparatory students were counted as one-half of an enrollment owing to the lesser resources committed to preparatory students.

Professional school enrollments also required special attention. Prior to 1890, the commissioner's reports did not combine data from professional schools at universities and colleges in the data of their host institution. Most professional schools, including law schools and medical schools, operated below the postsecondary level on a proprietary basis and required only one or two years of study and no examinations. Not really part of higher education prior to 1890, professional schools were effectively auxiliary enterprises, and separating their data from those of their host institutions seems justified in light of those conditions. But universities began to require their professional schools to elevate their academic standards in the 1880s, and the commissioner of education combined professional school data with the data of their affiliated universities for the first time in 1890 because this reflected a genuine expansion of higher education.[2] As a result, both the pre-1890 data and post-1890 data present information about higher education that can legitimately be compared.

"Capital" denotes the wealth of an institution, comprising all of its property and invested funds. Contrary to post-1930 usage, "property" in this study incorporates equipment and furnishings because the commissioner's reports did not separate equipment and furnishings until 1905.[3] Although recent scholars have generally not included the annual cost of capital in the production cost of higher education, economist Gordon Winston has shown that capital cost is an important annual expense for colleges and universities that incorporates the cost of depreciation, equipment, maintenance, supplies, and opportunity. Winston estimates that capital costs increase the cost of higher education by about 25 percent.[4] This percentage equals about one-third of the annual operating cost of higher education, as it is conventionally calculated.

2. See Kimball and Luke, "Measuring Cost Escalation," 205; Bruce A. Kimball, Jeremy B. Luke, and Jamie B. Brown, "The Formative Financial Era of 'the Major Professional Schools,'" in Adam and Bayram, *Economics of Higher Education*, 129–33.

3. The figures of Harvard, Yale, and Princeton do not include their property within their "capital" because those three rarely reported property values. A separate analysis revealed that the growth of permanent funds of Harvard, Yale, and Princeton was closely correlated with that of the total capital (including property). Consequently, the permanent funds of Harvard, Yale, and Princeton serve as a proxy for their total capital, since the change, not the absolute value, of capital is being studied. See Kimball and Luke, "Measuring Cost Escalation," 204.

4. Gordon C. Winston, "A Guide to Measuring College Costs" (discussion paper 46, Williamstown, MA, 1998); Gordon C. Winston, "Higher Education Costs, Prices, and Subsidies: Some Economic Facts and Fundamentals," in NCES, *Study of College Costs and Prices*, 125–26.

This fraction matches an earlier calculation by economist June O'Neill that the capital costs amounted to about 32 percent of operating costs in the 1929–30 academic year. In 1980, Howard R. Bowen reported that, between 1929 and 1976, "capital expenditures" were in the range of 20–25 percent of "current expenditures."[5] But that range of 20–32 percent seems low for the period 1875–1930, because one-third of the operating income (expense) during this period amounts to a total cost of only 3–6 percent of the capital, as can be computed from figures in appendix 3. Capital cost should be figured much higher than 3–6 percent of capital, particularly given the enormous material investment in new institutions during the formative period.

Considering the cost of capital on its own terms, Winston maintained that "depreciation is on the order of 2.5 percent of re-placement value while opportunity cost is, conservatively, 8 percent or more."[6] This "conservative" total of 10.5 percent of capital does not consider the expense of equipment and maintenance. O'Neill calculated the capital cost for 1929–30, the first year in her study, to be 7.8 percent of the total capital of land, buildings, and equipment. And she did not consider the opportunity cost of capital, which, per Winston's figure of 8 percent, would raise O'Neill's capital cost nearly to 16 percent.[7]

In light of these figures, this study estimates capital cost to be 15 percent of the value of capital during the period 1875–1930. But about 10 percent of that capital across all 32 institutions was invested permanent funds. Therefore, the capital cost has been discounted by 10 percent—from 15 percent to 13.5 percent—because the income, or cost, of the invested funds is already represented in the operating income. Multiplying the aggregate capital by 13.5 percent therefore yields the estimated capital cost for this study.

Dividing that capital cost by the enrollment produces the per-student capital cost, which actually exceeded the per-student operating income until 1915, as seen in appendix 6. This result of per-student capital cost running about 60 percent of total per-student cost greatly exceeds the range of 25–32 percent computed by Winston and O'Neill. But the higher pre-1930 percentage seems justified by the fact that most of the physical plant of colleges and universities was newly constructed during the formative period. If capital cost in the 2000s were calculated based on the replacement cost of the existing buildings, then the capital cost today would be much higher than the range of 25–32 percent, as Gordon Winston also observed.

---

5. June O'Neill, *Resource Use in Higher Education: Trends in Outputs and Inputs, 1930 to 1967* (Berkeley, CA, 1971), 90–91; H. Bowen, *Costs of Higher Education*, 35; see also 34–37, 145–51, 255–62.
6. Winston, "Higher Education Costs," 126.
7. O'Neill, *Resource Use in Higher Education*, 28–35, 91.

Capital, Income, and Enrollment of the Cross Section of 32 Institutions,
1875–1930

In the following tables, monetary figures are rounded to thousands of nominal dollars, and monetary "totals" in the right-hand columns are sums of the rows prior to rounding. See appendix 2 for discussion of the categories in the following tables. Further discussion and documentation concerning the data in these tables can be found in Kimball and Luke, "Measuring Cost Escalation," 212–16. The data in the commissioner's annual report for 1916 come from the year 1915 (US CommEd, *Report [June 30, 1916]*, 2:viii).

TABLE A3.1
Small Private Colleges, 1875–1930

	Amherst	Baylor	Centre	Earlham	Knox	Smith	Vassar	Wabash	Totals
1875									
Enrollment	335	95 [25]	169 [83]	287 [114]	42 [187]	17	225 [159]	86 [129]	1,256 [697]
Income	62	3	11	14	16	29	68	15	217
Capital	701	71	255	165	252	850	958	310	3,562
1880									
Enrollment	339	85 [35]	96 [84]	41 [144]	105	214	217 [86]	96 [84]	1,193 [433]
Income	25	3	10	9	10	30	58	21	167
Capital	811	96	246	120	276	643	1,060	340	3,591
1885									
Enrollment	335	5 [63]	95 [121]	92 [88]	166	296	238 [80]	89 [94]	1,316 [446]
Income	40	2	12	4	39	95	100	35	327
Capital	1,186	65	255	155	321	754	1,152	425	4,312
1890									
Enrollment	344	483 [204]	110 [94]	164 [78]	175	541	385	97 [166]	2,299 [542]
Income	75	15	16	15	60	161	132	35	510
Capital	1,500	251	335	240	392	925	1,636	511	5,790
1895									
Enrollment	439	338 [227]	218 [74]	168 [15]	581 [125]	787	532	137 [99]	3,200 [540]
Income	110	16	20	27	23	226	164	34	619
Capital	2,200	292	335	240	384	1,214	2,211	654	7,529
1900									
Enrollment	365	399 [350]	194 [80]	234 [12]	311	1,219	679	113 [65]	3,514 [507]
Income	101	30	20	21	28	185	316	35	735
Capital	2,500	332	355	500	513	1,811	3,224	918	10,153

1905

Enrollment	412	671 [238]	808 [360]	408	526 [81]	1,067	826	143	4,861 [679]
Income	303	65	74	58	29	236	478	35	1,278
Capital	2,900	740	726	512	522	2,477	3,821	770	12,467

1910

Enrollment	531	751 [257]	185 [60]	356	629 [54]	1,627	973	384	5,436 [371]
Income	262	71	43	98	75	609	574	54	1,787
Capital	2,588	870	802	716	804	3,439	4,827	999	15,045

1915

Enrollment	413	477	330	425	573	1,638	1,122	341	5,319
Income	222	149	57	118	71	733	670	58	2,078
Capital	4,209	1,173	1,241	981	1,186	5,021	6,607	1,180	21,599

1920

Enrollment	503	1,500	217	555	797	2,010	1,106	343	7,031
Income	109	309	71	166	141	561	875	69	2,301
Capital	6,857	1,686	1,680	1,016	1,593	6,110	8,168	1,298	28,409

1925

Enrollment	691	2,511	271	550	656	2,177	1,149	517	8,522
Income	564	436	93	288	295	1,746	1,590	145	5,158
Capital	12,087	2,199	1,737	1,515	2,627	10,769	10,977	2,057	43,969

1930

Enrollment	703	2,259	398	390	582	2,162	1,162	407	8,063
Income	691	570	135	246	313	2,259	1,958	202	6,375
Capital	11,404	2,361	1,841	2,143	3,046	14,267	13,786	2,935	51,782

Relatively Large, Wealthy, Eastern Universities, 1875–1930

	Columbia	Cornell	Harvard	Howard	Johns Hopkins	Princeton	Yale	Totals
1875								
Enrollment	154	333	776	18 [25]	35	474 [40]	582	2,372 [65]
Income	313	137	219	11	180	76	89	1,026
Capital	5,369	2,129	1,000	50	3,150	828	318	12,844
1880								
Enrollment	285	459	886	15 [18]	159	428	687	2,919 [18]
Income	338	171	360	13	180	84	183	1,327
Capital	5,669	1,930	3,960	516	3,631	1,083	1,293	18,082
1885								
Enrollment	296	563	1,067	110 [42]	290	434	657	3,417 [42]
Income	342	204	812	30	233	88	163	1,872
Capital	6,619	4,781	4,804	422	3,631	1,389	1,352	22,999
1890								
Enrollment	1,671	1,329	2,126	334 [31]	404	769	1,477	8,110 [31]
Income	726	330	1,013	44	114	128	212	2,567
Capital	9,754	6,355	7,030	690	3,872	1,698	3,148	32,547
1895								
Enrollment	1,943	1,689	3,290	441 [93]	589	1,109	2,300	11,361 [93]
Income	734	517	1,045	57	175	115	705	3,349
Capital	14,736	8,829	8,381	665	4,085	2,007	3,822	42,526
1900								
Enrollment	2,452	2,239	4,103	369 [145]	645	1,194	2,432	13,434 [145]
Income	973	664	1,377	50	171	272	770	4,275
Capital	21,785	9,380	12,615	945	4,115	2,317	4,942	55,098

	Col 1	Col 2	Col 3	Col 4	Col 5	Col 6	Col 7	Col 8
1905								
Enrollment	4,238	3,517	4,136	588 [279]	745	1,374	2,992	17,590 [279]
Income	1,142	996	1,626	146	303	234	853	5,300
Capital	26,623	11,790	18,036	2,271	6,200	2,880	7,317	74,946
1910								
Enrollment	3,474	4,227	4,046	905 [340]	679	1,400	3,297	18,028 [340]
Income	2,550	1,666	2,016	242	356	488	1,353	8,671
Capital	36,065	15,049	21,990	1,513	6,704	4,221	12,532	98,073
1915								
Enrollment	5,228	5,491	4,604	1,154 [298]	904	1,643	3,300	22,324 [298]
Income	4,047	2,970	2,866	204	575	899	1,777	13,337
Capital	48,796	23,382	28,471	1,616	10,672	5,563	16,153	134,652
1920								
Enrollment	8,510	5,765	4,650	1,487	2,715	1,850	3,300	22,277
Income	4,346	4,032	4,611	304	1,704	1,056	2,950	19,002
Capital	55,311	26,055	44,569	1,738	13,459	10,313	24,049	175,495
1925								
Enrollment	12,527	5,818	7,721	2,137	4,329	2,466	4,866	39,864
Income	15,181	7,152	9,484	718	1,856	1,835	5,233	41,460
Capital	76,347	34,763	76,022	2,650	30,585	15,000	45,604	280,970
1930								
Enrollment	15,903	5,893	9,475	2,559	5,027	2,489	5,330	46,676
Income	13,984	8,492	13,910	887	2,723	2,419	7,879	50,292
Capital	124,977	38,838	108,087	4,096	40,613	21,829	82,857	421,298

TABLE A3.3
Southern Universities, 1875–1930

	Alabama	Georgia	Louisiana State	Vanderbilt	Virginia	Totals
1875						
Enrollment	71	262	8	175	326	842
Income	39	36	7	26	15	123
Capital	150	573	220	700	634	2,257
1880						
Enrollment	140	83	122	191	347	883
Income	24	28	25	47	28	151
Capital	552	318	419	1,100	800	3,189
1885						
Enrollment	207	184	97 [60]	176	306	970 [60]
Income	86	29	25	55	40	234
Capital	552	577	618	1,300	900	3,947
1890						
Enrollment	206	319	72 [85]	637	483	1,717 [85]
Income	37	31	40	102	94	303
Capital	680	688	524	1,425	1,325	4,642
1895						
Enrollment	183	299	111 [91]	680	567	1,840 [91]
Income	27	52	57	107	147	390
Capital	550	1,025	368	1,739	1,758	5,441
1900						
Enrollment	411	337	234	814	655	2,451
Income	45	49	71	133	146	445
Capital	650	823	552	2,150	1,476	5,650
1905						
Enrollment	473	483	326	684	706	2,672
Income	54	62	112	134	164	526
Capital	1,315	1,051	729	2,300	1,978	7,373
1910						
Enrollment	611	531	511 [105]	1,007	803	3,463 [105]
Income	318	177	179	184	241	1,100
Capital	2,270	1,442	1,120	2,852	3,491	11,175
1915						
Enrollment	756	651	921	958	945	4,231
Income	210	286	271	268	342	1,377
Capital	2,179	1,802	1,326	4,000	4,295	13,602

1920						
Enrollment	1,171	1,360	1,128 [100]	1,042	1,638	6,339 [100]
Income	264	673	500	278	650	2,365
Capital	1,968	3,060	1,475	5,643	5,190	17,336
1925						
Enrollment	2,277	1,458	1,813	1,425	2,080	9,053
Total Income	591	1,391	1,244	755	1,163	5,144
Capital	3,310	3,906	6,469	14,387	7,010	35,083
1930						
Enrollment	3,603	1,868	2,132 [217]	1,485	2,458	11,546 [217]
Total Income	1,326	1,734	1,710	1,371	2,150	8,291
Capital	5,374	5,160	7,363	25,550	15,682	59,129

TABLE A3.4
Midwestern Public Universities, 1875–1930

	Indiana	Iowa State	Kansas	Michigan	Missouri	Nebraska	Ohio State	Wisconsin	Totals
1875									
Enrollment	134 [112]	126 [277]	78 [119]	324	132 [204]	35 [104]	99	201 [73]	1,129 [889]
Income	32	54	20	14	71	20	39	56	305
Capital	208	422	261	256	375	150	830	708	3,210
1880									
Enrollment	183 [172]	218	114 [251]	521	555	90 [168]	60 [93]	340 [31]	2,081 [715]
Income	32	39	38	163	52	25	58	77	485
Capital	230	617	348	1,140	377	150	1,060	854	4,776
1885									
Enrollment	157 [144]	234	180 [261]	524	573	142 [93]	64 [84]	313 [11]	2,187 [593]
Income	80	57	41	144	58	44	100	107	631
Capital	400	664	465	1,394	1,510	250	1,550	915	7,148
1890									
Enrollment	339 [99]	737	371 [138]	2,158	633 [104]	338 [138]	260 [165]	800	5,636 [644]
Income	99	101	83	145	73	110	129	203	943
Capital	740	503	665	1,750	1,074	1,630	2,039	2,051	10,454
1895									
Enrollment	780	1,133	875	2,818	614	978 [419]	755 [50]	1,520	9,473 [469]
Income	78	131	96	434	149	141	164	389	1,582
Capital	790	887	1,014	2,154	2,300	1,850	2,211	2,275	13,482
1900									
Enrollment	1,017	1,474	1,093	3,309	1,058	1,380 [345]	1,268	2,179	12,778 [345]
Income	138	296	183	555	193	254	316	370	2,303
Capital	900	995	1,010	2,599	2,286	1,731	3,224	2,087	14,832

1905									
Enrollment	1,538	1,512 [219]	1,446	3,742	1,892	2,289 [379]	1,835	3,010	17,264 [379]
Income	295	453	210	704	413	417	478	797	3,766
Capital	1,260	1,964	1,206	3,444	2,708	1,612	3,821	2,925	18,941
1910									
Enrollment	2,328	1,550 [219]	2,105	4,755	2,362	3,062	2,749	3,645	22,556 [219]
Income	369	610	487	1,448	706	605	932	1,768	6,926
Capital	1,619	2,933	1,891	4,761	3,665	2,726	4,827	5,686	28,109
1915									
Enrollment	2,056 [9]	2,923	2,478	5,763	3,140	3,832	4,597	5,128	29,917 [9]
Income	615	1,420	683	2,321	1,311	1,368	1,466	2,768	11,953
Capital	2,098	4,375	1,951	7,569	5,229	3,316	6,607	8,454	39,600
1920									
Enrollment	3,783	3,083 [951]	3,580 [120]	8,652	4,553 [125]	5,248 [511]	7,023	7,146 [148]	43,068 [1,855]
Income	927	2,274	1,149	3,855	1,794	2,447	2,653	3,723	18,822
Capital	3,078	5,246	3,882	11,592	6,011	6,082	8,168	10,010	54,070
1925									
Enrollment	4,503	4,109	4,548	9,923	4,517	6,836	9,963	8,392	52,791
Income	2,585	3,547	1,996	8,318	3,532	3,784	6,309	6,878	36,948
Capital	7,569	9,576	6,181	30,306	10,110	9,795	15,231	14,491	103,258
1930									
Enrollment	4,524	4,611 [90]	4,498	9,958 [340]	5,071 [141]	7,536 [564]	11,799	10,454 [377]	58,451 [1,512]
Income	3,510	4,098	2,304	10,532	3,925	4,165	8,607	8,581	45,722
Capital	8,935	18,134	7,603	41,224	9,355	12,273	21,193	20,310	139,028

TABLE A3.5
Western Public Universities, 1875–1930

	California	Colorado	Oregon	Texas	Totals
1875					
Enrollment	134	NA	NA	NA	134
Total Income	322	NA	NA	NA	322
Capital	1,560	NA	NA	NA	1,560
1880					
Enrollment	145	16 [64]	178	NA	339 [64]
Income	136	22	11	NA	169
Capital	2,476	75	130	NA	2,681
1885					
Enrollment	151	71 [51]	46 [147]	151	419 [198]
Income	130	43	15	126	313
Capital	2,678	120	180	634	3,612
1890					
Enrollment	701	75 [75]	292	307	1,375 [75]
Income	214	45	23	58	340
Capital	3,711	182	254	892	5,039
1895					
Enrollment	1,781	204 [192]	213 [177]	630	2,828 [369]
Income	284	65	42	74	465
Capital	3,987	320	320	944	5,571
1900					
Enrollment	2,457	445 [305]	183 [75]	1,002	4,087 [380]
Income	464	80	44	169	756
Capital	4,996	314	323	1,121	6,753
1905					
Enrollment	3,294	685 [415]	506	1,235	5,720 [415]
Income	829	150	60	252	1,291
Capital	8,088	400	345	1,446	10,279
1910					
Enrollment	3,858	1,108	874	1,863	7,703
Total Income	2,809	201	138	539	3,687
Capital	16,475	1,031	610	3,560	21,676
1915					
Enrollment	6,434	1,299	1,315	2,574	11,622
Income	2,667	293	202	603	3,765
Capital	16,372	1,516	990	4,626	23,504

1920					
Enrollment	12,630	2,090	2,172	4,418	21,310
Income	5,012	680	628	1,553	7,873
Capital	22,091	1,925	2,069	15,644	41,730
1925					
Enrollment	18,542	2,943	3,221	5,446	30,152
Income	12,012	2,017	1,447	2,508	17,984
Capital	37,167	6,307	3,594	24,948	72,016
1930					
Enrollment	18,689	3,260	3,512 [203]	6,681	32,142 [203]
Income	15,086	2,231	2,257	3,676	23,250
Capital	56,168	7,046	5,627	40,190	109,032

Note: Enrollment figures in brackets are the numbers of preparatory students.

Cumulative Percentage Increase of Aggregate Cost Index for 29 Colleges and Universities Compared to GNP, 1875–1930 (rounded to millions of constant dollars; 1860 = 1)

TABLE A4.1

Year	Annual operating income	Cumulative increase of income	Aggregate capital	Cumulative increase of capital	GNP	Cumulative increase of GNP
1875	1,510	—	17.8	—	5,500	—
1880	1,842	21%	26.1	47%	8,600	56%
1885	2,754	82%	35.4	99%	9,000	64%
1890	4,162	176%	52.4	195%	11,500	109%
1895	6,161	308%	72.2	307%	13,000	136%
1900	8,140	439%	90.8	411%	17,500	218%
1905	11,036	631%	114.9	547%	22,400	307%
1910	18,678	1,137%	148.1	734%	27,600	402%
1915	23,979	1,488%	172.4	870%	27,400	398%
1920	19,793	1,211%	123.9	597%	35,500	545%
1925	47,963	3,076%	238.3	1,241%	40,900	644%
1930	62,883	4,064%	363.7	1,947%	45,200	722%

Source: Data are calculated from appendix 3; Richard Sutch, "A Gross National Product and Gross Domestic Product: 1869–1929," in *Historical Statistics of the United States*, table Ca184–91.
Note: Data from the universities of Oregon, Colorado, and Texas are not included, as discussed in chapter 6.

Compound Annual Growth Rates (CAGR), 1875–1930

TABLE A5.1

CAGR of Aggregate Income and Capital for 29 Colleges and Universities Compared to GNP, 1875–1930 (percentages based on constant dollars; 1860 = 1)

Period	Annual operating income	Aggregate capital	GNP
1875–90	7.0%	7.5%	5.0%
1890–1915	7.0%	4.7%	3.4%
1915–30	7.1%	5.5%	3.6%
1875–1930	7.0%	5.6%	3.9%

Source: Amounts are computed from data in appendix 4.

TABLE A5.2

CAGR of Per-Student Production Cost of 32 Colleges and Universities, of the Commodities Price Index, and of GDP Per Capita, 1875–1930

Period	Total cost per student	Commodities price index	GDP per capita
1875–90	−0.17%	−2.20%	1.35%
1890–1915	0.51%	1.54%	2.53%
1915–30	0.96%	0.67%	4.47%
1875–1930	0.44%	0.29%	2.69%

Source: Amounts are computed from data in appendix 4 and *Historical Statistics of the United States,* table Cc125–37.

Index of Per-Student Production Cost for Cross Section of 32 Colleges and Universities, 1875–1930 (in constant dollars; 1860 = 1)

TABLE A6.I

Year	Operating income per student	Capital cost per student*	Production cost per student	Cumulative change in production cost per student
1875	230	366	596	—
1880	229	442	671	13%
1885	306	545	851	43%
1890	216	365	581	−3%
1895	215	338	553	−7%
1900	228	338	566	−5%
1905	234	322	556	−7%
1910	334	357	691	16%
1915	337	326	663	11%
1920	196	167	363	−39%
1925	362	245	607	2%
1930	424	334	758	27%

Source: Data are calculated from the tables in appendix 3. See Kimball and Luke, "Historical Dimensions of the 'Cost Disease,'" 49.

* Computed by multiplying aggregate capital by 13.5 percent and dividing by aggregate enrollment, as explained in appendix 2.

Approximate Enrollment in Degree-Granting, Non-profit and For-Profit Postsecondary Institutions, 1929–2019 (rounded to millions)

TABLE A7.1

Year	Total enrollment	Public institutions	Private institutions
1929*	1.1	0.5	0.6
1935	1.2	0.6	0.6
1939*	1.5	0.8	0.7
1945	1.7	0.8	0.8
1950	2.3	1.1	1.1
1955	2.7	1.5	1.2
1959*	3.6	2.2	1.4
1965	5.9	4.0	2.0
1970	8.6	6.4	2.2
1975	11.2	8.8	2.4
1980	12.1	9.5	2.6
1985	12.3	9.5	2.8
1990	13.8	10.9	3.0
1995	14.3	11.1	3.2
2000	15.3	11.8	3.5
2005	17.5	13.0	4.5
2010	21.0	15.1	5.9
2015	20.0	14.6	5.4
2019	19.6	14.5	5.1

Source: Data for 1929–59 are from *Historical Statistics of the United States*, table Bc523–36; data for 1979–2010 are from College Board, *Trends in College Pricing 2020*; NCES, *Digest of Education Statistics 2020*, table 303.25.
Notes: Enrollment includes full-time and part-time students and those in public two-year institutions. Some totals exceed subtotals owing to rounding. Data for 1929–45 represent enrollment during the academic year. Data for 1950–2010 represent enrollment during fall semester.
*Figures for the subsequent year unavailable.

Degree-Granting Colleges and Universities in the United States, 2010s

TABLE A8.1

Level	Institutional kind	2012–13	2019–20
Four-year			
	Non-profit	**2,244**	**2,340**
	Public non-profit	[689]	[772]
	Private non-profit	[1,555]	[1,568]
	For-profit	**782**	**339**
Subtotal		3,026	2,679
Two-year			
	Non-profit	**1,031**	**945**
	Public non-profit	[934]	[853]
	Private non-profit	[97]	[92]
	For-profit	**669**	**358**
Subtotal		1,700	1,303
Total		4,726	3,982

Source: NCES, *Digest of Educational Statistics 2013*, table 317.10; NCES, *Digest of Educational Statistics 2020*, table 317.10.

Endowment Market Value of the 100 Largest Endowments of Colleges and Universities at the End of Fiscal Year 2020 (rounded to billions of dollars)

TABLE A9.1

Rank	Institution	Market value
1	Harvard University	40.6
2	University of Texas System	32.0
3	Yale University	31.2
4	Stanford University	29.0
5	Princeton University	26.6
6	Massachusetts Institute of Technology	18.5
7	University of Pennsylvania	14.9
8	Texas A&M University System	13.6
9	University of Michigan	12.5
10	University of California System	12.1
11	University of Notre Dame	12.0
12	Columbia University	11.3
13	Northwestern University	11.0
14	Duke University	8.5
15	Washington University, St. Louis	8.4
16	University of Chicago	8.2
17	Emory University	8.0
18	University of Virginia	7.3
19	Cornell University	7.2
20	Vanderbilt University	7.0
21	Johns Hopkins University	6.8
22	Rice University	6.2
23	Dartmouth College	6.0
24	University of Southern California	5.9
25	Ohio State University	5.3

(continued)

Rank	Institution	Market value
26	Brown University	4.4
27	New York University	4.3
28	University of Pittsburgh	4.2
29	University of Minnesota	3.9
30	University of North Carolina, Chapel Hill	3.7
31	Pennsylvania State University	3.4
32	University of Wisconsin	3.2
33	University of Washington	3.1
34	Michigan State University	3.1
35	University of California, Los Angeles	2.9
36	Williams College	2.8
37	California Institute of Technology	2.8
38	Carnegie Mellon University	2.7
39	Purdue University	2.6
40	Boston College	2.6
41	Amherst College	2.6
42	University of Iowa	2.5
43	Boston University	2.4
44	Indiana University	2.4
45	University of Richmond	2.4
46	University of Illinois	2.4
47	University of Rochester	2.3
48	Rockefeller University	2.3
49	Wellesley College	2.3
50	Pomona College	2.3
51	Georgia Institute of Technology	2.2
52	University of California Berkeley	2.1
53	Swarthmore College	2.1
54	Grinnell College	2.1
55	University of California San Francisco	2.0
56	Virginia Commonwealth University	2.0
57	University of Toronto*	2.0
58	Smith College	2.0
59	Tufts University	2.0
60	Georgetown University	2.0
61	Case Western Reserve University	2.0
62	University of Florida	2.0
63	University of Kansas	1.8

Rank	Institution	Market value
64	George Washington University	1.8
65	Bowdoin College	1.8
66	University of Nebraska	1.7
67	University of Missouri	1.7
68	Liberty University	1.7
69	Texas Christian University	1.7
70	Southern Methodist University	1.7
71	Washington and Lee University	1.6
72	University of Colorado	1.5
73	University of Maryland System	1.5
74	Rutgers, State University of New Jersey	1.5
75	University of Delaware	1.5
76	Tulane University	1.5
77	University of Alabama	1.4
78	North Carolina State University	1.4
79	University of Cincinnati	1.4
80	Syracuse University	1.4
81	Baylor University	1.4
82	Lehigh University	1.4
83	University of Georgia	1.4
84	Wake Forest University	1.4
85	Virginia Tech University	1.3
86	University of Tennessee	1.3
87	University of Kentucky	1.3
88	Texas Tech University System	1.3
89	Trinity University	1.3
90	University of British Columbia*	1.3
91	Berea College	1.3
92	Medical College of Wisconsin	1.2
93	McGill University*	1.2
94	Oklahoma State University	1.2
95	University of Arkansas, Fayetteville	1.2
96	University of Alberta*	1.2
97	Baylor College of Medicine	1.2
98	Saint Louis University	1.2
99	Middlebury College	1.1
100	Princeton Theological Seminary	1.1

Source: NACUBO, *Endowment Study 2020* (April 2021).
*Canadian institutions.